Calypso Café

Cooking Up the Best Island Flavors From the Keys and the Caribbean

WRITTEN AND COMPILED BY BOB T. EPSTEIN

A portion of the proceeds from the sale of this book benefits The Florida Conservation Association.

Bob T. Epstein, Writer
Barbara M. Bachman, Cover and Book Design

Library of Congress Card Catalog Number: 95-61509
ISBN: 1-879958-29-5

For additional copies, use the order form in the back of the book,
or call
The Wimmer Companies, Inc., 1-800-727-1034

ACKNOWLEDGMENTS

Many thanks to writer **Bob T. Epstein**, former president and CEO of Florida Outdoor Writers Association and a photo-journalist of international acclaim, for the editorial sections of this cookbook and for working so hard to obtain the recipes found within. Bob is founder of the International Gamefish Release and Enhancement Foundation and president of Wildwater Productions. In addition, he is a public information officer and an official photographer for the Federal Emergency Management Agency (FEMA). Most of all, he loves Caribbean-style foods.

Cover and Book Design by Barbara M. Bachman, New York City

This cookbook would not be possible without the cooperation of the restaurant owners, managers, and chefs throughout the Keys and the Caribbean Islands who offered their delicious recipes found within. You, the reader and cook, will appreciate these folks each time you try one of their specialties. They encourage you to sample them in their restaurants as well as at home.

Special thanks to Irving R. and Jeane Eyster for the research involved developing the Keys' tidbits found throughout the book.

PREFACE

Gently caressed by tropic tradewinds, you are suddenly free when vacationing in the many islands of the Caribbean or Florida's sun-drenched Keys. Your nostrils are enlivened to the aromas and scents of native flora and the wafting delights of the sea air. Close your eyes in the pleasure of that moment of realization that your getaway is special and all encompassing.

Far away from the reality of everyday cares and work at home, you turn your thoughts to many things: amour—the sights, sounds, and ambiance of a romantic place in the sun; scuba diving or snorkeling in the azure water all around you; and, of course, tasting the foods of this particular getaway. Foods indigenous to the locale are always considered premier in the full enjoyment of a vacation paradise. In that respect, the Keys and the Caribbean Islands will not disappoint even the most jaded traveler. The traditional cuisine and flavors of the tropics translate into spicy, yes; vibrant, always; delicious, to say the least.

When the first settlers to the Caribbean reached its shores and learned the cooking customs of the local Indians, they added those foods, spices, and special cooking methods to their retinue of cooking traditions. In addition, rum, that old "devil," was created from the sugar cane and natural fermentation of airborne yeasts and became a potent addition to many of the dishes. Caribbean cooking, as we know it today, was born.

Islands by their very nature are surrounded by the sea. It's no wonder then that an abundance of seafood would be used in so many island recipes . . . mahi mahi (dolphin fish), yellowtail snapper, mackerel, conch, crab, shrimp, and lobster, in addition to dozens of other tasty species.

Many peppers, herbs, fruits, and seeds grown only in the tropics add to the specific nature of so many island dishes. One would need to be on the go throughout the Keys and Caribbean day in and day out to find the time and opportunity to taste all of what those islands offer in their particular specialties.

Whether you have been here for a visit or just want to get away to the islands without leaving your kitchen, this cookbook allows you to bring the flavors home. Restaurants throughout the Keys and the Caribbean Islands offer some of their favorite island recipes for you to test and taste in your own kitchen. So prepare a few, turn on that island music, and relax in that laid-back island style.

NOTE:

Many of the recipes in this book call for spices, seafood, and produce once only available in the Caribbean. Now many local markets are able to order specialty items for you on short notice. If that doesn't work, you can order from our list of suppliers on page 212.

CONTENTS

ABOUT THE KEYS PAGE 8

ABOUT THE CARIBBEAN PAGE 12

FLORIDA CONSERVATION ASSOCIATION PAGE 16

APPETIZERS & BEVERAGES

PAGE 17

THE KEYS page 18

SALADS PAGE 45

THE BAHAMAS page 46

SIDE DISHES & BREADS

PAGES 59

PUERTO RICO / DOMINICAN REPUBLIC / HAITI page 60

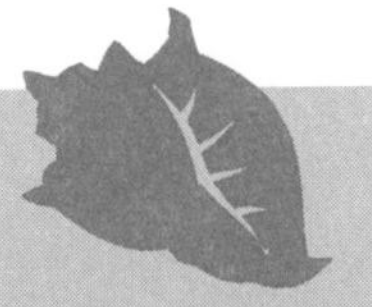

SOUPS & CHOWDERS

PAGE 71

VIRGIN ISLANDS page 72

FISH PAGE 97

LEEWARD ISLANDS page 98

SHELLFISH PAGE 141

WINDWARD ISLANDS page 142

MEATS, POULTRY, & MEATLESS

PAGE 165

BONAIRE / ARUBA / CURACAO page 166

DESSERTS PAGE 185

CANCUN / COZUMEL page 186

CARIBBEAN COMPLEMENTS

PAGE 209

JAMAICA / CAYMAN ISLANDS page 210

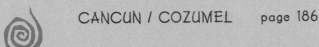

GLOSSARY page 211

DISTRIBUTORS page 212

RESTAURANTS page 213

MARINAS page 214

THE FLORIDA KEYS

This location immediately conjures up a tropical setting, fun-in-the-sun, with diving, snorkeling, fishing, and getting into that laid-back mood that puts all the world's troubles well behind on the back-burner of life. The Keys, actually hundreds of islands, incorporates just 32 inhabited ones for the visitor to enjoy—and all of these have their own personality and charm.

To reach the Keys by land you can travel down U.S.1 or for those in a hurry, Florida's Turnpike south to **Homestead** and **Florida City**, the gateway to the Keys. You'll travel through Monroe County, which is comprised mostly of the **Everglades National Park**. The park includes the Florida Bay, with its boundary on the Intracoastal Waterway along the southeastern border, about a mile or so from the Overseas Highway. The park area is about 1½ million acres, most of which are wetlands consisting of either fresh water or brackish flowing through the sawgrass. Similar to Yellowstone National Park, the Everglades was established to basically protect and preserve the wildlife and integrity of these major wetland areas. Visitors are encouraged to enjoy the park for fishing and wildlife photography. (Other national and state parks in the area include **Long Key State Park**, 291 acres about midway in the Keys, and **Bahia Honda State Park**, 256 acres in the Lower Keys. Bahia Honda is a gorgeous tropical part of the Keys with some of

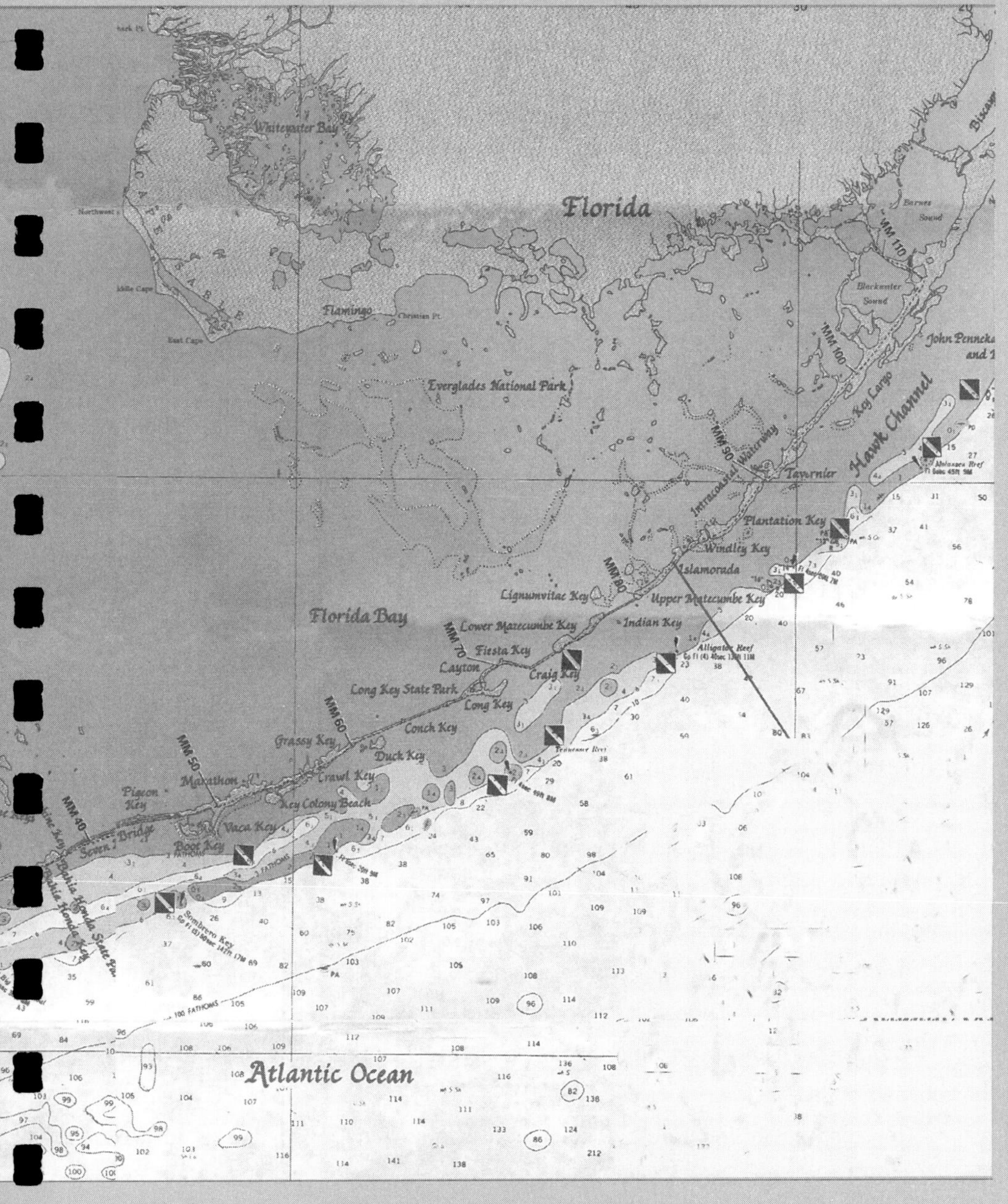

the best natural beaches. In all of the state parks the emphasis is on recreation.)

In the Upper Keys, visitors first reach **Key Largo**, made famous by Bogie & Bacall in the movie of the same name. **John Pennekamp Coral Reef State Park** is its main claim to fame and rightfully so, for the colorful and lively Pennekamp reefs are reputed to be the finest in the continental U.S. Dive boats, a glass-bottom boat, and numerous charter fishing boats are located in Key Largo, where the Florida Bay back country is as accessible as the Atlantic and the Gulf Stream. Pennekamp Park embraces 75 square miles of protected reef. There are tent and trailer spaces, a marina, picnic areas, a concession stand, a boardwalk through the mangroves, and a nature trail through a small stand of native tropical hardwood trees. There is also a small aquarium and center for education about the coral reefs and its denizens. More than 20 fine restaurants call Key Largo home, many of which are featured in Calypso Café.

Tavernier and **Plantation Key** are bedroom communities just 10 miles south of Key Largo, but also boast excellent marina facilities, restaurants, charter boat, and dive boat operations as well, but at a more laid-back pace and temper. Plantation Key received its name from the large pineapple plantations that were once prosperous there and later supplanted by Cuban pineapples and still later on Hawaiian "gold."

Going south, your next stop would be **Windley Key**. Originally known as Umbrella Key, Windley got its newer name during the railroad days. A homestead for a few farmers before 1900, Windley developed when the railroad joined two separate Keys together with fill and established a station there named Quarry. In addition to working rock pits for railroad track fill, the railroad also worked digging stone (old reef). These pits today are filled with fish and dolphin and are known as "Theatre of the Sea." The coral limestone that railroad engineers dug were used for riprapping, and the beautiful pattern from the fossilized rock was much prized for veneering house fronts and inside walls of Keys and South Florida homes. It has been sold under the name Keystone, and a visit to the Keys Hurricane monument just south in Islamorada will offer the visitor a first-hand look at this beautiful shell and limestone rock.

Islamorada houses major resorts, such as Cheeca Lodge, Holiday Isle, and the Chesapeake, which cater to visitors from around the world who come to the "Purple Isle." It has long been known as this due to the once-prolific purple sea-fans that dotted the shallows of the Atlantic.

Heading south you'll pass a number of sparsely inhabited islands such as **Matecumbe**, **Long Key**, **Duck Key** (which does have Hawks Cay), **Grassy Key**, and then come to the Middle Keys and the big island of **Marathon** with an airport, 50 restaurants, and a number of excellent resorts such as the Sombrero and the Buccaneer.

The world-renowned **Seven Mile Bridge**, which is even mentioned in Ripley's *Believe It or Not*, links Marathon and the Lower Keys and is an experience one won't soon forget. You will actually be driving over seas, thus the link with the mainland, U.S. 1 is also known as the Overseas Highway. Boats plying these waters catch tarpon, snapper, sharks, permit, and more than a dozen other species attracted by the artificial fish gathering device that the bridge abutments create.

On the other side of the bridge lies **Big Pine Key** and the home of the Key deer, a federally protected species of diminutive deer that looks exactly like its northern full size white-tailed variety, but these are the size of collie dogs trapped millenniums ago and evolving to a size that befitted their reduced food sources and territories.

Farther down the Keys heading toward Key West is an island known as **Little Palm,** which must be reached by ferry or private boat and is home to a Fijian look-alike resort known as Little Palm Island Resort, an upscale spot in the Keys island chain with a world-class restaurant.

As you head south, additional exciting islands open up before you as you cross a succession of 42 bridges. Leaving Big Pine, you will be headed for **Cudjoe Key** and waters will brighten to a rich aquamarine hue as the population decreases. Continue your journey and finally you'll reach Key West, about 132 miles from where you started in Florida City. Key West will open up the pages of its incredible history and modern-day tropical flavor.

Key West is as eclectic a place as you may find anywhere. From cat shows to sword swallowers on Mallory Square during daily sunset celebrations, to the world-famous Pier House Resort and restaurant, reputed to be about the best place to stay in Key West. Casa Marina Resort, Holiday Inn Beachside, and Sheraton Suites are just a few other wonderful places to drop your bags. On Duval Street, there's Fast Buck Freddies and a hundred or so other emporiums of tourist goodies for your shopping pleasure. Stop in at the legendary balladeer Jimmy Buffett's watering hole, The Margaritaville Cafe, which serves a great Conch Burger.

THE CARIBBEAN ISLANDS

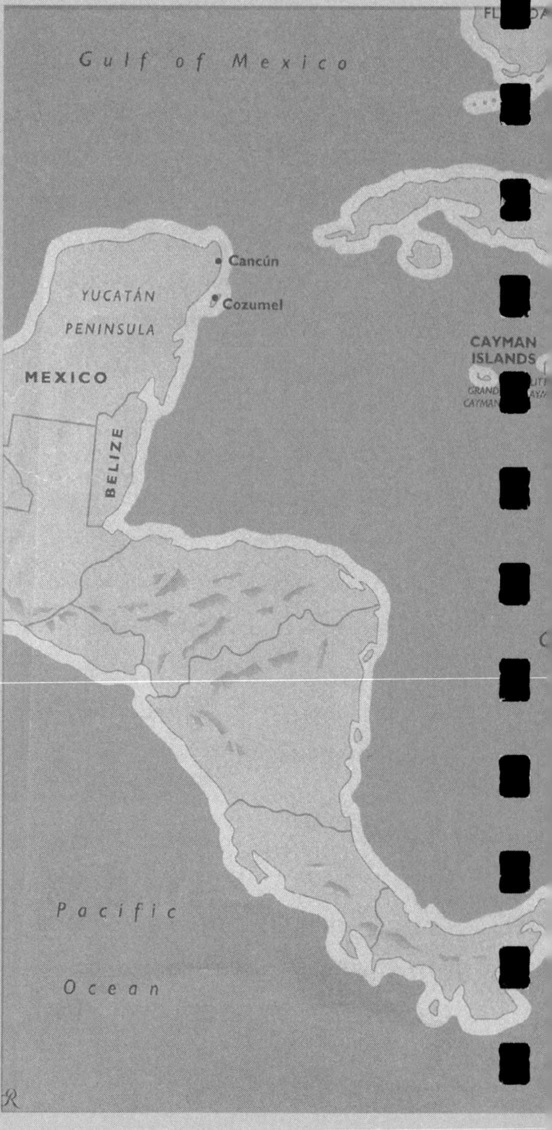

The Caribbean is more than giant expanses of sea, sand, and islands that punctuate crystalline waters. The Caribbean is an eco-paradise that has no equal. Perhaps you've visited one Caribbean country and had a wonderful time. Make no mistake; you have just reached a comma in your traveling essay on thousands of miles of blue-green waters and a magical landscape.

Besides the sights of jagged mountains, spring-fed swimming holes, cascading waterfalls, volcanoes, coral reefs, verdant lush tropical rain forests, and beaches as far as the eye can behold, there are also the sounds of peeper frogs in those rainforests, howls of raucous monkeys, calls of tropical birds, and steamy whooshes of a whale blowing off as it migrates to better feeding and calving grounds.

You'll experience the scents of jasmine and honeysuckle and the musk pungency of grasses and swamp cabbage. You'll taste the earth and its special aura in your nostrils—not heavy, but sweet and delectable, the way nature makes its presentation to one who quietly looks, listens, and takes in the total essence of a place made in God's mortar and pestle.

It's no wonder that the forefathers of the Europeans and Americans who now leave the death grip of winter to head to the sunny Caribbean fought for

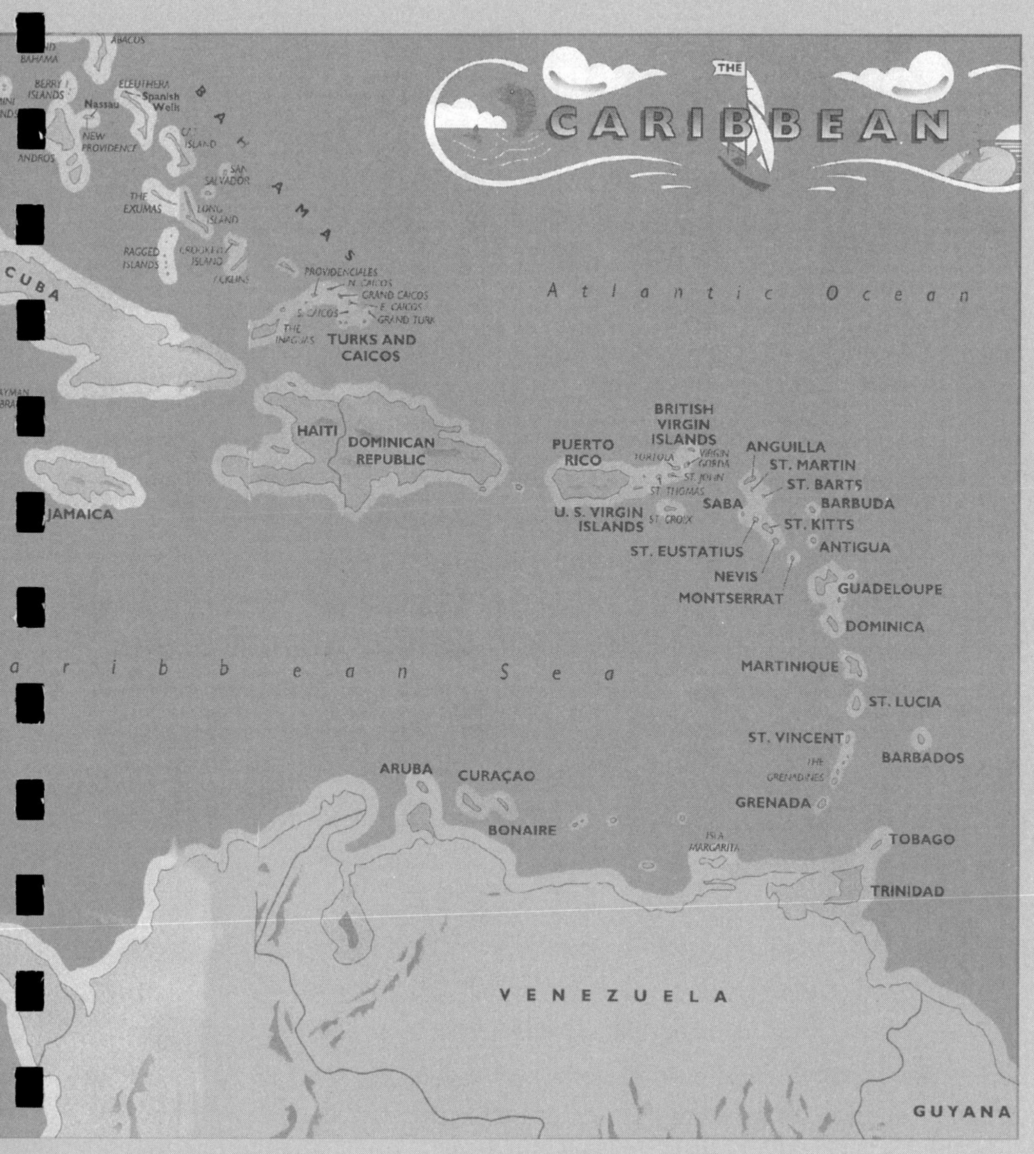

centuries to control the Caribbean Basin's island jewels and waterways. It's also fitting today that the millions of tourists who visit from around the world are captivated by the stunningly beautiful panoramas, powdery beaches, and warmth of the people and climate.

Most people have a chance to visit only one island at a time and enjoy the beauty and laid-back lifestyle by booking a fly-to destination vacation resort. This is a great way to get a good look at just one of the gemlike islands in the Caribbean.

Another way to visit the Caribbean is by booking a cruise ship holiday. These adventures leave little to the imagination on-board; they are floating hotels with gambling thrown in, and as many meals as you can stand, with full entertainment amenities day and night. But these giant ships visit an itinerary of Caribbean Islands, and this is a great way to get a touch of the tropics. Some 10-day cruises visit as many as 6 or 7 different ports of call. On each island there are opportunities to snorkel or dive their reefs and wrecks, try local food fare, and take photo memories of the most picturesque locations and specialties of that particular island. You can then return to your cabin, have dinner, take in a show, and wake up the next morning to another tropical island.

There are always opportunities for those who like to visit the wildlife of the island; you can even stroke a sting ray or take a photo with a sea turtle or a parrot, visit antique architecture, or do a culinary taste trip through the outdoor kiosks and corner shops serving Caribbean treats.

During your travels, you may find out that there is so much nutmeg on Grenada that the crushed shells are used for cooking fuel, garden mulch, or even on walkways to soften the path for bare feet. Nutmeg is key to Grenada's verdant island economy, as is clove, cinnamon, turmeric, allspice, ginger, bayleaf, peppers, and tonka bean, a substitute for vanilla. You might visit all the many distilleries found around the Caribbean, including Barbados' Cockspur rum or Pussers, Jamaica's dark aged Myer's Appleton Gold, or Puerto Rico's Bacardi, who first popularized white rum. One adventure interlude in the tropics is tasting the mélange of flavors and specialties that is known as Creole, which is guaranteed to make you loosen your waistband.

You can taste and enjoy these for yourself in air-conditioned restaurants, or at al fresco bistros or roadside stands. But a beachside location is the best for this kind of indulgence. Food will never taste so good, and a drink will never be so pure and delightful. and then when the body internal is soothed and excited, a splash in the pool or private secluded lagoon will temper the tropical sun and put you in the mood for a snooze and a dreamscape full of the best the Caribbean has to offer.

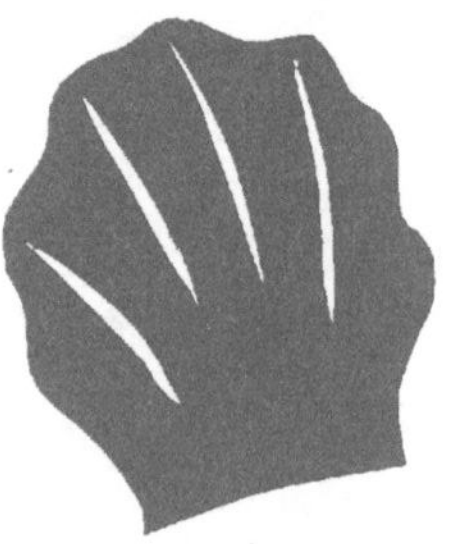

FLORIDA CONSERVATION ASSOCIATION

The Florida Conservation Association (FCA) was formed in 1985 by a group of conservation-minded saltwater anglers and their supporters who were concerned about the future of the state's fisheries. FCA is a nonprofit organization that is dedicated to the conservation and restoration of Florida's marine resources. We are a statewide membership organization made up of 28 chapters (and growing) with approximately 8,000 members. We also have many out-of-state members that support our conservation efforts and add to the strong voice we provide in favor of marine conservation.

FCA recognizes both the pleasure and positive impact that recreational fishing has on Florida. We do our best to ensure that the state's publicly owned marine resources are protected by supporting marine research, the development of effective resource management plans, and the enforcement of resource protection laws. Our efforts to protect and improve Florida's marine fisheries and other related natural resources include making the public aware of the importance and fragility of Florida's bounty today so that they will not destroy it through greed or lack of knowledge for tomorrow.

Our accomplishments have gained us recognition as an effective advocate for marine conservation. Specific successes include obtaining no-sale, gamefish status for the redfish, whose stocks were becoming seriously threatened by sudden market popularity. In fact, in 1989, FCA received the Florida Wildlife Federation's Conservation Organization of the Year Award for our work in protecting and restoring redfish.

FCA also supported the establishment of saltwater fishing license fees to raise revenue for marine research, conservation law enforcement, and habitat protection. We worked for the prohibition of fish traps in the South Atlantic and are now working to prohibit them in the Gulf of Mexico.

FCA was an active and driving force in the campaign for the Save Our Sealife constitutional amendment, which was overwhelmingly approved on election day in 1994. The amendment has been called the most significant mandate for marine conservation in Florida's history.

FCA is able to accomplish what we do through the support of foundations, corporations, and private donors who share our commitment to a healthy marine environment in our lifetime and for future generations. We are grateful to be the beneficiary of a portion of the proceeds from the sale of this cookbook. We know that these recipes will make your stomachs and hearts full!

Tight lines and...bon appetit!

Florida Conservation Association
Ted Forsgren, Executive Director
Izzie Berkson, Director of Development

APPETIZERS & BEVERAGES

THE KEYS

With more than 300 restaurants, the Florida Keys boasts something for everyone when it comes to dining in style, variety, and delectability. The Keys is home to the finest fish that swim the earth's oceans. It's no wonder that visitors worldwide come to expect the finest and freshest seafood dishes during their journey through these "enchanted" islands and find it almost everywhere they dine.

Chefs blend cooking influences from every continent with the colorful and flavorful resources and recipes of the Caribbean tropics, including the spicy Creole, into their recipes and specialties. For example, they embrace the "jerk" and pungent peppers from Jamaica; the down-to-earth, delicious black beans from Cuba; the vanilla bean of Madagascar; the yellow and distinct "flower essence" of saffron from Italy and Spain. White rice complements all the specialty meats and seafoods. Conch from the Bahamas finds its way into fritters, salads, stews, and chowders. The world's chefs find the delicate fleshed yellowtail snapper from the reefs of the Caribbean and the Keys and create novel recipes using tropical island rich fruits. They also create dishes with other fishes of the Caribbean, such as grouper, mackerel, mahi mahi (dolphin fish), and red snapper. And these chefs and their food emporiums prospered and made famous a cuisine for today's upbeat, well-traveled Calypso generation!

Sharkbites

- 1 pound shark steak, skinned and cubed
- Milk
- ¼ cup peanut oil
- ¼ cup white wine
- 1 tablespoon Cajun seafood seasoning
- ¼ cup orange juice
- 1 tablespoon lemon juice
- 1 tablespoon lime juice
- Pinch of cayenne pepper
- 1 tablespoon packed brown sugar
- 1 tablespoon teriyaki
- Orange wedges for garnish

Place shark in an airtight container. Cover with milk and refrigerate overnight or freeze until ready to use. Combine oil and next 8 ingredients in a sauté pan. Heat over low heat until sugar dissolves. Bring to a simmer. Drain shark and add to pan. Cook and toss for about 5 minutes. Shark will take on the color of the marinade and will flake with a fork when done. Serve over rice and garnish.

Yield: 4 servings

Blacktip, lemon shark, or mako shark steaks work well. If serving as a main dish, use ½ pound of shark per person and adjust other ingredients accordingly.

Pierre Relland
Smuggler's Cove
Islamorada

To make **Quick Old-style Keys Sour Seasoning,** mix a pint of Key lime juice (or regular lime juice) with a tablespoon of salt in a bottle. Leave the bottle uncapped for several days to ferment. When the mixture stops bubbling, it needs to be capped. Use on conch or fish dishes as a marinade.

Shrimp Rémoulade

- 1 gallon water
- 2 pounds (16-20 count) shrimp
- 3 tablespoons minced fresh cilantro
- 2 tablespoons minced fresh oregano
- 2 tablespoons minced fresh dill
- 2 tablespoons minced fresh basil
- 2 tablespoons minced fresh rosemary
- 2 tablespoons minced garlic in oil
- ¼ cup paprika
- 1 cup ketchup
- ¼ cup horseradish
- ½ cup olive oil
- ¼ cup Dijon mustard

Shrimp is a primary ingredient in Caribbean seafood recipes.

Bring water to a rolling boil. Stir in shrimp. Remove from heat and let stand 5 minutes. Drain shrimp and transfer to ice water to stop cooking process. When cool, peel and devein shrimp. Prepare sauce by combining cilantro and remaining 10 ingredients in a large bowl. Mix well. Add shrimp to sauce and marinate for 1 to 24 hours. To serve, place shrimp in lettuce-lined fruit cups topped with ¼ cup of sauce.

Yield: 7 servings

Bob Stoky
Sundowners
Key Largo

Kokomo Joe's Chicken Wings

- 6 chicken wings
- ½ cup all-purpose flour
- 1 teaspoon garlic salt
- 1½ sticks butter or margarine
- 6 tablespoons hot pepper sauce
- Oil for frying

Cut off chicken wing tips and discard. Separate wings at the joint to make two sections per wing. Combine flour and garlic salt. Thoroughly coat wing sections in flour mixture. Place wings in a plastic bag and close tightly. Refrigerate at least 1 hour, 30 minutes. Melt butter. Whip in hot pepper sauce. Keep warm. Heat oil to 350°. Fry wings 8 to 10 minutes or until browned on all sides. Drain wings and place in a serving bowl. Stir butter mixture and pour over wings. Shake bowl slightly to coat wings with sauce.

Joe Roth
Holiday Isle Resort and Marina
Islamorada

Columbus who sighted the Cayman Islands during his final voyage to the "New World" in 1503 named the islands Las Tortugas because the islands were loaded with sea turtles. The islands were later named *Caymanas*, which means crocodiles; however, few, if any, crocodiles ever made their home there.

Spicy Conch

- 4 ounces conch
- 1 cucumber
- 1 tablespoon kimchi sauce
- 1 tablespoon chopped scallion
- Sesame seeds

Pound conch with a mallet until very thin. Cut conch into about 7 pieces, each 2 inches square. Cut cucumber into two segments; then cut each segment into 4 strips. Combine conch, cucumber, kimchi sauce, and scallion. Sprinkle with sesame seeds.

Octopus can be substituted for conch.

Yield: 1 serving

Yoshi Mizuma
Ginza Sushi
Islamorada

Conch is a tough meat unless well beaten.

Dominican Wings

- 1 cup lime juice
- ½ cup dark rum
- 5 jalapeño peppers, thinly sliced
- ¼ cup soy sauce
- 10 pounds large chicken wings

Tips for Safe Boating in the Keys (from the Upper Keys Chapter of the American Red Cross): **Don't overpower or overload your boat, and don't overlook life jackets, anchor, oars, and a fire extinguisher. Always carry enough drinking water for at least 3 days in case you break down at sea. Be smart and play it safe by filing a float plan, keeping an eye on the weather, and making sure your boat is properly fueled with drain plug in place.**

Combine lime juice and next 3 ingredients. Cut off chicken wing tips and discard. Separate wings at the joint to make two sections per wing. Place in a container. Pour lime juice mixture over wings. Add enough water to cover wings. Refrigerate at least 24 hours. Drain wings and pat dry. Grill 5 to 6 minutes or until done, or coat with flour and fry in oil 4 minutes or until golden brown.

Yield: 10 servings

Serve wings with Jamaican pukka sauce on the side.

Frank Carlton
Snapper's
Key Largo

Zuppa de Clams

- 3 tablespoons chopped garlic
- 2 tablespoons olive oil
- Pinch of salt
- Pinch of black pepper
- Pinch crushed red pepper flakes
- Pinch of basil
- 1 cup clam juice
- 3 tablespoons white wine
- 14 to 15 fresh whole clams

Sauté garlic and next 5 ingredients together until golden brown. Add clam juice, wine, and whole clams. Cook until clams steam open.

Yield: 1 to 2 servings

Justin Green
Paradise Cafe
Long Key

Blue Crab Fritters

Fritters

- 3 bell peppers
- 3 red bell peppers
- 1 medium-size yellow onion
- 2 pounds blue crab claw meat
- 1 egg
- ½ teaspoon celery salt
- 2 tablespoons celery seed
- 1 teaspoon cayenne pepper
- 3 tablespoons baking powder
- 3 to 5 cups all-purpose flour
- Oil for frying

Bimini Sauce

- 1 cup mayonnaise
- ¾ cup ketchup
- 1 tablespoon mustard

Process bell peppers and onion in a blender or food processor until almost liquefied. Blend in crab and next 6 ingredients, adding enough flour to achieve a thick batter. Using a small ice cream scoop or a soup spoon, drop batter into 325° oil. Fry until golden brown. To prepare sauce, combine mayonnaise, ketchup, and mustard. Serve sauce with fritters.

Yield: 12 servings

Blue crab is a popular seafood in the Keys and Caribbean.

Islamorada Fish Co.
Islamorada

Cheeca Lodge Black Bean Fritters

Black Bean Fritters

- 1 cup cooked black beans, drained
- ½ red bell pepper, diced
- ½ yellow bell pepper, diced
- ¼ red onion, diced
- ½ chayote, diced
- ½ cup cornmeal
- ½ cup all-purpose flour
- ½ tablespoon baking powder
- 1 tablespoon packed brown sugar
- 1 egg
- 2 tablespoons buttermilk
- Salt and pepper to taste
- Peanut oil for frying

Mango-Passion Fruit Vinaigrette

- 1 mango
- ½ cup passion fruit juice
- ½ cup rice wine vinegar
- 3 tablespoons Key lime juice
- 1 cup peanut oil
- 2 tablespoons orange juice
- Salt to taste
- Honey to taste

Mix together black beans and next 8 ingredients. Add egg and buttermilk and toss lightly. Season with salt and pepper. Drop by spoonfuls into 350° peanut oil. Fry 3 to 5 minutes or until thoroughly cooked. To prepare vinaigrette, process mango and passion fruit juice in a blender. Combine vinegar and lime juice. With blender running, slowly add vinegar mixture and peanut oil, alternately. Mix in orange juice, salt, and honey. Serve vinaigrette with hot fritters.

Yield: 2 to 4 servings

Try the vinaigrette on salads or chicken, too.

Dawn Sieber
Cheeca Lodge
Islamorada

Sponges provide shelter for many marine animals. One large sponge that was harvested off a flat in the Keys was home to 12,000 small shrimp, 1,500 small shellfish, 18 various sea worms, and one fish.

Shrimp and Corn Fritters

- 1 pound shrimp
- 1 cup corn
- ½ cup diced onion
- ½ cup diced red bell pepper
- ½ cup chopped scallion
- ½ cup chopped fresh cilantro
- ½ cup diced fresh jalapeño pepper
- 1½ cups buttermilk pancake mix
- ½ cup all-purpose flour
- 1 teaspoon salt
- 1 teaspoon black pepper
- Juice of 1 lime
- 1 cup beer
- Oil for frying

Shrimp and corn are traditional ingredients found in Caribbean recipes.

Cook shrimp. Chill, peel, and devein. Coarsely chop shrimp. Cook corn and drain. Combine shrimp, corn, and next 11 ingredients. Refrigerate for at least 60 minutes. Using a small ice cream scoop or a soup spoon, drop batter into 350° oil. Fry 2 to 3 minutes or until golden brown. Place fritters on a paper towel to drain. Serve hot with cocktail or mustard sauce.

Yield: 6 to 10 servings

Konrad Jockum
Turtle Kraals Wildlife Bar and Grill
Key West

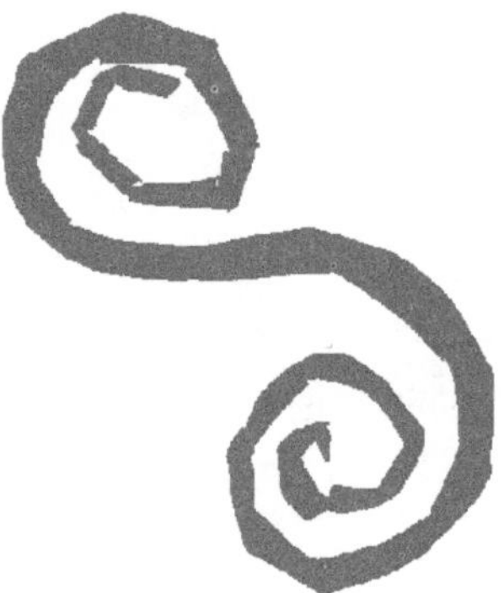

Fritters Calabaza

Calabaza, a member of the squash family, is a staple food in the Caribbean. It is usually sold in slices due to its large size.

- 2 pounds calabaza, cut in 1-inch cubes
- 1 egg, beaten
- 3 tablespoons butter
- ½ cup sugar
- ½ teaspoon nutmeg
- 1⅔ cups all-purpose flour
- Vegetable oil for deep-frying
- Salt to taste

Place calabaza in a large pan. Cover with water and bring to a boil. Reduce heat and simmer over low heat 25 minutes. Drain and mash. Combine 2 cups of mashed calabaza and next 3 ingredients in a large bowl. Mix until butter melts and is well blended. Stir in nutmeg. Add flour, ⅔ cup at a time and mix thoroughly. Drop by heaping spoonfuls into 375° oil. Fry about 6 fritters at a time for 4 to 6 minutes or until light brown. Drain on paper towels. Season with salt. Serve hot with onion or avocado dip.

Yield: 12 fritters

Monte Green
Olympia Bar and Grill
Dade County

Conch Fritters

- 1 pound conch, ground
- 2 eggs
- 3¼ cups all-purpose flour
- ½ bell pepper, chopped
- ½ red bell pepper, chopped
- ½ teaspoon cayenne pepper
- ½ tablespoon baking powder
- ½ cup beer
- Oil for deep-frying

Combine conch and next 6 ingredients. Add beer and mix thoroughly. Refrigerate 2 hours. Drop conch mixture by heaping spoonfuls into hot oil. Fry until golden. Serve on a bed of lettuce with cocktail sauce.

Yield: 4 servings

Chef Max, Bogies Cafe
Holiday Inn Resort and Marina
Key Largo

Shrimp With Smoked Andouille Sausage

- 4 large shrimp, peeled and deveined
- 6 (1-inch) slices andouille sausage
- 1 tablespoon olive oil
- 6 mushroom caps, quartered
- ½ cup Worcestershire sauce
- ½ cup heavy cream
- Salt and pepper to taste
- Chopped fresh parsley for garnish

Sauté shrimp and sausage in oil in a saucepan until shrimp turn translucent in color. Remove shrimp and sausage. Add mushrooms to saucepan and cook 1 minute. Add shrimp, sausage, Worcestershire sauce, and cream. Simmer 3 minutes or until sauce thickens. Season with salt and pepper. Garnish.

Yield: 2 servings

Mia Casey
Marriott's Frenchman's Reef Beach Resort
St. Thomas, U. S. Virgin Islands

Scallops and Artichoke Appetizer

Sea scallops accent this tropical recipe.

- 8 large sea scallops
- 4 artichoke hearts, halved
- ½ stick butter
- ½ teaspoon basil
- ½ cup white wine
- 1 tablespoon key lime juice
- 1 (15-ounce) can black beans, drained
- 2 tablespoons chopped parsley

Sauté scallops and next 3 ingredients together. Add wine and lime juice and cook to reduce sauce. Spread beans on a serving plate. Pour scallop mixture over top. Sprinkle with parsley. Serve with hot garlic bread.

Yield: 2 servings

Mohammad Motamedi
Coconuts
Key Largo

Frutta Di Mare

Best Times for Fishin' in the Keys: Early in the morning about an hour before dawn until the sun has risen for about an hour. An incoming tide is best, and second best is an outgoing tide. No tide movement usually means few fish biting. From about an hour before sunset until about midnight, fishing is also very good. But, there are many other factors that contribute to whether fishing will be good or poor no matter what the tides or the time of day or night.

4 ounces fish of choice
White wine
1 clove garlic, minced, divided
All-purpose flour for dredging
1 tablespoon butter
3 shrimp, peeled and deveined
2 ounces scallops

Combine fish, wine, and ½ clove garlic. Refrigerate overnight. Drain fish and dredge lightly in flour. Heat butter and remaining ½ clove garlic in a skillet. Add fish and sauté on one side. Turn fish and add shrimp. When shrimp are nearly cooked, add scallops. Cook until done. Serve on a bed of mixed salad greens.

Yield: 1 serving

Curried Shrimp Tropicale

Citrus Beurre Blanc Sauce

3 cups dry white wine
3 bay leaves
½ tablespoon peppercorn
¼ teaspoon dried thyme
½ onion, sliced
1 quart cream
4 sticks unsalted butter, softened
Salt and pepper to taste
¼ cup fresh lemon juice

Shrimp

8 jumbo shrimp, peeled and deveined
¼ cup curry powder
Olive oil for sautéing
1 teaspoon diced shallot
½ scallion, chopped
⅓ cup diced ripe mango
¼ cup diced ripe papaya
1 tablespoon Grand Marnier
1 tablespoon honey
Citrus Beurre Blanc Sauce
Salt and pepper to taste

Combine wine and next 4 ingredients in a saucepan. Cook until all liquid is absorbed. Add cream and cook until reduced by one-half. Whip in butter, salt, pepper, and lemon juice. Remove bay leaves. To prepare shrimp, dredge shrimp in curry powder. Sauté with olive oil and next 4 ingredients. Mix in Grand Marnier. Add honey and beurre blanc sauce. Season with salt and pepper.

Yield: 2 servings

John A. Potucek III / John A. Roy
The Old Tavernier
Tavernier

Shrimp Mykonos

- 1¼ pounds large shrimp, peeled and deveined
- ⅓ cup olive oil
- 3 cloves garlic, chopped
- 1 medium Spanish onion, chopped
- 4 ripe tomatoes, diced
- 1½ teaspoons salt
- ¼ teaspoon white pepper
- 4 teaspoons red wine vinegar
- 4 ounces feta cheese

Sauté shrimp in oil. In a separate pan, cook garlic, onion, and tomato over low heat for 15 minutes. Mix in salt, pepper, and vinegar. Place shrimp and vegetable mixture in a casserole dish. Top with cheese. Bake at 350° for 5 minutes.

Yield: 6 to 8 servings

This recipe is equally delicious served over rice as an entrée for 4 people.

Emmanouil Parissis
The Quay
Key West

Caribbean Escargot

- 12 snails, cleaned
- 1 tablespoon butter
- 1 clove garlic, chopped
- 2 to 3 puff pastry squares
- 1 egg, beaten
- Caribbean seasoning

Place 1 snail in each hole of 2 snail plates. Place ¼ teaspoon of butter on each snail. Top with garlic. Brush pastry squares with egg and sprinkle with seasoning. Use top of seasoning container to cut 12 quarter-size circles. Place one circle on each snail. Bake at 400° for 15 to 20 minutes.

Yield: 2 servings

Scott A. Price
Scooters
Tavernier

Shrimp Wellington

Shrimp

- 3 eggs, divided
- 4 ounces crabmeat, chopped
- ½ cup breadcrumbs
- ½ onion, chopped
- 1 teaspoon chopped garlic
- 4 large shrimp, peeled, deveined, and butterflied
- 4 (2-inch square) puff pastry sheets

Béarnaise Sauce

- ½ cup mayonnaise
- 2 teaspoons prepared mustard
- 1 teaspoon lemon juice
- Pinch of tarragon
- 2 tablespoons vinegar

Combine 2 eggs and next 4 ingredients to make a stuffing. Place 1 shrimp on each pastry sheet, allowing tail to hang over side. Cover the body of the shrimp with stuffing. Wrap pastry sheets around shrimp and stuffing. Beat remaining egg and brush over pastry. Bake at 375° for 15 minutes or until golden brown. While shrimp bakes, prepare béarnaise sauce. Combine mayonnaise, mustard, and lemon juice in a saucepan. Heat, but do not boil. Add tarragon and vinegar. Serve with shrimp.

Yield: 4 servings

Mohammad Motamedi
Coconuts
Key Largo

Boniata Chips

Boniatos are also known as Cuban sweet potatoes.

6 boniatos

Virgin olive oil for frying

Salt to taste

Pierce boniatos several times with a fork and place on the center rack of an oven. Bake at 400° for 40 to 50 minutes. Remove from oven and cool. Cut into ½-inch slices. Heat ¼-inch of oil in a skillet over high heat. Place 8 to 12 boniata slices at a time in skillet. Cook 2 minutes on each side or until brown. Drain on paper towels. Season with salt and serve immediately.

Yield: 6 servings

Monte Green
Olympia Bar and Grill
Dade County

Makoto Roll

5 ounces sushi rice

1 sheet dried seaweed

2 ounces cream cheese

1 scallion, sliced

5 ounces fresh salmon, thinly sliced

Spread rice over seaweed. Top with cream cheese, scallion, and salmon. Form into a roll. Cut in 8 to 10 slices. Deep-fry 5 to 7 minutes. Serve hot with mustard sauce.

Yield: 1 to 2 servings

Tony K. Liam
Makoto Japanese Restaurant
Key Largo

BEVERAGES

Mangorita

2 ounces tequila
½ ripe mango
Juice of 2 key limes
Sugar to taste
Crushed ice
Fresh strawberry for garnish

Process tequila and next 4 ingredients in a blender. Serve in a glass with strawberry garnish.

Yield: 1 serving

Alex Blanton
Cheeca Lodge
Islamorada

Cheeca Smoothy

3 ripe strawberries, divided
2 ounces dark rum
½ ripe banana
½ cup vanilla ice cream or frozen yogurt
Crushed ice

Process 2 strawberries and next 4 ingredients in a blender. Serve in a glass and garnish with remaining strawberry.

Yield: 1 serving

Alex Blanton
Cheeca Lodge
Islamorada

Reef Cooler

1¾ ounces vodka
Fresh limeade
Lime wheel for garnish

Combine vodka and limeade in a glass over crushed ice. Garnish.

Yield: 1 serving

Use Key limes to make limeade, if possible.

Alex Blanton
Cheeca Lodge
Islamorada

Manatee Bay

½ ounce white rum
1 ounce Tia Maria, or coffee-flavored liqueur
½ ounce crème de banane
½ ripe banana
½ cup vanilla ice cream
Crushed ice
Banana slice for garnish

Process rum and next 5 ingredients in a blender. Serve in a glass with garnish.

Yield: 1 serving

Alex Blanton
Cheeca Lodge
Islamorada

Key Lime Colada

2 ounces white rum
Juice of 4 large Key limes
3 ounces coconut milk
4 ounces pineapple juice
3 ounces sour mix
2 cups crushed ice
Fresh lime and pineapple for garnish

Process rum and next 5 ingredients in a blender. Freeze. To serve, place in a tall glass and garnish.

Yield: 1 serving

Madaline Robbins
Cracked Conch Café
Marathon

Jammer Slammer

2 ounces dark rum
2 ounces pineapple juice
1 ounce orange juice
1 ounce coconut milk
Orange slice and cherry for garnish

Mix rum and next 3 ingredients together well. Pour over ice into a glass and garnish.

Yield: 1 serving

John Bedell
Jammers
Islamorada

Margarita

1¼ ounces tequila	Ice
¼ ounce Triple Sec	Margarita salt
Sweet and sour mix	

This recipe comes from singer Jimmy Buffett's Margaritaville Café.

Place tequila and Triple Sec in a beverage shaker. Add sweet and sour mix. Fill with ice to near rim of shaker. Mix. Dip rim of a large cocktail glass in salt. Pour drink mixture into glass.

Yield: 1 serving

Ray Masiero and Billy Prokopf
Margaritaville Café
Key West

Barbados Rum Punch

½ ounce Barbados rum	1 ounce sour mix
½ ounce Faler rum	Dash of nutmeg

Combine all ingredients. Serve over ice.

Yield: 1 serving

Melody Mitchell
Sunset Bay and Hukilau
Key West

The Scorpion

- 1 ounce Puerto Rican Rum
- ¼ ounce gin
- ¼ ounce brandy
- 1 ounce papaya and mango nectar
- ¼ ounce amaretto

Combine all ingredients. Serve over crushed ice.

Yield: 1 serving

Melody Mitchell
Sunset Bay and Hukilau
Key West

Montego Bay Banana Cream Pie

- 1 ounce white rum
- ½ ounce cremè de banane
- ½ cup vanilla ice cream, or 2 ounces ice cream cocktail mix
- ½ banana, or 2 ounces banana frozen drink mix
- Crushed ice

Combine all ingredients in a blender. Process until thick. Pour into 2 large cocktail glasses. Garnish with a sprinkle of graham cracker crumbs, if desired.

Yield: 2 servings

Karen Young
Montego Bay Food and Spirits
Big Pine Key

Bananas and rum make this a delicious tropical cocktail or dessert drink.

Sangria

- 1 (26-ounce) bottle Spanish red wine
- 1 cup club soda
- 1 orange, thinly sliced
- 1 lemon, thinly sliced, or 2 Key limes
- 1 peach, chopped
- 1 apple, diced

Fruit and wine drinks are prevalent in the tropics.

Combine wine and soda in a serving pitcher. Stir in orange and remaining 3 ingredients. Chill and serve in large, ice-filled wine glasses.

Yield: 6 to 8 servings

Monte Green
Banana Patch
North Miami Beach

Cold Rum Toddy

- 1 teaspoon superfine sugar
- ¼ cup club soda
- 1 jigger dark rum
- Key lime twist for garnish

In a serving glass, dissolve sugar in soda. Add rum. Fill glass with ice cubes. Stir and garnish.

Yield: 1 serving

Monte Green
Coronado
Miami Beach

Planters Punch

- 1 jigger dark rum
- 1 jigger orange juice
- 1 teaspoon Key lime juice
- ½ teaspoon grenadine
- 1 maraschino cherry for garnish

Combine rum and next 3 ingredients in a beverage shaker. Shake to mix. Pour over ice into a glass. Top with cherry.

Yield: 1 serving

Monte Green
Unicorn Club
Cutler Ridge

Rum and Coconut Water

- 1 jigger white rum
- Fresh coconut milk
- Key lime twist for garnish

Fill a tall glass with ice. Add rum. Fill glass with coconut milk. Stir and garnish.

Yield: 1 serving

Monte Green
Unicorn Club
Cutler Ridge

Throughout the year there are numerous festivals in all of the Caribbean Islands that visitors can enjoy. From seafood festivals (including in the Keys) to art and crafts, dance and design—from the ridiculous to the sublime!

Piña Colada Extra

1 jigger dark rum
1 ounce coconut milk, chilled
1 tablespoon Key lime juice
¼ cup finely crushed pineapple
½ cup finely crushed ice
Cherry for garnish
Pineapple wedge for garnish

Process rum and next 4 ingredients in a blender until smooth. Pour into a tall glass. Spear cherry and pineapple with a swizzle stick and place on top.

Yield: 1 serving

Monte Green
Seabrook Lounge
Surfside

Cuban Coffee With Milk

2 tablespoons finely ground coffee
2 cups non-chlorinated water
2 cups milk
Sugar to taste

Brew coffee in water. While brewing, warm milk in a small saucepan over low heat. Divide coffee and milk evenly among 3 coffee cups. Add sugar and stir. Serve hot.

Yield: 3 servings

Monte Green
Executive Club
North Miami Beach

Papaya/Banana Batido

- ½ cup diced ripe banana
- 1 cup diced papaya
- 1 cup milk
- ½ cup crushed ice

Puree all ingredients in a blender. Pour into a large serving glass and serve immediately.

Yield: 1 serving

Monte Green
Executive Club
North Miami Beach

Spiced Calypso Punch

- 1 cup water, boiling
- ¼ cup honey
- 6 whole cloves
- ¼ teaspoon nutmeg
- ¼ teaspoon cinnamon
- 2 cups orange juice with pulp
- 1½ cups pineapple juice
- ¼ cup lime juice
- 1½ cups ginger ale
- Lime wedges for garnish
- Non-chlorinated crushed ice

Combine water and next 4 ingredients in a small bowl. Cool. Remove cloves. Combine water mixture, orange juice, and next 3 ingredients in a punch bowl. Garnish. Serve over ice in punch glasses.

Yield: 6 to 8 servings

Monte Green
Executive Club
North Miami Beach

Cuba Libre

2 jiggers cola
1 jigger light rum
2 lime wedges, divided

Combine cola and rum in an ice-filled glass. Squeeze juice from 1 lime wedge into glass. Stir and garnish with remaining lime wedge.

Yield: 1 serving

Monte Green
Executive Club
North Miami Beach

Ernest Hemingway's Mojito

Juice of 1 Key lime
1 teaspoon superfine sugar
2 ounces white rum
½ ounce club soda
Sprig of fresh mint for garnish

Combine lime juice and sugar in a tall glass. Stir until sugar dissolves. Fill glass three-fourths full with crushed ice. Add rum and soda. Mix well and garnish.

Yield: 1 serving

Monte Green
Venetion Isle Motel
Venetion Isle

Rum Swizzle

This drink is an old Cuban favorite.

1 jigger dark rum
½ ounce Key lime juice
Dash of bitters
Club soda
Key lime wedge for garnish

Combine rum, lime juice, and bitters in a tall, ice-filled glass. Fill to top with club soda. Mix well and garnish.

Yield: 1 serving

Monte Green
Venetion Isle Motel
Venetion Isle

Cuban Cocktail

2 ounces white rum
½ jigger apricot-flavored brandy
½ ounce lime juice

Combine all ingredients in an ice-filled glass. Stir.

Yield: 1 serving

Monte Green
Venetion Isle Motel
Venetion Isle

Conch's Dream

1¼ ounces Pussers gold rum
1½ ounces orange juice
1½ ounces pineapple juice
1½ ounces half-and -half
1½ ounces Coco Lopez
Nutmeg
Orange slice and cherry for garnish

Pour rum over ice in hurricane glass. In blender, mix next 4 ingredients and dash of nutmeg. Pour over rum and garnish with fruit.

Yield: 1 serving

Michelle Grenfell
The Conch Restaurant
Islamorada

Pineapple Daiquiri

1½ jiggers white rum
½ ounce Cointreau
½ ounce Key lime juice
½ cup crushed ice
½ cup crushed pineapple
Sugar to taste
Pineapple wedge for garnish

Process rum and next 5 ingredients in a blender until smooth. Pour into a daiquiri glass and garnish. Serve with a straw.

Yield: 1 serving

Monte Green
Venetion Isle Motel
Venetion Isle

Fishing is spectacular in most of the Caribbean. Reefs are covered with sea fans and riotously colored tropical fish. In the "deep," the powerful blue marlin, the swift wahoo, and acrobatic mahi mahi (dolphin fish) roam along with bull-tough yellowfin and blackfin tuna, to name a few.

Banana Daiquiri

- 1 jigger white rum
- ½ ripe banana, cut into several pieces
- 1 cup crushed ice
- ½ ounce Key lime juice
- ½ ounce Triple Sec
- Key lime twist for garnish

Process rum and next 4 ingredients in a blender until smooth. Pour into a daiquiri glass and garnish. Serve with a straw.

Yield: 1 serving

Monte Green
Venetion Isle Motel
Venetion Isle

Mango Daiquiri

- 4 jiggers light rum
- 1 ounce Curaçao
- ½ cup chopped ripe mango
- 1 tablespoon sugar
- 1 ounce Key lime juice
- 2 cups crushed ice
- Mango slices or chunks for garnish

Process rum and next 5 ingredients in a blender until smooth. Pour into 2 daiquiri glasses and garnish.

Yield: 2 servings

Monte Green
Venetion Isle Motel
Venetion Isle

SALADS

THE BAHAMAS

With this island chain's proximity to the Florida Keys and the east coast of Florida, it's no wonder that the influences of its "hey mon" folks, their culture and foods would be a great one. The 700 cays that make up the Bahamian chain, which is likened to a necklace of emeralds, are in their own ways as unique and varied as priceless jewels. New Providence Island is the most populated, although not the largest, island in the chain. Nassau is on New Providence, a city of commerce, industry, and communications. Old-world elegance and new-world vitality blend well, showcased by well-preserved colonial architecture, straw markets, picturesque surreys, casino gambling, world-class entertainment, duty-free shopping, and food — yes, foods that have influenced the Caribbean flavor of the tropics immeasurably.

The national dish of the Bahamas is conch, the fleshy creamy white meat of a large mollusk found off the shores of the Bahamas. The conch has been popular in the Keys, as well, so today the queen conch is endangered. Mounds of conch shells lie in Freeport, in the Bahamas — a testament to the take-without-giving-back, free-for-all these mollusks have been under for far too long. Today in the Caicos Islands on Providenciales there is a conch farm that proves they can be grown for commercial restaurant use and can be reseeded where they have been picked clean.

Dining in the Bahamas is rather extraordinary. There is just one five-star restaurant in the region, but many of the colorful local establishments qualify as great eateries, offering conch dishes (stews, fritters, and chowders) and steaks (sautéed, stuffed, or fried).

Grassy Key Dairy Bar's Conch Salad

- 1 pound conch, diced
- 2 medium onions, chopped
- 2 bell peppers, chopped
- 3 banana peppers, chopped
- 1 Scotch bonnet pepper, chopped
- 2 medium tomatoes, chopped
- 1 teaspoon thyme
- 1 teaspoon sugar
- 1 teaspoon ground allspice
- 1 teaspoon oregano
- 1 teaspoon chopped garlic
- ½ cup vegetable oil
- ¼ cup Worcestershire sauce
- ½ cup vinegar
- ¼ cup Key lime juice
- ¼ cup lemon juice
- Hot pepper sauce to taste

Marinated meats and fish are typical of Caribbean cuisine.

Combine all ingredients. Refrigerate at least 24 hours. Serve on a bed of lettuce.

Yield: 4 servings

The longer it marinates, the spicier this salad gets.

George and John Eigner
Grassy Key Dairy Bar
Marathon

Conch Salad

- 1 pound conch
- 1 small onion, sliced
- 1 small bell pepper, sliced
- 1 small red bell pepper, sliced
- 1 small yellow bell pepper, sliced
- 1 cup oil
- ½ cup water
- ¼ cup white vinegar
- ¼ cup Key lime juice
- 2 tablespoons Dijon mustard
- 1 teaspoon salt
- ½ teaspoon black pepper
- 1 tablespoon chopped garlic
- 2 tablespoons sugar

Tenderize conch by pounding with a mallet until it starts to fall apart. Dice conch and combine with onion and bell peppers. Whip together oil and remaining 8 ingredients. Pour over conch mixture. Mix well and marinate overnight in the refrigerator.

Yield: 4 servings

Edith Grenfell
The Conch Restaurant
Islamorada

Cayman Island Conch Salad

- 2 pounds conch
- 1 quart fresh lime juice
- 5 ounces hot pepper sauce
- 1½ tablespoons minced garlic
- 3 tablespoons minced fresh cilantro
- ½ cup diced bell pepper
- ½ cup diced red onion
- 1 cup diced tomato
- ½ cup diced celery
- 3 teaspoons salt
- Lime wedges for garnish

Before refrigeration or ice was available in the tropics, sauces, such as hot pepper sauce, were used to keep seafood fresh.

Pound conch with a mallet to flatten and tenderize. Place in a bowl and cover with lime juice. Marinate in refrigerator at least 24 hours. Drain conch, discarding lime juice. Dice into ¼-inch pieces. Combine conch, hot pepper sauce, and next 7 ingredients in a large bowl. Marinate 2 to 4 hours before serving. Serve on lettuce-lined salad plates with lime wedges on the side.

Yield: 7 servings

Bob Stoky
Sundowners
Key Largo

Caribbean Chicken Salad

- 3 cups cooked rice, cooled
- 2 cups diced cooked chicken or turkey
- 1 cup finely sliced celery
- ¼ cup chopped bell pepper
- 1 (20-ounce) can pineapple chunks, drained and halved
- 2 tablespoons sliced pimento
- ½ cup mayonnaise
- ¼ cup sour cream
- 1½ tablespoons lemon juice
- ½ teaspoon salt
- 1 teaspoon curry powder
- ¼ teaspoon black pepper
- Lettuce leaves

Combine rice and next 5 ingredients. In a separate bowl, blend mayonnaise and next 5 ingredients. Pour over rice mixture. Toss lightly and chill. Serve on lettuce leaves. If desired, garnish with scallions, parsley, tomato wedges, or ripe olives.

Yield: 6 servings

USA Rice Council

Tropical Chicken Salad

Marinated Chicken

1 cup coconut milk
½ cup soy sauce
2 tablespoons chopped garlic
2 tablespoons chopped ginger
½ cup orange juice
¼ cup lime juice
4 chicken breasts

Salad Dressing

1 cup sour cream
3 tablespoons curry powder
1 tablespoon lime juice
Sugar to taste

Salad

Mixed fresh salad greens
Sliced green apples for garnish
Alfalfa sprouts
Toasted coconut
Sliced almonds

Combine coconut milk and next 6 ingredients. Marinate until just prior to serving. Drain chicken and grill. Slice cooked chicken into strips. To prepare dressing, mix together sour cream and next 3 ingredients. To assemble salad, arrange greens on a serving platter. Place chicken strips on top. Garnish with green apple slices. Drizzle dressing over salad. Top with alfalfa sprouts, coconut, and almonds.

Yield: 4 to 6 servings

Ronney Sellack
Garden Cafe
Key West

Curried Coconut and Chicken Salad

- 3 cups coconut
- 2 oranges
- 1 cup raisins
- 2 cups cooked chicken, cubed
- 1 onion
- 1 (8-ounce) can jellied cranberry sauce, chilled and cut into ½-inch cubes
- 1 cup mayonnaise
- 1 teaspoon chicken base seasoning
- 2 teaspoons curry powder
- 1 teaspoon finely chopped ginger
- Salt and pepper to taste
- 1 tablespoon coconut flakes

Peel brown outer skin from coconut and slice as thinly as possible. Section oranges. In a large bowl, place coconut, orange, raisins, chicken, onion, and cranberry cubes; set aside. Combine mayonnaise, chicken seasoning, curry, ginger, and salt and pepper. Gently mix with chicken and fruit mixture. Chill well; sprinkle with coconut flakes before serving.

Yield: 4 servings

Michael Nighty
Holiday Inn
Grand Cayman Island

Served in Grenada and Trinidad, oildown stew is a mixture of salt pork and breadfruit that's stewed in coconut milk.

Avocado-Crab Salad

Avocados and crab are both commonly harvested in Caribbean areas.

2 ripe avocados, peeled and diced
2 hard-cooked eggs, diced
3 stalks celery, chopped
½ medium onion, chopped
¼ cup sweet pickle relish
Juice of 1½ limes
1 cup mayonnaise
8 ounces cooked crabmeat, flaked
Everglades seasoning to taste, or salt and pepper
Crumbled cooked bacon for garnish

Combine avocado and next 8 ingredients. Mix gently and chill. Serve on a bed of lettuce. Garnish with bacon sprinkled on top.

Yield: 6 servings

Valerie Mayfield
Jim and Val's Tugboat Restaurant
Key Largo

Fresh Tuna Salad

1 pound blackfin tuna
8 cups water, divided
⅔ cup milk, divided
Salt and pepper to taste
3 stalks celery, chopped
3 scallions, chopped
¼ cup chopped black olives
2 hard-cooked eggs, chopped
2 tablespoons mayonnaise

Place tuna in a pan. Cover with 4 cups water and ⅓ cup milk. Bring to a boil and cook 4 minutes. Discard water mixture. Add remaining 4 cups water and ⅓ cup milk to pan. Boil again for 4 minutes. Drain tuna and pat dry with paper towels. Remove blood vein, if present. Flake tuna with a fork. Combine tuna, salt, pepper, and next 4 ingredients. Mix well. Stir in mayonnaise.

Yield: 2 to 4 servings

Laura Brumm and Captain Allen King
Land's End Marina
Afternoon Delight III charter boat
Key Colony Beach

Sea turtles, a common visitor to Keys beaches each year, do not depend on land for any purpose other than to lay their eggs.

Spicy Tuna Salad

3 ounces fresh tuna
½ cup chopped cucumber
½ tomato, chopped
1 scallion, chopped
1 orange, peeled and chopped
Spicy sauce

Cook and chop tuna. Combine tuna and remaining 5 ingredients. Chill. Serve with sesame rice cakes and sliced ginger.

Yield: 1 serving

Tony K. Liam
Makoto Japanese Restaurant
Key Largo

Lentil Salad With Spiced Vinaigrette

9 cups water
2 tablespoons non-iodized salt
1 pound dried lentils
1 teaspoon cayenne pepper
⅓ cup virgin olive oil
1 teaspoon salt
⅓ cup white wine vinegar
½ teaspoon cumin
½ teaspoon ground coriander

Lentils, heavily cultivated in Grenada, are a nutritious staple for the islanders.

Bring water and non-iodized salt to a boil. Add lentils. Reduce heat to low and cook 30 minutes or until tender. Do not overcook. Drain, rinse with cold water, and drain again. In a large mixing bowl, combine lentils, cayenne pepper, and remaining 5 ingredients. Refrigerate at least 2 hours. Serve cold with Cuban bread or crackers.

Yield: 8 servings

Mari Green
Blue Horizons
Surfside

Jerked Shrimp Cobb

Salad

1 pound (31 to 35 count) shrimp, peeled and deveined

Salt and pepper to taste

¾ cup olive oil

4 ounces Caribbean jerk seasoning

Juice of 1 lemon

1 head romaine lettuce

4 plum tomatoes, sliced ⅛ inch thick

4 eggs, hard-cooked and sliced

1 ripe avocado, sliced

½ cup alfalfa sprouts

Jalapeño Vinaigrette

¾ cup oil

¼ cup red wine vinegar

3 jalapeño peppers, seeded

1 tablespoon sugar

Juice of 1 lemon

Combine shrimp, salt, pepper, and next 3 ingredients. Marinate in refrigerator overnight. Drain shrimp and grill just prior to serving salad. Clean lettuce leaves and cut into bite-size pieces. Place in a serving bowl. Arrange grilled shrimp, tomato, and next 3 ingredients on top. Prepare dressing by combining oil and remaining 4 ingredients in a blender. Serve dressing with salad.

Yield: 4 servings

Stephen Valentine
Marriott Key Largo Bay Beach Resort
Key Largo

Plantation Key was so called because of its pineapple plantations. R.J. Reynolds Tobacco Co. once owned the resort known today as Plantation Yacht Harbor. It was a pineapple plantation in the late 1800's and early 1900's.

Banana Nut Salad

Honey Dressing

¼ cup honey
¼ cup lime juice
Pinch of ground ginger

Salad

1 tablespoon peanut butter
1 banana, peeled and halved lengthwise
3 leaves lettuce
2 tablespoons chopped peanuts or English walnuts
4 orange sections for garnish
2 tablespoons red currant jelly for garnish
Honey dressing to taste

Heat honey. Stir in lime juice and ginger. To assemble salad, spread peanut butter on cut side of banana halves. Place halves, cut side up, on lettuce leaves. Sprinkle with chopped nuts. Garnish with orange sections and jelly. Drizzle honey dressing over top.

Yield: 1 serving

Bill Valet
Ballyhoo's Grille and Grog
Key Largo

Joe's Gorgonzola Salad

½ cup corn oil
Salt and pepper to taste
¼ cup cider vinegar
⅛ teaspoon garlic powder, or to taste
1 egg white
Crumbled Gorgonzola cheese

Combine oil, salt, pepper, and next 3 ingredients in a blender or food processor to make a dressing. To assemble salad, sprinkle cheese over a bed of lettuce, red cabbage, and diced onion. Top with dressing. Grind black pepper over salad, if desired.

Yield: 4 servings

Joseph H. Roth, Jr.
Holiday Isle Resort and Marina
Islamorda

Spain's sweet Valencia oranges became bitter, shriveled fruit in the tropical soil and climate of early Curacao. But the fruit's sun-dried skin yielded an extraordinary fragrant oil, which when combined with spices and distilled became what is today known as Curacao liqueur—the sunny essence of orange.

Curry Shrimp Salad

1 pound (21 to 30 count) shrimp, peeled and deveined
3 ounces mango chutney
½ cup mayonnaise
Curry powder to taste
1 stalks celery, chopped
Dash of cayenne pepper
Iceberg or Romaine lettuce inner leaves
1 plum tomato, cut into wedges
2 tablespoons finely diced red bell pepper

Cook shrimp. Drain and chop coarsely. Combine shrimp and next 5 ingredients. Chill. Arrange lettuce leaves on a serving plate. Mound shrimp mixture on leaves. Place tomato wedges around mound of shrimp and sprinkle top with bell pepper.

Yield: 4 or 5 servings

Carole Baker
Grove Park Cafe
Islamorada

Spicy Beef Salad

- ¾ pound beef
- 2 tablespoons fish sauce
- 2 tablespoons lime juice
- 10 chili peppers
- 1 cup sliced red or white onion
- 7 cucumber slices
- ½ tomato, thinly sliced
- 1 scallion, cut in 1-inch sections
- 3 leaves lettuce

Grill beef to a medium-rare doneness. Cut into thin slices. Combine fish sauce, lime juice, and chili peppers in a bowl. Add beef slices, onion, and next 3 ingredients. Mix thoroughly. Arrange lettuce on a serving platter. Place beef mixture on top. Garnish with parsley or tomato.

Yield: 2 servings

Panyaporn Russmetes
Num-Thai Restaurant and Sushi Bar
Key Largo

Hot Pepper Bottle

- 1½ cups white vinegar
- ½ cup vegetable oil
- ½ medium onion, diced
- 2 scallions, sliced
- 4 cloves garlic, chopped
- 1 ounce fresh thyme
- 3 Scotch bonnet or chili peppers, sliced

Combine all ingredients in a glass bottle. Refrigerate at least 2 days before using.

Yield: about 2¼ cups

This is a good dressing for salads or vegetables.

Mia Casey
Marriott's Frenchman's Reef Beach Resort
St. Thomas, United States Virgin Islands

Mango Vinaigrette

Mangoes are a tropical fruit commonly used in Caribbean cooking.

- 1 mango, mashed
- 1 shallot, minced
- 1 cup rice wine vinegar
- 2 cups oil
- 2 tablespoons chopped fresh cilantro
- 1 tablespoon chopped fresh mint

Combine mango and next 3 ingredients. Add cilantro and mint. Serve over the newer mixed greens or Oriental mixes on the market.

Yield: 8 to 10 servings

Wayne Kass
Sugarloaf Lodge
Sugarloaf Shores

Honey Key Lime Salad Dressing

- 2 shallots
- Salt and pepper to taste
- 2 cloves garlic
- 1 cup clover honey
- ¾ cup Key lime juice
- Extra virgin olive oil to taste

Process shallots, salt, pepper, and next 3 ingredients in a blender or food processor. Slowly blend in oil. Serve over salad.

Yield: 6 to 8 servings

Philip M. Smith
Mangoe's
Key West

Cou-Cou is a Barbadian side dish made of okra and cornmeal.

SIDE DISHES & BREADS

HAITI
DOMINICAN REPUBLIC
PUERTO RICO

The island of Hispaniola is home to both Haiti and the Dominican Republic. The diversity of both peoples, flora, and fauna makes this an interesting place to visit. Spicy succulent foods are devoured on both sides of the island. Seafood in the Monti Christi area of Dominicana is an early-century bargain. Not easy to get to, Monti Christi is a beautiful place with gorgeous hilly bluffs overlooking crystal clear waters filled with fish of all types.

Few places anywhere can match Dominicana as a fabulous place to play, fish, swim, dine, and stay. Virgin wild enclaves help to conserve one of the richest biological diversities on the planet. Bright-colored birds flutter among jungle vines and rainforest orchids. Ocean beaches and huge boulders and bluffs, as well as lush tropical reefs, shelter big grouper and colorful reef fish. The Dominican Republic has many restaurants that naturally serve fabulous Spanish-style dishes: from ropa vieja — shredded beef accompanied by black beans and rice — to that fabulous dessert called flan, which is a Spanish-style custard. In Haiti, at Port-au-Prince, Creole is the standard, with both fish and chicken meals served here.

Puerto Rico showcases lovely Spanish colonial towns, a lush and beautiful rainforest, quiet seaside restaurants, and golden-hued, kissed-by-the-sun beaches. In 1917, Puerto Ricans were granted U.S. citizenship. Today a harmonious mingle of American and Spanish cultures is the norm.

A visit to Puerto Rico will definitely entail some fine dining. Traditional Puerto Rican cuisine is a very flavorful mix of Spanish, Creole, and native Indian influences.

Lorelei's Jamaican Rice and Peas

- 1 cup cooked kidney beans, rinsed and drained
- 1 quart hot water
- 1 teaspoon chopped garlic
- 3 cups uncooked rice
- 2 stalks leeks, chopped
- Sprigs of fresh thyme to taste
- Salt to taste
- ¼ teaspoon black pepper
- 2 tablespoons coconut milk, or to taste

Combine kidney beans, water, and garlic in a pot. Cook until beans are tender but not overcooked. Add rice and remaining 5 ingredients. Cook over medium heat, stirring only a few times, until rice is tender. Add more water if needed to cook rice.

Yield: 6 to 8 servings

When adding rice, add a small amount of salt pork for extra flavor.

John Maloughney
Lorelei Restaurant
Islamorada

Empanadillas are crescent-shaped spicy pastries filled with everything from land crab to pork and served in various guises all over the Caribbean.

Caribbean Rice and Beans

- ¼ cup chopped onion
- 1 clove garlic, minced
- 1 tablespoon olive oil
- 1 tablespoon butter
- 4½ cups cooked beans, any type, drained
- Salt and pepper to taste
- 1 medium tomato, chopped
- ½ cup dry white wine
- ½ teaspoon chili powder
- ⅛ teaspoon ground cloves
- 2 tablespoons chopped fresh cilantro or parsley
- 4 cups hot cooked rice

Sauté onion and garlic in oil and butter until tender. Stir in beans, salt, pepper, and next 4 ingredients. Cover and simmer 20 minutes. Stir in cilantro. Serve over rice.

Yield: 6 to 8 servings

USA Rice Council

Caribbean Island Rice

- 1 cup uncooked rice
- 1 cup orange juice
- 1 cup chicken broth
- 1 teaspoon salt (optional)
- ¼ teaspoon white pepper
- ¼ cup flaked or grated coconut
- 1 tablespoon unsalted margarine
- 2 cups peeled and diced papaya

Combine rice and next 4 ingredients in a medium saucepan. Bring to a boil, stirring once or twice. Reduce heat and cover. Simmer 15 minutes or until rice is tender and liquid is absorbed. Remove from heat. Stir in coconut and margarine. Cover and let stand 10 minutes. Fold in papaya.

Yield: 6 servings

Replace papaya with fresh or canned mango or canned peach, if desired.

USA Rice Council

Straw markets, open-air events, are found everywhere in the Caribbean.

Caribbean Rice

- ½ cup unsweetened grated coconut
- 2 cups hot cooked rice
- 1 (11-ounce) can mandarin oranges, drained and coarsely chopped
- 1 (8-ounce) can crushed pineapple, drained
- ½ cup chopped red bell pepper
- ½ cup slivered almonds, toasted
- ⅓ cup sliced scallions
- 2 tablespoons mango chutney
- ¼ teaspoon ground ginger

Spread coconut on an ungreased baking sheet and toast in an oven at 300° for 1 minute. Combine coconut and remaining 8 ingredients in a large skillet over medium-high heat. Cook and stir to blend and thoroughly heat ingredients. Serve with grilled or broiled shrimp.

Yield: 4 servings

USA Rice Council

Yellow Rice

- 2½ cups chicken broth
- 2½ cups non-chlorinated water
- 4 tablespoons butter
- ½ teaspoon powdered saffron
- ½ teaspoon sea salt
- 2 cups uncooked long-grain rice

Combine broth and next 4 ingredients in a large pot. Bring to a boil over medium heat. Stir in rice. Reduce heat to medium-low and cover. Simmer, stirring often, 15 to 20 minutes or until rice is tender.

Yield: 6 servings

Monte Green
Banana Patch
North Miami Beach

This dish, also called Arroz Amarillo in Spanish, derives its yellow color from the saffron.

Fried Sweet Plantains

This is a standard Cuban side dish routinely served in restaurants with an entrée, beans, and rice.

- 3 ripe plantains, peeled
- 1 tablespoons virgin olive oil
- 4 tablespoons butter or margarine
- Juice of 1 Key lime or lemon
- Salt to taste

Cut plantains lengthwise into long slices. Heat oil and butter over medium-low heat in a skillet. Add plantain and fry 3 to 5 minutes on both sides. Shake skillet while cooking to prevent sticking. Drain plantain on paper towels. Place on a serving platter. Sprinkle with lime juice and salt. Serve warm.

Yield: 6 servings

Monte Green
Olympia Bar and Grill
Dade County

Funchi

- 1 cup yellow cornmeal
- 3 cups water, divided
- 4 tablespoons butter
- ½ cup sliced okra
- ½ teaspoon salt
- White pepper to taste

Combine cornmeal and 1 cup water in a bowl. Stir until smooth. Bring remaining 2 cups water to a boil in a medium saucepan. Add cornmeal mixture, butter, and remaining 3 ingredients. Cook 5 minutes, stirring constantly. Serve immediately when smooth and thick enough to scoop.

Yield: 2 servings

Mia Casey
Marriott's Frenchman's Reef Beach Resort
St. Thomas, U. S. Virgin Islands

Yuca With Garlic Sauce

- 1½ pounds yuca, peeled and cubed
- 1 teaspoon sea salt
- 5 cloves garlic, minced
- Juice of 1 large Key lime or lemon
- ⅔ cup virgin olive oil

Yuca is a favorite Caribbean side dish, often served with pork, beef, or chicken.

Place yuca in a saucepan. Add water to 1 inch above yuca. Add salt. Bring to a boil over high heat. Reduce heat and cover. Cook 30 minutes or until yuca is tender but not too soft. Drain yuca and transfer to a sauté pan. While tossing, add garlic, lime juice, and oil. Cook over medium heat, tossing lightly, for 5 to 6 minutes or until browned. Serve warm.

Yield: 4 servings

Mari Green
Blue Horizons
Surfside

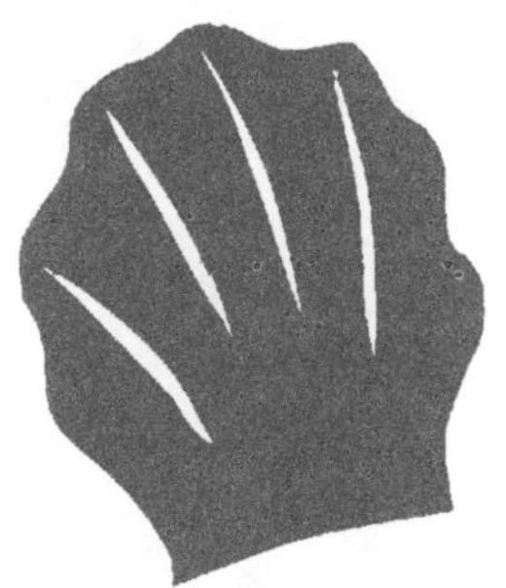

Shrimp Hash Cakes

- 1 pound round white potatoes
- 1 pound shrimp, peeled, deveined, and tails removed
- 1 egg, beaten
- 2 tablespoons chili oil
- ⅓ cup diced bell pepper
- ⅓ cup diced red bell pepper
- ⅓ cup diced yellow bell pepper
- 1 tablespoon diced poblano chili pepper
- ½ cup diced red onion
- 2 scallions, diced
- 3 tablespoons Parmesan cheese
- ½ cup chopped watercress
- ⅓ cup chopped parsley
- 1½ tablespoons chopped fresh chives
- ¼ teaspoon white pepper
- ½ teaspoon sea salt
- ½ cup breadcrumbs, plus extra for coating

Boil potatoes in their skins. Cook until outer potato is tender but center is still firm. Chill and peel. Break up half of the potatoes by hand. Finely grind the remaining potatoes and add to other potato. Saute shrimp until fully cooked. Cool and finely grind shrimp. Combine shrimp and egg and refrigerate. Sauté oil and next 6 ingredients until soft. Refrigerate until chilled. Combine potato and sautéed vegetables. Mix in cheese and next 5 ingredients. Fold in shrimp mixture. Add ½ cup breadcrumbs and mix. Refrigerate at least 60 minutes. Using about ½ cup of mixture each, form into patties. Press into extra breadcrumbs to coat. Fry in a skillet until golden brown on both sides.

Yield: 10 patties

Pat Tenney
Louie's Backyard
Key West

.The only living coral reefs on the North American continent are found paralleling the Keys.

BREADS

Caribbean-Style French Toast

6	eggs	2	tablespoons sugar
2	tablespoons cinnamon	¼	cup spiced rum (optional)
1	tablespoon vanilla	4	tablespoons butter
1	tablespoon baking powder		Bread of choice
			Powdered sugar for garnish

Beat eggs and next 5 ingredients together. Heat butter in a skillet over low heat. Dip bread in egg mixture. Place in skillet and cook until golden brown. Sprinkle with powdered sugar. Serve with syrup.

Yield: 4 to 6 servings

Wood carving, a popular and important craft in the Caribbean, turns out fish, whales, other animals, figurines, bowls, tables, statues—whatever you like—from teak, mahogany, blue mahoe, and a plethora of native woods.

Joe's Banana Bread Muffins

2 eggs
⅔ cup oil
1 teaspoon salt
1½ cups sugar
1½ cups all-purpose flour
1 teaspoon baking soda
½ cup water
1 cup pureed banana
¼ cup chopped nuts

Combine eggs and next 3 ingredients in a bowl. Stir in flour and remaining 4 ingredients. Pour batter into greased muffin tins or loaf pans. Bake at 350° for 15 to 20 minutes or until a toothpick inserted in the center comes out clean.

Yield: 1½ dozen muffins

Replace nuts with raisins, if desired, or use both in the recipe.

Joe Roth
Holiday Isle Resort and Marina
Islamorada

Banana Bread

Bananas are a major fruit and cooking ingredient in the Caribbean.

6 eggs
5 cups sugar
1 pint vegetable oil
4½ cups flour
¾ tablespoons salt
1¼ tablespoons baking powder
1¼ tablespoons baking soda
8 overripe bananas, pureed
1½ cups water
1 cup coconut
1 cup pecan pieces

Cream eggs, sugar, and oil together. Sift together flour and next 3 ingredients. Stir dry ingredients into creamed mixture. Mix well. Add banana. Slowly mix in water. Mix in coconut and pecan pieces. Divide into greased and floured loaf pans. Bake at 350° for 30 minutes or until bread is golden and begins to pull away from sides of pan.

Yield: 4 or 5 loaves

Bill Wiseman
Treetops
Key Largo

Old-fashioned Lemon Bread

Bread

- 1½ cups all-purpose flour
- 1 cup sugar
- 1 teaspoon baking powder
- ½ teaspoon salt
- 2 eggs
- ½ cup milk
- ½ cup oil
- 1½ teaspoons lemon or Key lime zest, or to taste

Lemon Glaze

- 4½ tablespoons lemon juice
- ⅓ cup sugar

Combine flour and next 3 ingredients in a large bowl. In a small bowl, beat together eggs and next 3 ingredients. Stir egg mixture into dry ingredients until just blended. Pour batter into a greased and floured 5x9 inch loaf pan. Bake at 350° for 40 to 45 minutes or until a toothpick inserted in the center comes out clean. While bread bakes, prepare lemon glaze by combining lemon juice and sugar in a small pan. Cook over medium heat, stirring constantly, until sugar dissolves. Remove from heat, but reheat when ready to use. When baked, remove bread from oven but leave in pan. While still hot, use a long skewer to poke holes to the bottom of the bread. Slowly drizzle hot glaze over top of bread. Cool in pan on a rack for 10 minutes. Turn out of pan and cool completely. Serve at room temperature.

Yield: 10 to 12 servings

Andrea Gallagher
Hungry Tarpon
Islamorada

Hurricane Terminology: ***Tropical Disturbance*—a moving area of thunderstorms. *Tropical Depression*—an area of low pressure, cloud pattern, and winds up to 38 miles per hour. *Tropical Storm*—is a counterclockwise cloud movement with winds from 39 to 74 mph. The tropical storm is assigned a name. *Hurricane*—a tropical storm that reaches 75 mph or more. *Advisory*–information made available to the public every six hours about storms and hurricanes.**

Bahamian Coconut Bread

Coconut is a common ingredient in Caribbean recipes.

- 3 cups unbleached flour
- 2 cups coarsely grated fresh coconut
- 1 cup sugar
- 1 tablespoon baking powder
- 1 teaspoon salt
- 1 teaspoon nutmeg
- 2 eggs
- 1 cup milk
- 2 tablespoons butter or margarine, melted, or oil
- 1 teaspoon vanilla

Combine flour and next 5 ingredients in a large bowl. In a separate bowl, beat together eggs and remaining 3 ingredients. Stir egg mixture into dry ingredients. Pour batter into a greased and floured 8-inch cast iron skillet. Bake at 350° for 45 to 60 minutes or until a toothpick inserted in the center comes out clean. Cool in skillet.

Yield: 10 to 12 servings

Serve bread with honey, or use as a dessert by topping a slice with ice cream and amaretto.

George McHugh
The Hungry Tarpon
Islamorada

SOUPS & CHOWDERS

BRITISH & U.S. VIRGIN ISLANDS

The British Virgin Islands consist of Anegada, Virgin Gorda, and Tortola, plus about 57 others. Spectacular white beaches and rich sapphire waters are punctuated by the verdant nature of this archipelago. Dining is quite informal in these islands. On Tortola, you'll find a variety of restaurants, many of which are located in historic old homes. Many of the fancier restaurants will require a boat ride to reach your location. Try some of the West Indian specialties, which consist of lots of fresh seafood.

Of the three U.S. Virgin Islands, St. Thomas is the busiest and most active. The port city of Charlotte Amalie is a picture-postcard waterfront that attracts thousands of tourists each year. Some of the most fabulous beaches in the West Indies stretch their powdery white trails along the waterway. If you love watersports, blue marlin fishing, sunbathing, or just want to relax and perhaps take in some duty-free shopping, then you'll love St. Thomas. In this vibrant place, enjoy American cuisine prepared with a Caribbean flair — or perhaps Chinese or French foods.

St. John is the smallest of the three islands, with half of this area preserved as a national park. Cruz Point is the arrival point here. Cruz Point is situated on a picturesque harbor at the west end of the island. Continental cuisine as well as Creole cooking will excite your taste buds here.

St. Croix, the largest of the three islands, is endowed with a diverse and gorgeous landscape. There is spiny desert vegetation, yet beautiful verdant hills and a lush rainforest in the western mountains. The island is skirted by white-sand beaches that are as breathtaking as the island's countryside. Delectable dinners of fresh fish and seafood sautéed or stuffed are the rule rather than the exception in these islands.

Hungary Tarpon Conch Chowder

20 ounces conch, cleaned and skinned
Olive oil
12 ounces red potatoes, peeled and diced
8 ounces onions, peeled and diced
½ bell pepper, chopped
1 (28-ounce) can Italian-style whole tomatoes
1 small smoked ham hock
Salt and pepper to taste
2 bay leaves
½ tablespoon dried thyme
1 tablespoon hot pepper sauce
Chopped garlic to taste
2 tablespoons sherry

Pound conch thoroughly with a tenderizing mallet. Cut across the grain into small strips. Sauté conch in a small amount of olive oil for 5 minutes or until strips begin to curl and change color. Transfer conch and any liquid rendered during sautéing to a large pot. Add potato, onion, and bell pepper. Press tomatoes through a sieve into the pot, scraping tomato on outside of sieve into pot. Discard seeds and pulp. Add ham hock, salt, pepper, and next 4 ingredients. Add water if needed to cover. Stir. Simmer over very low heat or in a crock pot 12 to 18 hours. Remove ham hock and bay leaves. Add sherry and adjust seasonings as desired. Serve with crackers and additional sherry on the side.

Yield: 8 (8-ounce) servings

George McHugh
The Hungry Tarpon
Islamorada

The thyme in this Bahamian recipe is similar to a native herb used by Bahamian cooks.

Joe's Famous Conch Chowder

- 8 ounces salt pork, chopped
- 2 medium onions, minced
- 1 large bell pepper, chopped
- 3 small potatoes, cubed
- 4 cloves garlic, chopped
- 1 (16-ounce) can tomatoes with basil, chopped and undrained
- 1 (12-ounce) can tomato paste
- 2 quarts water
- 1 teaspoon poultry seasoning
- 1 teaspoon basil
- ½ teaspoon hot pepper sauce
- 1 tablespoon oregano
- 1 tablespoon wine vinegar
- 6 bay leaves
- 2 tablespoons barbecue sauce
- 1½ teaspoons salt
- ½ teaspoon black pepper
- 8 ounces conch, pounded and chopped

Cook salt pork in a large pot until brown and crispy. Add onion and next 3 ingredients. Heat slowly to prevent burning. Add tomato and next 11 ingredients. Stir in conch. Simmer 2 hours. Remove bay leaves before serving.

Yield: 12 to 15 servings

Joe Roth
Holiday Isle Resort and Marina
Islamorada

Jammers Conch Chowder

- ½ tablespoon butter
- 1 slice bacon, diced
- 7 stalks celery, diced
- 2 cups diced bell pepper
- 3⅓ cups diced onion
- 2 (28-ounce) cans tomatoes, drained and diced
- 2 cups ketchup
- 1 quart water
- 1¼ teaspoons oregano
- 1 basil leaf, crushed
- 1 teaspoon red wine vinegar
- 1 clove garlic, crushed
- 2 tablespoons cooking sherry
- 18 ounces conch, ground

Melt butter in a large pot. Add bacon and cook until browned. Add celery, bell pepper, and onion. Sauté until vegetables are transparent. Stir in tomato and remaining 8 ingredients. Simmer until vegetables are soft.

Yield: 8 servings

Larry Thomas
Jammers
Islamorada

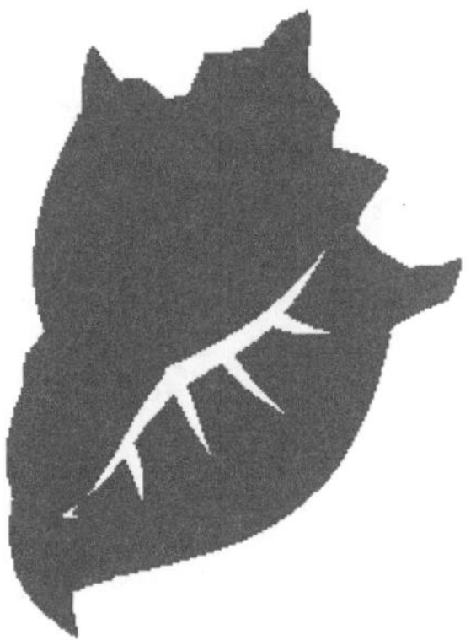

Escoveitch is a pickled fish that's served as a snack or full meal. The name is taken from the Spanish *escabeche.*

Smuggler's Cove Conch Chowder

This dish is a staple food in the Bahamian diet.

- 2 pounds conch
- 2 tablespoons butter
- 6 slices bacon
- 4 ounces ham, cubed
- 2 bay leaves
- 1 Spanish onion, diced
- 3 stalks celery, diced
- 4 large tomatoes, diced, or 1 (16-ounce) can crushed tomatoes
- 1 bell pepper, diced
- 1 large red potato, diced
- 1 cup fish broth
- Pinch of cayenne pepper
- Dash of lime juice
- Salt and pepper to taste

Tenderize conch with a mallet by pounding conch until it starts to fall apart. Dice conch; set aside. Sauté butter and next 4 ingredients in a large saucepan or pot. Add celery, tomato, and bell pepper. Continue cooking until vegetables are tender. Add conch, potato, and next 3 ingredients. Season with salt and pepper. Cook until potato is tender. Remove bacon and bay leaves. Serve with French bread or over pasta.

Yield: 4 to 6 servings

Homemade fish broth is best. If necessary, use canned chicken broth with some clam juice added for extra flavor.

Pierre Relland
Smuggler's Cove
Islamorada

Conch Gazpacho

- 1 (46-ounce) can spicy vegetable juice
- 1 (46-ounce) can tomato juice
- ½ cup lime juice
- ¼ cup sherry wine vinegar
- 10 drops hot pepper sauce
- 2 tablespoons Worcestershire sauce
- 2 cucumbers, diced
- 2 stalks celery, diced
- 1 bunch scallions, sliced
- 1 bell pepper, diced
- 2 pounds raw conch, diced
- 1 tablespoon celery salt
- 1 tablespoon black pepper
- 2 tablespoons minced garlic
- ¼ cup salad oil

Combine all ingredients. Chill 24 hours before serving.

Yield: 16 servings

Islamorada Fish Co.
Islamorada

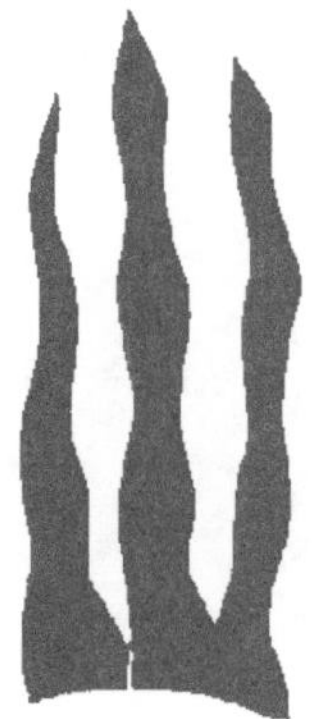

Coral reefs throughout the Caribbean are associations of ancient life forms that have been in existence about 200 million years, and the Keys is made up of the dead skeletons of these huge communities.

Conch Bisque

This rich and creamy bisque is one of many ways to prepare conch in a soup.

Bouquet Garni

- 2 sprigs fresh parsley
- 1 stalk celery
- 1 leek
- 1 large piece fresh ginger, halved

Bisque

- Bouquet garni
- 10 ounces conch, cleaned, peeled, and ground
- 2 quarts cold water
- 2 tablespoons salt
- 2 tablespoons butter
- ¼ cup all-purpose flour
- ½ cup heavy cream
- Sherry

To prepare bouquet garni, tie parsley and next 3 ingredients together with a string. Make bisque by placing bouquet garni and next 3 ingredients in a large pan. Bring to a boil. Reduce heat and simmer 1 hour, 30 minutes. Discard bouquet garni. Strain soup, reserving broth and setting conch aside. In a saucepan, melt butter. Stir in flour until smooth and thick. Slowly mix in reserved broth, stirring constantly until slightly thickened. Add conch. Bring to a boil. Reduce heat and simmer 15 minutes. Add cream and heat. Serve with sherry on the side, to be added according to taste.

Yield: 4 servings

Substitute chopped clams or whelk for conch, if desired.

Andre Mueller
Marker 88
Islamorada

White Conch Chowder

- 1½ gallons seafood broth
- ¼ cup chicken base
- 2 pounds conch, ground
- 2 bunches celery, diced
- 8 carrots, diced
- 2 medium-size white onions, diced
- 8 medium potatoes, cubed
- 1 quart heavy cream
- 2 tablespoons ground dill
- ¼ cup ground thyme
- 2 tablespoons black pepper
- ¼ cup chopped fresh parsley
- ¼ cup chopped fresh basil
- 2 tablespoons sea salt
- 1 cup all-purpose flour
- 2 sticks butter, melted

Bring broth to a boil. Reduce heat to medium and add chicken base. Mix well. Add conch, stirring to prevent conch from clumping. Add celery and next 3 ingredients. Cook, stirring occasionally, until potatoes are tender. Mix in cream and next 6 ingredients. Heat over high heat until almost boiling. Combine flour and butter. Stir until smooth. Blend flour mixture slowly into chowder until reaching desired consistency. Remove from heat.

Yield: 15 servings

Timothy J. Fodemski
Papa Joe's Landmark Restaurant
Islamorada

Caribbean Conch Consommé With Sweet Potato Tortellis and Seaweed Twists

Consommé

6 pounds conch
Zest of 1 lemon
1 white onion, chopped
3 leeks, chopped
1 head garlic, chopped
3 carrots, chopped
2 sticks butter
2 bunches lemon grass, chopped
1 quart dry white wine
1 gallon water
1 tablespoon black peppercorn
1 tablespoon coriander seed
Pinch of cayenne pepper
Salt to taste
16 egg whites, beaten
1 bunch cilantro, chopped, for garnish

Tortellis

1 pound sweet potatoes, peeled
½ bunch parsley, chopped
1 stick butter
Salt and pepper to taste
3 tablespoons water
3 tablespoons olive oil
Pinch of saffron
6 egg yolks
3 eggs
2¾ cup all-purpose flour

Seaweed Twists

4 (2-ounce) puff pastry sheets
4 roasted seaweed sheets
3 egg yolks, beaten

Boil conch and lemon zest for 1 minute. Strain and cool. Reserve large pieces of conch. Julienne these pieces and set aside for a garnish. Cut remainder of conch into cubes. In a large pot, sauté onion and next 4 ingredients together. Add lemon grass and cubed conch. Sauté 2 minutes. Stir in wine. Add water and cook over low heat for 1 hour, 30 minutes. Add black peppercorn and next 3 ingredients. Strain slowly through a fine sieve. Place egg white in pot and slowly pour in consommé. Mix together with a whisk. Cook over low heat until egg white absorbs the consommé color. Strain through a coffee filter into another pan. To prepare tortellis, cook sweet potatoes until tender. Puree with parsley, butter, salt, and pepper. Set aside. Bring water, oil, and saffron to a boil. Season with salt and pepper. Remove from heat and cool. Whip together cooled mixture, egg yolks, and eggs. Place flour in a bowl. Blend liquid mixture into flour. Let stand 1 hour. Working with half of the dough at a time, roll dough very thin into a rectangular shape. Cut into 3-inch squares. Place sweet potato mixture in the middle and fold squares in half. Seal and shape into rings. Boil tortellis in some of consommé for 1 minute. Make seaweed twists by rolling pastry sheets to twice the size of the seaweed sheets. Place a seaweed sheet on half of each pastry sheet. Fold pastry sheet over seaweed. Freeze. Cut sheets into fine strips. Twist each strip and place on a baking sheet. Brush with egg yolk and bake until golden brown. To serve, place a serving of tortellis in a soup bowl. Top with julienne pieces of conch. Pour consommé into the bowl. Sprinkle with chopped cilantro for garnish. Place seaweed twists on the side.

Yield: 20 servings

British Virgin Island Culinary Team
Peter Island Resort
Charlotte Amalie, Virgin Islands

Noted French painter Gauguin once brushed the images of the Caribbean. He was made famous by his sensuous paintings of Polynesia, but Gauguin in fact made his artistic breakthrough in Martinique in 1887. His paintings can be seen near the quaint little village of Carbet in Martinique.

Bouillabaisse

Abundant seafood highlights this Caribbean dish.

- ½ cup olive oil
- 3 cloves garlic, crushed, divided
- 2 medium onions, chopped
- 2 leeks, chopped
- 2 carrots, chopped
- Pinch of saffron
- Salt and pepper to taste
- 4 ripe tomatoes, chopped, or ½ cup canned
- 1 bay leaf
- 1 tablespoon chopped fresh fennel
- 1 sprig fresh thyme
- 5 sprigs fresh parsley, chopped, plus extra for garnish
- ¼ teaspoon orange zest
- 3 cups fish broth or water
- 2 pounds mixed fish
- 1 cup shrimp
- 1 cup clams
- 1 cup lobster meat
- 1 teaspoon lemon juice
- 1 cup white wine
- 8 (½-inch-thick) slices French bread
- 2 tablespoons butter, softened

Heat oil in a large pan. Add 2 cloves garlic and next 3 ingredients. Cook slowly until golden brown, stirring to prevent burning. Soak saffron in boiling water to dissolve. Add saffron, salt, pepper, and next 8 ingredients. Cover and cook 15 to 20 minutes. Add shrimp, clams, and lobster. Bring to a boil. Add lemon juice and wine. Adjust seasonings as needed. Bake bread in a warm oven until hard. Combine butter with remaining 1 clove garlic, salt, and pepper. Spread over bread slices. Place a slice of bread in bottom of each bowl. Pour bouillabaisse over top. Garnish with chopped parsley.

Yield: 8 servings

Jane Gahagen
Plantation Yacht Harbor Resort
Islamorada

Satay is marinated, grilled strips of pork or chicken, served with a peanut sauce. Usually found in Aruba, Curaçao, and Bonaire.

Cheeca Lodge's Jamaican Seafood Soup

Soup Base

- 2 ounces apple-smoked bacon, chopped
- ⅓ cup diced yellow onion
- ½ cup diced celery
- ½ cup diced leek
- 2 tablespoons packed dark brown sugar
- Pinch of cayenne pepper
- 1 ounce Jamaican jerk seasoning
- 2 cups fish broth
- 5 fresh plum tomatoes, diced
- ½ bunch fresh tarragon, chopped
- Salt to taste

Seafood

- 3 ounces shrimp, coarsely chopped
- 3 ounces snapper, dolphin, or grouper, coarsely chopped
- 3 ounces stone crabmeat, coarsely chopped
- 6 tablespoons butter

Cook bacon in a saucepan. Add onion, celery, and leek. Cook over low heat for 15 minutes or until vegetables are translucent. Add sugar and cook 3 minutes over low heat. Add cayenne pepper and jerk seasoning. Cook 1 minute. Stir in broth and tomato. Simmer 30 minutes. Add tarragon and salt. To prepare seafood, cook shrimp, snapper, and crabmeat in butter over low heat until done. Place in soup bowls. Top with hot soup base. Garnish with croutons, sliced scallions, or yogurt.

Yield: 4 servings

Dawn Sieber
Cheeca Lodge
Islamorada

King of the Sea

Seafood and chili peppers give this recipe a definite Caribbean quality.

- 1 stalk lemon grass, chopped
- 3 kaffir lime leaves, chopped
- 2 fresh mushroom caps
- Water
- ½ pound seafood
- 1½ tablespoons fish sauce
- 2 chili peppers, diced
- 1½ tablespoons lime juice
- 1 teaspoon chopped coriander for garnish

Boil lemon grass, lime leaves, and mushroom caps in water. Add seafood and fish sauce. Simmer until seafood is cooked. Remove from heat. Stir in chili pepper and lime juice. Sprinkle with coriander to garnish.

Yield: 1 serving

Try shrimp, scallops, crabmeat, squid, or your favorite seafood in this soup.

Panyaporn Russmetes
Num-Thai Restaurant and Sushi Bar
Key Largo

Curry-Ginger Chicken Bisque

- 1 large onion, diced
- 2 stalks celery, diced
- 1 teaspoon grated fresh ginger
- 1½ cups diced cooked chicken
- 2½ tablespoons chicken base
- 1 quart water
- ¼ cup curry powder, or to taste
- 1 quart heavy cream
- 5 bay leaves
- Salt and pepper to taste
- 1 stick butter
- ⅔ cup all-purpose flour

Curry powder and ginger give this dish its distinctive flavor.

Sauté onion and celery in a medium saucepan until transparent. Add ginger and next 3 ingredients. Cook until mixture reduces to about half. Add curry powder, cream, and bay leaves. Season with salt and pepper. In a separate pan, melt butter. Stir in flour until smooth. Slowly add to hot soup, stirring constantly, to thicken. Heat and serve.

Yield: 8 servings

Keith Norril
Caloosa Cove Resort
Lower Matecumbe

Pumpkin Soup

- 1 (8-pound) pumpkin, seeded, peeled, and cubed
- 2 quarts water
- 1 quart heavy cream
- 6 tablespoons sugar
- Dash of salt
- Dash of freshly ground black pepper
- 5 ounces Gouda cheese, grated

Boil pumpkin cubes in water 35 minutes or until soft. Drain cubes, reserving water. Puree cubes. Combine pumpkin puree, reserved water, cream, and next 3 ingredients. Heat and mix in cheese.

Yield: 18 servings

Kurt Biermanns
Boonoonoonoos Restaurant
Aruba

Grace's Bean and Rice Soup

This recipe uses two staple foods in Caribbean cooking — rice and beans.

- 1 pound dried navy beans
- 1 (14½-ounce) can tomatoes, chopped
- 2 medium onions, finely chopped
- ½ bell pepper, finely chopped
- ½ pound salt pork or ham bone with meat scraps
- Salt and pepper to taste
- ½ cup uncooked white rice

Soak beans in water overnight. Drain and rinse. Place beans and next 4 ingredients in a 6-quart Dutch oven. Add enough water to cover. Bring to a boil over medium-high heat. Reduce heat and simmer about 2 hours, 30 minutes, stirring frequently. Season with salt and pepper. Add rice. Cook over low heat for 30 minutes or until beans are creamy and rice is tender. Add extra water as needed. Remove salt pork before serving.

Yield: 8 servings

Garnish with avocado cubes dipped in lime juice, and this hearty soup becomes a whole meal.

Albert J. Amsterdam
Curry Mansion Inn
Key West

Spicy Caribbean Soup With Rice

- 1 cup chopped onion
- 1 clove garlic, minced
- 3 tablespoons butter or margarine
- 1 bay leaf
- ½ teaspoon crushed red pepper flakes, plus extra for garnish
- ½ teaspoon ground coriander
- ½ teaspoon ground allspice
- ¼ teaspoon salt
- ¼ teaspoon black pepper
- 4 cups chicken broth
- 4 cups cubed winter squash or pumpkin
- 2 cups cubed cooked chicken
- 3 cups hot cooked rice
- Sprigs of fresh cilantro for garnish (optional)

Cook onion and garlic in butter in a large saucepan or Dutch oven over medium-high heat. Add bay leaf and next 6 ingredients. Bring to a boil. Reduce heat and cover. Simmer 10 to 15 minutes. Add squash. Continue to simmer 10 to 15 minutes or until squash is tender but still slightly firm. Remove bay leaf. Reserve 1 cup squash cubes. Puree remaining mixture. Return pureed mixture and reserved squash cubes to saucepan. Stir in chicken. Cook until thoroughly heated. Serve soup topped with rice. Garnish.

Yield: 6 servings

USA Rice Council

Traveling to the Keys by land necessitates going through a portion of the southeastern part of the Everglades. The "Glades" is approximately 100 miles long and up to 70 miles wide. The Everglades is home to the ubiquitous alligator (once almost hunted to extinction, but now making a very strong comeback), deer, and a wide variety of other mammals, reptiles, fish, birds, insects, and amphibians.

Black Bean Chili

Serve this Cuban specialty as an appetizer or an entrée.

- 1 pound ground chuck
- ¾ pound chorizo, or other smoked sausage
- 2 cups dried black beans, soaked 12 hours minimum
- 6 cups water
- 1 large green or red bell pepper, chopped
- 2 medium to large onions, chopped
- 1¼ tablespoons minced garlic
- 2 stalks celery, chopped
- 3 cups peeled and chopped tomatoes
- ¼ cup white wine vinegar
- 1 cup beer
- 2 medium carrots, chopped
- ¾ cayenne pepper
- Chopped parsley and scallions for garnish

Brown and drain ground chuck. Brown and drain chorizo and cut into small pieces. Rinse and drain soaked beans. Combine beans and water in a large pot. Bring to a boil over medium-high heat. Stir in bell pepper and next 8 ingredients. Reduce heat to low and cover. Simmer 60 minutes or until beans are tender. Add browned chuck and chorizo. Simmer about 30 minutes longer. Let stand 5 minutes before serving. Garnish. Serve with rice, hot Cuban garlic bread or cornbread, and sangria.

Yield: 8 servings

To further enhance flavor of chili, prepare 1 day ahead and refrigerate overnight.

Monte Green
Banana Patch
Miami Beach

Jalapeño Corn Chowder

8 ears sweet corn, husks intact
1 gallon water
2 quarts heavy cream
2 jalapeño peppers, seeded and finely chopped
½ teaspoon salt
½ teaspoon white pepper
Juice of 1 lemon

Soak corn in water for at least 30 minutes. Drain. Roast corn over an open flame until kernels are tender. Remove husks and slice kernels from the cob. Divide corn into two equal halves, pureeing one half. In a saucepan, reduce cream over medium heat by one-fourth. Add all corn, jalapeño pepper, and remaining 3 ingredients. Simmer 15 minutes. Serve hot with corn chips or saltine crackers.

Yield: 8 servings

Sharon Hilbig
Bagatelle
Key West

Corn and jalapeño peppers are traditional ingredients in many Caribbean recipes.

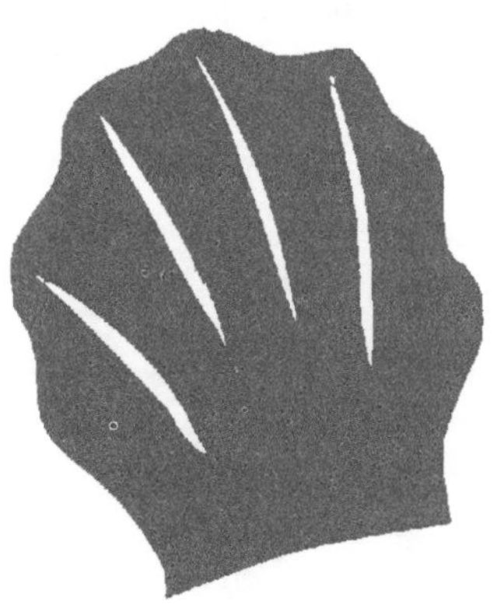

Flying fish is a small silvery delicately flavored fish found throughout warm Caribbean waters—and the official fish of Barbados. Flying fish is often marinated in lime juice and salt, then sprinkled with herbs and steamed, or breaded and pan-fried.

Black Bean and Tasso Soup

The beans and tasso in this recipe give it a Caribbean flair.

- 3½ quarts water, divided
- 2 cups dried black beans
- ½ cup soy sauce
- ½ cup red wine vinegar
- 2 tablespoons lime juice
- 4 tablespoons Worcestershire sauce
- 2 tablespoons unsalted butter
- 2 cups cubed tasso
- ½ cup diced bell pepper
- ½ cup diced red bell pepper
- ½ cup diced yellow bell pepper
- ¾ cup diced red onion
- 3 tablespoons chopped fresh rosemary
- 2 tablespoons chopped garlic
- 1 teaspoon cayenne pepper
- 3 bay leaves
- ¼ cup sherry
- ¼ cup sour cream for garnish
- ¼ cup chopped scallions for garnish

Combine 1½ quarts water and next 5 ingredients in a ceramic or stainless steel bowl. Soak overnight. Place butter and next 9 ingredients in a large pot. Cook over medium-low heat for 5 minutes. Turn to high heat and add sherry. Drain beans and add to pot. Add remaining 2 quarts water and simmer 60 minutes. Remove 2 cups of beans from soup and puree in a blender or food processor. Stir pureed beans back into soup and simmer 10 minutes. Remove bay leaves. Garnish each serving with a teaspoon of sour cream and a teaspoon of scallions.

Yield: 8 to 12 servings

Sharon Hilbig
Bagatelle
Key West

Tomato/Garlic Soup

2 heads garlic, peeled
7 tablespoons virgin olive oil, divided
1 pound tomatoes, finely diced
9 cups non-chlorinated water
1 teaspoon sea salt
1 bay leaf
3 tablespoons chopped fresh parsley
½ teaspoon paprika
Pinch of black pepper
6 slices Bahamian white bread
1 tablespoon sherry

Although enjoyed throughout the Caribbean, this soup is a Cuban and Puerto Rican specialty.

Combine garlic and 4 tablespoons olive oil in a pot. Sauté over medium-high heat 4 to 6 minutes or until browned. Add tomato and sauté 10 minutes. Stir in water and next 5 ingredients. Reduce heat to low and cover. Simmer 30 to 35 minutes, stirring often. Remove cover and simmer and stir 15 minutes longer. Remove bay leaf. Toast bread slices. Pour soup into bowls. Place 1 slice of bread in each bowl. Drizzle remaining 3 tablespoons olive oil and sherry over toast.

Yield: 6 servings

Pedro Gonzalez
Don Pedro Restaurant
Marathon

Tomato Basil Soup

1 (28-ounce) can pear-shaped tomatoes, undrained
3 ounces fresh basil
1 quart heavy cream
Salt and pepper to taste

Thoroughly blended tomatoes, basil, and cream in a blender or food processor. Season with salt and pepper. Chill before serving.

Yield: 8 to 10 servings

Joe's Summer Gazpacho

- 1 (46-ounce) can spicy vegetable juice
- 1 (28-ounce) can tomatoes, chopped
- 3 cucumbers, chopped
- 3 bell peppers, color of choice, chopped
- 1 bunch scallions, chopped
- 1½ teaspoons chopped garlic
- 3 tablespoons garlic wine vinegar
- 2 tablespoons olive oil
- Black pepper to taste
- Garlic salt to taste
- 3 dashes hot pepper sauce
- 2 dashes Worcestershire sauce
- Sour cream for garnish

Combine vegetable juice and next 11 ingredients. Serve with a scoop of sour cream of the side.

Yield: 6 to 8 servings

Joe Roth
Holiday Isle Resort and Marina
Islamorada

Cheeca Lodge White Gazpacho

Gazpacho

4 cups buttermilk
2 cups regular or fat-free sour cream
Juice of 4 limes
1 bell pepper, finely diced
1 red bell pepper, finely diced
1 yellow bell pepper, finely diced
2 English cucumbers, finely diced
6 Roma tomatoes, finely diced
Salt and pepper to taste

Pita Croutons

6 pita breads
Olive oil

Combine buttermilk, sour cream, and lime juice. Add peppers, cucumber, tomato, salt, and pepper, reserving a small amount of cucumber and tomato for garnish. Garnish with reserved cucumber and tomato and serve with pita croutons on the side. To prepare croutons, slice each pita bread into 8 wedges. Split wedges in half. Brush with olive oil and toast in oven until crisp.

Yield: 12 servings

Dawn Sieber
Cheeca Lodge
Islamorada

Strawberry Soup

Cold fruit soups are popular in the steamy tropics.

- 6 pints strawberries
- 3 cups orange juice
- 4 tablespoons tapioca
- ¼ teaspoon ground allspice
- ¼ teaspoon cinnamon
- 2 teaspoons lemon zest
- 2 cups sugar
- 1 tablespoon lemon juice
- 3 cups buttermilk

Process strawberries in a blender or food processor until smooth. Add orange juice. Place in a saucepan and heat slowly. In a mixing bowl, combine 1 cup of heated strawberry mixture and tapioca. Mix well and return to saucepan. Add allspice and next 3 ingredients. Bring to a boil. Cook 1 minute. Stir in lemon juice and buttermilk. Chill. Serve cold with sliced strawberries for garnish.

Yield: 12 servings

Bill Wiseman
Treetops
Key Largo, Florida

Aubergine Soup

- 1 pound eggplant (aubergine), peeled and cubed
- 6 tablespoons oil
- 4 tomatoes, peeled, seeded, and chopped
- 2 onions, diced
- 1 clove garlic, crushed
- ⅛ teaspoon basil
- ¼ teaspoon marjoram
- 2 (14½-ounce) cans chicken broth
- ½ teaspoon salt or to taste
- ¼ teaspoon pepper
- Parmesan cheese for garnish

Sauté eggplant in hot oil until brown. Add tomato and next 4 ingredients. Cook slowly until vegetables are soft. Add broth and cook 30 minutes. Season with salt and pepper. Chill. Serve cold with Parmesan cheese for garnish.

Yield: 10 to 12 servings

Lyla Naseem
Biras Creek Resort
Virgin Gorda, British Virgin Islands

Watercress Soup

- 2 bunches watercress
- 2 potatoes, peeled and sliced
- 1 onion, sliced
- 4 cups beef broth
- 1 bay leaf
- 1 clove garlic, chopped
- 1½ tablespoons butter
- ¼ cup heavy cream
- Nutmeg for garnish

Wash watercress thoroughly, discarding brown leaves and coarse stalks. Combine watercress and next 6 ingredients in a pan. Bring to a boil. Reduce heat and cover. Simmer until potato and onion are soft. Remove bay leaf and blend. Cool. Stir in cream before serving. Serve cold with a sprinkle of nutmeg.

Yield: 6 to 8 servings

Lyla Naseem
Biras Creek Resort
Virgin Gorda, British Virgin Islands

The Keys had a reputation as a **pirates' sanctuary** in past centuries. One pirate known as "Black Caesar" supposedly had a schooner and crew that hid out in the Keys after daring raids on passing ships. Caesar moved to the west coast of Florida after he retired from his raiding days and pirate ways on the Atlantic.

Carrot and Summer Squash Soup

- 4 medium summer squash, thinly sliced
- 4 large carrots, grated
- 1 medium red onion, diced
- 1 cup white wine
- 6 tablespoons clarified butter
- 1 pint heavy cream
- ½ cup grated Asiago or Parmesan cheese for garnish

Cook squash and next 4 ingredients together in a pot for 20 minutes or until vegetables are very tender. Puree vegetables in a blender and return to pot. Add cream. Cook 20 minutes longer. Do not boil. Serve in soup bowls with cheese sprinkled over the top.

Yield: 4 to 6 servings

Sharon Hilbig
Bagatelle
Key West

Chilled Papaya Soup

1 pound papaya, peeled and cut into cubes
½ cup water
1 tablespoon freshly squeezed lime juice
½ teaspoon nutmeg
¼ cup brandy (optional)

Cut about ¼ cup of the papaya cubes into smaller cubes, and set aside. Put remaining papaya into blender, and process with water for about 30 seconds or until smooth. Pour into bowl, add lime juice, nutmeg, and brandy. Refrigerate for 1 to 2 hours until well chilled. Serve with small cubes on top.

Yield: 6 servings

Michael Nighty
Holiday Inn
Grand Cayman Island

Island Blueberry Banana Bisque

¼ banana
Splash of crème de banane
Splash of blackberry-flavored brandy
¼ cup fresh or frozen blueberries, thawed
1 teaspoon powdered sugar
¼ cup half-and-half

Place all ingredients in a blender. Blend thoroughly. Serve immediately. Garnish with thin banana slices floated on top.

Yield: 1 to 2 servings

Andre Mueller
Marker 88
Islamorada

Snorkeling at underwater parks is big in the Keys and in the Caribbean. Hundreds of colorful fish and crustaceans can be seen over, in, and around the magnificent reefs of the Caribbean.

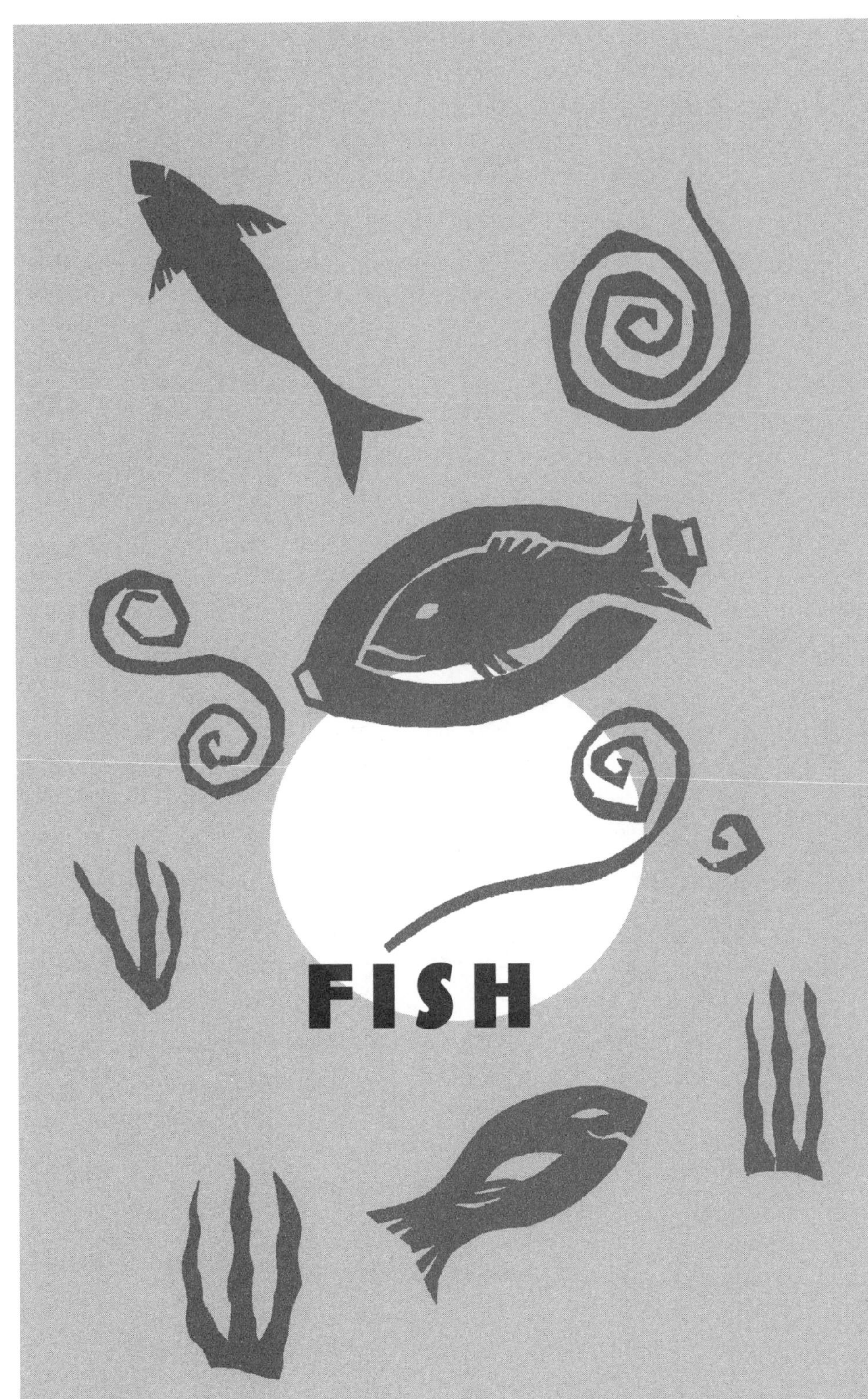

FISH

LEEWARD ISLANDS

So called because they are on the leeward side of the tropical tradewinds and are snuggled in a sense away from the heavier winds and fronts coming off of the African continent, the Leewards are comprised of Antigua, Barbuda, St. Kitts, Nevis, Anguilla, Montserrat, the Netherland Antilles, Saba, Sint Eustatius, Sint Maarten, the French Antilles, Guadeloupe, Saint-Martin, Saint Barthelemy, and Martinique.

Martinique is known for Mont Pelee, an active volcano, plus thickly forested mountains and green hills. An irregular coastline, with steep gorges and black sand. This is an exquisite French island that offers some fabulous cuisine. Martinque has some of the best dining in the entire Caribbean. More than 200 restaurants offer French and Creole cooking in a very relaxed atmosphere. One delicacy is the giant freshwater prawn shrimp grown on the island and served in a spicy Creole sauce.

All the other islands have much of the same type of vibrant and spicy dishes available throughout the Leewards. Antigua, Barbuda, and Anguilla are known for seafoods, with giant crawfish prepared in a dozen different ways. These are gemlike islands that offer the best the tropics has to offer.

St. Kitts and Nevis are vacation destination pearls with lush and lovely gold-sand beaches, exotic gardens, secluded coves, and great foods. From ramshackle beachfront bistros to the best of the best, the restaurants serve passion fruit-laced potions that enhance the entrees. One-pot meals and papaya soups that will spoil you are a hallmark of the areas dining possibilities.

Jamaican Jerk Fresh Fish Sandwich

Jerk Seasoning

- 1 tablespoon olive oil
- ½ onion, diced
- ⅛ teaspoon ground cloves
- ¼ teaspoon dried thyme
- 1 Scotch bonnet pepper, seeded and minced
- 2 scallions, diced
- 2 cloves garlic, minced
- ¼ teaspoon ground allspice
- 1 teaspoon salt

Sandwiches

- 2 (6-ounce) fish fillets
- Jerk seasoning
- 2 Kaiser rolls
- 2 leaves lettuce
- 2 slices tomato
- 2 wedges lemon

Heat oil in a saucepan. Add onion and next 7 next ingredients. Sauté, stirring constantly, until mixture turns a deep brown color. Cool. Rub seasoning into fish fillets. Refrigerate at least 60 minutes. Grill over medium-hot coals until done. To serve, place a fillet in each roll. Garnish with lettuce, tomato, and lemon.

Jim Ewing
Hawk Channel Bar And Grill
Islamorada

Fish Seminole

- 4 fish fillets
- ¼ cup seasoned flour
- 2 eggs, beaten
- Oil for sautéing
- ½ pound scallops
- ¼ cup diced shallot
- ½ pound fresh mushrooms, sliced
- ½ teaspoon salt
- 1 teaspoon chopped garlic
- ¼ teaspoon white pepper
- Butter for sautéing
- ½ pound cooked snow crabmeat

Dredge fish in flour and dip in egg. Sauté in a skillet in a small amount of oil until browned on both sides. Transfer to an oven and bake at 450° until fish flakes easily with a fork. To make topping, sauté scallops and next 5 ingredients together in a small amount of butter. Add crabmeat and cook until hot. Spoon topping over cooked fish.

Yield: 4 servings

For added flavor, top each serving with a lemon butter meunière sauce.

Edith Grenfell
The Conch Restaurant
Islamorada

When Spanish explorers reached the Keys in the mid-1500s, they found the Caloosa Indians were the dominant power in South Florida. The tribe had its chief villages in the Tampa Bay region on the west coast, but all of Florida's west coast and the Keys were under its sway.

Caribbean Fish

- ¼ cup clarified butter or margarine
- 2 eggs
- 1½ cups water
- 2 pounds fresh fish of choice, cleaned and boned

All-purpose flour for dredging

- 1 stick butter
- 1 ripe mango, peeled and cubed
- 1 ripe papaya, peeled and cubed
- 1 firm banana, cubed
- 1 peach, peeled and cubed
- ½ cup cubed pineapple
- ½ cup amaretto
- ½ teaspoon cinnamon

Chopped parsley for garnish

Heat clarified butter over medium heat in a skillet. Beat together eggs and water. Dredge fish in flour, shaking off excess. Dip fish in egg mixture and place in skillet. Sauté on both sides until golden brown. Transfer fish to a baking pan. Bake at 350° until fish flakes easily with a fork. While fish bakes, prepare fruit sauce. Melt butter in a skillet. Add mango and next 6 ingredients. Warm fruit over medium heat, being careful not to overcook the fruit or overheat the butter. Place baked fish on a serving platter. Using a slotted spoon, top fish with fruit. Ladle some of sauce over fish. Sprinkle with chopped parsley.

Yield: 4 servings

Andre Mueller
Marker 88
Islamorada

Fish Martinique

Tomato Concassee

- ⅓ cup chopped onion
- 2 cups peeled and chopped tomato
- 1 clove garlic, minced
- 1 teaspoon Italian seasoning
- Dash of salt
- Dash of white pepper
- Dash of sugar
- Tomato juice as needed

Entrée

- 4 bananas
- 4 tablespoons lemon juice, divided
- 1 teaspoon Worcestershire sauce
- 1 teaspoon salt
- ¼ teaspoon white pepper
- 2 pounds fish filets of choice, skinned and boned
- ½ cup clarified margarine
- 2 eggs
- ½ cup milk
- 1 tablespoon oil
- All-purpose flour for dredging
- 1½ sticks butter
- 1 tablespoon chopped parsley

To make tomato concassee, simmer onion and next 6 ingredients for 10 minutes. Add tomato juice if mixture is too dry. Prepare entrée by peeling bananas. Cut bananas into 2 sections each; then slice each section in half. Grill or sauté banana until cooked. Combine 2 tablespoons lemon juice and next 3 ingredients. Spread over fish. Heat clarified margarine in a skillet. Beat together eggs, milk, and oil. Dredge fish in flour; then dip in egg mixture. Place fillets in skillet and sauté on one side until lightly browned. Turn fish and sauté slowly until fish flakes easily with a fork. While sautéing, melt butter in a skillet. Mix in remaining 2 tablespoons lemon juice and parsley. Transfer cooked fish to a serving platter. Top with tomato concassee, cooked bananas, and butter mixture.

Yield: 4 servings

Yellowtail, snapper, grouper, or similar types of fish work well in this recipe.

Andre Mueller
Marker 88
Islamorada

Almond Encrusted Snapper With Avocado Beurre Blanc

Avocado Beurre Blanc

- 1 shallot, minced
- 2 bay leaves
- 1 sprig fresh thyme
- ¾ cup white wine
- Juice of 1 lemon
- 3 cups heavy cream
- Salt to taste
- ¼ cup ripe, finely diced avocado
- 2 sticks butter

Snapper

- 2 pounds yellowtail snapper
- 2 cups Italian-style breadcrumbs
- ½ cup sliced blanched almonds
- 4 eggs
- 2 cups milk
- 2 cups all-purpose flour
- Shaved avocado and orange garnish (optional)

Combine shallot and next 4 ingredients in a saucepan. Reduce at high heat to about a fourth of original volume. Add cream and salt and again reduce to about a fourth. Add avocado, and remove bay leaves. Cut butter into pieces and add to sauce. To prepare fish, cut yellowtail into 8-ounce portions. Combine breadcrumbs and almonds. Mix together eggs and milk. Dredge yellowtail in flour. Dip into egg mixture, then breadcrumb mixture. Sear yellowtail in a pan until golden brown. Transfer to an oven and bake until fish flakes easily with a fork. Serve with warm Beurre Blanc sauce. Garnish, if desired.

Yield: 4 servings

Stephen Valentine
Marriott Key Largo Bay Beach Resort
Key Largo

Snapper Macadamia With Mango Butter Sauce

Mango Butter Sauce

- ¾ cup sherry
- 1 tablespoon chopped shallot
- ¼ teaspoon salt
- ¼ teaspoon white pepper
- 2 ripe mangoes, peeled and pitted
- ¼ cup freshly squeezed orange juice
- 2 teaspoons rice wine vinegar
- 1 stick unsalted butter

Snapper Fillets

- 4 (7-ounce) snapper fillets
- 1½ cups finely ground macadamia nuts
- 1 cup clarified butter
- Salt and pepper to taste
- Sprigs fresh basil for garnish

In a medium pot over medium-high heat, reduce sherry and next 3 ingredients until almost all the liquid evaporates. While liquid is reducing, puree mangoes, orange juice, and vinegar until smooth. Add puree to remaining liquid and reduce heat to low. Cook to reduce sauce slightly. Using a whisk, thoroughly blend in butter, 1 tablespoon at a time. To prepare fish, press one side of each fillet into macadamia nuts. Sauté over low heat in clarified butter, nut side down. Cook 2 to 3 minutes or until nuts start to brown. Turn fillets and transfer to a 400° oven. Bake 8 to 12 minutes or until done. To serve, divide sauce evenly among 4 plates. Top with a fillet on each plate. Garnish. Serve with rice or linguine and clam sauce.

Yield: 4 servings

Sharon Hilbig
Bagatelle
Key West

Snapper Tropical

- 1 stick butter, divided
- 5 strawberries, sliced
- ½ banana, sliced
- ¼ cup pineapple juice
- 2 tablespoons lime juice
- 2 tablespoons white wine
- ¼ cup coconut-flavored rum
- 1 egg, beaten
- ¼ cup milk
- 4 (8-ounce) yellowtail snapper fillets, or fish of choice

All-purpose flour for dredging

This dish is a taste of the tropics with its fresh fish, tropical fruits, fruit juices, and rum.

Cook 4 tablespoons butter, strawberries, and banana over low heat until fruit begins to soften. Add pineapple juice and next 3 ingredients. Reduce sauce until thickened. While sauce cooks, combine egg and milk. Dredge fillets in flour; then dip in egg mixture. Cook fillets with remaining 4 tablespoons butter over medium-high heat. Turn fish when lightly browned. Continue cooking until fish flakes easily with a fork. Place fish on serving plates. Top with fruit sauce.

Yield: 4 servings

Bill Valet
Ballyhoo's Grille and Grog
Key Largo

The Presidential Snapper

President George Bush enjoyed this dish during frequent fishing trips to the Florida Keys.

Roasted Pepper/Orange Salsa

- 4 oranges, peeled, pith removed, and sectioned
- Salt and pepper to taste
- Juice of 2 Key limes
- ½ bunch cilantro, chopped
- 2 red bell peppers, roasted, peeled, and chopped
- ½ cup extra virgin olive oil

Sizzling Black Beans

- 1 cup cooked or canned black beans
- ¼ cup extra virgin olive oil

Yellowtail Snapper Entrée

- 1 eggplant
- 2 pounds yuca, peeled and finely grated
- 4 (7- to 8-ounce) yellowtail snapper fillets, skin intact
- Salt and pepper to taste
- ½ cup extra virgin olive oil, divided

Combine orange, salt, pepper, and next 4 ingredients to make salsa; set aside. To prepare beans, rinse, drain, and dry them. Heat oil until very hot. Add beans and sauté. Prepare entrée by cutting eggplant into 8 round slices. Grill or sauté until tender. Season yuca and fillets with salt and pepper. Mold yuca onto skinless side of fillets. Heat oil in a skillet. Place fillets, yuca side down, in skillet. Cook until golden brown. Turn fillets and finish cooking on skin side. To assemble, divide eggplant slices among 4 serving plates. Place a cooked fillet on each plate. Spoon salsa over top of fillets. Serve black beans on the side.

Yield: 4 servings

Substitute potatoes if yuca is not available.

Dawn Sieber
Cheeca Lodge
Islamorada

Fish Paradise

2 yellowtail snapper fillets
All-purpose flour for dredging
3 eggs, beaten
Oil for sautéing
2 tablespoons butter
2 tablespoons diced mango
2 tablespoons diced papaya
2 tablespoons diced banana
2 tablespoons diced pineapple
1 ounce coconut-flavored rum
Pinch of chopped parsley
2 tablespoons Key lime juice

Dredge fillets in flour; then dip in egg. Sauté in oil until done. In a separate pan, sauté butter and next 4 ingredients together. Add rum, parsley, and Key lime juice and heat. Serve over cooked fillets.

Yield: 2 servings

Justin Green
Paradise Cafe
Long Key

Dolphin Capri

4 (8-ounce) dolphin fillets
2 large tomatoes, chopped
½ cup chopped fresh basil, or 2 tablespoons dried
1 cup Parmesan cheese
6 ounces sliced mozzarella cheese, cut in strips
8 ounces pasta of choice
6 tablespoons butter, softened
2 cloves garlic, chopped

Place fillets in a greased baking dish. Top with tomato. Sprinkle with basil and Parmesan cheese. Place strips of mozzarella cheese over top. Bake at 375° for 15 to 20 minutes or until fish flakes easily with a fork. While fish bakes, cook pasta and drain. Sauté butter and garlic briefly. Add hot pasta to butter mixture and toss to coat. Serve fillets over pasta.

Yield: 4 servings

Madaline Robbins
Cracked Conch Café
Marathon

***Asopao* is Puerto Rico's thick, soupy chicken, fish, or shellfish stew ladled thickly on top of rice (arroz).**

Grilled Swordfish With Tropical Mango Salsa

Salsa

- 1½ mangoes, cubed, divided
- ½ red bell pepper, diced
- ½ yellow bell pepper, diced
- 1 (15¼-ounce) can pineapple chunks, drained
- ¼ red onion, diced
- 1 teaspoon salt
- Dash of black pepper
- ¼ cup honey
- ¼ cup molasses
- 1 (15-ounce) can black beans, rinsed and drained

Swordfish

- 2 swordfish steaks
- Olive oil
- Salt and pepper to taste

Puree one-third of mango cubes. Combine pureed mango and remaining mango cubes. Stir in red bell pepper and next 8 ingredients. To prepare swordfish, brush steaks with olive oil. Season with salt and pepper. Grill to a medium-well doneness. Serve with room temperature salsa spooned over top of steaks.

Yield: 2 servings

Philip M. Smith
Mangoe's
Key West

Sword of the Coral Lady

- 1 mango, diced
- 2 tablespoons lime juice
- 2 tablespoons chopped fresh cilantro
- 2 tablespoons chopped fresh parsley
- ¼ teaspoon cracked black pepper
- 1 clove garlic, minced
- 4 (8-ounce) swordfish steaks, skinned and boned
- ½ cup basil vinaigrette
- 1 cup fresh orange juice
- ¼ cup virgin olive oil
- 2 cloves garlic, sliced

Mango salsa is especially popular in the Yucatan area of Mexico.

Combine mango and next 5 ingredients. Refrigerate until needed. Marinate swordfish steaks in vinaigrette and orange juice at least 2 hours. Mix in ½ cup mango salsa. Marinate a minimum of 4 hours. Combine oil and garlic. Drain steaks, reserving marinade. Brush steaks with oil mixture. Broil steaks until done, basting with reserved marinade to keep fish from drying out. Serve with remaining mango salsa spooned over steaks.

Yield: 4 servings

Accompany this dish with cooked ears of sweet corn, steamed long-grain rice, and sliced ripe plantains coated with brown sugar.

George Neugent
Porky's Bayside
Marathon

Chef Pedro's Famous Whole Yellowtail

- 1 (12- to 16-ounce) whole yellowtail snapper, scaled and gilled
- ½ teaspoon salt
- ½ teaspoon black pepper
- 1 teaspoon garlic powder
- 1 lime, cut in wedges
- 2 cups vegetable oil
- Lettuce leaves for garnish
- 2 pimiento slices for garnish
- Fresh parsley for garnish

Make 2 angular cuts on side of fish to allow seasoning to penetrate. Combine salt, black pepper, and garlic powder. Sprinkle evenly over both sides of fish. Squeeze lime wedges over fish. Let stand 15 to 20 minutes before cooking. Heat oil in a deep pan over medium heat. Cook fish in oil for 10 minutes or until slightly browned on one side. Turn fish and cook 5 minutes longer. Serve on a bed of lettuce. Garnish with pimiento slices over the cuts on the side of the fish and parsley covering the gill space.

Yield: 1 or 2 servings

Pedro Gonzalez
Don Pedro Restaurant
Marathon

At various times, the Keys was colonized by Bahamians who came to these Florida islands as wreckers, timber cutters, seal hunters, and fishermen. Note: There are no seals in the Keys or anywhere in Florida today.

Yellowtail En Papillote

- 2 sticks butter, softened
- ¼ cup white wine
- 2 tablespoons minced garlic
- ½ cup sliced mushrooms
- ¼ cup chopped scallions
- 2 teaspoons chopped fresh cilantro
- 2 teaspoons salt
- 4 teaspoons lime juice
- Parchment paper
- 4 (8-ounce) yellowtail snapper fillets

Yellowtail is indigenous to all Caribbean islands that have reefs.

Combine butter and next 7 ingredients in a large bowl. Whip until liquid incorporates into butter. Cut paper into four (15-inch) squares. Place a fillet diagonally across the center of each square. Divide butter mixture over top of fillets. Fold squares corner to corner to form triangles. Beginning at a corner of each triangle, roll or fold paper in towards each fillet. Continue this all the way around the triangles. Bake at 350° for 12 to 15 minutes.

Yield: 4 servings

For an impressive presentation, serve after guests sit down. Place a triangle on each dinner plate and cut open paper for each guest.

Bob Stoky
Sundowners
Key Largo

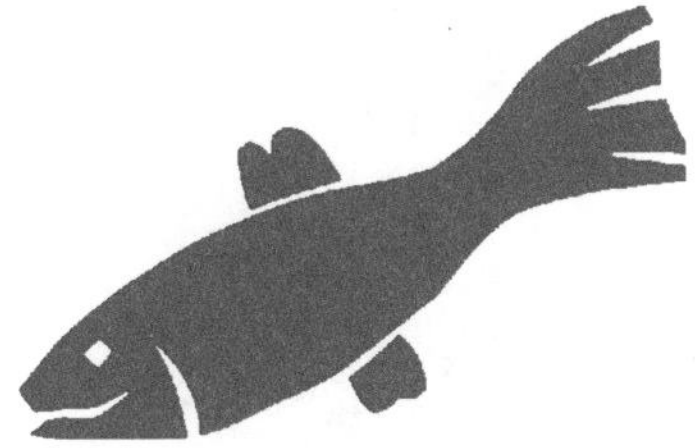

Yellowtail St. Croix

- 4 Key limes, divided
- ½ teaspoon chopped parsley
- 2 tablespoons unsalted butter, softened
- 3 eggs, beaten
- 2 tablespoons milk
- 2 (8-ounce) yellowtail snapper fillets, or snapper of choice
- ½ cup all-purpose flour for dredging
- 1 cup Japanese-style breadcrumbs
- 6 tablespoons clarified margarine or butter substitute

Freshly ground black pepper

In a small saucepan, warm juice from 2 Key limes and parsley. Remove from heat. Stir in unsalted butter until melted. Combine eggs and milk. Dredge fillets in flour; then dip in egg mixture. Coat fillets with breadcrumbs. Sauté in clarified margarine over medium-high heat until golden brown. Turn fillets and squeeze juice of 1 Key lime over fish. Sprinkle with black pepper. Cook until fish flakes easily with a fork. Transfer fillets to a serving platter. Drizzle Key lime sauce over top. Garnish with thin slices of remaining Key lime.

Yield: 2 servings

Herb Nordheimer
Squid Row
Islamorada

Pan-fried Yellowtail

2 eggs, beaten
Pinch of salt
Pinch of black pepper
½ teaspoon chopped garlic
2 (8-ounce) yellowtail snapper fillets
1 cup all-purpose flour
2 tablespoons margarine

Combine egg and next 3 ingredients. Dredge fillets in flour and dip into egg mixture. Repeat flour and egg mixture process. Heat margarine in a skillet. Place fillets in skillet and cook 3 to 5 minutes or until fish flakes easily with a fork. For extra flair, serve with Senator Sauce or Port of Spain Sauce.

Yield: 2 servings

Senator Sauce

2 sticks butter
2½ cups sliced fresh mushrooms
¾ cup sliced almonds, toasted
3 tablespoons lemon juice
2 tablespoons chopped parsley
⅓ cup diced scallions

Melt butter in a saucepan. Add mushrooms and remaining 4 ingredients. Cook until mushrooms are tender. Serve over sautéed fish.

Port of Spain Sauce

2 sticks butter
¾ cup diced apple
¾ cup diced banana
½ cup diced tomato
¼ cup diced pimiento
3 tablespoons lemon juice
2 tablespoons chopped parsley
⅓ cup diced scallions

Melt butter in a saucepan. Add apple and remaining 6 ingredients and sauté. Apples should remain slightly crisp. Do not overcook. Serve over sautéed fish.

Patricia Rodriquez
Rusty Anchor Restaurant
Key West

Yellowtail Caribbean Style

- 4 (8-ounce) yellowtail snapper fillets
- 1 ripe mango, chopped
- 2 ripe bananas, sliced
- 1½ papayas, chopped
- 1½ cups chopped watermelon
- 2 kiwis, peeled and sliced
- 1 cup Grand Marnier
- 1 tablespoon packed brown sugar
- 1 cup pineapple juice
- 2 sticks butter
- Grapes for garnish

Bake fillets at 400° for 10 minutes or until done. Transfer to a serving plate and keep warm. Combine mango and next 4 ingredients in a saucepan. Cook 3 to 4 minutes. Flambé with Grand Marnier. Add brown sugar and pineapple juice. Cook 1 minute. Add butter and cook until melted. Spoon over fillets and garnish.

Yield: 4 servings

Manny Glykas
Perry Seafood Restaurant
Key Largo

Yellowtail With Sweet Mango Cream Sauce

- 2 yellowtail snapper fillets
- All-purpose flour for dredging
- Olive oil
- 2 tablespoons diced shallot
- ½ cup white wine
- ½ mango, pureed
- ½ cup cream
- Salt and pepper to taste
- Fresh basil to taste

Dredge fillets in flour. Sauté on both sides in olive oil until golden brown. In a separate pan, cook shallot and wine for about 5 minutes. Add mango and cream. Season with salt, pepper, and basil. Simmer sauce over medium heat until cream reduces. Divide sauce between 2 serving plates. Place cooked fillets on top and serve.

Yield: 2 servings

Philip M. Smith
Mangoe's
Key West

Sautéed Yellowtail Snapper

4 shallots, chopped
Olive oil
1 bay leaf
10 peppercorns
¼ cup white wine
½ cup orange juice
¼ cup heavy cream
4 sticks unsalted butter
1 bunch basil, chopped
Salt and pepper to taste
4 (8-ounce) yellowtail snapper fillets
2 cups pearl onions, peeled and blanched
8 ounces golden chanterelle mushrooms, sliced
8 ounces lobster mushrooms, sliced
1 bunch asparagus, sliced

Sauté shallot briefly in olive oil. Add bay leaf, peppercorns, and wine. Cook until mixture reduces by half. Add orange juice and reduce by one-fourth. Add cream. Simmer 2 minutes. Add butter, 2 tablespoons at a time. Strain sauce. Stir in basil, salt, and pepper. Keep warm. Heat a small amount of olive oil in a large skillet. Add fillets and cook 2 minutes on each side. Finish cooking in a hot oven. In a separate skillet, sauté onions and remaining 3 ingredients in olive oil. Season with salt and pepper. To serve, ladle 2 to 3 ounces of sauce onto each serving plate. Place cooked fish on sauce. Arrange sautéed vegetables around fish. Garnish with fresh basil leaves.

Yield: 4 servings

Pat Tenney
Louie's Backyard
Key West

Baked Yellowtail With Banana Rum Glaze

Citrus Beurre Blanc Sauce

- 1½ cups dry white wine
- 2 bay leaves
- ¼ tablespoon peppercorn
- ⅛ teaspoon dried thyme
- ¼ onion, sliced
- 1 pint cream
- 2 sticks unsalted butter, softened
- Salt and pepper to taste
- ⅛ cup fresh lemon juice

Yellowtail

- 4 (8-ounce) yellowtail snapper fillets
- 8 tablespoons white wine
- 4 tablespoons lemon juice
- 8 teaspoons olive oil
- 4 teaspoons chopped shallot
- 2 scallions, chopped
- 2 ripe bananas, sliced
- 4 tablespoons honey
- 12 tablespoons coconut-flavored rum
- 1⅓ cups Citrus Beurre Blanc Sauce
- Salt and pepper to taste
- 1 cup sweetened coconut, toasted

Combine wine and next 4 ingredients in a saucepan. Cook until all liquid is absorbed. Add cream and cook until reduced by one-half. Whip in butter, salt, pepper, and lemon juice. Remove bay leaves; keep warm. To prepare entrée, combine fillet, wine, and lemon juice in a baking pan. Bake at 350° for 8 to 10 minutes or until fish flakes easily with a fork. While baking, heat oil in a sauté pan. Add shallot and next 3 ingredients. Stir in rum. Add beurre blanc sauce, salt, and pepper. Serve over baked fish. Sprinkle coconut on top.

Yield: 4 servings

John A. Potucek III and John A. Roy
The Old Tavernier
Tavernier

Fish Rangoon

Entrée

- 4 (8-ounce) yellowtail, snapper, or grouper fillets
- 1 teaspoon Worcestershire sauce
- 2 tablespoons lemon juice
- 1 teaspoon salt
- ¼ teaspoon white pepper
- 2 eggs, beaten
- 2 tablespoons milk
- 1 tablespoon oil
- All-purpose flour for dredging
- ½ cup clarified margarine
- ¼ teaspoon cinnamon
- 3 tablespoons currant jelly

Rangoon Sauce

- 4 tablespoons butter
- ½ cup diced banana
- ½ cup diced pineapple
- ½ cup diced mango
- ½ cup diced papaya
- 1 tablespoon chopped parsley
- 2 tablespoons lemon juice

Season fillets with Worcestershire sauce and next 3 ingredients. Combine egg, milk, and oil. Dredge fillets in flour; then dip in egg mixture. Heat clarified margarine in a skillet. Place fillets in skillet. Sauté until lightly browned on one side. Turn fillets and cook slowly until fish flakes easily with a fork. Remove to a serving platter. Sprinkle with cinnamon and spread jelly over top. Keep warm. To prepare rangoon sauce, melt butter in a clean skillet. Add banana and remaining 5 ingredients. Sauté until thoroughly heated. Do not overcook. Spoon some of sauce over each fillet.

Yield: 4 servings

Substitute peaches if mango or papaya is not available.

Andre Mueller
Marker 88
Islamorada

Yellowtail Macadamia

Papaya Mango Salsa

1 papaya, diced
Salt and pepper to taste
1 mango, diced
1 jalapeño pepper, diced
1 red bell pepper, diced
1 red onion, diced
Splash of olive oil
1 teaspoon cumin

Yellowtail Entrée

1 cup macadamia nuts
1 cup Japanese-style breadcrumbs
4 (7- to 8-ounce) yellowtail snapper fillets
2 eggs, beaten
Clarified butter for sautéing
1 cup papaya mango salsa

Combine papaya, salt, pepper, and next 6 ingredients to make salsa. Prepare entrée by processing nuts and breadcrumbs in a blender or food processor. Dip fillets in egg and then in nut mixture. Sauté in clarified butter until golden brown. Serve topped with salsa and with side dishes of rice and julienned vegetables.

Yield: 4 servings

Carole Baker
Grove Park Cafe
Islamorada

Cilantro Sauce

Cilantro, an herb used to flavor this delightful sauce, appears in many recipes originating from Cuba, Barbados, and Grenada.

⅓ cup finely chopped fresh cilantro
1 teaspoon lemon or Key lime juice
1 teaspoon capers
1 cup mayonnaise
⅓ cup sour cream
Sea salt to taste
Pinch of black pepper
Pinch of cayenne pepper

Combine all ingredients. Mix well and refrigerate. Serve cool or cold with seafood fritters or smoked fish.

Yield: 4 to 6 servings

Pedro Gonzalez
Don Pedro Restaurant
Marathon

Poncho Train

1 cup au jus or beef broth
Juice of 1 lemon
3 tablespoons white wine
Salt and pepper to taste
Cornstarch
2 (6-ounce) fish fillets
6 small shrimp
6 baby bay scallops
2 large mushrooms, diced
Olive oil for sautéing

Combine au jus, lemon juice, and wine. Season with salt and pepper. Bring to a boil. Thicken sauce with a mixture of cornstarch and cold water. Sauté fish and remaining 4 ingredients together until seafood is done. Place fish on a serving platter. Spoon shrimp, scallops, and mushrooms over fish. Pour sauce over the top.

Yield: 2 servings

Emmanouil Parissis
The Quay
Key West

Broiled Red Snapper Midori

2 (8-ounce) red snapper fillets
2 tablespoons butter, melted
¼ small cantaloupe, diced
¼ small pineapple, diced
¼ large mango, diced
¼ small honeydew melon, diced
½ cup diced watermelon
2 tablespoons Midori liqueur
2 tablespoons heavy cream
Salt and pepper to taste

Broil fillets, basting occasionally with melted butter. Sauté cantaloupe and next 4 ingredients in butter. Add liqueur and cream. Season with salt and pepper. Serve sauce over cooked fish.

Yield: 2 servings

Arthur Paterson
Green Turtle Inn
Islamorada

Yellowtail Morocco

- 3 tablespoons butter or margarine, divided
- ½ cup plus 1 tablespoon all-purpose flour, divided
- 1 cup beef broth
- 2 cups grated potato
- ½ white onion, sliced
- ½ cup sliced bell pepper
- ½ cup sliced mushrooms
- 2 tablespoons brandy
- ½ cup broccoli flowerettes, blanched
- 1 egg, beaten
- ½ cup milk
- ⅓ cup oil
- 2 (8-ounce) yellowtail snapper fillets, boned and skinned
- ½ cup grated Monterey Jack cheese
- ½ teaspoon nutmeg

Make a brown sauce by melting 1 tablespoon butter in a small saucepan. Mix in 1 tablespoon flour until smooth. Cook and stir until lightly browned. Add broth and bring to a boil. Reduce heat and simmer 20 to 30 minutes. While sauce simmers, form potato into 2 hash brown patties on a greased skillet. Cook until done. Melt remaining 2 tablespoons margarine in a saucepan. Add onion, bell pepper, and mushrooms and sauté 2 to 3 minutes. Add brown sauce, brandy, and broccoli. Turn heat to low and cook 5 to 10 minutes. Combine egg and milk. Heat oil in a large skillet. Dredge fillets in remaining ½ cup flour. Dip in egg mixture and then place in skillet. Cook on both sides until fish flakes easily with a fork. To serve, place hash browns in a shallow casserole dish. Lay fillets on top. Spoon vegetables and sauce mixture over fillets. Sprinkle with cheese. Broil until cheese melts. Sprinkle with nutmeg to garnish.

Yield: 2 servings

Timothy Fodiemski
Papa Joe's Landmark Restaurant
Islamorada

Grouper Phillipe With Almond Mango Chutney

Almond Mango Chutney

- 1¼ pounds mango, diced
- ¼ onion, diced
- ½ cup raisins
- ½ pineapple, diced
- 1½ teaspoons chili powder
- 2 tablespoons peeled and diced ginger root
- ¾ teaspoon cinnamon
- Dash of mace
- Dash of ground allspice
- Dash of ground cloves
- 1½ teaspoons dry mustard
- ¾ teaspoon ground coriander
- 1 bay leaf
- ¾ cup rice vinegar
- 1¾ cup packed brown sugar
- ½ cup white wine
- ½ cup breadcrumbs
- ¾ cup chopped almonds, toasted

Grouper Phillipe

- 6 (7-ounce) grouper fillets
- Almond mango chutney
- Salt and pepper
- 1 pound spinach
- 1 clove garlic, chopped
- ½ tablespoon lemon juice
- 12 thin slices pancetta or regular bacon
- 1 ripe plantain, thinly sliced
- Caul fat

Combine mango and next 15 ingredients in a saucepan. Using medium-low heat, reduce sauce by one-half. Stir in breadcrumbs. Just prior to stuffing fillets, add almonds. Use half of chutney per 6 grouper fillets. To prepare grouper, butterfly fillets to about ¼ inch thick. Place equal amounts of chutney on each fillet. Wrap fillets around the chutney. Season fish with salt and pepper. Sauté spinach, garlic, and lemon juice together. Add salt and pepper to spinach mixture as needed. Layer each fillet with spinach mixture, pancetta, and plantain. Hold each fillet and its toppings together with a small amount of caul fat. Bake at 400° for 35 minutes. If fillets begin to brown too much while baking, cover with foil.

Yield: 6 servings of grouper, 12 servings of chutney

Phillip Heimer
Pier House Restaurant
Key West

Grouper Lucea

- 4 (8-ounce) grouper fillets
- ½ cup all-purpose flour
- 1 cup breadcrumbs
- ¼ cup chopped fresh parsley
- 2 tablespoons garlic powder
- ¼ cup clarified butter

Salt and pepper to taste

Coat fillets with flour. Sear briefly in a hot, greased skillet or on a grill. Combine breadcrumbs, salt, pepper, and remaining 3 ingredients. Roll fillets in breadcrumb mixture. Return fillets to skillet and sauté until done. Serve with Jamaican yellow squash or black beans and rice.

Yield: 4 servings

Larry Lower
Montego Bay Food and Spirits, Inc.
Big Pine Key

Yellowtail Papillote

Yellowtail snapper is abundant and easily caught in the warm waters of the Caribbean.

- 4 (8-ounce) yellowtail snapper fillets
- 4 square sheets parchment paper
- 1 stick butter, softened
- 12 leaves fresh basil
- 4 sprigs fresh thyme
- 4 sprigs fresh rosemary
- 4 cloves garlic, crushed
- 1 cup dry white wine

Center a fillet on each square of paper. Spread butter evenly over fillets. Divide basil and next 3 ingredients equally among the fillets. Sprinkle wine over each portion. Fold paper into pouches and secure at top with a staple. Place pouches on a baking sheet and bake at 350° for 15 minutes. Serve with pasta and clam sauce or yellow rice.

Yield: 4 servings

John Daverio
The Pilot House Restaurant
Key Largo

Eigner's Caribbean Fish

- 1 lemon
- 4 (6-ounce) fish fillets
- Salt and pepper to taste
- All-purpose flour for dredging
- 5 eggs, beaten
- Virgin olive oil
- 1 cup coconut-flavored rum
- 1 stick butter
- 1½ oranges, peeled and sliced
- 1½ bananas, peeled and sliced
- 1 cup cubed fresh pineapple

Squeeze lemon over fish. Season with salt and pepper. Dredge fish lightly in flour. Dip in egg. Fill a skillet ½ inch deep with olive oil. Heat oil and add fillets. Sauté until golden brown on both sides. Place fillets on a serving plate. In a small saucepan, reduce rum by one-half. Add butter and swirl until creamy. Add orange, banana, and pineapple. Heat until warm. Pour over fish. Serve with rice and black beans.

Yield: 4 servings

George and John Eigner
Grassy Key Dairy Bar
Marathon

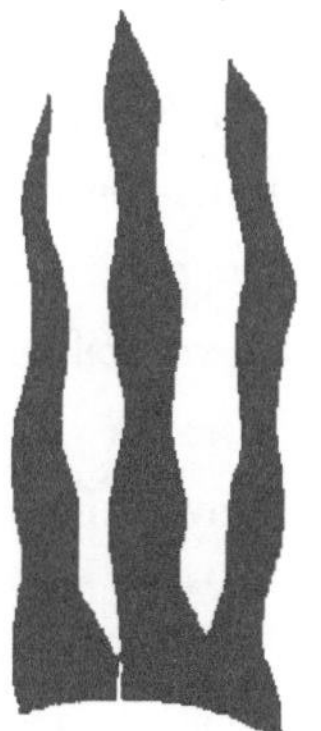

The Keys were formed 100,000 years ago by corals building the reef that we travel, live, and play on today. Indians lived on these islands almost 4000 years ago. but the first written history of the Keys was by Ponce de Leon in 1513. He sailed through the Keys (calling them *Los Martires*) and stopped at Indian Key on his way back to Puerto Rico.

Bagatelle Stuffed Grouper

Grouper is plentiful in the Caribbean and commonly used in cooking.

Stuffing

- ⅓ cup chopped Spanish onion
- ⅓ cup chopped carrot
- ⅓ cup chopped celery
- 1½ tablespoons chopped fresh thyme leaves
- 6 tablespoons unsalted butter
- 6 tablespoons clam reduction
- ¾ cup chopped shrimp
- ¼ cup sherry
- Pinch of salt
- Pinch of black pepper
- 1½ cups breadcrumbs

Grouper

- 4 (6-ounce) grouper fillets
- 1 tablespoon butter

Shrimp and Lobster Butter Cream Sauce

- 2 tablespoons diced onion
- 1 stick unsalted butter, divided
- ⅓ pound shrimp, chopped
- 1 (9-ounce) lobster tail, chopped
- 2 tablespoons all-purpose flour
- 3 tablespoons clam broth
- 1 pint heavy cream, divided
- Pinch of cayenne pepper
- ¼ cup sherry
- Pinch of salt
- Pinch of black pepper
- Paprika for garnish

In a large pot, sauté onion and next 4 ingredients until onion is tender. Add clam reduction and shrimp and cook until shrimp turns pink. Add sherry, salt, and pepper. Remove from heat. Stir in breadcrumbs until all liquid is absorbed. Stuffing should form into balls without being tacky and without falling apart. To stuff grouper fillets, make a vertical cut down the center of each fillet to within ¼ inch from the bottom. Be careful not to cut through the fillet. Form stuffing pockets by making horizontal cuts on both sides of the inside of the first cut. Stuff pockets with grouper stuffing. Place fillets in a broiling pan. Add butter and ½ inch of water. Bake at 375° for 10 to 15 minutes or until stuffing is golden brown and fish cooks to desired degree of doneness. While the grouper bakes, prepare the sauce. Sauté onion in 4 tablespoons unsalted butter until soft. Add shrimp and lobster and sauté until pink. Mix in flour and cook 3 minutes. Add clam broth and remaining 4 tablespoons unsalted butter. While stirring, slowly add 1 cup cream. Add cayenne pepper and continue to cook and stir. When sauce begins to thicken, add remaining 1 cup cream, sherry, salt, and pepper. To serve, place cooked grouper on serving plates. Cover with cream sauce and sprinkle with paprika.

Yield: 4 servings

Sharon Hilbig
Bagatelle
Key West

Sautéed Wahoo in Seaweed Crust With Butternut Squash and Lime Sauce

- 1 small butternut squash, peeled, seeded, and cubed
- 2 cups Chardonnay
- ½ cup lime juice
- 1 stick unsalted butter
- Coarse salt to taste
- White pepper to taste
- ¼ ounce arame seaweed
- ¼ ounce wakame seaweed
- ¼ ounce hijiki seaweed
- 1 (7-ounce) wahoo fillet
- ½ tablespoon clarified butter

Wahoo, a member of the mackerel family of fish, has a slightly sweet flavor.

Poach squash in Chardonnay until soft. Puree in a blender or food processor until smooth. Mix in lime juice. Blend in unsalted butter, 1 tablespoon at a time. Season with salt and white pepper. Grind together seaweeds in a spice grinder or coffee mill. Press the fillet, serving side down, into the seaweed mixture. Sauté the fillet, seaweed side down, in clarified butter. Turn fillet halfway through cooking and sauté until done. To serve, pour sauce onto a serving plate. Place fillet on top.

Yield: 1 serving

Sharon Hilbig
Bagatelle
Key West

Caribbean Stew Grouper

- 3 pounds whole grouper
- 1 onion, diced
- 2 stalks celery, diced
- 2 carrots, sliced
- 2 cups fish broth
- 2 potatoes, peeled and cubed
- ½ ripe tomato, diced
- 6 sprigs parsley
- ½ teaspoon salt, or to taste
- ½ teaspoon black pepper

Fillet grouper, using the center bone and head to make fish broth. Cut grouper fillets into cubes. In a large pot, sauté onion and celery. Add carrot and fish broth. Simmer until carrot starts to soften. Add fish, potato, and remaining 4 ingredients. Cook 10 to 15 minutes. Serve with steamed rice.

Yield: 8 servings

Arthur Paterson
Green Turtle Inn
Islamorada

Sailing in prime seas awaits the Caribbean sailor. The British Virgin Islands and Antigua are delightful locations for a sailing adventure due to their deep water access and broad and brilliant vistas.

Grilled Tuna Islamorada-Style

Tuna

- 1 green bell pepper, chopped
- 1 red bell pepper, chopped
- 1 yellow bell pepper, chopped
- ½ cup chopped pineapple with juice
- 1 red onion, chopped
- ½ cup Key lime juice
- 4 (7-ounce) tuna fillets or steaks
- Salt and pepper to taste
- Hollandaise Sauce
- ¾ cup fresh orange juice

Combine green bell pepper and next 5 ingredients. Let stand 60 minutes. Season tuna with salt and pepper. Grill tuna to desired degree of doneness. Combine Hollandaise Sauce and orange juice. Place tuna on a serving plate. Top with bell pepper mixture and Hollandaise.

Hollandaise Sauce

- 2 egg yolks
- 2 tablespoons lemon juice
- 1 stick butter
- ¼ teaspoon salt

To prepare sauce, beat together egg yolks and lemon juice in a saucepan. Cut stick of butter in half. Heat saucepan and stir in half of butter until melted. Add other half of butter to sauce and stir until melted. Mix in salt.

Yield: 4 servings

Brad Harding
The Conch Restaurant
Islamorada

Seared Tuna With Yellow Bell Pepper Sauce

- 1 tablespoon unsalted butter
- 1 tablespoon minced shallot
- 1 clove garlic, crushed
- 1 small sprig fresh thyme
- 2 large yellow bell peppers, chopped
- 2 cups fish broth
- 2 tablespoons sugar, or to taste
- Salt and pepper to taste
- ¼ cup hot pepper sauce
- 2 (6-ounce) tuna steaks

Melt butter in a sauté pan. Add shallot, garlic, and thyme. Cook about 2 minutes, being careful not to brown. Add bell pepper, broth, and sugar. Simmer about 20 minutes. Remove thyme and pour mixture into a blender. Puree until mixture is smooth and glossy. Season with salt, pepper, and hot pepper sauce. Sear steaks on a grill for 3 minutes on each side or until done. Place steaks on a serving plate and lightly cover with sauce.

Yield: 2 servings

Lyla Naseem
Biras Creek Resort
Virgin Gorda, British Virgin Islands

Local Broiled Grouper

- 2 (8-ounce) grouper fillets, skin intact
- Salt and pepper
- Garlic powder
- Lime juice
- Clarified butter
- Breadcrumbs
- Dried parsley

Place fillets, skin side down, in a greased broiler pan. Add a small amount of water. Season fillets with salt, pepper, garlic powder, and lime juice. Drizzle a small amount of butter over top. Sprinkle with breadcrumbs and parsley. Broil at 350° for 10 minutes or until done.

Yield: 2 servings

Patricia Rodriquez
Rusty Anchor Restaurant
Key West

Jerk Tuna

Salsa

- ½ pineapple, diced
- 1 mango, diced
- 1 bunch scallions, thinly sliced
- ½ red bell pepper, diced
- ½ bunch cilantro, chopped

Coconut Rice

- 1½ cups water
- 1½ cups coconut milk
- 1½ cups rice
- 1 tablespoon chopped garlic
- 1 teaspoon salt
- 2 tablespoons diced red bell pepper

Tuna

- 4 (6-ounce) yellowfin tuna fillets
- 4 ounces jerk seasoning, preferably in paste form

Combine pineapple and next 4 ingredients to make a salsa. To prepare rice, bring water and coconut milk to a boil. Add rice, garlic, and salt. Cook, covered, until rice is tender. Stir in bell pepper. Prepare tuna by coating one side of fillets with jerk seasoning. Sear on seasoned side in a pan. Transfer to an oven and bake to desired degree doneness. Serve tuna on a bed of coconut rice. Top each fillet with 2 to 3 tablespoons of room temperature salsa.

Yield: 4 servings

Frank Carlton
Snapper's
Key Largo

Tuna and jerk are typically Caribbean seafood and spice combinations.

Fish Tropical

- 2 (8-ounce) dolphin, grouper, or snapper fillets
- Salt and pepper
- ¼ cup all-purpose flour
- 2 eggs, beaten
- 4 tablespoons clarified margarine
- 1 stick butter, softened
- Juice of ½ lemon or lime
- 1 large banana, sliced
- 8 strawberries, slices
- ¼ pineapple, cut into chunks
- 1 orange, cut into chunks
- 2 tablespoons crème de banane
- ½ cup sliced almonds, toasted

Season fillets with salt and pepper. Dredge in flour; then dip in egg. Cook fillets in clarified margarine over medium heat until edges are golden brown. Turn fillets and add butter. When butter melts, turn heat to medium-high. Add lemon juice and next 5 ingredients. Cook until banana is tender and fish flakes easily with a fork. Serve fillets with fruit and some of sauce spooned over the top. Sprinkle with almonds.

Yield: 2 servings

Craig Belcher
Craig's Restaurant
Tavernier

Ackee: The cooked yellow pulp of this fruit resembles scrambled eggs and is served with saltfish as the Jamaican national dish.

Grilled Wasabi Cobia

- 4 tablespoons butter, melted
- ¼ teaspoon garlic powder
- ¼ teaspoon black pepper
- 4 (8-ounce) cobia fillets, or any firm fresh fish fillets
- 1 cup finely chopped fresh horseradish root
- ⅔ cup finely chopped fresh ginger root
- 2 tablespoons soy sauce
- 1 teaspoon minced garlic
- 3 tablespoons honey, or packed brown sugar
- ¾ cup mayonnaise

Combine butter, garlic powder, and black pepper. Brush fillets with butter mixture. Broil on a charcoal grill until done. While fish cooks, process horseradish root and remaining 5 ingredients in a blender or food processor. Mix well. Top each cooked fillet with a generous portion of horseradish root mixture. Broil fillets until sauce starts to bubble. Serve immediately.

Yield: 4 servings

Prepare the wasabi sauce ahead of time and refrigerate until ready to use, if desired. The sauce gives the fish a little "bite" without being overpowering.

George and John Eigner
Grassy Key Dairy Bar
Marathon

Queen Trigger Fish

Known to Virgin Islanders as "Old Wife," trigger fish live in tropical waters near coral reefs.

- 2 (7-ounce) fish fillets
- 2 limes
- 4 sprigs fresh thyme
- 2 cloves garlic, chopped
- 1 tablespoon finely minced Scotch bonnet pepper, or chile pepper
- ¼ teaspoon salt
- 4 tablespoons butter, divided
- 1 medium bell pepper, julienned
- 1 medium red bell pepper, julienned
- 1 large Spanish onion, julienned

Lay fillets flat in a pan. Squeeze juice of limes over the fish. Top with thyme and next 3 ingredients. Cover pan with plastic wrap and marinate in a refrigerator 60 minutes. Sauté 2 tablespoons butter and remaining 3 ingredients in a saucepan until onions are translucent. Add fish and all of marinade ingredients. Cook over medium heat 3 to 4 minutes. Add remaining 2 tablespoons butter and stir to melt and create a sauce. Serve on a bed on spinach, okra, and onions with fungi on the side.

***Yield:* 2 servings**

Grouper or red snapper work best in this authentic West Indian dish.

Mia Casey
Marriott's Frenchman's Reef Beach Resort
St. Thomas, U. S. Virgin Islands

Dolphin Jalamango

Roasted Bell Pepper

- 1 tablespoon oil
- 1 bell pepper, quartered

Dolphin Jalamango

- 1½ cups diced mango
- ¼ cup diced red onion
- 3 tablespoons diced roasted bell pepper
- 3 tablespoons diced pickled jalapeño pepper
- 1½ teaspoons jalapeño pepper pickling juice
- ½ teaspoon lemon zest
- 1½ teaspoons cider vinegar
- 6 (6-ounce) dolphin fillets
- Salt to taste
- 1 tablespoon butter or margarine

Brush oil over skin of bell pepper. Broil, skin side up, until black and bubbly. Place in a paper bag for 10 minutes. Remove from bag and peel off skin. To prepare Dolphin Jalamango, combine mango and next 6 ingredients to make a salsa. Season fillets with salt. Melt butter in a pan over medium-high heat. Add fillets and cook 3 minutes on each side. Transfer fish to a hot serving platter. Place salsa mixture in pan and warm thoroughly. Spoon salsa over fish. Serve with yellow rice and a salad.

Yield: 6 servings

Miles Madenwald
Herbies
Marathon

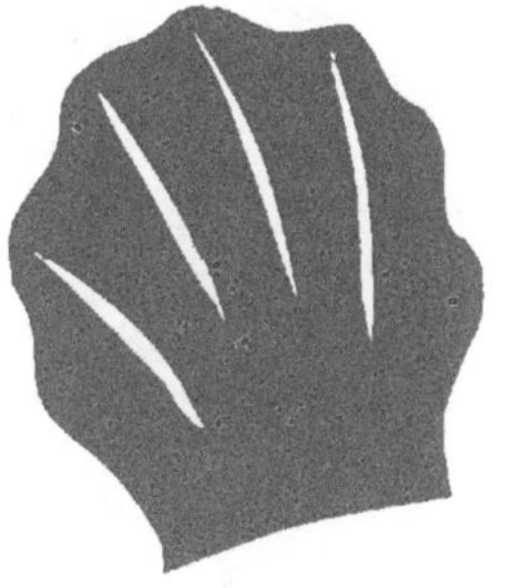

Fish Sicily

Several of the ingredients used in this recipe commonly appear in Caribbean and Mediterranean cooking.

- 4 (8-ounce) grouper fillets, or fish of choice
- ¾ cup regular or fat-free ranch dressing
- 2 cups Japanese-style breadcrumbs
- ¼ cup oil or clarified margarine
- 2 cups sliced mushrooms
- 2 tablespoons chopped garlic
- ½ cup white wine
- 1 cup chopped scallions
- ½ tablespoon chopped shallot (optional)
- 4 tablespoons butter

Dip fillets in dressing. Roll in breadcrumbs to evenly coat. Place fillets in a hot skillet with oil. Cook until lightly browned on both sides. Place fish on a baking tray and bake at 350° for 8 minutes. In a clean skillet, combine mushrooms, garlic, and wine. Cook until mushrooms soften. Add scallions, shallot, and butter. Cook until butter melts. Place fish on a serving plate. Spoon mushroom mixture over top.

Yield: 4 servings

Bill Wiseman
Treetops
Key Largo

Grilled Mahi-Mahi With Tropical Fruit Salsa in Mango Sauce

- 2 kiwi fruits, peeled and diced
- ½ ripe papaya, diced
- 1/6 cantaloupe, diced
- ½ pint strawberries, diced
- ¾ cup diced and seeded watermelon
- 1 ripe mango, pureed
- ½ tablespoon sugar
- 2½ tablespoons water
- 2 tablespoons chopped fresh cilantro
- 5 (8-ounce) mahi-mahi fillets
- Salt and pepper to taste
- Sprigs of cilantro for garnish

Mango and papaya are extremely popular Caribbean fruits.

Combine kiwi fruit and next 4 ingredients. In a separate container, combine mango, sugar, and water. Pour over fruit mixture. Stir in cilantro. Grill fillets for 5 to 8 minutes or until done. Season with salt and pepper. Spoon salsa over cooked fillets. Garnish.

Yield: 5 servings

The Tropical Fruit Salsa in Mango Sauce is also excellent over chicken.

Linda Meehan
Lazy Days Ocean Front Bar and Seafood Grill
Islamorada

Pompano in Island Spices With Date, Rum, and Coconut Milk Sauce

Fish, spices, coconut milk, and rum all contribute to the Caribbean style of this recipe.

- 12 medium dates, pitted
- 1½ cups dark rum
- 1¼ cups coconut milk
- 1 tablespoon butter
- ½ teaspoon Madras curry powder
- ½ teaspoon ground allspice
- ½ teaspoon cardamom
- ½ teaspoon coriander
- 1 teaspoon cinnamon
- ½ teaspoon fennel
- 1 teaspoon five-spice powder
- ½ teaspoon crushed red pepper flakes
- ½ teaspoon salt
- ½ teaspoon white pepper
- ¼ teaspoon ground ginger
- ⅛ teaspoon nutmeg
- ¼ teaspoon ground cloves
- 4 (7-ounce) African pompano fillets

Combine dates and rum in a medium saucepan. Cook over high heat for 10 minutes. Flambé the mixture until all alcohol burns off. Place in a food processor. Add coconut milk and butter. Blend sauce until smooth. Combine curry powder and next 12 ingredients. Press fillets, serving side down, into the spice mixture. Barbecue fillets, spice side down, on a hot grill. Turn fillets halfway through cooking and grill until done. To serve, divide sauce among 4 serving plates. Top with a cooked fillet on each plate.

Yield: 4 servings

Sharon Hilbig
Bagatelle
Key West

Sautéed Cobia With Black-eyed Pea / Corn Salsa and Avocado Aioli

Avocado Aioli

- 2 ripe avocados
- Juice of 1 lemon
- 1½ teaspoons chopped garlic
- 1 teaspoon salt
- ½ teaspoon white pepper
- ½ cup olive oil

Black-eyed Pea / Corn Salsa

- 1½ cups dried black-eyed peas
- 1½ quarts water
- 4 large ears sweet corn, husks intact
- 1 medium red onion, finely diced
- 1 medium bell pepper, finely diced
- 1 medium red bell pepper, finely diced
- ¼ bunch cilantro, chopped
- Juice of 2 limes
- Salt and pepper to taste

Cobia Fillets

- 4 (7-ounce) cobia fillets
- ½ cup buttermilk
- ¼ cup cornmeal
- Clarified butter

Puree avocados in a blender or food processor. Mix in lemon juice and next 3 ingredients. With blender running, slowly add oil to mixture. To make salsa, soak peas in 1½ quarts water for 3 hours. Cook peas in remaining liquid for 30 minutes or until tender. Add more water if needed. Drain peas and cool. Soak ears of corn in water for 30 minutes. Drain. Roast over an open flame, turning occasionally, for 60 minutes or until corn is tender. Remove husks and cut kernels from the cob. Combine peas, corn kernels, onion, and bell peppers. Add cilantro. Mix in lime juice, salt, and pepper. Prepare cobia by soaking fillets in buttermilk for 30 minutes. Drain and shake off excess liquid. Coat one side of each fillet with cornmeal. Sauté fillets, cornmeal side down, in clarified butter. Cook 2 minutes or until lightly browned. Turn fillets and cook 5 minutes or until fish flakes easily with a fork. To serve, divide aioli evenly onto 4 serving plates. Place a cooked fillet, cornmeal side up, on each plate. Spoon salsa over the top.

***Yield:* 4 servings**

Sharon Hilbig
Bagatelle
Key West

Dos Equis XX Seafood Extravaganza Paella

This is a major Cuban party dish.

- ½ pound chicken breast, cubed
- ½ pound pork loin, cubed
- Olive oil for sautéing
- 4 cups converted rice
- 1 (10-ounce) can whole baby clams, undrained
- 2 (6½-ounce) cans chopped clams, undrained
- 3½ (12-ounce) bottles Dos Equis XX beer
- 1½ cups chopped onion
- 1½ cups chopped bell pepper
- 3 tablespoons chicken base
- 1 teaspoon white pepper
- 1 tablespoon onion flakes
- 1 tablespoon garlic flakes
- 1 tablespoon chopped garlic
- 1 tablespoon hot pepper sauce
- ½ pound smoked sausage, cubed
- ½ pound ham, cubed
- ½ pound grouper, cubed
- 1 (3⅔-ounce) can mussels, drained
- 1 pound scallops
- 1 pound large shrimp
- ½ pound steamed crab claws
- 1 (10-ounce) package frozen green peas, thawed, for garnish
- ½ red bell pepper, diced, for garnish
- 1 (1-ounce) jar pimiento for garnish
- 4 hard-cooked eggs, sliced, for garnish

In a large skillet, sauté chicken and pork in olive oil. Add rice and sauté a bit longer. Transfer mixture to a large roasting pan. In a large pot, combine undrained cans of whole and chopped clams, beer, and next 8 ingredients. Bring to a boil. Add boiling mixture to rice mixture. Stir in sausage and ham. Cover and bake at 350° for 35 to 40 minutes or until liquid is absorbed. Remove from oven and mix thoroughly. Stir in grouper, mussels, and scallops. Place shrimp and crab claws on top of mixture. Bake 25 minutes longer. Remove from oven. Set shrimp and crab claws on the side. Spoon mixture into a paella pan or a serving dish. Place shrimp and crab claws on top. Garnish with peas, bell pepper, pimiento, and egg.

Yield: 15 servings

Michael P. Bradley
Mexican Cantina
Islamorada

Fast Creole Sauce

- 1 (28-ounce) can Italian-style tomatoes, drained
- 1 (6-ounce) can tomato paste
- ½ teaspoon salt
- 1 tablespoon onion juice
- ½ teaspoon sugar
- ¾ cup chopped bell pepper
- ¾ cup chopped onion
- ¾ cup chopped celery
- ¾ cup chopped olives
- ¾ cup chopped pimiento
- 1-2 small green chile peppers, chopped

Garden-grown vegetables, such as those used in this recipe, help liven up meals for self-sufficient islanders.

Combine tomatoes and next 4 ingredients in a saucepan. Bring to a boil. Reduce heat to low and cover; simmer 20 minutes. Add bell pepper and remaining 5 ingredients. Cook until hot. Serve with seafood, eggs, or chicken.

Yield: 6 servings

Add cheese to sauce for a zesty and robust flavor.

Bill Valet
Ballyhoo's Grille and Grog
Key Largo

Cucumber Sauce

- ¾ cup heavy cultured or sweet sour cream
- 2 tablespoons lemon or lime juice, or apple cider vinegar
- ¼ teaspoon sea salt
- ⅛ teaspoon paprika
- 1 tablespoon chopped chives or dill
- 1 large cucumber, finely diced

Beat sour cream. Slowly mix in lemon juice. Season with salt, paprika, and chives. Fold in cucumber. Serve with cold fish or meats.

Yield: 1½ cups

Bill Valet
Ballyhoo's Grille and Grog
Key Largo

Key Lime-Avocado Salsa

- 2 ripe avocados, peeled and cubed
- 3 Key limes, peeled, seeded, and chopped
- 1 red onion, diced
- 1 clove garlic, minced
- 1 shallot, minced
- 1 teaspoon cumin
- 1 red bell pepper, diced
- 2 tablespoons chopped fresh cilantro
- 2 tablespoons extra virgin olive oil
- Salt and pepper to taste

Combine all ingredients. Refrigerate one hour to blend flavors. Serve as an accompaniment for fish, chicken, or shrimp.

Yield: 4 to 8 servings

Philip M. Smith
Mangoe's
Key West, FL

Windley Key was also called Umbrella Key at one time. In the early 1900s, Windley Key quarry furnished stone for railway fill and large blocks for piling and bridge abutments. One of the few places the coral reef can be studied without getting wet, the quarry is a Geologic Historic Site

Key Lime Beurre Blanc

- 2 shallots, sliced
- 4 sprigs fresh thyme
- 1 tablespoon extra virgin olive oil
- ¾ cup fresh Key lime juice
- ¾ cup Chablis
- ¼ cup heavy cream
- 4 sticks butter, softened
- Salt and pepper to taste
- Avocado and papaya slices for garnish

In a shallow pan, sauté shallots and thyme in oil. Add Key lime juice and Chablis. Reduce mixture over medium heat by one-half. Add cream and again reduce by one-half. While stirring, slowly add butter. Strain sauce. Season with salt and pepper. To serve, pour sauce on serving plates. Top each plate with a grilled or sautéed fish fillet. Garnish.

Yield: 8 servings

Philip M. Smith
Mangoe's
Key West

SHELLFISH

WINDWARD ISLANDS

Dominica, St. Lucia, St. Vincent, the Grenadines, Grenada, Carriacou, Trinidad, Tobago, Isla de Margarita, and the Venezuelan Islands make up the Windward Islands. (Bonaire, Curaçao, and Aruba are also Windwards, but are discussed on page 166.) These are the islands that take your breath away with their beauty and diversity.

From Dominica to Trinidad and Tobago, virtually every menu offers fresh fish and seafoods. Together with yams, sweet green bananas, guava, and pineapple, the quickest way to dining heaven can be found here. Exotic rum punches can set the stage for the real meaning in "Creole." On Grenada, known as the "Isle of Spice," conch, oysters, and lobster with a true cornucopia of fresh fruits and vegetables can have you swooning with every taste and tempting bite of its foods. Luxuriant is the word for Grenada.

Barbados is like stepping back in time. From boats to vehicles to hotels and even to the music, you will think you've gone back to the 50s. Barbados offers a plethora of restaurants as perfect preludes to some calypso and jazz or reggae later in the tropical night air. After sipping a Cuba Libre or mango punch, dine on anything from gourmet to Caribbean to French or Chinese. Barbados is the perfect spot for getting down to the business of living life to the fullest.

At St. Lucia, you'll marvel at the weekly Friday night "jump in" at Gros Inlet. At sundown, the streets are closed to traffic and bands set up for a nights riotous music. Batches of skewered lambi (conch), spicy chicken, and fresh fish are hawked — pure delights to the palate. This is the biggest block party in the Caribbean.

Lobster Thermador

- 4 (20-ounce) Florida lobster tails
- ⅓ cup oil
- 8 ounces mushrooms, sliced
- 4 bunches scallions, chopped
- 2 ripe tomatoes, diced
- 2 tablespoons chopped garlic
- 1 pint heavy cream
- 1 cup Parmesan cheese
- Salt and pepper to taste
- ½ pound mozzarella cheese, thinly sliced

Split lobster tails in half, lengthwise. Remove meat and set aside. Place shells on a baking sheet and bake at 350° for 10 minutes. Arrange shells on a serving platter. Chop lobster meat. Sauté lobster with oil and next 4 ingredients until lobster is half cooked. Add cream and simmer 3 minutes. Add Parmesan cheese, salt, and pepper. Cook until creamy. Spoon mixture into lobster shells. Top with mozzarella cheese. Bake at 350° until cheese melts.

Yield: 8 servings

Manny Glykas
Perrys Restaurant
Key Largo

Lobster Mexical

Mornay Sauce

2 tablespoons butter

2 tablespoons all-purpose flour

1 cup milk

1 shallot, minced

1 egg yolk

2 tablespoons cream

2 tablespoons Parmesan cheese

2 tablespoons grated Gruyère cheese

Pinch of cayenne pepper

Entrée

1½ pounds lobster, chopped

4 tablespoons butter

1 clove garlic, minced

¼ cup chopped onion

¼ cup chopped bell pepper

¼ cup chopped red bell pepper

¼ cup chopped yellow bell pepper

2 tablespoons chopped pimiento

1 cup sliced mushrooms

Fresh parsley for garnish

Melt butter in a saucepan. Blend in flour until smooth. Slowly stir in milk and cook until mixture starts to thicken. Add shallot and next 5 ingredients. Cook, stirring frequently, for 5 minutes. While sauce cooks, prepare entrée by sautéing lobster in butter and garlic. When almost cooked, add onion and next 5 ingredients. Continue to sauté until done. Serve topped with sauce. Garnish.

Yield: 4 servings

For added appeal, serve in lobster shells with rice on the side.

Brad Harding
The Conch Restaurant
Islamorada

Colombo is a French West Indian stew that can be made of anything from conch to sea urchin.

The Pilot's Lobster Pie

Creamy Garlic Sauce

- 1 quart milk
- ¼ large onion, sliced
- 1 quart heavy cream
- Salt and pepper to taste
- 1 tablespoon chicken base
- 1 tablespoon lobster base
- 1 tablespoon chopped garlic
- 1 tablespoon chopped parsley
- ¼ cup white wine
- ¼ teaspoon onion salt
- 3 tablespoons butter or margarine
- 3 tablespoons all-purpose flour

Pie

- 2 pounds lobster meat, steamed and chopped
- 4 teaspoons pine nuts, toasted
- 8 mushrooms, sliced
- ½ cup diced provolone cheese
- ½ cup diced scallions
- 2 cups creamy garlic sauce
- 6 to 8 sheets puff pastry, thawed
- 2 eggs, beaten

Simmer milk and onion 45 minutes. Strain. Add cream, salt, pepper, and next 6 ingredients. Simmer 60 minutes. In a small saucepan, melt butter. Stir in flour until smooth to make a roux. Use roux to thicken milk mixture, stirring in a small amount at a time until sauce reaches desired thickness. To assemble pie, combine lobster meat and next 5 ingredients. Divide among 6 to 8 single-serving casserole dishes. Top each dish with a puff pastry sheet. Brush with egg. Bake at 350° for 15 minutes.

Yield: 6 to 8 servings

John Daverio
The Pilot House Restaurant
Key Largo

Conch Sauté

Conch sauté is a Caribbean specialty.

- 12 ounces conch, slightly frozen
- All-purpose flour for dredging
- 4 tablespoons butter
- 4 tablespoons vegetable oil
- 1 large onion, quartered
- 20 snow pea pods
- 1 cup button mushrooms
- 4 teaspoons soy sauce
- 4 teaspoons sake
- ½ teaspoon salt, or to taste
- ½ teaspoon black pepper, or to taste

Cut conch while slightly frozen into thin slices. Dredge in flour. Heat butter and oil in a saucepan. Add conch and sauté for 5 seconds. Add onion and remaining 6 ingredients. Continue to sauté 4 to 7 minutes. Serve hot.

Yield: 4 servings

Yoshi Mizuma
Ginza Sushi
Islamorada

Ramon's Conch Steak

Conch (pronounced conk) is any of various large spiral-shaped marine gastropod mollusks. Natives of the Keys are also referred to as "conchs."

- 2 (8-ounce) conch steaks
- 2 eggs, beaten
- 2 tablespoons water
- ½ teaspoon chopped garlic
- ½ teaspoon salt
- ½ teaspoon black pepper
- 1 cup all-purpose flour
- ½ teaspoon oregano
- ½ teaspoon lime juice
- ½ teaspoon garlic powder
- Vegetable oil

Beat conch with a mallet to tenderize. Combine egg and next 4 ingredients. Dip conch into flour, then egg mixture, and back into flour. Sprinkle conch with oregano, lime juice, and garlic powder. Place conch in oil for 1 minute. Transfer conch to a hot sauté pan. Sauté 2 minutes or until firm and slightly browned on both sides. Serve with cocktail and lime sauce.

Yield: 2 servings

Patrica Rodriguez
Rusty Anchor Restaurant
Key West

Bahamian Conch Steak

Conch Steak

4 (7-ounce) conch steaks

All-purpose flour for dredging

3 tablespoons clarified butter

Sauce

4 tablespoons unsalted butter, divided

1 tablespoon chopped shallot

2 tablespoons all-purpose flour

½ cup white wine

¼ cup lime juice

¾ cup water

1 tablespoon chopped fresh parsley

Salt and pepper to taste

Pound conch steaks with a tenderizing mallet. Dredge in flour. Sauté in clarified butter in a very hot skillet until golden brown on both sides. Hold cooked steaks in a warm oven while preparing remaining steaks and sauce. To prepare sauce, melt 2 tablespoons unsalted butter in a saucepan. Add shallot and cook briefly. Mix in flour until smooth. Cook 1 minute. Add wine, lime juice, and water. Cook 2 minutes or until sauce starts to thicken. Add remaining 2 tablespoons unsalted butter and parsley. Cook and stir until butter melts and blends into sauce. Season with salt and pepper. Spoon sauce over cooked conch steaks.

Yield: 4 servings

Sharon Hilbig
Bagatelle
Key West

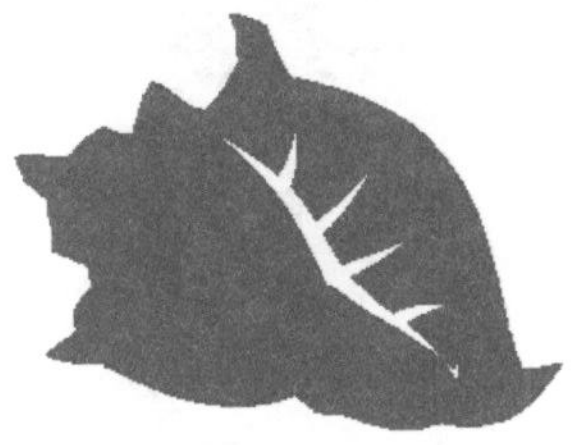

Conch, the giant snail of the Caribbean, has a beautiful, spiral-shaped shell.

If you want to stroke a **stingray,** head over to the Cayman Islands and snorkel Stringray City, a clear patch of water about 12- to 15-feet deep. Dive masters have gotten these rays so tame by feeding them for so long that you can have a safe close encounter with these saucers of the deep.

Cracked Conch With Crabmeat Stuffing

- 1½ pounds conch
- 1 cup crabmeat stuffing, commercially prepared or homemade
- 2 eggs, beaten
- 2 tablespoons water
- 1 cup seasoned cracker crumbs
- Oil for frying
- Scallion tops, thinly sliced, for garnish
- Lime slices for garnish

Tenderize conch by pounding with a mallet until meat resembles lace. Piece together conch into two 6x8-inch rectangles. Combine egg and water. Use some of egg mixture as a glue to hold conch pieces together. Place even amounts of stuffing across the center of each rectangle. Wrap conch around stuffing. Dip in egg mixture and then roll in cracker crumbs. Deep-fry in 350° oil until golden brown. Top with Lobster Sauce (page 164) or hollandaise sauce. Garnish.

Yield: 4 servings

Valerie Mayfield
Jim and Val's Tugboat Restaurant
Key Largo

Most of the Spanish Treasure Fleet returning to Spain in July 1733 was destroyed by a hurricane.

Sautéed Caribbean Conch Joseph

½ pound conch
All-purpose flour for dredging
3 tablespoons clarified butter
12 (16 to 20 count) shrimp, peeled and deveined
1 cup diced tomato
1 teaspoon chopped fresh parsley
Pinch of salt
Pinch of black pepper
2 tablespoons sherry
3 tablespoons butter
4 slices white American cheese
1 (8-ounce) package linguini, cooked al dente

Tenderize conch with a mallet. Cut into small pieces and dredge lightly in flour. Heat clarified butter in a large sauté pan over medium heat. Add conch and shrimp and turn heat to medium-high. Sauté 1 minute. Turn to high heat and sauté 1 minute more. Add tomato and next 3 ingredients. Cook and stir until tomato is hot. Add sherry and flambé. Remove from heat. Stir in butter until melted. Cover with cheese and place under a broiler until cheese melts. Serve immediately over hot linguini.

Yield: 4 servings

Thomas Jay Mercier
Cracked Conch Café
Marathon

Orange Conch

- 4 (6-ounce) conch steaks
- 1 teaspoon salt
- 1 teaspoon black pepper
- 2 eggs, beaten
- ½ cup all-purpose flour
- Clarified butter for sautéing
- ¼ cup white wine
- ⅓ cup fresh orange juice
- 2 tablespoons butter
- Orange sections for garnish

Tenderize conch steaks with a mallet. Sprinkle with salt and pepper. Dip in egg; then coat with flour. Sauté in a saucepan in clarified butter until lightly browned on both sides. Transfer to a serving platter and keep warm. Deglaze saucepan with white wine and reduce by one-half. Add juice and again reduce by half. Swirl in butter, 1 teaspoon at a time. Pour sauce over conch. Garnish.

Yield: 4 servings

Frank Carlton
Snapper's
Key Largo

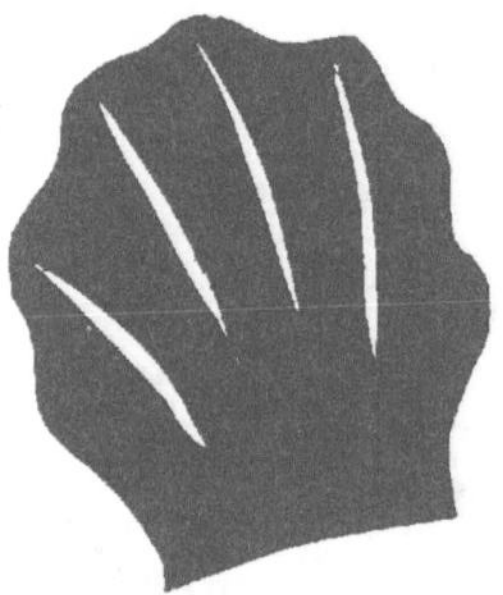

Conch Burger

Out Island Sauce

- 1 cup mayonnaise
- ¼ cup ketchup
- 1 teaspoon hot pepper sauce

Sandwiches

- 1 pound conch
- 2 eggs
- ¼ cup milk
- 1 cup all-purpose flour
- 1½ cups Japanese-style breadcrumbs
- Oil for frying
- 4 Kaiser rolls
- 4 leaves lettuce
- 4 slices tomato
- 4 wedges lemon

Mix together mayonnaise, ketchup, and hot pepper sauce with a whip. Refrigerate sauce until needed. Pound conch to tenderize. Cut into small pieces. Beat eggs and milk together. Dredge conch in flour. Dip in egg mixture and then press into breadcrumbs. Deep-fry in hot oil until golden brown. Divide conch evenly between rolls. Garnish with lettuce, tomato, and lemon. Serve with sauce.

Yield: 4 servings

Jim Ewing
Hawk Channel Bar and Grill
Islamorada

Grilled Keys Shrimp

- ¼ cup Chardonnay
- 2 tablespoons lime juice
- 4 tablespoons butter
- 8 (16 to 20 count) shrimp, peeled and deveined

Combine Chardonnay, lime juice, and butter in a shallow saucepan. Heat to melt butter. Mix in shrimp. Cook until shrimp turn bright pink. Remove shrimp from saucepan and broil or grill 5 to 10 seconds. Serve with marmalade, mango chutney, or cocktail sauce.

Yield: 1 serving

Tracy A. Holder
Royal Pelican Restaurant, Holiday Inn
Marathon

Shrimp Amelia

- 24 jumbo shrimp, peeled and deveined
- ½ cup all-purpose flour
- 1 cup clarified butter
- 2 cups sliced shiitake mushrooms
- 1 large shallot, chopped
- 2 cloves garlic, chopped
- 2 cups Burgundy wine
- 2 sticks butter, cut into pats
- Salt and pepper to taste
- 4 cups cooked pasta

Lightly dust shrimp in flour. Combine shrimp, clarified butter, and next 3 ingredients in a large skillet. Sauté over medium-high heat 3 to 4 minutes or until shrimp turn pink. Remove shrimp mixture and deglaze pan with wine. Bring to a boil. Roll pats of butter in flour and add to wine. Stir and remove from heat. Season with salt and pepper. Divide hot pasta among 4 serving plates. Place shrimp mixture over pasta. Ladle wine sauce over top.

Yield: 4 servings

Brian W. Duffy
Snooks Bayside
Key Largo

Coconut Shrimp

Sweet Caribbean Sauce

3 ounces orange juice

2 tablespoons chopped banana

2 tablespoons chopped mango

2 tablespoons chopped fresh parsley

2 tablespoons butter

1 ounce coconut-flavored rum

Shrimp

1 cup grated coconut

1 cup crushed corn flakes

1 pound shrimp, peeled, deveined, and butterflied

1 cup all-purpose flour

4 eggs, beaten

2 cups peanut oil

Prepare sauce by reducing orange juice by a third over medium-high heat. Add banana and next 4 ingredients and reduce again by a third. Cool before serving. To prepare shrimp, combine coconut and corn flakes. Dip shrimp in flour and then egg. Press both sides of each shrimp firmly into coconut mixture. Cook shrimp in 325° oil until golden brown. Serve with Sweet Caribbean Sauce.

Yield: 2 servings

Justin Green
Paradise Cafe
Long Key

Deep-fried Coconut Shrimp With Coconut Rum Sauce

- 7 ounces water, divided
- ½ cup coconut-flavored rum
- 1 cup heavy cream
- 1 tablespoons sugar
- 1 tablespoon cornstarch
- 2 eggs, beaten
- 1 cup milk
- 24 (16 to 20 count) shrimp, peeled, deveined, and butterflied
- 1 cup all-purpose flour
- Coconut flakes
- Oil for deep-frying
- Chopped parsley for garnish

In a small saucepan, combine 4 ounces water and next 3 ingredients. Bring to a boil. Mix cornstarch with remaining 3 ounces water. Add cornstarch mixture to saucepan. Reduce heat and simmer 5 minutes. Mix together eggs and milk. Dredge shrimp in flour; then dip in egg mixture. Press shrimp into coconut flakes. Deep-fry shrimp in oil for 2 minutes, 30 seconds or until golden brown. Place shrimp on a serving plate. Pour sauce over shrimp. Sprinkle with parsley for garnish. Serve with grilled plantain.

Yield: 4 servings

Arthur Paterson
Green Turtle Inn
Islamorada

Easy Coconut Shrimp

- 1 (8-ounce) box tempura batter flour
- ½ cup grated coconut
- 8 (16 to 20 count) shrimp, peeled and deveined
- ½ cup coconut syrup
- Oil for frying

Combine flour and coconut. Dip shrimp in coconut syrup, then roll in flour mixture. Dip again in syrup, then back in flour mixture. Drop shrimp individually into hot oil and cook until golden brown. Serve with orange marmalade.

Yield: 1 serving

Tracy Holder
Royal Pelican Restaurant, Holiday Inn
Marathon

Souse, a pickled vegetable and pig parts concoction, is a traditional Bajan dish.

Hurricane Shrimp

- 1 pound (11 to 15 count) white or pink shrimp, peeled and deveined
- 1 tablespoon coarse salt
- 1 tablespoon fresh thyme, or 1 to 2 teaspoons dried
- 2 cloves garlic, sliced
- Pinch of crushed red pepper flakes
- Pinch of cayenne pepper
- Juice of 2 Key limes
- 1 teaspoon black pepper

Place shrimp and salt in an ice water bath while preparing marinade. Mix thyme and remaining 5 ingredients in a blender or food processor. Drain shrimp. Combine shrimp and thyme mixture and marinate for at least 30 minutes. Broil shrimp on a barbecue grill or in an oven for 10 minutes or until done.

Yield: 3 to 4 servings

Annabella Dolan
Twin Landings Waterfront Bar and Restaurant
Key Colony Beach

Chef Pedro's Shrimp Scampi

- ½ cup olive oil
- 1 pound shrimp, peeled and deveined
- 4 cloves garlic, crushed
- ½ teaspoon salt
- 1 teaspoon hot pepper sauce
- 2 bay leaves
- ¼ teaspoon ground cumin
- 2 tablespoons dry white wine
- 2 tablespoons chopped fresh parsley

Heat oil in a large skillet for 30 seconds. Add shrimp and sauté until shrimp are pink. Add garlic and next 4 ingredients. Cook and stir for 30 seconds. Mix in wine and parsley. Cook another 1 to 2 minutes, being careful to not overcook shrimp. Remove bay leaves. Garnish with sprigs of parsley.

Yield: 3 to 4 servings

Pedro Gonzalez
Don Pedro Restaurant
Marathon

Stone Crab Cakes With Avocado Aioli

Avocado Aioli

- 2 ripe avocados
- Juice of 1 lemon
- 1½ teaspoons chopped garlic
- 1 teaspoon salt
- ½ teaspoon white pepper
- ½ cup olive oil

Crab Cakes

- 1 pound crabmeat, cleaned
- ½ cup finely diced bell pepper
- ½ cup finely diced red bell pepper
- ½ cup finely diced yellow bell pepper
- ½ cup finely diced red onion
- 1 tablespoon coarse salt
- 2 teaspoons black pepper
- 1 teaspoon cayenne pepper
- 1 tablespoon Worcestershire sauce
- 1 tablespoon chopped fresh dill
- 1 tablespoon chopped fresh parsley
- 1 cup breadcrumbs
- 1 egg, lightly beaten
- 1 cup mayonnaise
- Clarified butter

Puree avocados in a blender or food processor. Mix in lemon juice and next 3 ingredients. With blender running, slowly add oil to mixture. To prepare crab cakes, combine crabmeat and next 10 ingredients in a large bowl. Toss in breadcrumbs. Fold in egg and mayonnaise. Divide into 8 cakes and sauté in a small amount of clarified butter over medium heat. To serve, divide aioli evenly onto 4 serving plates. Place 2 crab cakes on each plate. Garnish with chopped tomatoes, lemon wedges, and sprigs of dill.

Yield: 4 servings

Sharon Hilbig
Bagatelle
Key West

Crabmeat Omelet

- 3 eggs, or egg substitute equivalent
- 2 ounces water
- 6 ounces crabmeat, or baby shrimp
- 3 tablespoons cocktail sauce
- Dash of salt

Whip together eggs and water. Cook over medium heat in a pan or skillet. When eggs set, add crabmeat, cocktail sauce, and salt. Cook until golden brown. Fold over omelet and transfer to a serving plate. Top with a spoonful of cocktail sauce. Serve with home-fried potatoes or grits and toast.

Yield: 2 servings

Lee G. Ganim
Ganim's Kountry Kitchen
Key Largo

Seafood Special

- 4 tablespoons margarine
- ½ medium onion, chopped
- 1 tomato, chopped
- 1 bell pepper, chopped
- 1 stalk celery, chopped
- 4 ounces shrimp, chopped
- 5 ounces fish, diced
- 4 ounces squid, cleaned and chopped
- 4 ounces boiled and cleaned octopus
- 2 ounces scallops
- ¼ teaspoon salt
- Black pepper to taste

Melt margarine in a preheated sauté pan. Add onion and next 3 ingredients. Simmer 3 minutes. Add shrimp and next 4 ingredients. Season with salt and pepper. Sauté until seafood is cooked.

Yield: 3 to 4 servings

Maduro Wyki
Mi Cushina
Aruba

Keys Seafood Pasta

This recipe features seafood and pasta, perfectly matched ingredients in Caribbean cooking.

- 1 teaspoon chopped shallot
- 4 tablespoons clarified butter, divided
- 1 quart heavy cream
- 2 tablespoons dry sherry
- 1 cup grated Asiago cheese
- Salt and pepper to taste
- 8 ounces lobster
- 8 (11 to 16 count) shrimp
- 12 ounces firm white fish
- 1 tablespoon chopped garlic
- 1 cup sliced button mushrooms
- ¼ bunch parsley, chopped
- 1 (16-ounce) package linguine, cooked al dente

Briefly cook shallot in 2 tablespoons clarified butter. Add cream and reduce over low heat by a third. Remove from heat and add sherry. Use a whip to completely mix in cheese. Sauté remaining 2 tablespoons clarified butter, salt, pepper, and next 3 ingredients for 2 minutes. Add garlic and mushrooms and sauté 2 minutes longer. Stir in cream sauce and parsley. Continue to heat. Add linguine and cook until thoroughly heated.

Yield: 4 servings

Sharon Hilbig
Bagatelle
Key West

Seafood Collins

- 1 pound medium shrimp
- ½ pound medium scallops
- 4 tablespoons clarified margarine or oil
- Salt and pepper to taste
- 4 tablespoons butter, softened
- 2 tablespoons chopped garlic
- ⅛ teaspoon paprika
- 1 large tomato, diced
- 1 pound mushrooms, sliced
- 1 cup heavy cream

Shrimp and scallops highlight this delicious tropical recipe.

Sauté shrimp and scallops in clarified margarine 4 minutes. Season with salt and pepper. Stir in butter until melted. Add garlic and next 3 ingredients. Sauté briskly for about 2 minutes. Add cream. Cook to reduce sauce. When thickened, serve over rice or pasta.

Yield: 3 to 4 servings

Craig Belcher
Craig's Restaurant
Tavernier

Old Tavernier Seafood Cioppino

- 2 tablespoons olive oil
- 3 (11 to 15 count) shrimp
- 4 ounces large sea scallops
- 8 littleneck clams
- 10 mussels
- ½ Florida lobster tail
- 3 ounces grouper, cubed
- 3 ounces mahi-mahi, cubed
- 1 tablespoon chopped shallot
- Salt and pepper
- 2 tablespoons minced garlic
- ½ cup sliced mushrooms
- ¼ cup chopped scallions
- ¼ cup chopped tomato
- ½ jalapeño pepper, diced
- ½ tablespoon crushed red pepper flakes
- ½ cup tomato sauce
- ¾ cup clam juice

Heat olive oil in a large skillet. Add shrimp and next 6 ingredients and sauté. Add shallot, salt, pepper, and remaining 8 ingredients. Mix together and cover. Cook 5 minutes or until seafood cooks thoroughly and clams and mussels open. Discard any clams or mussels that fail to open.

Yield: 2 servings

John A. Potucek III and John A. Roy
The Old Tavernier
Tavernier

Goat Water is a ragout of goat meat and vegetables that's served in Montserrat and Anguilla and elsewhere in the islands.

Paella

- 6 mussels, scrubbed
- 2 quarts water
- 3 cups uncooked long-grain rice
- ½ cup olive oil
- 4 cloves garlic, chopped
- ½ pound chorizo, cut in ¼-inch slices
- ½ pound pork, cubed
- 4 chicken breasts
- 4 chicken thighs
- 4 chicken legs
- 6 rock lobster tails
- 1 onion, chopped
- 1 bell pepper, chopped
- 1 red bell pepper, chopped
- ½ cup tomato sauce
- ⅛ teaspoon saffron powder
- 1 teaspoon salt
- ¼ teaspoon black pepper
- 1½ quarts chicken broth
- 12 large shrimp, peeled and deveined
- 6 cherrystone clams, scrubbed
- 1 pound calamari
- 1 pound scallops
- 1 cup frozen peas
- 1 tomato, peeled, seeded, and diced

Paella is a Cuban specialty.

Soak mussels in cold water for 30 minutes to remove salty taste. Discard any shells that open while soaking. Drain. Bring 2 quarts water to a boil. Add rice and cook for 1 minute. Rinse with cold water and drain. Heat oil in a large skillet. Leave oil in skillet after each addition and removal of ingredients that follow. Add garlic and cook until browned. Remove garlic and discard. Add chorizo and cook until browned on both sides. Remove to drain. Add pork, brown, and remove to drain. Add chicken pieces and fry until golden brown and thoroughly cooked. Remove from skillet and drain. Add lobster to skillet and fry just until shells turn pink. Remove and drain. Add onion and sauté 5 minutes or until tender. Stir in bell peppers and sauté with onion. Mix in tomato sauce and simmer until thick. Add drained rice, saffron, and next 3 ingredients. Bring to a boil. Arrange mussels, chorizo, pork, chicken, lobster, shrimp, and next 3 ingredients on rice mixture. Scatter peas and tomato on top. Cover tightly. Simmer 30 to 45 minutes or until rice is tender, shrimp and lobster meat turn white, and mussel and clam shells open. Remove from heat and let stand, covered, 10 minutes. Serve hot in pan.

Yield: 6 to 8 servings

Pedro Gonzalez
Don Pedro Restaurant
Marathon

Seafood Pie

- 2 (9-inch) pastry shells, unbaked
- 3 tablespoons butter or margarine
- 3 tablespoons minced scallions
- 1 tablespoons tomato paste

Cayenne pepper to taste

- 3 tablespoons sherry
- 4 eggs, beaten
- 1½ cups heavy cream
- 1½ cups diced, cooked seafood

Salt and pepper to taste

- ¼ cup grated Gruyère cheese

Prick bottom of pastry shells with a fork. Bake at 375° for 15 minutes. Cool. Melt butter in a skillet. Add scallions and sauté about 2 minutes. Add tomato paste, cayenne pepper, and sherry. Cook and stir until boiling. Cool to lukewarm. Mix in egg and cream. Add seafood and season with salt and pepper. Pour into pastry shells. Sprinkle cheese over top. Bake at 375° for 30 minutes.

Use shrimp, scallops, lobster, or other seafood according to preference and availability.

Yield: 12 servings

Jane Gahagen
Plantation Yacht Harbor Resort
Islamorada

Papaya Chutney

- 1 medium to large onion, chopped
- 2 cups diced ripe papaya
- ½ cup sugar
- 1 large red bell pepper, diced
- ½ teaspoon ground allspice
- 1 teaspoon ground ginger
- ½ cup cider vinegar
- 1 cup non-chlorinated water
- ½ teaspoon sea salt
- Dash of hot pepper sauce

This tasty condiment is a blend of several Caribbean ingredients, including papaya, allspice, and ginger.

Combine all ingredients in a large pot. Simmer over low heat 45 minutes. Cool. Serve over crab cakes, lobster, shrimp, or broiled fish.

Yield: 6 servings

Pedro Gonzalez
Don Pedro Restaurant
Marathon

Octopus Pasta Sauce

- 1 cup virgin olive oil
- 1¼ cups peeled, seeded, and chopped tomato
- 1 teaspoon salt
- 2 cloves garlic, chopped
- 1½ cups cooked and chopped octopus
- 1 (16-ounce) package linguine, cooked al dente

Octopus is a warm water Caribbean seafood.

Heat oil in a large saucepan over medium-high heat. Add tomato, salt, and garlic. Simmer 20 minutes. Stir in octopus and simmer 20 minutes longer. Toss with drained linguine and serve immediately.

Yield: 2 servings

Bill Valet
Ballyhoo's Grille and Grog
Key Largo

Lobster Sauce

- 4 tablespoons butter
- ¼ cup all-purpose flour
- 2 teaspoons lobster base
- 2 cups milk
- ½ cup tomato juice
- 1 tablespoon white wine

Melt butter in a small saucepan. Mix in flour until smooth. Cook and stir for 2 to 3 minutes. Mix lobster base with enough water to dissolve. Add lobster base mixture, milk, and tomato juice to saucepan. Cook and stir constantly until sauce thickens. Add wine. Serve over seafood entrée of choice.

Yield: 2½ cups

Jim and Val Mayfield
Jim and Val's Tugboat Restaurant
Key Largo

Conch Key was the last of the keys true fishing villages. It is located in the bay at mile marker 62 on the Overseas Highway. It has a single circular road passing between wooden houses with docks and lobster traps. In the 1960s, this was the most densely populated island in the Keys.

MEATS, POULTRY, & MEATLESS

Today part of Aruba is as rugged and rocky as it was when the Dutch first rowed ashore hundreds of years ago. Cacti and divi-divi trees spread across the center of the island. Wild donkeys roam near the shore, and new luxury hotels entice visitors to gourmet restaurants, active casinos, and "hot" nightlife. Add to this, duty-free shopping and every watersport you can imagine, and Aruba is worthy of any tourist's dream vacation.

An interesting culinary blend is an understatement in Aruba. Fresh seafood and fish are specialties in most restaurants. Some highlights include Keshi yena, a large round of baked Edam cheese, which is hollowed out and filled with shrimp, meat or chicken, tomatoes, onions, olives, pickles, and raisins; stoba, a lamb or goat stew; and sopa di pisca, a combination of fish fillets, tomatoes, onions, red pepper, garlic, carrots, and olives. You'll want to try the ubiquitous fresh fish the way the locals do — with funchi, or the typical Aruban pan bati, a cornmeal and flour pancake; cala, bean fritters; and pastiche, a meat-stuffed turnover.

Just 35 miles north of Venezuela, Curaçao, the largest and most populated of the Netherlands Antilles, is 180 square miles of Caribbean delight. The friendly, accommodating residents are a unique combination of Dutch, Portuguese, Spanish, English, African, and Indians. There are restaurants all around the picturesque capital of Willemstad that reflect the island's international influences.

Dining alfresco as you're caressed by sea breezes is what you'll find on Bonaire. Antillean foods are specialties — such as snapper and shrimp served with rice and beans, fried bananas, and boiled cornmeal. International cuisines eaten to the tune of steel bands and folkloric groups will lull you into the laid-back life of the island.

Lorelei's Redbone Island Pork Barbecue

Honey Ginger Sauce

- 1 (8-ounce) can sweetened tamarind nectar
- 1 tablespoon honey
- 2 inches ginger root, ground
- 1 tablespoon commercial dry jerk seasoning
- 1 tablespoon soy sauce
- 1 teaspoon water
- 1 teaspoon cornstarch

Simple Jerk Sauce

- 1 onion
- 1 cup soy sauce
- 2 teaspoons chopped garlic
- 1 Scotch bonnet pepper, chopped

Jamaican Jerk Rub

- 1 onion, diced
- 2 teaspoons chopped fresh thyme
- 1 teaspoon ground allspice
- ½ teaspoon cinnamon
- 1 teaspoon black pepper
- ½ cup diced scallions
- 2 teaspoons salt
- ¼ teaspoon nutmeg
- 4 Scotch bonnet peppers, minced

Jerk Pork Roast

- 1 (3- to 5-pound) boneless pork loin
- Jamaican jerk rub

Seasoning jerk recipes is done through use of a rub, marinade, or dry seasoning. This rub recipe was discovered near Runaway Bay, on the northern coast of Jamaica. Store the Jamaican jerk rub in a tightly sealed bottle for up to 1 month. Add extra Scotch bonnet peppers to make the rub spicier.

Mix together tamarind nectar and honey. Bring to a boil and cook until mixture reduces by a third. Add ginger root, jerk seasoning, and soy sauce. Stir together water and cornstarch. Add to sauce and continue to cook until thickened. Make simple jerk sauce by cutting onion into slices. Cut onion slices in half. Combine onion and next 3 ingredients in a saucepan. Simmer until thoroughly cooked. To prepare jerk rub, combine onion and next 8 ingredients in a blender or food processor. Blend until mixture forms a paste. Coat the outside of the pork loin with jerk rub. Cover tightly with plastic wrap and refrigerate 24 hours. Cook slowly in an oven until the internal temperature reaches 160°. Cool 10 minutes before slicing. Serve with honey ginger sauce or simple jerk sauce.

Yield: 6 to 8 servings

John Maloughney
The Lorelei
Islamorada

Caribbean Pork Risotto

- 3/4 pound boneless pork tenderloin, cut into strips
- Salt to taste
- Ground ginger to taste
- Ground cloves to taste
- 1 tablespoon oil
- 1 cup diced bell pepper
- 1 tablespoon packed brown sugar
- 1 clove garlic, minced
- Juice of 1 lime
- 1/2 cup chopped onion
- 1 tablespoon butter
- 1 cup uncooked rice
- 2 tablespoons rum
- 2 cups chicken broth, divided
- 3 cups water
- 1 (8-ounce) can pineapple tidbits in juice, undrained

Season pork with salt, ginger, and cloves. Sauté pork in oil in a large non-stick skillet over high heat. Add bell pepper and next 3 ingredients. Cook 1 to 2 minutes longer. Remove pork mixture from skillet and set aside. Add onion and butter to skillet. Cook until tender. Add rice and cook and stir 2 to 3 minutes. Add rum and stir until absorbed. Decrease heat to medium-high and stir in 1 cup broth. Cook uncovered, stirring frequently, until absorbed. Continue stirring and add remaining 1 cup broth and water, 1 cup at a time, allowing each cup of liquid to be absorbed before adding another. Add liquid until rice is tender and mixture is creamy. Stir in pineapple and pork mixture. Serve immediately.

Yield: 4 servings

USA Rice Council

Besides being a place of pleasures, dreams, and fantasies, the Florida Keys also have occasional storms and hurricanes. But the beauty of the Keys still draws people from far and wide to its diving opportunities, wonderul fishing, and American-Caribbean sunsets.

Caribbean Roast Pork Loin

Pork Loin

- ¼ cup Dijon mustard
- 1 (4-pound) boneless pork loin
- ¼ cup sugar
- ½ cup jerk seasoning

Apple Compote

- 12 Granny Smith apples, peeled and diced
- Butter for sautéing
- 1 cup golden raisins
- ½ cup sugar
- 1 teaspoon cinnamon
- 1 teaspoon nutmeg

Spread mustard over entire pork loin. Combine sugar and jerk seasoning. Coat pork loin with an even layer of sugar mixture. Bake at 300° for 60 minutes to 1 hour, 30 minutes. Serve with warm or cold chunky applesauce or apple compote. To prepare apple compote, sauté apple in butter. Add raisins and remaining 3 ingredients. Cook until softened.

Yield: about 10 servings

Carole Baker
Grove Park Cafe
Islamorada

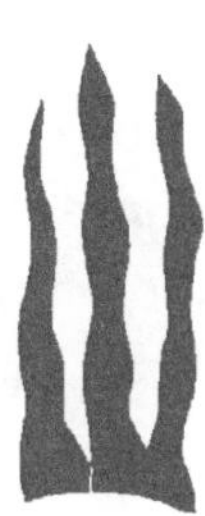

Smoked Caribbean Pork Roast

- 1 (5-pound) pork loin roast
- 2 tablespoons adobo spice
- 2 tablespoons black peppercorn
- 3 tablespoons lime juice
- 2 jalapeño peppers, halved
- 4 (12-ounce) cans beer

Rub roast thoroughly with adobo spice. Place meat in a roasting pan just larger than the roast. Add leftover adobo spice and remaining 4 ingredients to pan. Cover and refrigerate 2 hours. Remove cover and place pan in a smoker for 5 to 6 hours. Baste meat with pan juices several times while cooking. Serve with coconut salsa or jalapeño barbecue sauce.

Yield: 4 to 6 servings

Use a combination of mesquite and hickory wood in the smoker for best results.

Tracy A. Holder
Royal Pelican Restaurant, Holiday Inn
Marathon

Caribbean Lamb

- 1 pound boneless lamb, cut in ¾-inch cubes
- 1 teaspoon salt
- 1 tablespoon oil
- 1 cup diced red bell pepper
- 2 teaspoons curry powder
- 1 (8-ounce) can pineapple tidbits, undrained
- 3 cups cooked rice
- ⅓ cup raisins

Season lamb with salt. Sauté in oil in a large skillet over medium-high heat 2 to 3 minutes, or until browned. Add bell pepper and curry powder and cook until bell pepper is crisp-tender. Add pineapple, rice, and raisins. Simmer, uncovered, 5 minutes or until lamb is cooked.

Yield: 4 servings

USA Rice Council

Jerk Spaghetti

- 2 tablespoons olive oil or butter
- ¼ cup chopped onion
- 8 ounces jerk sausage, diced
- 1 clove garlic, chopped

Salt and pepper to taste

- 3 pounds fresh tomatoes, chopped
- 1 teaspoon jerk seasoning
- 2 tablespoons chopped fresh basil
- 1 (8-ounce) package spaghetti, cooked al dente

Heat oil in a heavy skillet. Add onion and sauté until tender. Add sausage and garlic. Cook 3 minutes. Mix in salt, pepper, and next 3 ingredients. Simmer 10 minutes. Serve over hot spaghetti.

Yield: 4 servings

Evita's Restaurant
Jamaica

Cuban Roasted Pork

- 1 small pork shoulder or loin roast
- 1 cup orange juice

Juice of 2 lemons

- 4 tablespoons salt
- 3 tablespoons black pepper
- 3 tablespoons oregano
- 6 cloves garlic, minced
- 1 small onion, sliced

Marinate pork roast in orange juice and lemon juice 2 to 3 hours. Remove pork from juice. Season with salt and next 3 ingredients. Place in a roasting pan and cover with foil. Bake at 300° for 2 hours, 30 minutes or until internal temperature reaches 160°. Remove foil and bake at 350° for 15 minutes to brown meat. Remove from oven and let stand 5 to 10 minutes. Cut in ¾-inch slices. Top with sliced onion for garnish.

Yield: 6 servings

Pedro Gonzalez
Don Pedro Restaurant
Marathon

It's hard to imagine a more infectious music than **calypso.** Created in Trinidad and known for its insistent beat, sun-soaked melodies, and sly word play, calypso eclipses reggae as the music the people of the Caribbean love best.

Stewed Goat

- 1 pound goat meat, cubed
- 1 tablespoon salt
- 1 stick margarine
- ½ medium onion, chopped
- 1 bell pepper, chopped
- 1 stalk celery, chopped
- 1 tomato, chopped
- Curry powder to taste
- Nutmeg to taste
- Basil to taste
- Garlic to taste

Place goat meat, salt, and enough water to cover in a pot. Bring to a boil and cook 60 minutes or until tender. Remove meat from water and transfer to a sauté pan. Add margarine and remaining 8 ingredients. Simmer 30 minutes.

Yield: 2 servings

Maduro Wyki
Mi Cushina
Aruba

Latin-Style Roast Pork

Roast pork is a staple food in the Caribbean.

- 3 cloves garlic, chopped
- 2 teaspoons cumin
- 1 cup olive oil
- 1 cup bitter orange juice
- 2 teaspoons black pepper
- 1 (12-pound) fresh ham, leg, or shoulder cut

Combine garlic and next 4 ingredients to make a marinade. Pierce meat with numerous 2-inch-deep knife slits. Rub marinade over entire ham and into slits. Place ham and remaining marinade in a plastic bag. Refrigerate a minimum of 6 hours. Bake, uncovered, at 325° for at least 6 hours. Meat will fall from bone when done. Serve with red beans and rice and with onions that have been sautéed in remaining marinade.

Yield: 24 servings

Captain Alan R. Horn
Porkers
Key Largo

Veal Scaloppine Ocho Rios

Brown Sauce

- 1 small onion, chopped
- 1 stalk celery, chopped
- 1 carrot, chopped
- ½ teaspoon thyme
- 1 bay leaf
- ½ teaspoon rosemary
- 2 cups beef broth
- ¼ cup vegetable oil
- ½ cup all-purpose flour

Veal

- 4 (4-ounce) veal cutlets, pounded thin
- All-purpose flour for dredging
- 2 tablespoons clarified butter
- ½ cup sliced button mushrooms
- ¼ cup sliced portabella mushrooms
- 1 clove garlic, chopped
- 1 clove shallot, chopped
- 2 ounces sherry
- 1 cup brown sauce

Combine onion and next 5 ingredients in a saucepan. Sauté until vegetable start to brown. Add broth and simmer about 60 minutes. In a separate pan, combine oil and flour over medium heat. Stir until smooth. Strain broth and slowly stir into flour mixture. Cook until thickened. To prepare veal, dredge cutlets in flour. Sear in a sauté pan over medium heat. Place cutlets on a serving plate. Add butter and next 4 ingredients to pan. Sauté until mushrooms soften. Carefully add sherry and flambé. Stir in brown sauce. Spoon over cutlets.

Yield: 2 servings

Larry Lower
Montego Bay Food and Spirits Inc.
Big Pine Key

Pea & Rice refers to kidney beans, pigeon beans, or black-eyed peas served over a Caribbean dish containing onions, salt pork, and rice.

Jamaican Chicken

1 ounce olive oil
2 tablespoons Caribbean jerk seasoning
1½ ounces dark rum
1 ounce Triple Sec
2 chicken breasts

Combine oil and next 3 ingredients. Mix thoroughly. Marinate chicken in oil mixture 3 minutes. Remove chicken from marinade. Cook on a charcoal grill until done. Serve with coconut salsa or honey mustard and ginger sauce.

Yield: 2 servings

Tracy A. Holder
Royal Pelican Restaurant
Marathon

James Bond (agent double 0 seven) always asked for a pot of Jamaican Blue Mountain coffee with his breakfast. He wasn't the first to prize the delicious coffee with a mellow flavor and full-bodied taste of Arabica coffee beans grown in eastern Jamaica's Blue Mountains. This coffee sells for $30 to $40 per pound in the U.S.

Chicken Saltenbuca

½ pound spinach, cleaned and stemmed
4 large chicken breasts, skinned and boned
1 pound ham, sliced
½ pound provolone cheese, sliced
¾ pound prosciutto, sliced thin
3 bunches basil, chopped fine
3 cups heavy cream
Salt and pepper to taste

Sauté spinach in a small amount of oil; set aside. Pound chicken breasts flat. Divide ham evenly over breasts. Add layers of cheese and spinach. Roll chicken and wrap with prosciutto. Bake at 400° for 15 minutes or until done. Turn rolls frequently while baking. While chicken bakes, prepare a sauce by combining basil and cream in a saucepan. Cook and reduce sauce until thick and creamy. Season with salt and pepper. To serve, slice chicken rolls and top with sauce.

Yield: 4 servings

Manny Glykas
Perrys Seafood Restaurant
Key Largo

Black and Bleu (Blackened Chicken Sandwiches)

Bagatelle Blackening Spice Mix

8 ounces paprika
1 ounce onion powder
1 ounce garlic powder
1 ounce cayenne pepper
2 teaspoons white pepper
2 teaspoons black pepper
1 ounce dried basil
1 ounce dried thyme
1 ounce dried oregano
1 ounce coarse salt

Sandwich

4 (5-ounce) skinless and boneless chicken breasts
Clarified butter or oil
4 tablespoons blackening spice mix
8 ounces bleu cheese, crumbled

Combine paprika and next 9 ingredients. Store in an airtight container until ready to use. To prepare sandwiches, dip one side of each chicken breast in clarified butter. Coat greased side of chicken with spice mix. Place breasts, spice side down, in a very hot, dry skillet. Cook on this side until bottom of breasts reach an even black color. Turn and cook on other side for 1 minute. Divide cheese evenly over chicken. Place each breast in a sandwich roll.

Yield: 4 servings

Store extra spice mix in an airtight container for future use.

Sharon Hilbig
Bagatelle
Key West

Blackened cooking is a popular preparation technique in Caribbean recipes.

Spanish Chicken Rice

- 1 chicken, quartered
- All-purpose flour for dredging
- Oil for sautéing
- ½ cup Spanish olives
- ¼ cup large capers
- 2 tablespoons chopped onion
- 2 tablespoons chopped bell pepper
- 2 tablespoons chopped red bell pepper
- 2 tablespoons halved mushrooms
- 1 (16-ounce) can plum tomatoes
- 1 cup rice
- 2 cups water

Dredge chicken pieces in flour. Sauté in oil in a large skillet. Add olives and next 5 ingredients and continue cooking until vegetables become tender. Add tomatoes, rice, and water. Bring to a boil. Transfer skillet to an oven. Bake at 350° for 30 minutes or until chicken is cooked and rice is tender. Remove from pan when finished cooking to prevent rice from sticking.

Yield: 4 servings

Chicken and rice are staples in Caribbean dishes, especially in Cuba and Jamaica.

Justin Green
Paradise Cafe
Long Key

Rotisserie Chicken

- ¾ cup lemon juice
- ¾ cup orange juice
- ¾ cup pineapple juice
- 2 cloves garlic, sliced
- ½ onion, sliced
- ½ teaspoon salt, or to taste
- ¼ teaspoon coarse black pepper, or to taste
- ½ teaspoon seasoning salt, or to taste
- 1 chicken

Make a marinade by combining lemon juice and next 7 ingredients. Place chicken in a container and add marinade. Refrigerate 24 hours. Remove chicken from marinade and place in a rotisserie. Cook chicken for 2 hours, basting with marinade every 30 minutes.

Yield: 2 to 4 servings

To prevent bacterial contamination, do not baste with marinade during final few minutes of cooking time.

Rip Tosun
Rip's Island Rib n_ Chicken Restaurant
Islamorada

The early settlers in the Keys came from the Bahamas. They depended on the sea and nature for their everyday needs. Their pillows and mattresses were stuffed with soft silk grass found near the beaches. They used the skin of the trigger fish for scouring and scrubbing. Bread was made from the sweet potato and baked in outdoor ovens. Lime cement was made from shells. Many homes and furnishings were constructed of driftwood or lumber from wrecks. The pioneer "Conch" raised pineapples, limes, and melons.

Tropical Chicken

Any combination of citrus or tropical juices produces an excellent marinade for chicken.

- 1 teaspoon ground ginger
- 2 tablespoons packed brown sugar
- Salt and pepper
- 1 cup peanut oil
- 1 cup orange juice
- ¼ cup lemon juice
- ¼ cup lime juice
- 1 teaspoon crushed garlic
- 1 tablespoons soy sauce
- 1 chicken, halved or quartered

Prepare a marinade by combining ginger, brown sugar, salt, and pepper in a bowl. Add peanut oil and next 5 ingredients. Mix thoroughly. Place marinade and chicken in an airtight container. Refrigerate overnight or freeze until ready to use. Drain chicken, reserving marinade. Bake at 350° for 45 to 60 minutes or cook on a barbecue grill. If using a grill, place marinade in a saucepan and bring to a boil. Use marinade to baste chicken while barbecuing. Serve with fried plantain and rice and black beans.

Yield: 2 to 4 servings

Pierre Relland
Smuggler's Cove
Islamorada

Chicken Angela

1 (5-ounce) boneless, skinless chicken breast

1 cup thinly sliced mushrooms, soaked in water

3 sun-dried tomatoes, julienne

Pinch of chopped garlic

¼ cup sliced almonds, lightly toasted

1 cup cooked tri-colored angel hair pasta

2 tablespoons light cream

Dash of all-purpose flour (optional)

Salt and pepper to taste

Grill chicken lightly; then cut into slices. Place chicken and next 3 ingredients in a skillet. Sauté, using mushroom and tomato juices to braise chicken. Add almonds, pasta, and cream. Cook until pasta is hot and sauce starts to thicken. Add flour, if desired, to thicken further. Season with salt and pepper.

Yield: 1 serving

Bill Wiseman
Treetops
Key Largo

Chicken Breast With Orange, Pineapple, and Ginger Sauce

2 (6-ounce) boneless, skinless chicken breasts

Olive oil

Salt and pepper to taste

2 tablespoons grated ginger

1 small pineapple, cut in chunks

½ cup chicken broth

1 tablespoon cornstarch

15 segments fresh mandarin orange

Scallion strips for garnish

Marinate chicken in oil for 60 minutes. Season with salt and pepper. Grill 2 minutes on each side. Combine ginger, pineapple, and broth in a saucepan. Bring to a boil. Mix cornstarch with enough water to make a thin paste. Stir cornstarch mixture into saucepan. Add orange and simmer 2 minutes. Place chicken on serving plates. Spoon sauce over top. Garnish. Serve with grilled pineapple slices and orange wedges.

***Yield:* 2 servings**

Lyla Naseem
Biras Creek Resort
Virgin Gorda, British Virgin Islands

Puerto Rico is an island that offers so many vacation experiences that it calls itself "The Continent of Puerto Rico." Beaches, a rainforest, forts, and Old San Juan alone can fill up a week or month itinerary.

Roasted Herb Chicken

- 1 chicken, halved
- ½ cup olive oil
- 1 teaspoon chopped garlic
- 1 teaspoon rosemary, plus extra for potatoes
- 1 teaspoon basil
- 1 teaspoon Old Bay seasoning, plus extra for potatoes
- 2 red potatoes, cubed
- Salt and pepper
- 1½ cups water, divided
- 2 tablespoons all-purpose flour

Place chicken in a baking pan. Combine oil and next 4 ingredients. Brush oil mixture over chicken. Bake at 400° for 15 minutes; then lower to 350° for 30 minutes. Season potato with rosemary, Old Bay seasoning, salt, and pepper. Add potato to baking pan and bake 30 minutes longer or until done. Transfer chicken and potato to a serving dish. Add ½ cup water to pan juices and bring to a boil. Mix flour with remaining 1 cup water. Stir flour mixture slowly into juices. Cook and stir until thickened. Pour over chicken and potato.

Yield: 2 servings

Mohammed Motamedi
Coconuts
Key Largo

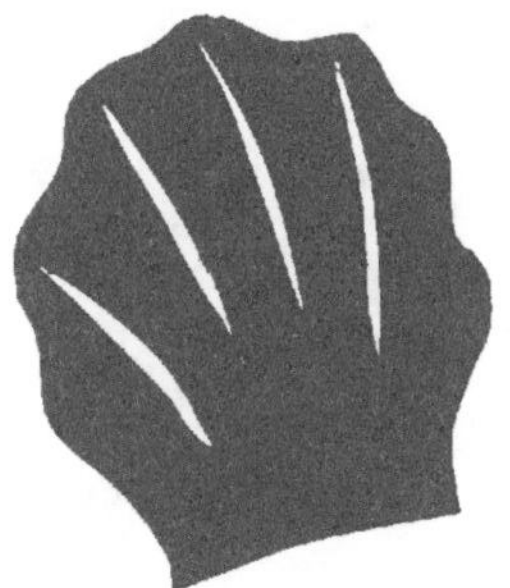

Snooks Hazelnut Chicken

- 4 (4-ounce) boneless, skinless chicken breasts
- ½ cup all-purpose flour
- 4 eggs, beaten
- 2 cups ground hazelnut
- ¾ cup clarified butter
- ¼ cup Frangelico
- 2 tablespoons dried thyme
- 1 pint heavy cream
- 1 (11-ounce) can mandarin oranges, drained

Dip chicken in flour and then in egg. Roll in hazelnut. Sauté in butter until lightly browned on each side. Finish cooking chicken in oven. In a separate pan, combine Frangelico and thyme. Flambé. When flame dies down, add cream and bring to a boil. Cook until liquid reduces to a sauce consistency. Place cooked chicken on a serving plate. Cover with sauce. Sprinkle oranges on and around chicken.

Yield: 4 servings

Brian W. Duffy
Snooks Bayside
Key Largo

Key Lime Chicken

- 4 chicken breasts, boned and skinned
- 1 cup Spanish barbecue sauce
- ¼ cup Key lime juice
- ¾ cup water
- Butter, melted
- Cajun seasoning
- Lime slices for garnish

Butterfly each chicken breast. Combine chicken and next 3 ingredients. Refrigerate 2 to 3 hours. Remove chicken from marinade. Brush with melted butter and sprinkle with Cajun seasoning. Cook on a grill or in a skillet about 5 minutes on each side. Garnish. Serve with yellow rice and a green salad.

Yield: 4 servings

Valerie and Jim Mayfield
Jim and Val's Tugboat Restaurant
Key Largo

Chicken a la Snooks With Caramelized Apples

4 (4-ounce) boneless, skinless chicken breasts
½ cup all-purpose flour
½ cup clarified butter
¾ cup spiced rum
1¼ cups heavy cream, divided
Salt and pepper to taste
3 ounces soft caramel candies
1 large apple, thinly sliced

Dust chicken in flour. In a medium sauté pan, heat butter. Add chicken and cook over medium heat 5 to 6 minutes on each side. Remove chicken from pan. Deglaze pan with rum, holding it away from flame. Add chicken and ¾ cup cream. Cook until liquid reduces to a sauce consistency. Season with salt and pepper. While sauce reduces, melt together candy and remaining ½ cup cream in a double boiler or a microwave. Add extra cream, if needed, to reach desired consistency. To assemble, fan apple slices on half of a serving platter and top with caramel sauce. Fan chicken on other half of platter and top with cream sauce.

Yield: 4 servings

Brian W. Duffy
Snooks Bayside
Key Largo

Quick Tomato Sauce

1 (28-ounce) can Italian-style tomatoes, drained
1 (6-ounce) can tomato paste
½ teaspoon salt
1 tablespoon onion juice, or 2 tablespoons finely grated onion
½ teaspoon sugar

Combine all ingredients in a saucepan. Bring to a boil. Reduce heat to low and cover; simmer 20 minutes. Serve over pasta.

Yield: 4 servings

Bill Valet
Ballyhoo's Grille and Grog
Key Largo

The wrecking business was the most profitable occupation for many years as ships were going aground or breaking up on the reefs. In spite of a false reputation as being pirates, these were the "good guys." There were no lighthouses or Coast Guard, and maps of the time were of no use except as art. The wreckers braved storms and hurricanes to save ships, people, and cargo. For this, they received a percentage of the value of the salvage.

Lasagne Rasta

Béchamel Sauce

- 1 quart milk
- 2 sticks butter
- 2 cups all-purpose flour
- Salt to taste

Lasagne

- 1 pound ackee
- ¾ cup chopped onion
- 1 clove garlic, chopped
- ¼ cup olive oil or butter
- ½ pound carrot, thinly sliced
- 1 pound calaloo, chopped
- 1 pound zucchini, sliced
- 1 pound tomatoes, chopped
- 2 teaspoons salt
- 2 teaspoons white pepper
- 12 lasagne noodles
- Béchamel sauce
- 1 pound mozzarella cheese, grated

Bring milk to a boil. Remove from heat. Melt butter in a skillet. Blend in flour. Whip in milk until smooth and thick. Season with salt. Cook and stir 5 minutes. To prepare lasagne, cook ackee. Set aside. Sauté onion and garlic in oil. Add carrot, calaloo, and zucchini. Cook until tender. Add ackee, tomato, salt, and pepper. In a large pot of salted water, cook noodles 7 minutes. Drain and rinse with cold water. Pat dry with a towel. Brush with oil, if desired, to prevent sticking. Add a small amount of juice from vegetable mixture to the bottom of a 12x9x2-inch pan. Line pan with 3 noodles. Spoon 1 cup béchamel sauce over noodles. Spread one-fourth of vegetable mixture on top. Sprinkle with 1 cup cheese. Repeat layers 3 times. Bake at 350° for 45 minutes. Remove from oven and let stand 10 minutes before cutting.

Yield: 9 servings

Evita's Restaurant
Jamaica

Big Pine is the largest island and the main home of the tiny Key deer. In the 1920s, its main industry was a shark factory owned by Ocean Leather Inc. of New York. The hides were turned into expensive leather, referred to as "Shogreen."

DESSERTS

CANCUN & COZUMEL

Cancun is on the Yucatan Peninsula, showing a smiling face to the Caribbean Sea. There are two parts to Cancun; a hotel zone, with powder beaches as the attraction, and the downtown district, a booming city on the mainland proper.

Between the two areas lies Laguna Nichupté. The whole area was a small fishing village just a few years back, but today the place is a world-class resort.

Cancun eclipses all other sunny vacation meccas in Mexico, leading the pack as Mexico's leading tourist destination. Just 8 miles off the shores of Cancun is Isla Mujeres, a special place for fishing. People there are descendants of the Mayans and really know how to cook. Seafoods and all types of Mexican foods can be found both in Cancun and Isla Mujeres.

Cozumel is located farther south along the mainland of the Peninsula on an island that measure 29 miles by 9 miles. San Miguel, the main town on the island, is charming and a fun place to shop and dine. The Maya considered this place a sacred shrine, and it's no wonder; it looks like God has shone down on this lushly beautiful place. Sport fishing boats are waiting to take you out to tackle the white and blue marlin and the sailfish, tuna, and mahi mahi. The reefs here are spectacular, and snorkeling and scuba diving allow you to explore the wonder of nature's reefs.

Some typical recipes that date back thousands of years can be enjoyed here. The most familiar of which is mole, a complicated sauce for chicken made with 30 different ingredients, including chocolate, three types of chiles, garlic, onions, nuts, and anise seeds, all of which must be finely ground and pureed.

Aunt Sally's Key Lime Pie

- 4 eggs, separated
- ½ cup Key lime juice
- 1 (14-ounce) can sweetened condensed milk
- 1 (8-inch) graham cracker crust
- ¼ teaspoon cream of tartar
- ⅓ cup sugar
- Thin slices of lime for garnish

Beat egg yolks until thick and lemon-colored. Blend in lime juice. Stir in milk until mixture thickens. Pour mixture into crust. Beat egg whites and cream of tartar until stiff. Gradually mix in sugar, beating until glossy peaks form. Spread over pie to the edge of the crust. Bake at 350° for 20 minutes or until golden brown. Chill and garnish.

Yield: 8 servings

Edith Amsterdam
Curry Mansion Inn
Key West

Key Lime Pie was first created in the Curry Mansion by Aunt Sally, a cook who worked for the Curry family in 1894.

The Key lime is a small round lime that is usually more yellow than it is green. It can easily be found in Florida and in specialty produce and gourmet markets throughout the rest of the U.S. These great limes are "key" to perfect Key Lime Pies.

Bagatelle's Key Lime Pie

Crust

- 1½ cups graham cracker crumbs
- 1 tablespoon sugar
- Pinch of salt
- 6 tablespoons unsalted butter, melted
- ¼ teaspoon vanilla

Filling

- 6 egg yolks
- 1 (14-ounce) can sweetened condensed milk
- Zest of 1 lime
- 4½ ounces Key lime juice
- 1 tablespoon lemon juice
- Whipped cream for topping

Combine crumbs, sugar, and salt in a bowl. Combine butter and vanilla and slowly mix into crumb mixture. Press into a 9-inch pie pan. Bake at 350° for 10 minutes. Remove from oven and cool completely. To prepare filling, combine egg yolks, milk, and zest in a bowl. Gradually add lime juice and lemon juice. Stir until smooth and creamy. Pour into prepared crust. Bake at 350° for 10 minutes. Chill and top with whipped cream before serving.

Yield: 8 servings

Sharon Hilbig
Bagatelle
Key West

Through **Eco-Tourism,** which is already a popular concept in the Caribbean, visitors can enjoy a country's natural beauty, while being asked and shown how to preserve and protect it.

Margaritaville Key Lime Pie

Crust and Filling

1 (9-inch) graham cracker pie crust
2 egg yolks
1 egg white
1 (14-ounce) can sweetened condensed milk
½ cup Key lime juice

Topping

5 egg whites
2 teaspoons cream of tartar
½ cup sugar

This tropical dessert recipe comes from singer Jimmy Buffett's Margaritaville Café.

Bake pie crust at 350° for 5 minutes. Beat egg yolks with an electric mixer 2 minutes. Beat egg white with electric mixer until fluffy. Blend yolk into milk. Gently fold white into mixture. Fold in lime juice. Pour filling into pie crust. Refrigerate 2 to 3 hours before adding topping. To make topping, whip egg whites and cream of tartar with electric mixer until foamy. Continue to whip while slowly adding sugar. Beat until peaks form. Score filling with a fork. Spread topping over filling. Bake at 425° for 5 minutes or until topping starts to brown.

Yield: 8 servings

Ray Masiero
Margaritaville Café
Key West

Cheeca Key Lime Pie

All along the Keys, one bird—the ubiquitous **osprey**—symbolizes the free-wheeling nature of the area. Nests both natural and manmade are all along the Overseas highway. This fish-eating eagle catches fish that swim just under the surface of the water by diving and grasping them with their curved sharp talons. Ospreys mate for life, and they nearly disappeared due to pesticide poisoning. However, they have made a remarkable comeback.

Graham Cracker Crust

- 1½ cups graham cracker crumbs
- ½ cup sugar
- 6 tablespoons butter, melted

Filling

- 4 eggs, beaten
- 1 cup sugar
- ½ cup lime juice
- 1 stick butter
- 1 teaspoon unflavored gelatin
- Zest of 2 limes
- Whipped cream for topping

Combine crumbs, sugar, and butter. Press into a pie pan. To make filling, cook eggs and next 3 ingredients in a double boiler until thick. Remove from heat. Soften gelatin with cold water. Stir gelatin and zest into filling. Pour into prepared crust. Top with whipped cream.

Yield: 8 servings

Dawn Sieber
Cheeca Lodge
Islamorada

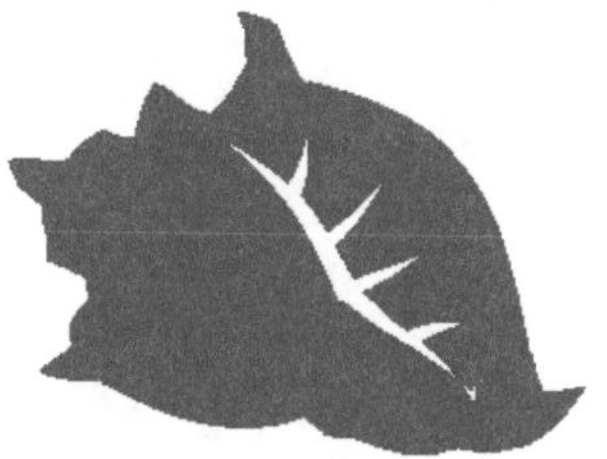

Lorelei's Frozen Key Lime Pie

3 limes
1 (8-ounce) container frozen whipped topping, thawed
1 (16-ounce) can condensed milk
3 ounces Key lime juice
1 teaspoon cream of tartar
1 (9-inch) deep-dish pie crust, baked

Remove and reserve zest of limes. Cut away white pith, membrane, and seeds from limes. Puree remaining fruit, reserving juice and pureed fruit. Combine lime zest, juice, pureed fruit, whipped topping, and next 3 ingredients. Blend until mixture reaches a pudding consistency. Spoon into pie crust. Freeze overnight.

Yield: 8 servings

Use two regular (8-inch) pie crusts instead of one deep-dish crust, if desired.

John Maloughney
The Lorelei
Islamorada

Mangoes Islamorada

½ cup sliced almonds, blanched and roasted
½ teaspoon cinnamon
4 large scoops vanilla ice cream
2 large ripe mangoes, peeled and diced
½ cup chocolate syrup
¼ cup Grand Marnier
1 cup heavy cream, whipped

Combine almonds and cinnamon. Place a scoop of ice cream in each of 4 serving dishes. Divide mango evenly over ice cream. Top with chocolate syrup, Grand Marnier, and almond mixture. Surround ice cream and toppings with whipped cream.

Yield: 4 servings

Andre Mueller
Marker 88
Islamorada

By 1900, one-third of Key Largo was owned by railroad companies. Flagler's railway reached this Key in 1906 and brought the fishermen followed by the developers and the land boom. It reached its crescendo in the late 1920s.

Three Milks Cake

Cake

- 1 (18-ounce) box butter cake mix
- 1 (12-ounce) can evaporated milk
- 1 (14-ounce) can sweetened condensed milk
- 1 cup heavy cream
- ½ teaspoon vanilla
- 2 egg yolks

Meringue

- 2 egg whites, room temperature
- ½ cup sugar
- ½ cup light corn syrup
- ⅛ cup water

Prepare cake mix according to package, being sure to use butter as the added fat. Cool cake. Combine evaporated milk and next 4 ingredients. Poke holes in cake with a fork. Pour mixture over cake. Refrigerate at least 2 hours to allow mixture to saturate cake. To prepare meringue, combine egg whites and remaining 3 ingredients in a mixing bowl. Use an electric mixer on high speed to whip for 15 to 30 minutes or until stiff. Spread meringue over cake.

Yield: 12 servings

Pedro Gonzalez
Don Pedro Restaurant
Marathon

A worldwide web of air transportation and cruise ships makes daily visits to all the Caribbean Islands.

Coconut Custard Pie

- 1 cup sugar
- 6 tablespoons cornstarch
- ¼ teaspoon salt
- 1 quart milk
- 8 egg yolks
- 2 tablespoons margarine
- 2 cups grated coconut
- 1 (9-inch) deep-dish pie crust, unbaked
- Whipped cream for topping (optional)

Combine sugar, cornstarch, and salt in a pan. Slowly stir in milk. Cook over medium heat, stirring constantly, until thickened. Beat egg yolks until thick and lemon-colored. Gradually mix about a quarter of the hot mixture into egg yolk. Add back into pan, stirring constantly. Cook 2 minutes. Remove from heat and stir in margarine and coconut. Spoon into crust. Bake at 350° for 10 to 15 minutes. Chill and top with whipped cream before serving.

Yield: 8 servings

Use two regular (8-inch) pie crusts instead of one deep-dish crust, if desired.

Lee G. Ganim
Ganim's Kountry Kitchen
Key Largo

During prohibition, Key Largo and most of the Keys were unknown ports of entry for the rum trade due to their proximity to Miami and hidden docks in the remote jungles.

Coconut Phyllo Napoleon With Mango Mousse, Caribbean Cocoa, and Passion Fruit Sauce

Mango Mousse

- 1½ tablespoons unflavored gelatin
- 1¼ cup plus 1 tablespoon water, divided
- ½ cup sugar
- 1 cup pureed and strained mango
- 1 tablespoon fresh lime juice
- 4 egg yolks
- 1 teaspoon vanilla
- 1 cup heavy cream
- 2 tablespoons dark rum

Caribbean Cocoa Sauce

- 4 ounces semi-sweet chocolate
- 1½ cups water
- 6 ounces cocoa
- ¾ cup confectioners' sugar
- 2 tablespoons butter

Coconut Phyllo

- 4 sheets phyllo dough
- 2 sticks butter, melted
- ¾ cup granulated sugar
- 1 cup coarsely grated coconut

Passion Fruit Sauce

- 12 ounces pureed passion fruit
- 1 pound sugar
- Juice of 1 lemon
- ½ cup passion fruit juice
- ¼ cup cornstarch
- ½ cup water

Combine gelatin and ¼ cup water in a small bowl. In a saucepan, bring sugar and 1 cup water to a boil, stirring until dissolved. Remove from heat and stir in gelatin mixture. Allow to cool. Process gelatin mixture, mango, and lime juice in a blender. Transfer to a bowl and whip by hand for 2 to 3 minutes. Refrigerate. Combine egg yolks and remaining 1 tablespoon water in a stainless steel bowl. Place bowl over a saucepan of hot, but not boiling, water. Whip until egg yolk is pale and stiff. Stir in vanilla. Add egg yolk mixture to gelatin mixture. Whip cream until soft peaks form. Add rum and continue to whip to form slightly stiffer peaks. Fold cream into gelatin mixture. Refrigerate 1 hour, 30 minutes. To prepare cocoa sauce, boil chocolate in water for 10 minutes. Mix well with a wooden spoon. Add cocoa and simmer 15 minutes, stirring occasionally. When smooth, beat in sugar and butter. To make coconut phyllo, lay a sheet of phyllo dough on plastic wrap. Brush with butter, sprinkle with sugar, and top with coconut. Place a second layer of phyllo dough on the first. Repeat the toppings as on the first. Do the same for a third sheet of phyllo dough. Place the fourth sheet on the top. Brush with butter and cover with plastic wrap. Place a baking sheet on top of phyllo layers and press down firmly. Transfer to a freezer for 10 minutes. Cut phyllo dough into triangles and place on a baking sheet lined with parchment paper. Bake at 350° for 6 to 7 minutes. Make passion fruit sauce by combining pureed passion fruit and next 3 ingredients in a saucepan. Bring to a boil and cook 2 minutes. Dissolve cornstarch in water and add to saucepan. Boil 1 minute. Remove from heat and strain. Cool to room temperature. To serve, form a row of 4 coconut phyllo triangles, holding the triangles together with layers of mango mousse. Drizzle cocoa sauce and passion fruit sauce in a design on a serving plate. Place row of triangles in middle of plate. Repeat as desired with remaining triangles, mousse, and sauces.

Yield: 20 servings

British Virgin Island Culinary Team
Peter Island Resort
Charlotte Amalie, Virgin Islands

In 1860, Key West was the second largest city in Florida. There were more people there than in either Jacksonville or Tallahassee.

Easy Florida Keys Key Lime Cheesecake

Filling

- 1 cup heavy cream
- 2 (¼-ounce) envelopes unflavored gelatin
- 1¾ cups sugar
- Dash of salt
- 1 cup milk
- 2 eggs, well beaten
- 1 (24-ounce) container creamed cottage cheese
- ¼ cup Key lime juice, strained

Topping

- ¾ cup graham cracker crumbs
- 1 tablespoon sugar
- 2 tablespoons butter or margarine, softened

Whip cream and chill. Combine gelatin, sugar, and salt in a double boiler. Stir in milk and egg. Cook, stirring constantly, for 5 minutes or until gelatin in dissolved. Blend cottage cheese and lime juice with an electric mixer or in a blender on high speed until smooth. Add gelatin mixture and mix well. Stir in whipped cream and blend well to avoid lumps. Pour into an 8x8x2-inch pan or a glass casserole dish. Chill until partially set. Prepare topping by combining crumbs, sugar, and butter. Sprinkle over filling. Chill until firm.

Yield: 10 to 12 servings

Joe Roth
Holiday Isle Resort and Marina
Islamorada

Flamboyants, brilliant red-orange trees also known as flame trees or royal poincianas, grow on many of the Caribbean islands and the Keys.

Key Lime Cheesecake

Crust

1 cup graham cracker crumbs

2 tablespoons butter, softened

½ cup sugar

Filling

3 (8-ounce) packages cream cheese, softened

¾ cup sugar

1 cup sour cream

3 eggs

3 tablespoons all-purpose flour

1 cup Key lime juice

2 teaspoons vanilla

Topping

1 cup sour cream

½ cup sugar

2 teaspoons vanilla

Mix together graham cracker crumbs, butter, and sugar. Pack into the bottom of a springform pan to make a crust. To prepare filling, beat cream cheese until soft. Continue beating and mix in sugar and sour cream. Beat in eggs one at a time. Mix in flour slowly. Add lime juice and beat until smooth. Blend in vanilla. Pour into springform pan. Bake at 350° for 15 minutes. Lower temperature to 300° and bake another 55 minutes. Remove from oven carefully and cool. Make topping by mixing together sour cream, sugar, and vanilla. Spread over cooled cake. Bake at 400° for 10 minutes. Refrigerate 24 hours before serving.

Yield: 12 to 16 servings

Islamorada Fish Company
Islamorada

Macadamia Banana Cream Pie

Crust

- 1 cup plus 2 tablespoons all-purpose flour
- ¼ teaspoon salt
- ⅓ cup shortening
- 5 tablespoons plus 1 teaspoon cold water

Filling

- ¾ cup sugar
- 3 tablespoons cornstarch
- ¼ teaspoon salt
- 2 cups whole milk, divided
- 2 egg yolks
- 1 tablespoon unsalted butter
- 1 teaspoon vanilla
- 1 cup sliced banana
- ½ cup coarsely chopped macadamia nuts
- Whipped cream for topping
- Sprigs of fresh mint for garnish

Combine flour and salt in a mixing bowl. Cut in shortening until particles are pea-size. Do not overmix. Sprinkle with water, 1 tablespoon at a time, tossing lightly with a fork until all particles have been dampened. Use only enough water to hold pastry together when pressed between fingers. Pastry should not feel wet. Roll dough into a ball, handling as little as possible. Roll out onto a lightly floured board into a circle ⅛-inch-thick and 1 inch larger than the diameter of a pie pan. Transfer dough into pie pan. Trim edge with dough extending ½ inch over rim. Turn edge under and flute with fingers to make a standing rim. Prick shell several times with a fork to prevent air bubbles. Bake at 450° for 10 minutes. Cool to room temperature. To prepare filling, combine sugar, cornstarch, and salt in a double boiler. Stir in 1½ cups milk and cook over medium-high heat until thickened to a pudding consistency. In a small bowl, beat together egg yolks and remaining ½ cup milk. Slowly add egg mixture to filling and cook 2 minutes longer, stirring constantly. Remove from heat and stir in butter, vanilla, and banana. Pour into cooled crust. Bake at 350° for 10 minutes. Sprinkle nuts over top of pie and bake 5 minutes longer. Cool completely before serving. Top with whipped cream and garnish.

Yield: 8 servings

Sharon Hilbig
Bagatelle
Key West

Cheeca's Passion Fruit Pie

Graham Cracker Crust

1½ cups chocolate sandwich cookie crumbs

½ cup sugar

6 tablespoons butter, melted

Filling

4 eggs, beaten

1 cup sugar

½ cup passion fruit juice or concentrate

¼ cup lime juice

1 stick butter

1 teaspoon unflavored gelatin

Zest of 1 lime

Whipped cream for topping

To make crust, mix together crumbs, sugar, and butter. Pat into a pie pan. Prepare filling by placing eggs and next 4 ingredients in a double boiler. Cook until thick, whisking occasionally. Soften gelatin in cold water. Stir gelatin and zest into egg mixture. Cool before pouring into prepared crust. Chill. Top with whipped cream.

Yield: 8 servings

Dawn Sieber
Cheeca Lodge
Islamorada

Tropical Coconut and Key Lime Cheesecake

Toasted coconut and Key limes combine for a tropical delight.

Crust

- 2 cups graham cracker crumbs
- 6 tablespoons butter, melted
- 1½ cups coconut, toasted, divided

Filling

- 3 (8-ounce) packages cream cheese, softened
- 2 teaspoons lime zest
- ¼ cup Key lime juice
- 1 (¼-ounce) envelope unflavored gelatin
- 1 cup water, divided
- 3 eggs, separated
- 1 cup sugar
- 1 cup heavy cream

Combine graham cracker crumbs and butter. Press into the bottom of a 9-inch springform pan. Spread 1 cup coconut evenly over crust. To prepare filling, beat cream cheese 5 minutes or until smooth. Mix in lime zest and lime juice. Set aside. Mix together gelatin and ¼ cup water in a small saucepan. Add remaining ¾ cup water, egg yolks, and sugar. Heat, stirring constantly, until mixture is steaming. Do not boil. Pour into a bowl and refrigerate 10 minutes. While mixture cools, beat egg whites in a large bowl until stiff. In a separate bowl, beat cream until stiff, being careful not to overbeat. Fold together cream cheese mixture, refrigerated mixture, egg white, and cream. Use a whisk if necessary to blend ingredients well. Pour into prepared crust. Sprinkle remaining ½ cup coconut over top. Refrigerate overnight. Garnish, if desired, with lime slices or whipped cream.

Yield: 12 to 16 servings

Jamille Cucci
Garden Café
Key West

Coconut Square

- 2¼ cups graham cracker crumbs, divided
- 3 large coconuts, grated
- 2 (14-ounce) cans sweetened condensed milk
- 1 teaspoon nutmeg
- 1 teaspoon cinnamon
- 2 teaspoon vanilla
- 8 ounces semi-sweet chocolate

Combine 2 cups graham cracker crumbs and next 5 ingredients. Mix well. Sprinkle remaining ¼ cup graham cracker crumbs in a greased and floured 13x9x2-inch pan. Pour coconut mixture into pan. Smooth top of mixture with a spatula. Bake at 350° for 15 to 20 minutes. Remove from oven and cool. Melt chocolate in a double boiler. Spread hot chocolate over cooled dessert. Allow chocolate to cool. Cut in 2-inch squares. Serve with vanilla ice cream.

Yield: 24 servings

Evita's Restaurant
Jamaica

Carib Indians were the region's primary residents of the tropics, along with the Arawaks, Maya, Tainos, Incas and Olmecs. Their demise was due to Spanish Conquistadors, European diseases, and gold fever, among other causes.

Island Spice Cake

1¼ cups water, boiling
1 cup oats
1 stick butter, softened
1 cup packed brown sugar
1 teaspoon vanilla
2 eggs
1⅓ cups all-purpose flour
1 teaspoon cinnamon
½ teaspoon ground allspice
1 teaspoon salt
1 teaspoon baking soda

Pour water over oats. Let stand 20 minutes. Cream butter and next 3 ingredients together. Add to oats and mix well. Sift together flour and remaining 4 ingredients. Mix dry ingredients into oat mixture. Pour into a greased 9-inch cake pan. Bake at 350° for 35 to 40 minutes or until center of cake springs back when lightly touched. Cool in pan. Serve with whipped cream and pecans.

Yield: 6 to 8 servings

Jim Harrison
Porkers
Key Largo

Planter was the first village on Key Largo with a post office. It had 10 houses, a church, and a store. Thousands of pineapples were shipped from the Planter docks. The village was destroyed by the 1909-1910 hurricanes and the people moved to Tavernier, which was on the railway.

Chocolate Brownies

½ (2½-pound) box baking mix
1½ pounds chocolate chips
6 eggs
2 cups sugar
1¼ cups milk
6 ounces cocoa powder
2 cups black coffee
8 ounces pecans

Mix all ingredients. Spread into a lined large sheet pan. Bake at 325° until brownies start to pull away from sides of pan.

Yield: 16 to 20 servings

John Daverio
The Pilot House Restaurant
Key Largo

Mango Mascarpone Tart

Crust

1½ sticks butter
2 cups all-purpose flour
1 teaspoon salt
4 tablespoons ice water

Filling

1 medium mango, peeled, or 1 (10-ounce) can
½ cup sugar
2 teaspoons vanilla
2 teaspoons lemon juice
3 eggs
1 pound mascarpone cheese
⅓ cup apricot preserves
¼ cup water

Red Wine Caramel Sauce

1 cup sugar
½ cup water
1 cup red wine

Cut butter into flour and salt until mixture resembles coarse meal. Add ice water, 1 tablespoon at a time, until mixture just forms a ball. Flatten and cover with plastic wrap. Refrigerate 30 minutes. Roll out dough on a floured surface to a ¼-inch thickness. Line an 11-inch removable-bottom tart pan with dough. Trim sides and refrigerate 20 minutes. Pierce bottom with a fork several times. Line dough with aluminum foil filled with uncooked rice. Bake at 350° for 20 minutes or until sides of tart set. Remove rice and foil and bake 10 minutes longer. Cool. To prepare filling, cut mango into ¼-inch slices. Combine sugar and next 3 ingredients in a mixing bowl. Beat with and electric mixer until light and airy. Add cheese and whip until thoroughly blended. Do not overmix. Line bottom of baked crust with half of mango slices. Spread cheese mixture over slices. Arrange remaining mango slices on top. Bake at 350° for 20 to 25 minutes or until center is set and top begins to brown. In a small saucepan, heat preserves with water until melted. Brush tart with preserves mixture while still warm. Cool. To make sauce, heat sugar and water until mixture turns golden brown. Do not overcook. Add wine and continue to cook until sugar dissolves and sauce is smooth. Cool before drizzling over tart.

Yield: 8 servings

Mia Casey
Marriott's Frenchman's Reef Beach Resort
St. Thomas, United States Virgin Islands

Rumrunner Salsa

Tropical fruits and rums give this recipe its Caribbean flavor.

- ¾ cup dark rum
- 6 tablespoons coconut-flavored rum
- ¾ cup rumrunner mix
- 1 (10-ounce) package frozen strawberries, thawed and undrained
- 1 cup pineapple juice
- 1 pint fresh strawberries, divided
- 4 bananas, divided
- 2 cups diced pineapple
- 1 pint blueberries
- 1 pint blackberries

Combine dark rum and next 4 ingredients. In a blender, mix 1 cup fresh strawberries and 2 bananas. Add to rum mixture. Cut remaining fresh strawberries in half. Cube remaining bananas. Add halved strawberries, cubed banana, and remaining 3 ingredients to rum mixture. Cover tightly and refrigerate up to 1 week. Serve over shortcake or pound cake. Garnish with whipped cream.

Yield: 8 servings

Konrad Jockum
Turtle Kraals
Key West

Piña Colada Pie

- 4 ounces cream cheese
- 8 ounces sweetened condensed milk
- ½ cup pineapple juice
- 4 ounces shredded coconut
- 3 cups whipped topping, divided
- 4 ounces crushed pineapple, drained
- 2 (9-inch) chocolate cookie pie crusts

Combine cream cheese, milk, and pineapple juice in a mixing bowl. Beat until thoroughly mixed. Add coconut, 1½ cups whipped topping, and pineapple. Mix until well blended. Divided between pie crusts. Top with remaining whipped topping. Garnish with toasted coconut or shaved chocolate, if desired. Freeze.

Yield: 16 servings

John Daverio
The Pilot House Restaurant
Key Largo

Bimini Apple Betty

- 1¼ cups sugar
- 1½ teaspoons cinnamon
- 1 teaspoon nutmeg
- 1 lemon
- ½ cup butter, melted
- 3 cups bimini or whole wheat breadcrumbs
- 2 tablespoons water
- 5 large Granny Smith apples, unpeeled and thinly sliced, divided

Combine sugar, cinnamon, and nutmeg. Add zest of lemon. Reserve juice of lemon for later use. Mix together butter and breadcrumbs. Combine reserved lemon juice and water. Spread one-third of breadcrumb mixture in a greased 2-quart round pan. Cover with half of apple slices. Sprinkle half of sugar mixture over top. Layer with another third of breadcrumb mixture. Top with remaining apples and sugar mixture. Distribute remaining breadcrumbs on top. Sprinkle with lemon juice mixture. Dot with butter. Cover with foil and place in a 450° oven. Reduce heat immediately to 350° and bake 40 minutes. Uncover and bake 10 to 15 minutes or until golden. Cool 15 minutes. Invert onto a serving plate. Serve warm or cold with whipped cream or vanilla or cinnamon ice cream.

Yield: 8 servings

Jim Harrison
Porkers
Key Largo

Pineapple Ice Cream

2 cups whole milk
1 cup sugar
4 eggs
1 tablespoon vanilla
½ cup chopped fresh pineapple

Bring milk to a boil over high heat. Remove from heat and cool slightly. In a large saucepan, combine hot milk and next 3 ingredients. Cook and stir over medium heat until hot, but do not boil. Mixture should thicken to a light paste consistency. Fold in pineapple and cool. Place in an electric ice cream maker and churn until stiff and cold.

Yield: 4 servings

If desired, substitute 1 cup pureed guava for the pineapple.

Pedro Gonzalez
Don Pedro Restaurant
Marathon

Coconut Ice Cream

4 cups heavy cream, divided
1 teaspoon vanilla
1 cup sugar
½ cup flaked coconut, toasted

Heat 1 cup cream, vanilla, and sugar over low heat. Do not boil. Remove from heat and cool slightly. Stir in remaining 3 cups cream and coconut. Place in an electric ice cream maker and churn until stiff and cold.

Yield: 4 to 6 servings

Pedro Gonzalez
Don Pedro Restaurant
Marathon

Dark Chocolate Walnut Fudge

Fudge

- 3 sticks butter
- 6 cups sugar
- 1⅓ cups evaporated milk
- 24 ounces dark, non-tempering chocolate
- 1 cup chopped walnuts
- ¼ cup Barbados rum
- 2 (7-ounce) jars marshmallow creme

Butter Cream Icing

- 2 sticks butter, softened
- 2 pounds powdered sugar
- 2 tablespoons Barbados rum
- 1 teaspoon heavy cream

Combine butter, sugar, and milk in a saucepan. Bring to a boil. Stirring constantly, boil 5 minutes or until temperature reaches 234° on a candy thermometer. Remove from heat. Stir in chocolate until melted. Add walnuts, rum, and marshmallow creme. Pour into a lined sheet pan and cool at room temperature. To prepare icing, mix butter and remaining 3 ingredients with an electric mixer on high speed until creamy. Spread over cooled fudge.

Yield: 16 to 20 servings

John Daverio
The Pilot House Restaurant
Key Largo

Dark chocolate and walnuts are ingredients used in many Caribbean desserts.

Papaya Sherbet

- 1 pound papaya, peeled, seeded, and diced
- 1 can sweetened condensed milk
- 1 teaspoon vanilla
- ½ teaspoon nutmeg
- 1 pound ice cubes

In a blender, combine papaya, milk, vanilla, nutmeg; blend for 30 seconds. Add half of ice cubes and continue to blend 10 seconds; add remaining ice and blend until creamy. Serve immediately.

Yield: 6 to 8 servings

Michael Nighty
Holiday Inn
Grand Cayman Island

Piña Colada Cake

- 6 egg whites
- 1½ cups sugar, divided
- 4 egg yolks
- ½ cup vegetable oil
- ½ cup water
- 1 teaspoon vanilla
- 1½ cups flour
- 3 teaspoons baking powder
- Dash of salt
- ¼ cup pineapple juice
- 2 tablespoons white rum
- ¼ cup cream of coconut
- 6 tablespoons butter
- 1 pound powdered sugar, sifted
- 1 egg
- ¼ cup cream
- 1 teaspoon vanilla
- 1 teaspoon coconut or almond extract
- 8 ounces shredded coconut
- ¼ cup crushed pineapple
- 1 tablespoon dark rum
- Toasted coconut

Preheat oven to 350*. Beat egg whites until soft peaks form. Gradually add ½ cup sugar while continuing to beat until very stiff. Whisk together egg yolks, oil water, and vanilla in a small bowl. Sift together 1 cup sugar, flour, baking powder, and salt. Fold flour mixture into beaten yolks and mix well. fold in beaten egg whites. Pour into two 8-inch cake pans. bake for about 25 minutes at 350° until sides shrink and top springs back when touched. Turn out and cool on cake racks. In a small bowl, mix together pineapple juice, rum, and cream of coconut. Brush both cake layers with this combination. Beat butter and next 6 ingredients together until smooth and creamy. Combine half of this frosting with crushed pineapple and spread between layers as a filling. Stir dark rum into remaining frosting. Frost cake and sprinkle with toasted coconut.

Yield: 8 servings

Joanna Samuels-Watson
Sugar Mill Hotel
Tortola, British Virgin Islands

Sugarloaf Key is said to have achieved its name from the pineapple. Some of the early Spanish believed the name came from an Indian mound, which resembled a loaf of sugar. In early times, sugar was made and sold in loaves.

CARIBBEAN
COMPLEMENTS

JAMAICA & THE CAYMAN ISLANDS

Jamaica rivers, high peaks of the Blue Mountains, and waterfalls help keep you cool in hot Jamaica. You can drift lazily down a river on a bamboo raft or climb the rocks near Dunn's River Falls. Pirate hangouts and ancient Indian sites are around the island. The Jamaican people are an interesting multi-racial mix. Arabic, European, Chinese, and East Indian ancestry is in evidence here. Montego Bay is probably one of the most popular tourist destinations in the entire Caribbean. A bustling port and the second largest city in Jamaica, Montego Bay is punctuated by Georgian architecture known for its classic designs and proportions. Fresh seafood — in a variety of spicy dishes — awaits your palate here. Italian and Jamaican specialties are available.

The Cayman Islands area is a diving mecca that has as its capital, George Town, on Grand Cayman. But, two other islands also make up this azure-watered paradise: Cayman Brac and Little Cayman. Bonefishing is popular here, and anglers from around the world and the Caribbean (many from Jamaica) head to Grand Cayman for a chance to land the biggest blue marlin during Million Dollar Month in June.

In the Caymans, visit the turtle farm, and then head over to Liberty's Restaurant to eat "legal" turtle steak with beans and rice. Wild sea turtles are protected internationally today as many species were brought to the brink of extinction by overharvesting. Cayman Brac is known for its dramatic bluff, running down the middle of the 12-mile length of the island.

Cayman foods and dining is as varied as all the world's continental cuisine. Besides fresh fish, there is turtle steak and stew, conch fritters and chowders, and large rock crawfish (they call them lobster there).

Caribbean Glossary

Ackee or akee: a bright-red tropical fruit, which is only ripe when it bursts open to reveal three large black seeds and a soft creamy white flesh.

Accras de Morue: the French West Indies term for fritters made of salted codfish or bacalao (called "stamp and go" in Jamaica and bacalitos in Puerto Rico). They're a pillar of Caribbean cuisine.

Avocado: a rich fruit native to tropical regions and known for its buttery texture and nutlike flavor. Used in salads and mashed to make Guacamole.

Boniato: a Cuban favorite that is similar to a sweet potato.

Breadfruit or breadnut: bumpy green skin and a bland-tasting cream-colored center. It can be treated like squash: baked, broiled, grilled, fried.

Calabaza: a staple in the Caribbean, it's a member of the squash family.

Callaloo or calaloo: two different types of greens and also a soup that uses these greens as one of the main ingredients.

Carailla: a pale-green pod-shaped vegetable that's bitter when ripe. It's usually sautéed or used in stir frys or curries.

Cassava or yuca: tuberous root vegetables that are 6 to 12 inches in length, tough brown skin with white flesh.

Cristophene or chayote squash: a gourdlike fruit similar to a large pear. Can be prepared like summer squash.

Coconut: a tropical fruit whose creamy white meat is eaten fresh or dried. The coconut juice and oil is also very useful in cooking.

Conch (pronounced conk): a large mollusk found inside the pink conch shell is used throughout the Keys and Caribbean in chowders, stews, salads, fritters, etc. The meat is very tough and needs to be pounded and marinated before cooking.

Cumin: a distinctive East Indian spice whose seeds and leaves are used in cooking. Cumin is an ingredient in curry powder.

Dasheen: one of the many root vegetables found in the West Indies. The young leaves are known as callaloo.

Eddo: another name for dasheen.

Guava: a fruit that's sweet and aromatic and eaten stewed or used to make jelly.

Habanero: an extremely hot chile pepper that's native to the Caribbean and the Yucatan.

Jackfruit: closely related to breadfruit but grows on short stalks closely attached to the bark. Often curried.

Jerk: a Jamaican cooking technique in which pork, chicken, beef, and even fish is marinated in a special fiery concoction of "jerk" spices then slowly grilled over a wood fire.

Mango: a delectable fruit that grows in warm regions. Great in fruit salads and chutneys.

Mauby: the bark of some small trees found in the Caribbean. Boiled with spices, orange peel, and sugar, it's a refreshing drink when served over ice.

Okra: green podlike vegetables added to soups and stews for thickening.

Papaya or paw paw: yellow-orange fruit that can be eaten fresh or used in drinks, fruit salads, or jams.

Passion Fruit: a tropical fruit with a soft, golden flesh that is sweet-tart and fragrant. Serve plain or in sauces, salads, or beverages.

Pineapple: the fruit of a perennial herbaceous plant found in the Caribbean and South America.

Plantain: a fruit similar to bananas but usually longer and more angular with a sweeter taste. Can be boiled or fried, used in various dishes, or made into chips.

Roti: various breads brought to the Caribbean by the East Indians. Usually cooked on a special griddle or large flat frying pan.

Satay or sate: small marinated strips or cubes of meat, fish, or poultry threaded on skewers and grilled. Usually served with a peanut sauce.

Soursop: a heart-shaped fruit with a prickly green skin and white flesh.

Star Apple: a glossy purple fruit with a smooth thick skin. Usually eaten raw or in fruit salads.

Tamarind or tamarin: brown pods 2 to 4 inches long. Flesh is tart and spicy when ripe. Used for drinks, candy, and preserves. When unripe, used in chutneys and curries.

Yellowtail fish: a large game fish related to pompano but with a flavor and texture similar to tuna. Found in the waters off Florida and in the Caribbean, and also in southern California.

Where to Find Caribbean Foods

Your local grocery store is a good place to start when trying to order specialty items. If they cannot obtain them, then this list of distributors will gladly help you with your Caribbean foods needs:

Henry Lee Co.: 3301 NW. 125th St., Miami, FL 33167; (305) 685-5851. A complete food service distributorship of most Caribbean products, including jerk and island spices and herbs.

Green Turtle Seafood Market and Cannery: Islamorada, FL; (305) 664-4918. Will ship conch, chowders, fish etc. anywhere in the Continental U.S.

Salada Foods Jamaica Limited: Kingston, Jamaica; (809) 923-7114. Carries all kinds of coffee products, Caribbean beans, mixes, and condiments.

Walker's Wood, The Taste of Jamaica: 3020 NW. 75th St., Miami, FL 33147; 1-800-827-0769. Offers jerk seasonings, spices, preserves, hot pepper sauces, cooking sauces.

Restaurants

Many restaurants throughout the Keys and in the Caribbean shared their wonderful recipes in this book. Here are their locations and phone numbers. They would be pleased to the pleasure of your company when you make your visit beyond Calypso Café.

Bagatelle
Key West
(305) 296-6609

Ballyhoo's Grille and Grog
Key Largo
(305) 852-0822

Biras Creek Resort
Virgin Gorda, British Virgin Islands

Bogies Cafe
Holiday Inn Resort and Marina
Key Largo
(305) 451-2121

Boonoonoonoos Restaurant
Aruba

British Virgin Island Culinary Team
Peter Island Resort
Charlotte Amalie, Virgin Islands
(809) 495-2000

Caloosa Cove Resort
Lower Matecumbe
(305) 664-8811

Cheeca Lodge
Islamorada
(305) 664-4651

Coconuts
Key Largo
(305) 453-9794

Cracked Conch Café
Marathon
(305) 743-2233

Craig's Restaurant
Tavernier
(305) 852-9424

Curry Mansion Inn
Key West
(305) 294-5349

Don Pedro Restaurant
Marathon
(305) 743-5247

Eigner's Grassy Key Dairy Bar
Marathon
(305) 743-3816

Evita's Restaurant
Jamaica

Ganim's Kountry Kitchen
Key Largo
(305) 451-2895

Garden Cafe
Key West
(305) 294-2991

Green Turtle Inn
Islamorada
(305) 664-9031

Grove Park Cafe
Islamorada
(305) 664-0116

Hawk Channel Bar and Grill
Islamorada
(305) 664-0020

Herbies
Marathon
(305) 743-6373

Holiday Inn, Seven Mile Beach
Grand Cayman Island

Holiday Isle Resort and Marina
Islamorada
(305) 664-2321

Islamorada Fish Co.
Islamorada
(305) 664-9271

Jammers
Islamorada
(305) 852-8786

Jim and Val's Tugboat Restaurant
Key Largo
(305) 453-9010

Land's End Marina
Afternoon Delight III charter boat
Key Colony Beach

Lazy Days Ocean Front Bar and Seafood Grill
Islamorada
(305) 664-5256

Louie's Backyard
Key West
(305) 294-1061

Makoto Japanese Restaurant
Key Largo
(305) 451-7083

Mangoe's
Key West
(305) 292-4606

Margaritaville Café
Key West
(305) 292-1435

Marker 88
Islamorada
(305) 852-5503

Marriott Key Largo Bay Beach Resort
Key Largo
(305) 453-0000

Marriott's Frenchman's Reef Beach Resort
St. Thomas
U. S. Virgin Islands

Mexican Cantina
Islamorada
(305) 664-3721

Mi Cushina
Aruba

Molasses Reef Marina
Key Largo
(305) 451-9411

Montego Bay Food and Spirits
Big Pine Key
(305) 872-3009

Num-Thai Restaurant and Sushi Bar
Key Largo
(305) 451-5955

Papa Joe's Landmark Restaurant
Islamorada
(305) 664-2290

Paradise Cafe
Long Key
(305) 664-4900

Perry Seafood Restaurant
Key Largo
(305) 451-1834

Pier House Restaurant
Key West
(305) 296-4600

Pilot House
Key Largo
(305) 451-3142

Plantation Yacht Harbor Resort
Islamorada
(305) 852-2381

Porkers
Key Largo
(305) 451-1988

Porky's Bayside
Marathon
(305) 289-2065

Rip's Island Rib n' Chicken Restaurant
Islamorada
(305) 664-5300

Royal Pelican Restaurant
Marathon
(305) 289-0222

Rusty Anchor Restaurant
Key West
(305) 296-2893

Scooters
Tavernier
(305) 852-9272

Smuggler's Cove
Islamorada
(305) 664-5564

Snapper's
Key Largo
(305) 852-5956

Snooks Bayside
Key Largo
(305) 453-3799

Squid Row
Islamorada
(305) 664-9865

Sugar Mill Hotel
Tortola British Virgin Islands
(809) 495-4355

Sugarloaf Lodge
Sugarloaf Shores
(305) 745-3741

Sundowners
Key Largo
(305) 451-4502

Sunset Bay and Hukilau Bar
Key West
(305) 296-7277

The Conch Restaurant
Islamorada
(305) 664-4590

The Hungry Tarpon
Islamorada
(305) 664-0535

The Lorelei
Islamorada
(305) 664-4656

The Old Tavernier
Tavernier
(305) 852-6012

The Quay
Key West
(305) 294-4446

Treetops
Key Largo Sheraton
Key Largo
(305) 852-5553

Turtle Kraals Wildlife Bar and Grill
Key West
(305) 294-2640

Twin Landings Waterfront Bar and Restaurant
Key Colony Beach
(305) 289-0141

Thanks also to the USA Rice Council in Houston, Texas. (713) 270-6699.
Rice is found in many Caribbean dishes.

Marinas

The entry point for most anglers in the Keys and Caribbean is the boating and fishing marina. Marinas serve numerous purposes for the boating angler. This is where boat fueling, bait, ice, and actual access to the waters of the Atlantic, Gulf of Mexico, and the Caribbean Sea is accomplished. Numerous charter boats big and small ply the fish-prolific waters of South Florida, the Keys, and the Caribbean. Many anglers from around the world seek the giant powerful tarpon known as the "silver king" inshore and the active showy sailfish and dorado (dolphin fish) offshore. At most restaurants, the dolphin fillets of the day are turned into magnificent fish dishes for dinnertime. Most restaurants cheerfully cook your catch. Numerous fish, such as bonefish on the shallow flats or the ocean and gulfside of the Keys waterways, are caught for fun only. Tarpon too are not a food fish and their battle is the reward not their fillets.

However, from snapper, to mackerel and grouper, wahoo, tuna, cobia, and dolphin offshore, there is never any lack of fish for the Caribbean's or Keys' visitors to enjoy in so many different ways as evidenced by the many fabulous recipes contained in Calypso Café!

The following list of marinas are full service businesses handling the needs a visiting boater, be it power or sail, and or angler could use. Contact them or the Chambers of Commerce for a list of fishing captains to fulfill your wildest angling dreams!

America Outdoors Marina
Key Largo (305) 852-9121

Banana Bay Resort & Marina
Marathon (305) 743-3500

Barefoot Cay Marina
Key Largo (305) 451-5400

Bayside Marine, Inc.
Islamorada (305) 664-9491

Blue Fin Marina
Key Largo (305) 852-2025

Blue Waters Marina
Tavernier (305) 652-5141

Bud N' Mary's Fishing Marina
Islamorada (305) 664-2461

Caloosa Cove Marina
Lower Matecumbe
(305) 664-4455

Calusa Camp Resort Marina
Key Largo (305) 451-3433

Campbell's Marina
Tavernier (305) 852-8390

Caribee Boat Sales & Storage
Islamorada (305) 664-3431

Coconut Cover Resort & Marina
Islamorada (305) 664-0123

Coconut Palma's Marina
Grassy Key (305) 743-0552

Coral Bay Marina
Islamorada (305) 664-3111

Cudjoe Gardens Marina & Dive
Cudjoe Key (305) 745-2357

Curtis Marine Inc.
Tavernier (305) 852-5218

Duck Key Marina, Inc.
Duck Key (305) 289-0161

Faro Blanco Marine Resort
Marathon (305) 743-9018

Garden Cover Marina/Storage
Key Largo (305) 451-4694

Gilbert's Holiday Island of Key Largo
Key Largo (305) 451-1133

Grassy Key Marina
Marathon (305) 743-3372

Harborside of Marathon
Marathon (305) 743-3099

Hawk's Cay Resort & Marina
Marathon (305) 743-7000

Hobo's Marina
Key Largo (305) 451-4684

Holiday Inn & Marina of Marathon
Marathon (800) 224-5053

Italian Fisherman Marina
Key Largo (305) 451-3726

Key Biscayne Marine, Inc.
Key Biscayne (305) 361-9224

Key Colony Beach Marina
Key Colony Beach
(305) 289-1310

Key Largo Bay Beach Resort
Key Largo (305) 453-0000

Key Largo Harbour
Key Largo (305) 451-0045

Key Largo Ocean Resort Cafe & Marina
Key Largo (305) 852-1168

Key West Oceanside Marina, Inc.
Key West (305) 294-4676

Knight's Key Campground & Marina
Marathon (305) 743-4343

Lagoon Resort & Marina
Marathon (305) 743-5463

Mandalay Marina
Key Largo (305) 852-5450

Marathon Marina
Marathon (305) 743-6575

Marie's Yacht Harbor Club
Marathon (305) 743-2442

Mariner Resort
Big Pine Key (305) 872-2222

Matecumbe Marina
Islamorada (305) 664-2402

Max's Marine & Boat Yard
Islamorada (305) 664-8884

Ocean Bay Marina
Key Largo (305) 451-3109

Oceanside Cafe & Marina
Key Largo (305) 852-1168

Oceanside Marine Services, Inc.
Marathon (305) 743-6666

Papa Joe's Marina & Fishing Team
Islamorada (800) 539-8326

Pelican Cay Harbor Marina
Key Largo (305) 451-2128

Pinellas Marina & Dive Center
Marathon (305) 743-5317

Plantation Key Marina
Tavernier (305) 852-5424

Plantation Yacht Harbor Resort & Marina
Plantation Key (305) 852-2381

Rock Harbor Marina
Key Largo (305) 852-2753

Rowell's Marina
Key Largo (305) 451-1821

Sea Horse Marina
Key West (305) 292-9880

Shelter Bay Marina
Marathon (305) 743-7008

Sisters Creek Marina
Marathon (305) 743-2383

Sugarshack Marina
Sugarloaf Shores (305) 745-3135

Sunshine Key Marina & RV Resort
Sunshine Key (305) 872-2217

Tavernier Creek Marina
Tavernier (305) 852-5854

The Boat House
Marathon (305) 289-1323

Treasure Harbor Marine, Inc.
Plantation Key (305) 852-2458

INDEX

A

Aioli, Avocado 137, 156
ALMOND
Almond Encrusted Snapper With Avocado Beurre Blanc 103
Almond Mango Chutney 121
APPETIZERS
Blue Crab Fritters 23
Boniata Chips 32
Caribbean Escargot 30
Cheeca Lodge Black Bean Fritters 24
Conch Fritters 26
Curried Shrimp Tropicale 29
Dominican Wings 22
Fritters Calabaza 26
Frutta Di Mare 28
Kokomo Joe's Chicken Wings 21
Makoto Roll 32
Scallops and Artichoke Appetizer 27
Sharkbites 19
Shrimp and Corn Fritters 25
Shrimp Mykonos 30
Shrimp Rémoulade 20
Shrimp Wellington 31
Shrimp With Smoked Andouille Sausage 27
Spicy Conch 21
Zuppa de Clams 22
APPLES
Apple Compote 169
Bimini Apple Betty 205
Chicken a la Snooks With Caramelized Apples 183
Artichoke Appetizer, Scallops and 27
Aubergine Soup 94
Aunt Sally's Key Lime Pie 187
AVOCADO
Avocado Aioli 137, 156
Avocado Beurre Blanc 103
Avocado-Crab Salad 52
Key Lime-Avocado Salsa 140

B

Bagatelle Stuffed Grouper 124
Bagatelle's Key Lime Pie 188
Bahamian Coconut Bread 70
Bahamian Conch Steak 147
Baked Yellowtail With Banana Rum Glaze 116
BANANA
Banana Bread 68
Banana Daiquiri 44
Banana Nut Salad 55
Fish Martinique 102
Island Blueberry Banana Bisque 96
Joe's Banana Bread Muffins 68
Macadamia Banana Cream Pie 198
Barbados Rum Punch 36
BEANS (See Black Beans also)
Caribbean Rice and Beans 62
Grace's Bean and Rice Soup 86
Béarnaise Sauce 31
Beef Salad, Spicy 57
BEVERAGES
Banana Daiquiri 44
Barbados Rum Punch 36
Cheeca Smoothy 33
Cold Rum Toddy 38
Conch's Dream 43
Cuba Libre 42
Cuban Cocktail 43
Cuban Coffee With Milk 40
Ernest Hemingway's Mojito 42
Jammer Slammer 35
Key Lime Colada 35
Manatee Bay 34
Mango Daiquiri 44
Mangorita 33
Margarita 36
Montego Bay Banana Cream Pie 37
Papaya/Banana Batido 41
Piña Colada Extra 40
Pineapple Daiquiri 43
Planters Punch 39
Reef Cooler 34
Rum and Coconut Water 39
Rum Swizzle 42
Sangria 38
Spiced Calypso Punch 41
The Scorpion 37
Bimini Apple Betty 205
Black and Bleu (Blackened Chicken Sandwiches) 175
BLACK BEANS
Black Bean and Tasso Soup 90
Black Bean Chili 88
Cheeca Lodge Black Bean Fritters 24
Sizzling Black Beans 106
Black-eyed Pea / Corn Salsa 137
Blue Crab Fritters 23
Blueberry Banana Bisque, Island 96
Boniata Chips 32
Bouillabaisse 82
BREADS
Bahamian Coconut Bread 70
Banana Bread 68
Caribbean-Style French Toast 67
Joe's Banana Bread Muffins 68
Old-fashioned Lemon Bread 69

Broiled Red Snapper Midori 119
Brown Sauce 173
Brownies, Chocolate 202

C

CAKES
Island Spice Cake 202
Piña Colada Cake 208
Three Milks Cake 192
Calabaza, Fritters 26
Caribbean Chicken Salad 49
Caribbean Cocoa Sauce 194
Caribbean Conch Consommé With Sweet Potato Tortellis and Seaweed Twists 80
Caribbean Escargot 30
Caribbean Fish 101
Caribbean Island Rice 62
Caribbean Lamb 170
Caribbean Pork Risotto 168
Caribbean Rice 63
Caribbean Rice and Beans 62
Caribbean Roast Pork Loin 169
Caribbean Stew Grouper 126
Caribbean-Style French Toast 67
Carrot and Summer Squash Soup 95
Cayman Island Conch Salad 49
Cheeca Key Lime Pie 190
Cheeca Lodge Black Bean Fritters 24
Cheeca Lodge White Gazpacho 93
Cheeca Lodge's Jamaican Seafood Soup 83
Cheeca Smoothy 33
Cheeca's Passion Fruit Pie 199
CHEESECAKES
Easy Florida Keys Key Lime Cheesecake 196
Key Lime Cheesecake 197
Tropical Coconut and Key Lime Cheesecake 200
Chef Pedro's Famous Whole Yellowtail 110
Chef Pedro's Shrimp Scampi 155
CHICKEN
Black and Bleu (Blackened Chicken Sandwiches) 175
Caribbean Chicken Salad 49
Chicken a la Snooks With Caramelized Apples 183
Chicken Angela 179
Chicken Breast With Orange, Pineapple, and Ginger Sauce 180
Chicken Saltenbuca 174
Curried Coconut and Chicken Salad 51
Curry-Ginger Chicken Bisque 85
Dominican Wings 22
Jamaican Chicken 174
Key Lime Chicken 182
Kokomo Joe's Chicken Wings 21
Roasted Herb Chicken 181
Rotisserie Chicken 177
Snooks Hazelnut Chicken 182
Spanish Chicken Rice 176
Spicy Caribbean Soup With Rice 87
Tropical Chicken 178
Tropical Chicken Salad 50
Chili, Black Bean 88
Chilled Papaya Soup 96
Chocolate Brownies 202
CHUTNEY
Almond Mango Chutney 121
Papaya Chutney 163
Cilantro Sauce 118
Cioppino, Old Tavernier Seafood 160
Citrus Beurre Blanc Sauce 116
Clams, Zuppa de 22
COCONUT
Bahamian Coconut Bread 70
Coconut Custard Pie 193
Coconut Ice Cream 206
Coconut Phyllo Napoleon 194
Coconut Rice 129
Coconut Shrimp 153
Coconut Square 201
Curried Coconut and Chicken Salad 51
Deep-fried Coconut Shrimp With Coconut Rum Sauce 154
Easy Coconut Shrimp 154
Piña Colada Cake 208
Piña Colada Pie 204
Tropical Coconut and Key Lime Cheesecake 200
Cold Rum Toddy 38
CONCH
Bahamian Conch Steak 147
Caribbean Conch Consommé With Sweet Potato Tortellis and Seaweed Twists 80
Cayman Island Conch Salad 49
Conch Bisque 78
Conch Burger 151
Conch Fritters 26
Conch Gazpacho 77
Conch Salad 48
Conch Sauté 146
Cracked Conch With Crabmeat Stuffing 148
Grassy Key Dairy Bar's Conch Salad 47
Hungary Tarpon Conch Chowder 73
Jammers Conch Chowder 75
Joe's Famous Conch Chowder 74
Orange Conch 150
Ramon's Conch Steak 146
Sautéed Caribbean Conch Joseph 149
Smuggler's Cove Conch Chowder 76
Spicy Conch 21
White Conch Chowder 79
Conch's Dream 43
CORN
Black-eyed Pea / Corn Salsa 137
Jalapeño Corn Chowder 89

Shrimp and Corn Fritters 25
CRAB
Avocado-Crab Salad 52
Blue Crab Fritters 23
Crabmeat Omelet 157
Cracked Conch With Crabmeat Stuffing 148
Fish Seminole 100
Stone Crab Cakes With Avocado Aioli 156
Cracked Conch With Crabmeat Stuffing 148
Creamy Garlic Sauce 145
Cuba Libre 42
Cuban Cocktail 43
Cuban Coffee With Milk 40
Cuban Roasted Pork 171
Cucumber Sauce 139
Curried Coconut and Chicken Salad 51
Curried Shrimp Tropicale 29
Curry Shrimp Salad 56
Curry-Ginger Chicken Bisque 85

D

Dark Chocolate Walnut Fudge 207
Date, Rum, and Coconut Milk Sauce 136
Deep-fried Coconut Shrimp With Coconut Rum Sauce 154
DESSERTS (See Cakes, Cheesecakes, Ice Cream and Pies also)
Bimini Apple Betty 205
Coconut Phyllo Napoleon 194
Coconut Square 201
Dark Chocolate Walnut Fudge 207
Mango Mascarpone Tart 203
Mangoes Islamorada 191
Rumrunner Salsa 204
DOLPHIN
Dolphin Capri 107
Dolphin Jalamango 133
Dominican Wings 22
Dos Equis XX Seafood Extravaganza Paella 138

E

Easy Coconut Shrimp 154
Easy Florida Keys Key Lime Cheesecake 196
Eigner's Caribbean Fish 123
Ernest Hemingway's Mojito 42
Escargot, Caribbean 30

F

Fast Creole Sauce 139
FISH (See individual listings also)
Caribbean Fish 101
Cilantro Sauce 118
Dolphin Capri 107
Dolphin Jalamango 133
Dos Equis XX Seafood Extravaganza Paella 138
Eigner's Caribbean Fish 123
Fish Martinique 102
Fish Paradise 107
Fish Rangoon 117
Fish Seminole 100
Fish Sicily 134
Fish Tropical 130
Frutta Di Mare 28
Grilled Mahi-Mahi With Tropical Fruit Salsa in Mango Sauce 135
Grilled Wasabi Cobia 131
Grouper Phillipe With Almond Mango Chutney 121
Jamaican Jerk Fresh Fish Sandwich 99
Makoto Roll 32
Pompano in Island Spices With Date, Rum, and Coconut Milk Sauce 136
Poncho Train 119
Queen Trigger Fish 132
Sautéed Cobia With Black-eyed Pea / Corn Salsa and Avocado Aioli 137
Sautéed Wahoo in Seaweed Crust With Butternut Squash and Lime Sauce 125
Sharkbites 19
Fresh Tuna Salad 52
Fried Sweet Plantains 64
FRITTERS
Blue Crab Fritters 23
Cheeca Lodge Black Bean Fritters 24
Conch Fritters 26
Fritters Calabaza 26
Shrimp and Corn Fritters 25
FRUIT (See individual listings also)
Rumrunner Salsa 204
Tropical Fruit Salsa 135
Frutta Di Mare 28
Fudge, Dark Chocolate Walnut 207
Funchi 64

G

GAZPACHO
Cheeca Lodge White Gazpacho 93
Conch Gazpacho 77
Joe's Summer Gazpacho 92
Goat, Stewed 172
Grace's Bean and Rice Soup 86
Grassy Key Dairy Bar's Conch Salad 47
Grilled Keys Shrimp 152
Grilled Mahi-Mahi With Tropical Fruit Salsa in Mango Sauce 135
Grilled Swordfish With Tropical Mango Salsa 108
Grilled Tuna Islamorada-Style 127
Grilled Wasabi Cobia 131
GROUPER
Bagatelle Stuffed Grouper 124

Caribbean Stew Grouper 126
Fish Sicily 134
Grouper Lucea 122
Grouper Phillipe With Almond Mango Chutney 121
Local Broiled Grouper 128

H

Hollandaise Sauce 127
HONEY
Honey Dressing 55
Honey Ginger Sauce 167
Honey Key Lime Salad Dressing 58
Hot Pepper Bottle 57
Hungary Tarpon Conch Chowder 73
Hurricane Shrimp 155

I

ICE CREAM
Coconut Ice Cream 206
Papaya Sherbet 207
Pineapple Ice Cream 206
Island Blueberry Banana Bisque 96
Island Spice Cake 202

J

Jalapeño Corn Chowder 89
Jalapeño Vinaigrette 54
Jamaican Chicken 174
Jamaican Jerk Fresh Fish Sandwich 99
Jamaican Jerk Rub 167
Jammer Slammer 35
Jammers Conch Chowder 75
Jerk Seasoning 99
Jerk Spaghetti 171
Jerk Tuna 129
Jerked Shrimp Cobb 54
Joe's Banana Bread Muffins 68
Joe's Famous Conch Chowder 74
Joe's Gorgonzola Salad 56
Joe's Summer Gazpacho 92

K

KEY LIMES
Aunt Sally's Key Lime Pie 187
Bagatelle's Key Lime Pie 188
Cheeca Key Lime Pie 190
Easy Florida Keys Key Lime Cheesecake 196
Honey Key Lime Salad Dressing 58
Key Lime Beurre Blanc 140
Key Lime Cheesecake 197
Key Lime Chicken 182
Key Lime Colada 35
Key Lime-Avocado Salsa 140
Lorelei's Frozen Key Lime Pie 191
Margaritaville Key Lime Pie 189
Tropical Coconut and Key Lime Cheesecake 200
Keys Seafood Pasta 158
King of the Sea 84
Kokomo Joe's Chicken Wings 21

L

Lamb, Caribbean 170
Lasagne Rasta 184
Latin-Style Roast Pork 172
Lemon Bread, Old-fashioned 69
Lentil Salad With Spiced Vinaigrette 53
Lime Sauce 125
LOBSTER
Lobster Mexical 144
Lobster Sauce 164
Lobster Thermador 143
Shrimp and Lobster Butter Cream Sauce 124
The Pilot's Lobster Pie 145
Local Broiled Grouper 128
Lorelei's Frozen Key Lime Pie 191
Lorelei's Jamaican Rice and Peas 61
Lorelei's Redbone Island Pork Barbecue 167

M

Macadamia Banana Cream Pie 198
Makoto Roll 32
Manatee Bay 34
MANGO
Almond Mango Chutney 121
Caribbean Fish 101
Mango Butter Sauce 104
Mango Daiquiri 44
Mango Mascarpone Tart 203
Mango Mousse 194
Mango Sauce 135
Mango Vinaigrette 58
Mangoes Islamorada 191
Mangorita 33
Papaya Mango Salsa 118
Sweet Mango Cream Sauce 114
Sword of the Coral Lady 109
Tropical Mango Salsa 108
Mangorita 33
Margarita 36
Margaritaville Key Lime Pie 189
Meringue 192
Montego Bay Banana Cream Pie 37
Mornay Sauce 144
Muffins, Joe's Banana Bread 68

O

Octopus Pasta Sauce 163

Old Tavernier Seafood Cioppino 160
Old-fashioned Lemon Bread 69
ORANGE
Orange Conch 150
Orange, Pineapple, and Ginger Sauce 180
Out Island Sauce 151

P

Paella 161
Paella, Dos Equis XX Seafood Extravaganza 138
Pan-fried Yellowtail 113
PAPAYA
Caribbean Fish 101
Chilled Papaya Soup 96
Papaya Chutney 163
Papaya Mango Salsa 118
Papaya Sherbet 207
Papaya/Banana Batido 41
PASSION FRUIT
Cheeca's Passion Fruit Pie 199
Passion Fruit Sauce 194
PASTA
Jerk Spaghetti 171
Keys Seafood Pasta 158
Octopus Pasta Sauce 163
Peas, Lorelei's Jamaican Rice and 61
PIES
Aunt Sally's Key Lime Pie 187
Bagatelle's Key Lime Pie 188
Cheeca Key Lime Pie 190
Cheeca's Passion Fruit Pie 199
Coconut Custard Pie 193
Lorelei's Frozen Key Lime Pie 191
Macadamia Banana Cream Pie 198
Margaritaville Key Lime Pie 189
Piña Colada Pie 204
PINEAPPLE
Orange, Pineapple, and Ginger Sauce 180
Piña Colada Cake 208
Piña Colada Pie 204
Pineapple Daiquiri 43
Pineapple Ice Cream 206
Plantains, Fried Sweet 64
Planters Punch 39
Pompano in Island Spices With Date, Rum, and Coconut Milk Sauce 136
Poncho Train 119
PORK
Black Bean and Tasso Soup 90
Caribbean Pork Risotto 168
Caribbean Roast Pork Loin 169
Cuban Roasted Pork 171
Latin-Style Roast Pork 172
Lorelei's Redbone Island Pork Barbecue 167
Smoked Caribbean Pork Roast 170
Port of Spain Sauce 113
POTATOES
Boniata Chips 32
Fried Sweet Plantains 64
Shrimp Hash Cakes 66
Pumpkin Soup 85

Q

Queen Trigger Fish 132
Quick Tomato Sauce 183

R

Ramon's Conch Steak 146
Rangoon Sauce 117
Red Wine Caramel Sauce 203
Reef Cooler 34
RICE
Caribbean Island Rice 62
Caribbean Pork Risotto 168
Caribbean Rice 63
Caribbean Rice and Beans 62
Coconut Rice 129
Grace's Bean and Rice Soup 86
Lorelei's Jamaican Rice and Peas 61
Spanish Chicken Rice 176
Yellow Rice 63
Risotto, Caribbean Pork 168
Roasted Herb Chicken 181
Roasted Pepper/Orange Salsa 106
Rotisserie Chicken 177
Rum and Coconut Water 39
Rum Swizzle 42
Rumrunner Salsa 204

S

SALADS
Avocado-Crab Salad 52
Banana Nut Salad 55
Caribbean Chicken Salad 49
Cayman Island Conch Salad 49
Conch Salad 48
Curried Coconut and Chicken Salad 51
Curry Shrimp Salad 56
Fresh Tuna Salad 52
Grassy Key Dairy Bar's Conch Salad 47
Jerked Shrimp Cobb 54
Joe's Gorgonzola Salad 56
Lentil Salad With Spiced Vinaigrette 53
Spicy Beef Salad 57
Spicy Tuna Salad 53
Tropical Chicken Salad 50
SALAD DRESSINGS
Honey Dressing 55
Honey Key Lime Salad Dressing 58
Hot Pepper Bottle 57
Jalapeño Vinaigrette 54
Mango Vinaigrette 58

SALSA
Black-eyed Pea / Corn Salsa 137
Papaya Mango Salsa 118
Roasted Pepper/Orange Salsa 106
Tropical Fruit Salsa 135
Tropical Mango Salsa 108
SANDWICHES
Black and Bleu (Blackened Chicken Sandwiches) 175
Jamaican Jerk Fresh Fish Sandwich 99
Sangria 38
SAUCES
Avocado Aioli 137, 156
Avocado Beurre Blanc 103
Béarnaise Sauce 31
Brown Sauce 173
Caribbean Cocoa Sauce 194
Cilantro Sauce 118
Citrus Beurre Blanc Sauce 116
Creamy Garlic Sauce 145
Cucumber Sauce 139
Date, Rum, and Coconut Milk Sauce 136
Fast Creole Sauce 139
Hollandaise Sauce 127
Honey Ginger Sauce 167
Key Lime Beurre Blanc 140
Key Lime-Avocado Salsa 140
Lime Sauce 125
Lobster Sauce 164
Mango Butter Sauce 104
Mango Sauce 135
Mornay Sauce 144
Octopus Pasta Sauce 163
Orange, Pineapple, and Ginger Sauce 180
Out Island Sauce 151
Passion Fruit Sauce 194
Port of Spain Sauce 113
Quick Tomato Sauce 183
Rangoon Sauce 117
Red Wine Caramel Sauce 203
Senator Sauce 113
Shrimp and Lobster Butter Cream Sauce 124
Simple Jerk Sauce 167
Sweet Caribbean Sauce 153
Sweet Mango Cream Sauce 114
Tomato Concassee 102
Yellow Bell Pepper Sauce 128
SAUSAGE
Jerk Spaghetti 171
Shrimp With Smoked Andouille Sausage 27
Sautéed Caribbean Conch Joseph 149
Sautéed Cobia With Black-eyed Pea / Corn Salsa and Avocado Aioli 137
Sautéed Wahoo in Seaweed Crust With Butternut Squash and Lime Sauce 125
Sautéed Yellowtail Snapper 115
SCALLOPS
Fish Seminole 100
Frutta Di Mare 28
Scallops and Artichoke Appetizer 27
SEAFOOD (See individual listings also)
Bouillabaisse 82
Cheeca Lodge's Jamaican Seafood Soup 83
Dos Equis XX Seafood Extravaganza Paella 138
Keys Seafood Pasta 158
King of the Sea 84
Old Tavernier Seafood Cioppino 160
Paella 161
Seafood Collins 159
Seafood Pie 162
Seafood Special 157
Seared Tuna With Yellow Bell Pepper Sauce 128
Seaweed Twists 80
Senator Sauce 113
Sharkbites 19
Sherbet, Papaya 207
SHRIMP
Chef Pedro's Shrimp Scampi 155
Coconut Shrimp 153
Curried Shrimp Tropicale 29
Curry Shrimp Salad 56
Deep-fried Coconut Shrimp With Coconut Rum Sauce 154
Easy Coconut Shrimp 154
Frutta Di Mare 28
Grilled Keys Shrimp 152
Hurricane Shrimp 155
Jerked Shrimp Cobb 54
Shrimp Amelia 152
Shrimp and Corn Fritters 25
Shrimp and Lobster Butter Cream Sauce 124
Shrimp Hash Cakes 66
Shrimp Mykonos 30
Shrimp Rémoulade 20
Shrimp Wellington 31
Shrimp With Smoked Andouille Sausage 27
SIDE DISHES (See individual listings also)
Funchi 64
Shrimp Hash Cakes 66
Simple Jerk Sauce 167
Sizzling Black Beans 106
Smoked Caribbean Pork Roast 170
Smuggler's Cove Conch Chowder 76
SNAPPER (See Yellowtail also)
Almond Encrusted Snapper With Avocado Beurre Blanc 103
Broiled Red Snapper Midori 119
Fish Paradise 107
Snapper Macadamia With Mango Butter Sauce 104
The Presidential Snapper 106
Snooks Hazelnut Chicken 182
SOUPS
Aubergine Soup 94
Black Bean and Tasso Soup 90

Black Bean Chili 88
Bouillabaisse 82
Caribbean Conch Consommé With Sweet Potato Tortellis and Seaweed Twists 80
Carrot and Summer Squash Soup 95
Cheeca Lodge White Gazpacho 93
Cheeca Lodge's Jamaican Seafood Soup 83
Chilled Papaya Soup 96
Conch Bisque 78
Conch Gazpacho 77
Curry-Ginger Chicken Bisque 85
Grace's Bean and Rice Soup 86
Hungary Tarpon Conch Chowder 73
Island Blueberry Banana Bisque 96
Jalapeño Corn Chowder 89
Jammers Conch Chowder 75
Joe's Famous Conch Chowder 74
Joe's Summer Gazpacho 92
King of the Sea 84
Pumpkin Soup 85
Smuggler's Cove Conch Chowder 76
Spicy Caribbean Soup With Rice 87
Strawberry Soup 94
Tomato Basil Soup 91
Tomato/Garlic Soup 91
Watercress Soup 95
White Conch Chowder 79
Zuppa de Clams 22
Spanish Chicken Rice 176
Spiced Calypso Punch 41
Spicy Beef Salad 57
Spicy Caribbean Soup With Rice 87
Spicy Conch 21
Spicy Tuna Salad 53
SQUASH
Carrot and Summer Squash Soup 95
Fritters Calabaza 26
Sautéed Wahoo in Seaweed Crust With Butternut Squash and Lime Sauce 125
Stewed Goat 172
Stone Crab Cakes With Avocado Aioli 156
Strawberry Soup 94
Sweet Caribbean Sauce 153
Sweet Mango Cream Sauce 114
Sweet Potato Tortellis 80
Sword of the Coral Lady 109
SWORDFISH
Grilled Swordfish With Tropical Mango Salsa 108
Sword of the Coral Lady 109

T

Tart, Mango Mascarpone 203
The Pilot's Lobster Pie 145
The Presidential Snapper 106
The Scorpion 37
Three Milks Cake 192
TOMATOES
Quick Tomato Sauce 183
Tomato Basil Soup 91
Tomato/Garlic Soup 91
Tomato Concassee 102
Tropical Chicken 178
Tropical Chicken Salad 50
Tropical Coconut and Key Lime Cheesecake 200
Tropical Fruit Salsa 135
Tropical Mango Salsa 108
TUNA
Fresh Tuna Salad 52
Grilled Tuna Islamorada-Style 127
Jerk Tuna 129
Seared Tuna With Yellow Bell Pepper Sauce 128
Spicy Tuna Salad 53

V

Veal Scaloppine Ocho Rios 173
VEGETABLES (See individual listings also)
Lasagne Rasta 184

W

Wahoo in Seaweed Crust With Butternut Squash, Sautéed 125
Watercress Soup 95
White Conch Chowder 79

Y

Yellow Bell Pepper Sauce 128
Yellow Rice 63
YELLOWTAIL SNAPPER
Baked Yellowtail With Banana Rum Glaze 116
Chef Pedro's Famous Whole Yellowtail 110
Fish Rangoon 117
Pan-fried Yellowtail 113
Sautéed Yellowtail Snapper 115
Snapper Tropical 105
Yellowtail Caribbean Style 114
Yellowtail En Papillote 111
Yellowtail Macadamia 118
Yellowtail Morocco 120
Yellowtail Papillote 122
Yellowtail St. Croix 112
Yellowtail With Sweet Mango Cream Sauce 114
Yuca With Garlic Sauce 65

Z

Zuppa de Clams 22

CALYPSO CAFÉ

Wimmer Cookbook Distribution
4210 B. F. Goodrich Boulevard
Memphis, Tennessee 38118

Please send ________ copies of ***Calypso Café***

@ $17.95 each______________

Tennessee residents add sales tax @ $ 1.48 each______________

Postage and handling @ $ 5.00 each______________

Total______________

Charge to Visa ( ) or MasterCard ( )

______________________________ Expiration Date______________

Signature ____

Name ____

Address ____

City ________________________ State __________ Zip ___________

COOKBOOK LOVERS TAKE NOTE...

If you've enjoyed ***Calypso Café***, The Wimmer Companies, Inc., has a catalog of 250 other cookbook titles that may interest you. To receive your free copy, write:

The Wimmer Companies, Inc.
4210 B. F. Goodrich Boulevard
Memphis, Tennessee 38118
or
call 1-800-727-1034

OXFORD WORLD'S CLASSICS

C. P. CAVAFY

The Collected Poems

Translated by

EVANGELOS SACHPEROGLOU

Greek Text Edited by

ANTHONY HIRST

With an Introduction by

PETER MACKRIDGE

UNIVERSITY PRESS

OXFORD
UNIVERSITY PRESS

Great Clarendon Street, Oxford OX2 6DP

Oxford University Press is a department of the University of Oxford.
It furthers the University's objective of excellence in research, scholarship,
and education by publishing worldwide in

Oxford New York

Auckland Cape Town Dar es Salaam Hong Kong Karachi
Kuala Lumpur Madrid Melbourne Mexico City Nairobi
New Delhi Shanghai Taipei Toronto

With offices in

Argentina Austria Brazil Chile Czech Republic France Greece
Guatemala Hungary Italy Japan Poland Portugal Singapore
South Korea Switzerland Thailand Turkey Ukraine Vietnam

Oxford is a registered trade mark of Oxford University Press
in the UK and in certain other countries

Published in the United States
by Oxford University Press Inc., New York

First published as an Oxford World's Classics paperback 2007
Reissued 2008

British Library Cataloguing in Publication Data
Data available

Library of Congress Cataloging in Publication Data
Cavafy, Constantine, 1863–1933.
[Poems. English & Greek]
The collected poems / C.P. Cavafy ; translated by Evangelos Sachperoglou ;
Greek text edited by Anthony Hirst ; introduction by Peter Mackridge.
p. cm. – (Oxford world's classics)
Poems in Greek and in English translation.
ISBN 978–0–19–955595–6 (alk. paper)
1. Cavafy, Constantine, 1863–1933–Translations into English. I. Sachperoglou, Evangelos,
1941– II. Hirst, Anthony, 1945– III. Title.
PA5610.K2A2 2007
889'.132–dc22
2007015833

ISBN 978–0–19–955595–6

19

Typeset by Cepha Imaging Private Ltd., Bangalore, India
Greek typesetting by Ioanna Stavridis

Printed and bound in Great Britain by Clays Ltd, Elcograf S.p.A.

OXFORD WORLD'S CLASSICS

THE COLLECTED POEMS

C. P. CAVAFY was born in 1863 into a well-to-do Greek mercantile family in Alexandria, Egypt. After his father's death and the beginning of the family's financial difficulties, the young Cavafy moved with his mother and brothers to England, where they spent the period 1872–7 in Liverpool and London. Apart from three years in Constantinople from 1882 to 1885, he spent the rest of his life in Alexandria, where he worked, until his retirement in 1922, as a senior clerk in the Irrigation Department, living alone (after the departure of his brother Paul in 1908) in a relatively large apartment near the centre of the city. He visited Greece on only four occasions. He began publishing poetry in periodicals in 1886, but abandoned many of his early poems, and self-publication gradually became his preferred means of disseminating his work. By the time of his death in 1933 his poetry was widely known—though the subject of much controversy—throughout the Greek-speaking world and beyond.

EVANGELOS SACHPEROGLOU was born in Piraeus in 1941. He has taught Economics and History at Athens College and Deree College in Athens, where he lives.

ANTHONY HIRST is a part-time Lecturer in Modern Greek at Queen's University Belfast. He is the author of *God and the Poetic Ego* (2004), a study of the use and abuse of religious language in the work of three modern Greek poets, and of many critical articles on Cavafy and other Greek authors.

PETER MACKRIDGE is Emeritus Professor of Modern Greek at Oxford University. His books include *The Modern Greek Language* (1985) and *Dionysios Solomos* (1989). He has co-authored two grammars of Modern Greek (1997 and 2004) and has published many articles on medieval and modern Greek literature.

OXFORD WORLD'S CLASSICS

For over 100 years Oxford World's Classics have brought readers closer to the world's great literature. Now with over 700 titles—from the 4,000-year-old myths of Mesopotamia to the twentieth century's greatest novels—the series makes available lesser-known as well as celebrated writing.

The pocket-sized hardbacks of the early years contained introductions by Virginia Woolf, T. S. Eliot, Graham Greene, and other literary figures which enriched the experience of reading. Today the series is recognized for its fine scholarship and reliability in texts that span world literature, drama and poetry, religion, philosophy and politics. Each edition includes perceptive commentary and essential background information to meet the changing needs of readers.

CONTENTS

Introduction xi

Note on the Greek Text xxxiv

Note on the Translation xl

Select Bibliography xlii

A Chronology of C. P. Cavafy xlv

THE COLLECTED POEMS

ΠΟΙΗΜΑΤΑ 1910 [1897–1909]/POEMS 1910 [1897–1909]

Φωνὲς 2	Voices 3
Ἐπιθυμίες 2	Desires 3
Κεριὰ 2	Candles 3
Ἕνας γέρος 4	An old man 5
Δέησις 6	Supplication 7
Ἡ ψυχὲς τῶν γερόντων 6	The souls of old men 7
Τὸ πρῶτο σκαλὶ 6	The first step 7
Διακοπὴ 8	Interruption 9
Θερμοπύλες 10	Thermopylae 11
Che fece . . . il gran rifiuto 10	*Che fece . . . il gran rifiuto* 11
Τὰ παράθυρα 12	The windows 13
[Τρῶες]	[Trojans]
Τείχη 12	Walls 13
Περιμένοντας τοὺς βαρβάρους 14	Waiting for the barbarians 15
[Μονοτονία]	[Monotony]
Ἀπιστία 18	Perfidy 19
Ἡ κηδεία τοῦ Σαρπηδόνος 20	The funeral of Sarpedon 21
Τὰ ἄλογα τοῦ Ἀχιλλέως 22	The horses of Achilles 23
[Ἡ συνοδεία τοῦ Διονύσου]	[The retinue of Dionysus]
[Ὁ βασιλεὺς Δημήτριος]	[King Demetrius]
[Τὰ βήματα]	[The footsteps]
[Οὗτος Ἐκεῖνος]	[That is the Man]

ΠΟΙΗΜΑΤΑ (1905–1915)/POEMS (1905–1915)

Ἡ πόλις 28	The city 29
Ἡ σατραπεία 28	Satrapy 29
Σοφοὶ δὲ προσιόντων 30	Wise men 31
Μάρτιαι εἰδοὶ 32	The ides of March 33
Τελειωμένα 32	Finished 33

Ἀπολείπειν ὁ θεὸς Ἀντώνιον 34	The god forsakes Antony 35
Ὁ Θεόδοτος 34	Theodotus 35
Μονοτονία 36	Monotony 37
Ἰθάκη 36	Ithaca 37
Ὅσο μπορεῖς 38	As best you can 39
Τρῶες 40	Trojans 41
Ὁ βασιλεὺς Δημήτριος 42	King Demetrius 43
Ἡ δόξα τῶν Πτολεμαίων 42	The glory of the Ptolemies 43
Ἡ συνοδεία τοῦ Διονύσου 44	The retinue of Dionysus 45
Ἡ μάχη τῆς Μαγνησίας 44	The Battle of Magnesia 45
Ἡ δυσαρέσκεια τοῦ Σελευκίδου 46	The displeasure of the Seleucid 47
Ὀροφέρνης 48	Orophernes 49
Ἀλεξανδρινοὶ βασιλεῖς 52	Alexandrian kings 53
Φιλέλλην 54	Philhellene 55
Τὰ βήματα 56	The footsteps 57
Ἡρώδης Ἀττικὸς 56	Herod Atticus 57
Τυανεὺς γλύπτης 58	Sculptor of Tyana 59
Λυσίου γραμματικοῦ τάφος 60	Tomb of the grammarian Lysias 61
Εὐρίωνος τάφος 60	Tomb of Eurion 61
Οὗτος Ἐκεῖνος 62	That is the Man 63
Τὰ ἐπικίνδυνα 62	Perilous things 63
Μανουὴλ Κομνηνὸς 64	Manuel Comnenus 65
Στὴν ἐκκλησία 64	In church 65
Πολὺ σπανίως 66	Very seldom 67
Τοῦ μαγαζιοῦ 66	Of the shop 67
Ζωγραφισμένα 68	Painted 69
Θάλασσα τοῦ πρωϊοῦ 68	Morning sea 69
Ἰωνικὸν 70	Ionic 71
Στοῦ καφενείου τὴν εἴσοδο 70	At the entrance of the café 71
Μιὰ νύχτα 70	One night 71
Ἐπέστρεφε 72	Come back 73
Μακρυὰ 72	Far away 73
Ὀμνύει 74	He vows 75
Ἐπῆγα 74	I went 75
Πολυέλαιος 74	Chandelier 75

ΠΟΙΗΜΑΤΑ (1916–1918)/POEMS (1916–1918)

Ἀπ' τὲς ἐννιὰ— 78	Since nine o'clock— 79
Νόησις 78	Perception 79
Ἐνώπιον τοῦ ἀγάλματος τοῦ Ἐνδυμίωνος 80	Before the statue of Endymion 81
Πρέσβεις ἀπ' τὴν Ἀλεξάνδρεια 80	Envoys from Alexandria 81
Ἀριστόβουλος 82	Aristoboulos 83
Καισαρίων 84	Caesarion 85
Ἡ διορία τοῦ Νέρωνος 86	Nero's term 87
Εἰς τὸ ἐπίνειον 88	In the harbour town 89

Ένας θεός των 88	One of their gods 89
Λάνη τάφος 90	Tomb of Lanes 91
Ἰασῆ τάφος 90	Tomb of Iases 91
Ἐν πόλει τῆς Ὀσροηνῆς 92	A town in Osroene 93
Ἰγνατίου τάφος 92	Tomb of Ignatius 93
Ἐν τῷ μηνὶ Ἀθὺρ 92	In the month of Athyr 93
Γιὰ τὸν Ἀμμόνη, ποὺ πέθανε 29 ἐτῶν, στα 610 94	For Ammones, who died aged 29, in 610 95
Αἰμιλιανὸς Μονάη, Ἀλεξανδρεύς, 628–655 μ.Χ. 96	Aemilianus Monaë, Alexandrian, A.D. 628–655 97
Ὅταν διεγείρονται 96	When they are roused 97
Ἡδονῇ 98	To sensual pleasure 99
Ἔτσι πολὺ ἀτένισα — 98	So long I gazed — 99
Ἐν τῇ ὁδῷ 98	In the street 99
Ἡ προθήκη του καπνοπωλείου 100	The tobacconist's window 101
Πέρασμα 100	Passage 101
Ἐν ἑσπέρᾳ 102	In the evening 103
Γκρίζα 102	Grey 103
Κάτω ἀπ' τὸ σπίτι 104	Outside the house 105
Τὸ διπλανὸ τραπέζι 104	The next table 105
Θυμήσου, σῶμα . . . 106	Body, remember . . . 107
Μέρες τοῦ 1903 106	Days of 1903 107

ΠΟΙΗΜΑΤΑ 1919–1933/POEMS 1919–1933

Ὁ ἥλιος τοῦ ἀπογεύματος 110	The afternoon sun 111
Νὰ μείνει 110	Has come to rest 111
Τῶν Ἑβραίων (50 μ.Χ.) 112	Of the Hebrews (A.D. 50) 113
Ἴμενος 114	Imenos 115
Τοῦ πλοίου 114	On the ship 115
Δημητρίου Σωτῆρος (162–150 π.Χ.) 116	Of Demetrius Soter (162–150 B.C.) 117
Εἴγε ἐτελεύτα 118	If dead indeed 119
Νέοι τῆς Σιδῶνος (400 μ.Χ.) 120	Young men of Sidon (A.D. 400) 121
Γιὰ νἄρθουν — 122	That they come — 123
Ὁ Δαρεῖος 124	Darius 125
Ἄννα Κομνηνὴ 126	Anna Comnena 127
Βυζαντινὸς Ἄρχων, ἐξόριστος, στιχουργῶν 126	A Byzantine Nobleman, in exile, composing verses 127
Ἡ ἀρχή των 128	Their origin 129
Εὔνοια τοῦ Ἀλεξάνδρου Βάλα 128	The favour of Alexander Balas 129
Μελαγχολία τοῦ Ἰάσωνος Κλεάνδρου· ποιητοῦ ἐν Κομμαγηνῇ· 595 μ.Χ. 130	Melancholy of Jason, son of Kleander, poet in Commagene, A.D. 595 131
Ὁ Δημάρατος 130	Demaratus 131
Ἐκόμισα εἰς τὴν Τέχνη 132	I brought to Art 133
Ἀπὸ τὴν σχολὴν τοῦ περιωνύμου φιλοσόφου 134	From the school of the renowned philosopher 135

Τεχνουργὸς κρατήρων 136	Craftsman of craters 137
Ὑπὲρ τῆς Ἀχαϊκῆς Συμπολιτείας πολεμήσαντες 136	Those who fought for the Achaean League 137
Πρὸς τὸν Ἀντίοχον Ἐπιφανῆ 138	To Antiochus Epiphanes 139
Σ' ἕνα βιβλίο παληὸ— 138	In an old book— 139
Ἐν ἀπογνώσει 140	In despair 141
Ὁ Ἰουλιανός, ὁρῶν ὀλιγωρίαν 140	Julian, noticing negligence 141
Ἐπιτύμβιον Ἀντιόχου, βασιλέως Κομμαγηνῆς 142	Epitaph of Antiochus, king of Commagene 143
Θέατρον τῆς Σιδῶνος (400 Μ.Χ.) 144	Theatre of Sidon (A.D. 400) 145
Ὁ Ἰουλιανὸς ἐν Νικομηδείᾳ 144	Julian in Nicomedia 145
Πρὶν τοὺς ἀλλάξει ὁ Χρόνος 146	Before they are changed by Time 147
Ἦλθε γιὰ νὰ διαβάσει— 146	He came to read— 147
Τὸ 31 Π.Χ. στὴν Ἀλεξάνδρεια 148	In Alexandria, 31 B.C. 149
Ὁ Ἰωάννης Καντακουζηνὸς ὑπερισχύει 148	John Cantacuzenus prevails 149
Τέμεθος, Ἀντιοχεύς· 400 Μ.Χ. 150	Temethos, Antiochian, A.D. 400 151
Ἀπὸ ὑαλὶ χρωματιστὸ 152	Of coloured glass 153
Τὸ 25ον ἔτος τοῦ βίου του 152	The 25th year of his life 153
Εἰς Ἰταλικὴν παραλίαν 154	On an Italian shore 155
Στὸ πληκτικὸ χωριὸ 154	In the dreary village 155
Ἀπολλώνιος ὁ Τυανεὺς ἐν Ρόδῳ 156	Apollonius of Tyana in Rhodes 157
Ἡ ἀρρώστια τοῦ Κλείτου 156	Kleitos' illness 157
Ἐν δήμῳ τῆς Μικρᾶς Ἀσίας 158	In a township of Asia Minor 159
Ἱερεὺς τοῦ Σεραπίου 160	A priest of the Serapeum 161
Μέσα στὰ καπηλειὰ— 160	In the wine taverns— 161
Μεγάλη συνοδεία ἐξ ἱερέων καὶ λαϊκῶν 162	A great procession of priests and laymen 163
Σοφιστὴς ἀπερχόμενος ἐκ Συρίας 164	Sophist leaving Syria 165
Ὁ Ἰουλιανὸς καὶ οἱ Ἀντιοχεῖς 164	Julian and the Antiochians 165
Ἄννα Δαλασσηνὴ 166	Anna Dalassene 167
Μέρες τοῦ 1896 166	Days of 1896 167
Δύο νέοι, 23 ἕως 24 ἐτῶν 168	Two young men, 23 to 24 years old 169
Παλαιόθεν ἑλληνὶς 170	Greek since ancient times 171
Μέρες τοῦ 1901 172	Days of 1901 173
Οὐκ ἔγνως 172	You didn't understand 173
Ἕνας νέος, τῆς Τέχνης τοῦ Λόγου—στὸ 24ον ἔτος του 174	A young man of Letters—in his 24th year 175
Ἐν Σπάρτῃ 174	In Sparta 175
Εἰκὼν εἰκοσιτριετοῦς νέου καμωμένη ἀπὸ φίλον του ὁμήλικα, ἐρασιτέχνην 176	Portrait of a 23-year-old man, painted by a friend of the same age, an amateur artist 177
Ἐν μεγάλῃ Ἑλληνικῇ ἀποικίᾳ, 200 Π.Χ. 178	In a large Greek colony, 200 B.C. 179
Ἡγεμὼν ἐκ Δυτικῆς Λιβύης 180	The potentate from Western Libya 181

Κίμων Λεάρχου, 22 ἐτῶν, σπουδαστὴς Ἑλληνικῶν γραμμάτων (ἐν Κυρήνῃ) 182
Kimon, son of Learchos, 22 years old, student of Greek letters (in Cyrene) 183
Ἐν πορείᾳ πρὸς τὴν Σινώπην 184
On the march to Sinope 185
Μέρες τοῦ 1909, '10 καὶ '11 186
Days of 1909, '10 and '11 187
Μύρης· Ἀλεξάνδρεια τοῦ 340 Μ.Χ. 186
Myres: Alexandria, A.D. 340 187
Ἀλέξανδρος Ἰανναῖος, καὶ Ἀλεξάνδρα 190
Alexander Jannaeus, and Alexandra 191
Ὡραῖα λουλούδια κι ἄσπρα ὡς ταίριαζαν πολὺ 192
Lovely flowers and white such as befitted well 193
Ἄγε ὦ βασιλεῦ Λακεδαιμονίων 194
Come, O king of the Lacedaemonians 195

Στὸν ἴδιο χῶρο 196
In the same space 197
Ὁ καθρέπτης στὴν εἴσοδο 196
The mirror in the entrance 197
Ρωτοῦσε γιὰ τὴν ποιότητα— 198
He was asking about the quality— 199

Ἂς φρόντιζαν 200
If only they had seen to it 201
Κατὰ τὲς συνταγὲς ἀρχαίων Ἑλληνοσύρων μάγων 202
According to the recipes of ancient Greco-Syrian magicians 203
Στὰ 200 Π.Χ. 204
In the year 200 B.C. 205
Μέρες τοῦ 1908 206
Days of 1908 207
Εἰς τὰ περίχωρα τῆς Ἀντιοχείας 208
In the outskirts of Antioch 209

Explanatory Notes 213

Glossary 229

Chronological List of Poems 231

Index of Greek Titles 235

Index of English Titles 237

INTRODUCTION

Cavafy's 'slight angle to the universe'

K. P. Kavafis (known in English as C. P. Cavafy) died in Alexandria on 29 April 1933, seventy years to the day after he was born there into a well-to-do Greek family. His parents, who originated from Constantinople (Istanbul), moved to Alexandria in 1855, only eight years before the poet's birth. His father was part of a family trading company that enjoyed considerable success until it more or less collapsed shortly after his death in 1870. Cavafy lived in Alexandria for the whole of his almost entirely uneventful life, except for two periods. He spent five years (1872–7) in Liverpool and London with his mother and the rest of his family after his father's death, and he spent the period 1882–5 in Constantinople, which at that time was both the capital of the Ottoman Empire and a great traditional centre of Greek culture. From at least 1892 to 1922 the poet held a part-time clerical job, working mornings only, in the Egyptian government's Irrigation Office. He only visited Greece four times: he went there for touristic and family reasons in 1901, 1903, and 1905, and in order to undergo a tracheotomy for cancer of the throat in 1932. In his personal life Cavafy was reticent and secretive, and although he wrote openly about homoeroticism in his poetry, he hardly ever revealed any details about his own sexual life.

Few people of European origin lived in Egypt between the time of the Arab conquest in the seventh century AD and the early nineteenth century. During the nineteenth century, however, Alexandria became a cosmopolitan city whose citizens spoke various languages and practised different religions, even though it was treated by most of its European residents as a European trading colony on the shores of an alien continent. In 1882—the high point in the proportion of foreign residents—foreign nationals made up more than a fifth of the population of Alexandria. Greeks moved to Egypt in large numbers during the nineteenth century. Of the population of Alexandria in 1927, almost 50,000 originated from Greece or Cyprus, representing 8.5 per cent of the total but more than half of all the inhabitants of foreign origin.[1] The most successful Greeks in Alexandria were engaged in banking and the export of wheat, especially from the 1830s onwards, and later in the production and export of cotton. The Greek community had its own churches, schools, cemeteries, and social clubs.

In Cavafy's day, as in Hellenistic times, Egypt was at the centre of power-struggles: between the Ottoman Empire and the British Empire in Cavafy's day and between Greece and Rome in ancient times. For most of Cavafy's life (at least from 1882 onwards) Britain exerted a high degree of economic and political control over Egypt, which was ruled by members of a non-native dynasty descended from Muhammad Ali (ruled 1805–48), who was of Albanian origin but was born—like Alexander the Great—in Macedonia. It was not difficult for people living in Egypt at the time to see the situation of these rulers as being similar to that of the Greek kings who ruled Egypt under Roman supervision.

The English novelist E. M. Forster, who was stationed in Alexandria during the First World War, wrote that 'modern Alexandria is scarcely a city of the soul', and he went on to describe it as 'founded upon cotton with the concurrence of onions and eggs'.[2] Europeans settled in Alexandria primarily in order to make money, and there was little Greek cultural life there before Cavafy's time. For this reason, it is perhaps not surprising that it took the poet so long to realize that Alexandria, in both its ancient and its modern phases, had the potential to become the most appropriate symbolic embodiment of his outlook on life; the earliest of the poems explicitly set in Alexandria that he later allowed to enter his 'canon' of approved poems is 'The god forsakes Antony', which dates from 1911, when he was already 48 years old.

As a poet, Cavafy went through a long process of maturation; he is often called a 'poet of old age'. Once he had reached maturity, he abandoned most of his earlier work. In the absence of major poets and major artistic movements in his immediate vicinity, he had to develop his poetic craft all on his own. Nevertheless, he read widely in the

[1] Robert Mabro, 'Alexandria 1860–1960: The Cosmopolitan Identity', in Anthony Hirst and Michael Silk (eds.), *Alexandria, Real and Imagined* (Aldershot: Ashgate, 2004), 248, 254, 256.

[2] E. M. Forster, 'The Poetry of C. P. Cavafy', in *Pharos and Pharillon* (Richmond: Hogarth Press, 1923), 75.

poetry of Victorian England and nineteenth-century France, as well as Greek literature of the Classical and Hellenistic periods.

Of the English Victorians, Robert Browning helped him to develop his technique of dramatic monologue, in which an entire poem is placed in the mouth of a fictional character living at a particular historical period. He learned valuable lessons from two French poetic movements, Parnassianism and Symbolism. Many Parnassian poems by poets such as Leconte de Lisle and José-Maria de Hérédia consist of antique scenes, and they often aspired to resemble sculptures. In a somewhat similar way, most of Cavafy's best poems achieve a 'sculptural' aesthetic autonomy and a distance from the situation depicted, and some actually include depictions of sculptures and sculptors. Symbolist poetry (particularly that of Charles Baudelaire and Paul Verlaine), which aspired to the state of music rather than sculpture, helped Cavafy to make use of suggestive symbols, to express vague, fleeting impressions and feelings, and to exploit the evocative musical resources of language.

Cavafy was also influenced by the Decadent and Aesthetic movements in nineteenth-century France and England.[3] From these he developed the view that experience is primarily an aesthetic matter, that art is the antithesis of nature, and that the senses need to be refined and new sensations pursued. Cavafy's presentation of exquisitely beautiful works of art, including jewels and fabrics as well as sculptures and paintings, was influenced by the Aesthetic movement, which subscribed to a belief in 'art for art's sake', in other words, the doctrine that art serves no social, spiritual, or moral purpose. It is symptomatic of Cavafy's adherence to Aestheticism that he never actually published a book of poetry, in the sense of one that is offered for sale; instead, he printed his poems singly and in collections, which he gave or sent free of charge to select individuals whom he considered capable of appreciating his work.

His chief influence from ancient Greek literature was the epigram. The earliest Greek epigrams were actually epitaphs, that is, they were composed to be inscribed on tombs; this type of epigram is recalled in the poems Cavafy wrote in the guise of epitaphs for fictional ancient Alexandrians. The most famous epigrammatist was Callimachus, who worked in Alexandria during the third century BC. The epigrams

[3] For an account of Cavafy's debt to the Decadent movement see Christopher Robinson, *C. P. Cavafy* (Bristol: Bristol Classical Press, 1988), 2–9.

of Callimachus and other Hellenistic poets helped Cavafy develop his characteristically brief, laconic poems, sometimes with an unexpected twist at the end.[4]

E. M. Forster painted a vivid picture of Cavafy in the street as 'a Greek gentleman in a straw hat, standing absolutely motionless at a slight angle to the universe'.[5] That this phrase has become a cliché does not alter the fact that it is one of the most perceptive comments ever made on Cavafy's view of the world, and it can be a useful key for exploring his poetic universe.

Critics have remarked on Cavafy's eccentric perspective, his unique angle on history and geography, sexuality and language. His geographical distance from Greece allowed him to stand aloof from the Greek poetic fashions of his time, which included the worship of Classical Greek antiquity, Greek nature, folk culture, and the language of the rural population. As a Greek living outside Greece but in a region once dominated by Greek culture, his view of Hellenism is at once more distant and more inclusive.

Cavafy writes about geographical, historical, and human peripheries.[6] The Greeks who people those of his poems that are set in ancient times are both geographically and historically situated outside Classical Greece: they live beyond its geographical limits and after the Golden Age of Classical Athens in the fifth and fourth centuries BC. The Egyptian and Syrian Greeks in a poem that remained unpublished at his death, characteristically entitled 'Return from Greece', look upon Greece itself—supposedly the origin of their language and the basis of their high culture—as a foreign country.

All this is typical of Cavafy's decentring viewpoint. In his poetry, he often adopts a betwixt-and-between position, encapsulated in the phrase 'In part . . . in part . . .' ('Perilous things'). Many of his characters are betwixt and between in their ethnic, religious, and sexual identities, while he himself was betwixt and between in his use of language, metre, and rhyme. Even his own name, Konstantinos Kavafis, is a combination of the Latin Constantinus (the founder of the city of Constantinople and of what later came to be known as the

[4] See Valerie A. Caires, 'Originality and Eroticism: Constantine Cavafy and the Alexandrian Epigram', *Byzantine and Modern Greek Studies*, 6 (1980), 131–56.

[5] Forster, 'The Poetry of C. P. Cavafy', 75.

[6] Willis Barnstone, 'Real and Imaginary History in Borges and Cavafy', *Comparative Literature*, 29 (1977), 54–6.

Byzantine Empire) and the Arabic-Turkish word *kavaf*, meaning 'dealer in cheap shoes'. Many of his characters have multiple and shifting identities, combining Greek with African or Asian blood, temperament, and behaviour, and in some cases combining different religions. Yet the result of this is usually a harmonious fusion of races, religions, and cultures rather than conflict. This is one of the aspects of Cavafy's poetry that make it seem more and more modern as the years go by.

In most of Cavafy's poems the speaker cannot be identified with the poet himself. These poems do not seem to present the poet's own experiences, thoughts, and feelings; they are like fictions that create, explore, and experiment with alternative and parallel lives. In Cavafy's poetic oeuvre there are no fewer than 251 named characters, 130 of them historical, sixty-four mythological, and fifty-seven fictional, in addition to a large number of anonymous figures.[7]

Cavafy's poetic oeuvre

The poet himself wrote in 1927: 'Cavafy . . . has three areas—the philosophical (or the area of thought), the historical, and the hedonic (or sensual).'[8] In each of his poems one or more of these thematic areas is dominant.

Cavafy tacitly divided the first half of his poetic oeuvre into philosophical, historical, and sensual poems, with the hedonic as a subcategory of the sensual. For instance, he classified 'As best you can' as philosophical, 'King Demetrius' as historical, and 'Painted' as sensual. He made no distinction between poems with historical and mythical themes; he classified all these as historical. Within each group of 'historical' poems, the poems are arranged in chronological order of the periods in which they are set.

In the 154 poems of Cavafy's canon there is no properly historical (as opposed to mythical and philosophical) poem dating from before 1906 ('King Demetrius'). Conversely, the philosophical category

[7] Kyriakos Delopoulos, *Historika kai alla prosopa sten poiese tou Kavafe* (Athens, 1972). Delopoulos confined his survey to the 154 poems of Cavafy's 'canon' and the so-called 'unpublished poems'.

[8] *Alexandrine Techne*, 1.6 (May 1927), 39–40; later in the same volume (p. 210), the word 'area' is interpreted as 'category of themes'. 'Hedonic' means voluptuous, pertaining to sensual pleasure.

gradually disappeared as his work progressed, and after 1915 we find no more allegorical uses of history and mythology.[9]

Yet, as might be expected from Cavafy's 'betwixt-and-between' outlook, there are many crossovers between the three thematic areas. For instance, he classified didactic poems such as 'Waiting for the barbarians' as philosophical, despite their antique dress, since they are intended to be read as conveying a message of universal significance. The same is true of the didactic poems dating from up to 1911 ('The Ides of March', 'The god forsakes Antony', 'Ithaca', 'Trojans'); all of these are metaphorical and allegorical non-narrative poems in the present tense which generalize on some incident from history or mythology. Similarly, Cavafy classified 'Perception' as a philosophical poem rather than a sensual one, despite its obvious sensual content.

In later philosophical-sensual poems such as 'Come back', 'Body, remember', and 'When they are roused', Cavafy uses the second-person singular and the imperative mood that he had previously used in the philosophical-historical poems he published in 1911. The sensual category includes 'In church', in which, ironically, despite the speaker's statement of Christian and national piety, he focuses exclusively on the sensual aspects of the Orthodox liturgy: the visual spectacle, the harmonious sounds, and the 'fragrances of incense'. Although the poems whose themes are taken from late Byzantine history have no overt erotic content, many of the other historical poems contain some sensual element, albeit merely in the form of a handsome youth. But all of the historical poems share with the sensual a sense of the loss of the past, whether national or personal, and the attempt to revive it: in both cases, the poet tries to capture the fleeting moment.

Some of the poems dating from before 1905 (especially those inspired by Homer's *Iliad*) are infused with tragic pessimism, fatalism, and defeatism, and are obsessed with the relationship between men and gods. Human beings are doomed to defeat. Gods break their own promises to mortals ('Perfidy'), and even they are sometimes powerless to alter destiny ('The funeral of Sarpedon'). Such poems depict the omnipotence of an unjust fate and the transitory nature of beauty and happiness. In the historical poems of Cavafy's later

[9] For details of the division into the three thematic areas see Anthony Hirst, 'Philosophical, Historical and Sensual: An Examination of Cavafy's Thematic Collections', *Byzantine and Modern Greek Studies*, 19 (1995), 33–93.

oeuvre, however, the gods are replaced by history as a force against which we are powerless, but of which we have a moral duty to be aware. The sentimental fatalism of the early poems is superseded in later poems by stoicism: some characters are depicted bearing adversity with dignity and fortitude and courageously refusing to harbour comforting illusions. Whereas the poetic voice in some of the early poems appears to believe in the gods, it is only historical and fictional characters that entertain such beliefs in the later poems.

The apparently direct expression of an outlook by the poet himself in 'Walls' and 'Windows' is superseded in 'The city' by a dialogue between two conflicting attitudes. This in turn gives way to the embodiment of attitudes in a specific, objectively presented situation in the later poem 'If only they had seen to it', where the character who speaks is placed at a historical and ironic distance from the poet and the reader. It is characteristic of the differences between Cavafy's earlier and later poetry that in 'Walls', 'Windows', and 'The city' the central symbol is specified from the outset in the title, whereas the title of 'If only they had seen to it' is a quotation from near the end of the poem and is incomprehensible until we have read the whole text (and this title is practically impossible to translate into any other language).

Despite the differences between the philosophical, historical, and sensual areas, and between the earlier and later poems, there are characteristics that immediately strike the reader as being typically Cavafian: a distinctive tone of voice, a combination of irony and sensuality, and an attempt to deal with loss through the reanimation of the past.

Art, memory, and time

The settings of Cavafy's poems are, like those of Baudelaire's, enclosed spaces and city streets. Cavafy's poetry is anti-Romantic: nature and the countryside are hardly mentioned. In the poem 'In the evening' the speaker finds respite from nostalgia by going out onto his balcony and looking at the 'beloved city' with its bustling streets and shops. In 'Morning sea' the speaker's fantasies, his memories, and his visions of sensual bliss prevent him from fixing his gaze on a natural scene.

In place of nature, Cavafy's poetry promotes art and artifice. In 'Of the shop' artificial flowers, beautiful as the artist-character has willed them—as he *sees* them in his mind's eye—are promoted above the real flowers that he *has happened to see* in nature. In 'So long I gazed—' the speaker's vision is full of the beauty that he has gazed upon. These poems set up a complex relationship between seeing and visualizing, between gazing and musing—a relationship that oscillates between collaboration and conflict. In 'So long I gazed—' the speaker's gaze enhances, idealizes, and makes whole and permanent the fragmentary beauty that he briefly glimpses. In the same poem art is even presented as a model for the perception of the real.

In many of the poems with a modern setting, physical beauty or erotic experience is viewed by the speaker through the mediation of memory. Five of Cavafy's poems have titles consisting of the formula 'Days of . . .' plus a year or years; in each case there is a gap of at least fourteen years between the year specified in the title and the date of the poem's composition. Thus sensual experience is decentred by being refracted through the prism of memory rather than being viewed directly. In 'Craftsman of craters' the figure of the beloved youth engraved inside the silver wine-mixing bowl is created through memory—the 'leg immersed | knee-deep in the water' symbolizing the position of the dead beloved, partly in and partly outside reality—while the whole composition being created by the fictional artist is intended to be viewed through liquid.

Memory is deliberately summoned up in poems such as 'Come back', 'Body, remember' (both of which talk about bodily memories), and 'One night' (where the poet, through the process of writing, re-experiences an erotic thrill from the past). By contrast, in another group of poems memory is involuntarily triggered by a chance encounter with an object or a person, as in the work of Marcel Proust, where the chance repetition of a set of sense impressions reawakens in a person's mind and body a whole world of past experience. Examples of this in Cavafy's poetry include 'Grey' and 'Outside the house'; in the second of these the erotic thrill is reawakened in the speaker as he happens to pass a house where the relevant experience had taken place.

Sometimes an erotic encounter or simply a glimpse of a beautiful body is so vivid that it is like an epiphany of the sort evoked by James Joyce: an experience that seems to transcend time and provide a glimpse of eternity within the physical world. In 'Their origin' the memory of a sexual encounter is able to cross time and become the starting-point for a poem. In 'Days of 1908' the sight of a young man's naked body is described as a 'miracle'. Despite the sensuality that pervades Cavafy's poetry, there is a definite Platonic dimension to his vision of ideal beauty, as can be seen in the phrase 'an Apollonian vision' ('Tomb of Eurion'), and in the reference to 'Plato's Charmides' ('A town in Osroene'). The Platonic ideal can be related to dreams, since dreams may sometimes contain images that express or symbolize our ideals. Individual experiences, then, combined in memory, become timeless, because they are fitted to an ideal pattern, which then comes to be seen as having pre-existed. This sense, not merely of the recuperation of the individual past, but of the attainment of the timeless ideal Platonic Form, leads to a sense of the transfiguration of one's individual experiences and the redemption of one's past, of one's whole existence, and ultimately of the whole of past time. It is no coincidence that transfiguration and redemption are Christian concepts; the transcendence of time through eros, memory, and art in Cavafy's poetry can be interpreted as an attempt to compensate for the loss of religion.

Art and homosexuality

Cavafy was one of the earliest writers to deal openly with homosexual love. In the poems that he published before 1919, there is no unequivocal reference to the gender of the loved one, but from that year onwards ('On the ship') he began to produce poems in which a first-person speaker who is not obviously fictional speaks about a male beloved.

The vast majority of the characters depicted in Cavafy's poetry are male; he seldom depicts female characters except as the mothers of sons. The poems set in ancient times depict both homosexual and heterosexual characters. Those set in Byzantium present only one character who is clearly homosexual, while all the characters in the poems set in modern times may be seen as homosexual.

In the five 'epitaphs' written for fictional young men in ancient Alexandria, Cavafy presents youths who have been greatly loved and admired by their contemporaries for their beauty or for their learning, or for both. Their death provides the occasion for the poet to juxtapose love and death and to contrast their transitory living presence with the enduring character of their writing. The homosexual characters in the historical poems never suffer because of their sexual orientation.

By contrast, many of the poems with a modern setting depict young, anonymous, working-class men who are socially stigmatized and economically marginalized because of their sexuality.

Cavafy seems to have believed that one is born, rather than made, a homosexual:[10] in 'Days of 1896' the poet characterizes homosexuality as 'a sexual inclination . . . strongly forbidden, and much despised (nevertheless innate)'. In his poetry homosexual love is often described with the kind of vocabulary used by the society in which he lived: 'aberrant pleasure' ('A young man of letters . . .'), 'a love that's barren and deprecated' ('Theatre of Sidon (A.D. 400)')—the opposite of 'healthful love' ('In an old book'). Yet Cavafy wrote in a private note in 1902 that 'perversion' is 'the source of greatness'.[11]

A poem entitled 'December 1903', addressed to a young man he had recently met in Athens, but not published during the poet's lifetime, ends with these lines: 'the days of September that rise in my dreams | give shape and colour to my words and phrases, | whatever theme I touch, whatever thought I utter.' This has been interpreted as suggesting that 'homosexual desire finally manages to mold and color all words and phrases, to permeate every theme and thought' of his poetry[12]—including even poems that have no apparent sensuous content. In other words, Cavafy sees his particular artistic sensibility as having been created by homoerotic desire.

Cavafy's poetic inspiration, then, is inextricably bound up with eroticism and erotic memory. In fact, his poetry identifies the aesthetic response to beauty with the erotic response to it, whether this beauty is an attribute of a human body or of a work of art. Eros belongs to the realm of art, not to the realm of nature. Eros is nourished by transient beauty, while art makes beauty permanent. The very act of writing is presented as an erotic experience ('One night'). Art depends on the experience of abandonment to the senses ('Perception'). There is also a sense that erotic experiences were destined to form the basis of poetry, even though only Art was aware of this at the time ('Their origin'). Cavafy's later poetry implies that Techne (Art) and Eros are benevolent deities, providentially controlling the destiny of those they have selected as being worthy of their patronage ('I brought

[10] K. P. Kavaphes, *Anekdota semeiomata poietikes kai ethikes*, ed. G. P. Savvides (Athens: Hermes, 1983), 36.

[11] Ibid. 29.

[12] Dimitris Papanikolaou, '"Words that Tell and Hide": revisiting C. P. Cavafy's Closets', *Journal of Modern Greek Studies*, 23 (2005), 242.

to Art'). This is in contrast to the early poems, in which the gods are indifferent to human fate. In the poem 'At the entrance of the café' Eros is said to be an artist who has fashioned a youthful body of consummate beauty. Other benevolent deities play a role too: 'Passage' presents a personification (or apotheosis) of *hedone* (sensuality) and *methe* (intoxication), which are depicted as agents acting upon the body of a young man who is carried away by sensuality and whose life intersects with art in the erotic act; he has become worthy of the artist's interest because of his abandonment to his sexual desires. Even Tyche (Chance) is presented as an artist in 'Before they are changed by time', where a pair of lovers are forced by economic necessity to separate, thus ensuring that each one remains forever in the memory of the other just as he was at the peak of his beauty.

For Cavafy, art has the power to complete what is incomplete in life: brief glimpses and furtive (sometimes unconsummated) encounters are transformed through poetry into timeless, transcendent experiences. This is implied in 'I went' ('pleasures that were partly real, | partly swirling in my mind'), 'I have brought to art' ('some vague memories | of unfulfilled affairs'), and 'It has come to rest' ('half-opened clothes; | quick baring of the body'). Thus the process is circular, for the shaping of his 'poetic will' and the mapping of 'the territory of [his] art' depend on the 'sensuous life' of his youth ('Perception'), while in his maturity Art comes to complete the process that she herself had initiated.

In Cavafy's view, then, art is not an abstract concept, but an activity, a vital creative force. Art doesn't represent reality, or imitate life, or copy nature; instead, it imposes its will upon the art-object, removing it from the contingencies that dominate the natural and social worlds. Poems and other works of art, enshrining ideal beauty, correct the deficiencies of nature and society. Cavafy rebels against what he sees as the unholy alliance between nature and society: to be free is to contravene laws and conventions, whether these be natural or social, and this violation leads to a special kind of pleasure. Nevertheless, in Cavafy's poetry the relationship between the sensual realm of eros and art on the one hand and the social realm of conventional morality, economics, and commerce on the other is not a straightforward antithesis. In many of the poems set in modern times sensual and socio-economic forces are shown as interacting: in 'Days of 1909, '10 and '11' the young man prostitutes himself to earn the money to buy a shirt or tie that will make him into an attractive sexual partner; in 'Lovely flowers and white . . .' one of the reasons why a young man returns to his former lover is the lure of money; in 'A young man of Letters . . .' a character feels that the fact that he is poor and unemployed is one of the causes of his sense of sexual unfulfilment with his lover; while conversely, in 'Two young men, 23 to 24 years old' a chance win at cards feeds the lovers' erotic bliss.

In its ideal form, however, erotic—and especially homoerotic—experience is indissolubly linked by Cavafy to art, in that it likewise involves a relationship that is entered into on an equal and consensual basis, and it is thus exempt from historical, social, economic, and natural contingencies. For Cavafy, homoeroticism is—in a positive sense—'unnatural' in that it doesn't lead to biological reproduction, and 'antisocial' in that it doesn't lead to marriage; like art, it has no end outside itself. Thus eros and art are equally linked to creation rather than procreation.

The Egyptian historian Khaled Fahmy assumes that the modern objects of the Cavafian gaze, with their 'poetic eyes', 'pale face', and 'intoxicating lips', are 'Arab-speaking locals',[13] yet most Greek readers assume that these anonymous young men are Alexandrian Greeks. The fact is that, while most of the young men in the poems set in the historical past are given names and ethnic identities, the handsome youths depicted in the poems with a modern setting never speak and rarely move; they are certainly never named. In fact, they are seldom individualized through the description of specific features of either their bodies or their personalities.[14]

Cavafy frequently uses adjectives that idealize the young men he depicts: *idanikos* and *ideodes* (ideal), *teleios* (perfect), *aitherios* (ethereal), *exaisios* (exquisite), *horaios* (lovely), *poietikos* (poetic), *hedonikos* (made to give and take sensual pleasure), *erotikos* (made for eros). Indeed, Cavafy's young men are sometimes portrayed (as in 'Portrait of a 23-year-old man' and 'So long I gazed—') as though they were already an artistic representation: a statue or a painting that has transcended the specific features of its individual model and transfigured it into an ideal embodiment of aesthetic beauty and sexual desire.

[13] Khaled Fahmy, 'For Cavafy, with Love and Squalor', in Hirst and Silk, *Alexandria, Real and Imagined*, 273.

[14] As Evangelos Sachperoglou has pointed out to me, in 'The mirror in the entrance' the young man who is an amateur athlete on Sundays is likely to be a Greek, whereas the 'member of the household' in the same poem is likely to be an Egyptian servant.

Homoerotic code-words are frequently used in Cavafy's poetry. They are not intended to conceal, but rather to be understood by sensitive and sympathetic readers. Chief among them are the following (each accompanied by the title of one of the poems in which it appears): *aisthesis*, 'sense, sensation' ('Come back'); *aisthema*, 'feeling' ('At the entrance of the café'); *aisthetikos*, 'aesthetic and sensual' ('Orophernes'); *sympathetikos*, 'likeable' ('Caesarion'); *synkinesis*, 'emotion' (but here with connotations of an erotic thrill: 'Ithaca'); *eklektos*, 'select, special' ('In an old book—').

History

How much history are Cavafy's readers expected to know? Cavafy published his poems without historical notes or commentary, but explanatory notes have normally been provided by later editors, as is the case with the present edition. The chief periods in which Cavafy sets his historical poems are the Hellenistic (fourth to first centuries BC), the Roman (first century BC to fourth century AD), and the late Byzantine (eleventh to fourteenth centuries).

The Hellenistic period was dominated by Egypt and Syria, which were ruled by kings and queens descended from generals in Alexander the Great's Macedonian Greek army. These Greek kingdoms, together with the Greek mainland, gradually came under Roman control between 197 and 31 BC, when Egypt became fully incorporated into the Roman Empire. Cavafy also writes about the lesser kingdoms of Commagene, Cappadocia, and Judaea, whose rulers at the time were dominated by Greek culture.

For most people who study Ancient History, the Greek history they learn about ends with the death of Alexander the Great. As for the period from 250 BC onwards, we learn chiefly about Roman history, so the little we hear about the Greeks from then on is within the context and from the viewpoint of Roman culture. Cavafy redresses the balance by substituting the periphery for the centre and looking at the Roman world from a Greek perspective.

Cavafy's ancient world centres around the kingdoms that followed the decline of the Classical city states of Athens and Sparta. Hellenistic Egypt was ruled by a dynasty known as the Ptolemies (after the first king, Ptolemy I) or the Lagids (because Ptolemy I was the son of Lagus). Syria was ruled by the Seleucid dynasty, named after the first king, Seleucus I. Many of Cavafy's poems are set in Alexandria between the early years of the Hellenistic kingdom of Egypt in 300 BC and the Arab conquest of the country in the seventh century AD. Others are set in the Syrian cities of Antioch, Seleucia (now Antakya and Silifke in Turkey), and Beirut (the capital of modern Lebanon).

Cavafy had no feeling for the culture of pre-Ptolemaic Egypt, the Egypt of the Pharaohs. In fact, the Ptolemies, who ruled Egypt for almost 300 years, constituted the longest-ruling dynasty in the country's 5,000-year history. During the Ptolemaic period Alexandria was the largest city in the world and one of the greatest centres of art, scholarship, and science. In those of Cavafy's poems that are set in ancient Alexandria, the various characters from diverse ethnic and religious backgrounds are united by the Greek language and Greek culture. Some characters are Coptic Christians, while others are Jewish. Yet the peaceful coexistence of two polytheistic religions (Egyptian and Greek) allowed great freedom of choice to the inhabitants of Hellenistic Egypt. Some ancient tombs in Alexandria contain two sets of wall-paintings depicting death and rebirth, one Egyptian and the other Greek, each one featuring its own gods in the appropriate style.[15] This kind of religious syncretism is adopted by a number of characters in Cavafy's historical poems. By contrast, monotheism is shown to be divisive and to preclude such freedom of choice (see especially 'Myres: Alexandria, A.D. 340').

As for Byzantium, Cavafy was fascinated by the fourth-century emperor Julian the Apostate, who attempted to turn the clock back by returning from Christianity to a particularly intolerant version of paganism. Julian is the subject of no fewer than six of the 154 poems that make up Cavafy's canon, including his very last. The Apostate is viewed, from the perspective of the Christians of Antioch, as a pedantic, puritanical, and narrow-minded bigot.[16] Apart from Julian, Cavafy's poetic interest in Byzantium is confined to two periods of history: the flowering of the Comnenian dynasty in the late eleventh and early twelfth centuries, and the political decline of the empire under the Palaeologan dynasty in the fourteenth, which ended with the fall of Constantinople to the Ottoman Turks in 1453.

[15] Anne-Marie Guimier-Sorbets and Mervat Seif ed-Din, 'Life After Death: An Original Form of Bilingual Iconography in the Necropolis of Kawm al-Shuqafa', in Hirst and Silk, *Alexandria, Real and Imagined*, 133–41.

[16] For more on Cavafy's Julian poems see G. W. Bowersock, 'The Julian Poems of C. P. Cavafy', *Byzantine and Modern Greek Studies*, 7 (1981), 89–104.

Cavafy is reported to have said: 'I am a *poietes historikos* [historical poet or poet-historian]; I would never be able to write a novel or a play, but I feel 125 voices inside me telling me I could write history.'[17] Cavafy's phrase can be seen in the light of the following passage from Aristotle's *Poetics* (1551b): 'the essential difference [between the historian and the poet] is that the one tells us what happened and the other the sort of thing that would happen. That is why poetry is at once more like philosophy and more worth while than history, since poetry tends to make general statements, while those of history are particular.'[18] Indeed, in 'Wise men' Cavafy implies that the poet is a philosopher who looks at the human condition down the long avenue of history and learns lessons from it in order to be able to foresee imminent historical disasters. Yet, despite his denial of his ability to write drama or fiction, Cavafy presents his historical material partly in dramatic mode, with the use of monologues, dialogues, and dramatic irony, and sometimes employing narrative techniques appropriate to fiction, through which he records his characters' thoughts, emotions, and sense-impressions.

'Caesarion' shows how even reading dry historical sources can arouse the sensual memory. Cavafy draws 'archaeological' inspiration from ancient objects such as inscriptions, literary works (especially Homer in his early poems), and other ancient primary sources. Inspiration from ancient coins—the meeting-point of history, art, and commerce—can be found in 'Philhellene' and 'Orophernes'. Cavafy also draws on the writings of historians, both ancient—particularly Plutarch, with his *Parallel Lives* of Greek and Roman heroes—and modern.

Cavafy's historical poems focus both on the attitudes of real and fictional individuals bound up in the historical process, and on the attitudes of people outside historical events (including not only historians but also the poet and his readers) towards these events. In 'Orophernes' and 'Caesarion' Cavafy presents a contrast between

[17] G. Lechonites, *Kavaphika autoscholia* (Athens: Denise Harvey, 1977), 19–20. The poet George Seferis made the following helpful comment on this quotation: 'Like everything said on the spur of the moment, this is rather lacking in clarity. Nevertheless, I don't think *poietes historikos* means a poet who also writes history or who versifies history; if the word "poet" has any meaning at all, it means someone who possesses a historic sense' (G. Sepheres, *Dokimes* (Athens: Ikaros, 1974), i. 340).

[18] D. A. Russell and M. Winterbottom (eds.), *Classical Literary Criticism* (Oxford: Oxford University Press, 1989), 62.

what historians have written about these historical figures and what is more precious, namely their living image. Orophernes' death 'was recorded somewhere and then lost; | or perhaps history passed it by | and—with good reason—a thing as trivial as that . . .', while the figure of Caesarion is evoked by 'a small insignificant mention' in a historical work. Here the poet shows his emotional and sensual participation with characters ignored or marginalized by history; in both cases Cavafy uses the adjective *asemantos* (trivial, insignificant). In this way the 'poet-historian' subverts the work of the historian in order to see, by means of sensual intuition, something different in it, something personal, individual, and subjective, and to present an alternative view to the prevailing one. In the Aristotelian rivalry between poetry and history, poetry is victorious, as in 'Darius', where the fictional poet Phernazes mobilizes history—both the history of the Persian king Darius and that of his own time—in the service of poetry, rather than vice versa.[19] Far from putting history into poetry by rewriting it as verse, Cavafy puts poetry into history.

In his mature poetry Cavafy looks at the human predicament with the detachment of the historian who takes a long-term view. Cavafy is aware of the multiple causes and effects at work in the historical process. He is fascinated not only by the fortunes of individuals but also by the fate of whole dynasties and whole nations, especially the Greeks as they gradually lose their independence to Rome. The beginnings of the Roman conquest are referred to obliquely in 'In 200 B.C.', 'In a large Greek colony', 'The Battle of Magnesia', and even 'Craftsman of craters', while the impact of the Battle of Actium (31 BC) is reflected obliquely in various other poems, such as 'The god forsakes Antony', 'Alexandrian kings', 'In a township of Asia Minor', 'Caesarion', and 'In Alexandria, 31 B.C.'.

In the poems set in Hellenistic and Roman times Cavafy deals with a period of Greek history when Greece itself was no longer at the centre of world culture and politics. Attica became culturally subordinated to Egypt and Syria, and eventually all of these became politically subjugated to Rome. Cavafy's historical characters are mainland Greeks, diaspora Greeks, and non-Greeks that Keeley calls 'pretenders to Hellenism' ('Philhellene', 'The potentate from

[19] Katerina Karatasou, '"Pos douleuei to myalo tou Phernaze"', in M. Pieres (ed.), *He poiese tou kramatos* (Herakleio: Panepistemiakes Ekdoseis Kretes, 2000), 264.

Western Libya').[20] The old centre is viewed from the former periphery, while the old periphery is viewed from even more peripheral areas: the Athenian orator Herod Atticus is viewed from the standpoint of Syrian Greeks, while the non-Greek 'Philhellene' has sophists and versifiers (not philosophers and poets!) from Syria bringing him Greek culture.

Cavafy tends not to look directly at the great events themselves or at the powerful historical characters who played a central part in them, but to show the impact of these events on the consciousness of less famous or else totally fictitious characters. This is another aspect of his eccentric perspective: historical events are refracted through the thoughts and emotions of individuals. Thus Antony and Octavian—at the centre of the power-struggle for the control of the Roman Empire—are viewed merely as interchangeable names in the poem 'In a township of Asia Minor'. In 'On an Italian shore' the sack of the Greek city of Corinth by the Romans in 146 BC is seen from the viewpoint of a hedonistic young man in Sicily as he watches the spoils being unloaded. In some poems ('Darius' and 'Demaratus') Cavafy depicts a character in later—but still ancient—times writing about a 'Classical' one.

By adopting an individual character's restricted and biased view of an event or situation, Cavafy provides relative perspectives on history: partial views, in both senses of the word 'partial'. These are subjective rather than objective perspectives on history—though the perspectives are not the poet's own. History is viewed not with hindsight but as experienced at the time by an individual subjectivity.

Yet, like any work of art, Cavafy's poetry cannot be isolated from the period of history in which it was written. Although he never made any explicit connections between the past historical periods about which he wrote and the period in which he lived, Cavafy's interest in and sympathy with the historical fortunes of Hellenism (in the sense of the Greeks in general, rather than merely the Greek state and its citizens) led him to keep abreast with the contemporary historical fate of the Greeks, especially during the First World War and the subsequent conflict between Greece and Turkey, which resulted in the victory of Turkey in 1922 and the obligatory transfer of up to one-and-a-half million Orthodox Christians from Turkey to Greece.

[20] Edmund Keeley, *Cavafy's Alexandria* (new edn., Princeton: Princeton University Press, 1996), 174.

Like the 'Wise men' in the poem of that title, Cavafy was able to hear 'the secret sound | of approaching events'.

Irony

In Cavafy's poetry even the ironic is sensual—perhaps because it is based on uncertainty and an openness to different possibilities. Cavafian irony emerges from a discrepancy between different degrees of knowledge: in the early 'Interruption' and the later 'Envoys from Alexandria' the ironies are pointed out quite unambiguously, yet in most of the later poems irony and ambiguity go hand-in-hand. In some poems a character is deprived of choice ('Interruption'), while in others the protagonist refuses to weigh up the options available to him ('Nero's term'). The irony of fate (or the disparity between a belief or attitude and the 'truth'), which is frequently presented in his early poetry, later gives way to a disparity between attitudes (of the same or different characters).

The character who speaks in the poem is often situated at the time of the action in the past, and his limited perspective contrasts with the omniscience brought to the poet-historian by hindsight. Yet there is a difference between historical and fictional characters: we cannot be sure what to think about the latter because we don't know their ultimate fate, and for this reason we have to withhold judgement.

For instance, 'From the school of the renowned philosopher' presents a cynical fictional character who successively takes up and then abandons philosophy, politics, and the Church—then decides to give himself over to debauchery, at which he's far more successful. Meanwhile he is encouraged by the thought that when, after ten years or so, he ceases to be a sought-after sexual partner, he will be able to return to philosophy or politics and gain respectability by doing his duty to his country. Now it is obvious that Cavafy isn't taking this character's side. But we can't be sure whether the irony lies in this man's *belief* in his ability to return to philosophy after his complete abandonment to sensual enjoyment, or in his cynical *aspiration* to return to philosophy and politics only after he has exhausted his potential for pleasure.

The characters that are clearly ironized are those who act in blithe and wilful ignorance of what fate might have in store for them. As Edmund Keeley has pointed out, the lack of 'a proper degree of self-awareness [is] the least forgivable sin in Cavafy's mythical world'.[21] This is what Nero is guilty of in 'Nero's term' and (comically) the Delphic priests in 'Envoys from Alexandria'. These are people who refuse to investigate what the likely outcome of their actions and situations may be, thereby depriving themselves of the freedom and the power to choose. Yet readers are not exempt from this ironic play: Cavafy makes us realize that we ourselves are in the same position as these characters, since we cannot know what the future holds for us.

One of the most complex examples of verbal and situational irony in Cavafy's poetry is 'Kimon, son of Learchos...' The closing line of the poem-within-the-poem, placed in the mouth of the dead Marylos ('I ended my days well amid undivided affection') is a statement based on the fictional epitaph-writer's incomplete knowledge of the situation, whereas Marylos' cousin knows very well that Marylos had 'stolen' Hermoteles from him.

The most truly tragic irony is to be found in 'Myres: Alexandria, A.D. 340', Cavafy's longest and perhaps most compassionate and moving poem. As he sees his beloved Myres being removed from him and appropriated by Christianity in death, the pagan narrator becomes aware for the first time of the discrepancy between the actions and the thoughts of his lover, and comes to suspect that Myres has always been alien to him. The inner gulf that separates people of different religions ultimately suggests, perhaps, that each of us is barred from total communication with the inner life of even our closest friends and lovers.

Language and style

Two rival Greek literary languages had developed in the nineteenth century, namely *katharevousa* (a hybrid of ancient and modern Greek vocabulary and grammar) and demotic (a standardized version of the modern spoken language). Cavafy exploited the full resources of the Greek language, from its most formal and archaic to its most colloquial registers, thus mixing the two versions of modern Greek that almost all other Greek poets kept apart. His use of a mixed language enabled him to incorporate passages from ancient and medieval texts, both in titles and in the poems themselves.

[21] Keeley, *Cavafy's Alexandria*, 106.

The central figures of some of Cavafy's poems are painters and sculptors, and his oeuvre depicts a number of works of visual art. The visual nature of much of its content is probably behind the oft-repeated claim that his poetry is itself predominantly visual rather than oral. It has been rightly said that 'In the month of Athyr' is 'a poem that can't be read aloud'[22]—yet this is the exception that proves the rule. By contrast, the typographical layout (spacing and indentation) of 'Waiting for the barbarians', together with the different verse-forms used by the two speaking voices in this poem, can be considered as conveying indications concerning oral delivery.

Cavafy's diction is more sensuous than most critics have made out, and insufficient emphasis has been placed on the oral aspects of Cavafy's poetry.[23] We often hear voices in Cavafy's poems, either the poet's own or that of some historical or fictional character. One significant indicator of orality is Cavafy's use of the exclamation 'Ah!' (represented in Greek by the single letter 'A!'), which appears in no fewer than fifteen poems. This 'Ah' is combined with suspension points [. . .] in 'Far away', where the poetic voice is struggling to recall an erotic memory from the past. These suspension points, like rests in musical notation, are visual signs of an audible pause, pregnant with unstated meaning.

Cavafy pays particular attention to the musicality, rhythm, melody, and harmony of his poems. At times he plays elaborate games with the sounds of the words. Even in a poem that is as much about vision as 'So long I gazed—', the central word is the adjective *achtenista* (unkempt), which chimes with the verb of the title, *atenisa* (I gazed). This chiming, in which all the sounds of the verb are contained within the adjective, and in the same order, is part of the sensual structure of the poem and is a key to understanding the complex relationship between sound, vision, and sense in Cavafy's poetry.

Cavafy developed a kind of loose iambic verse, corresponding to the so-called 'liberated' Alexandrine line in French. Every verse of the poems in his canon can be scanned as iambic (that is, crudely put, ti-TUM-ti-TUM-ti-TUM-ti-TUM, etc.), but he varies the lengths of the lines within a poem, and he allows himself to follow the versification conventions of both *katharevousa* and demotic when he deals with

[22] David Ricks, 'Cavafy's Alexandrianism', in Hirst and Silk, *Alexandria, Real and Imagined*, 347.

[23] A notable exception is the section entitled 'Poetic Technique' in Robinson, *C. P. Cavafy*, 31–63.

two vowels that follow one after the other. *Katharevousa* conventions treat every vowel sound as forming a separate syllable, while the demotic conventions, inherited from the Greek folk songs, normally count two adjacent vowel sounds belonging to two consecutive words as forming a single syllable.

Some of Cavafy's poems are elaborately rhymed (e.g. 'Before the statue of Endymion'), while most of them do not employ rhyme at all. When rhyme is present, it tends to be used unconventionally. For instance, 'Caesarion' uses rhyme in the first ten lines, which convey a rather prosaic message, while the last sixteen lines, which are more lyrical, dispense with rhyme altogether. In 'On an Italian shore' the rhyme is apparently rather random, yet the insistent repetition of the two-syllable sequence *lían*—at the end of *paralían* 'shore' in the title, at the end of the first half-line of l. 5 (a word meaning 'very'), then *paralían* again, then *melancholían* 'melancholy'—eventually leads up to *lían* in l. 8 (here meaning 'booty, loot'), which is repeated in the following line. This system of rhymes, which manages to be both sensual and ironic at the same time, contributes to the rich and complex phonic texture of this poem.

'On an Italian shore' is one of a type of poem that Cavafy wrote from 1917 onwards, in which every typographical line consists of two metrical lines separated from each other by a space. All of these poems have a significant sensual content. They are among the most tightly structured of Cavafy's poems: each metrical line contains either six or seven syllables. (The English translations of the poems in paired lines reproduce the metre of the original as faithfully as possible.) The inspiration for this unusual verse-form may have originated in a set of Byzantine religious hymns composed in the late ninth century in pairs of seven-syllable lines and written with a gap between them. Cavafy's practice here represents a daring combination of erotic content and ecclesiastical verse-form.

The historical poems tend to be narrative or dramatic, while most of the sensual poems are lyrical, and there are concomitant differences in style and diction. But even the philosophical poems may be lyrical ('The god forsakes Antony') or dramatic ('Waiting for the barbarians') in form. Most of his poems after 1920 are either narratives (short stories) or dramatic monologues.[24] In his narrative poems Cavafy

[24] Katerina Karatasou, 'O "Demaratos" tou Kavaphe', *Mikrophilologika*, 2 (Autumn 1997), 26–7.

makes use of a variety of narrative techniques. Sometimes he uses an omniscient narrator (as in 'Before they are changed by time') who knows more about the characters' situation than they do themselves, whereas in other poems he employs the technique of restricted point of view, as developed and promoted by the American novelist Henry James. In a number of poems Cavafy employs free indirect discourse, a technique perfected by the French novelists Gustave Flaubert and Émile Zola, and consisting of the narration of a scene from the viewpoint of a character, using that character's supposed words or thoughts but presenting them in the third person. As well as spoken monologue ('Sculptor of Tyana') he also uses interior monologue (that is, the supposedly unmediated transcription of a character's thoughts) as used by James Joyce in his novel *Ulysses* (1922).

The poem 'Darius' is a particularly sophisticated example of Cavafy's narrative technique. It is a short story consisting of a single brief scene of crisis, in which Cavafy orchestrates a complex combination of straightforward narrative—albeit with the use of a present tense that suggests a running commentary ('But he is interrupted by his servant')—free indirect discourse ('Just as he felt certain that with his "Darius" . . .'), interior monologue ('Are we a match for them, we Cappadocians?'), and direct speech (the servant's words, 'The bulk of our army has crossed the border').

Afterlife

Cavafy's poetic canon was first collected in a single volume published in 1935, two years after his death. It seems remarkable today that his poems went through only four Greek editions before the centenary of his birth in 1963, which saw the publication of G. P. Savidis's standard edition. From then on his popularity and reputation among Greeks were assured.

Cavafy's personality and poetic work were first brought to the attention of the English-speaking world by E. M. Forster in his book about Alexandria, *Pharos and Pharillon*, published in 1923, which contains an essay on Cavafy and some of the earliest English translations of his poetry. The first complete translation of the Cavafy canon, by John Mavrogordato, appeared in 1951, and it was followed in the next few years by the translation by Rae Dalven (1961) and that by Edmund Keeley and Philip Sherrard (1975).

Cavafy's reputation in the English-speaking world has been immense, and the impact of his personality and poetry can be traced in the work of a large number of British and American writers and artists. This impact is most obvious in Lawrence Durrell's set of four novels entitled *The Alexandria Quartet* (1957–60), where the memory of Cavafy still haunts Alexandria as 'the old poet of the city'. Other British and American writers and artists who have been clearly influenced by Cavafy include W. H. Auden, Stephen Spender, James Merrill, David Hockney, D. J. Enright, Christopher Middleton, Peter Porter, Roy Fuller, Paul Muldoon, Rachel Hadas, and Duane Michaels. Cavafy is the only modern Greek writer whose complete poems have been published in more than one English translation, and the only one to have provided the English language with quotations, the most famous of these being used for the title of J. M. Coetzee's novel *Waiting for the Barbarians* (1980).[25]

Cavafy's poetry implicitly poses searching questions concerning national, cultural, ethnic, religious, and sexual identity, free will, the sources of artistic creativity and its personal and social functions. Because his poetic oeuvre is suffused with irony, it is open to multiple (and sometimes contradictory) interpretations. Various interest-groups, such as gays, socialists, and Greek nationalists, have attempted to appropriate it for themselves, arguing that a single aspect of Cavafy's life and personality is the most basic to the interpretation of his poetry. Other critics have objected to this kind of appropriation. When all is said and done, while it is certain that Cavafy was a homosexual, it is by no means certain that he was a socialist or a nationalist.

It is to a large extent because of the ambivalence of his poetry—its constant openness to different readings—that his reputation is now firmly established, both in Greece and abroad, as one of the world's leading poets.

Peter Mackridge

[25] An anthology of poems written by non-Greek poets and inspired by Cavafy contains 153 poems by 135 poets from 30 countries: N. Vagenas (ed.), *Synomilontas me ton Kavaphe* (Salonica: Kentro Hellenikes Glossas, 2000).

NOTE ON THE GREEK TEXT

Cavafy's self-published collections

Cavafy was his own publisher, and the 154 poems in this volume of *The Collected Poems* are 'collected' in the very specific sense that Cavafy himself included all but two of them in one or more of the many privately printed collections which he distributed between 1905 and his death in 1933; and the other two poems, the very earliest and very latest of the 154 poems in this volume, 'Walls' (1897) and 'In the outskirts of Antioch' (1933), may be regarded (as explained below) as collected by implication.

Cavafy's first self-published collection was *Poems 1904*, printed early in 1905. It contained fourteen poems arranged thematically. In 1910 there followed an augmented version, known as *Poems 1910*, with seven additional poems. The twenty-one poems of this latter collection were all first published (mainly in periodicals) in the period 1897–1909. In 1912 Cavafy began to circulate, alongside *Poems 1910*, his post-1909 poems arranged chronologically by date of first publication (*Poems 1910–1912*; the end date changing annually as new poems were added). In 1918 he put together a new thematic collection, *Poems (1909–1911)*,[1] containing the 1909 poems from *Poems 1910* and all the poems first published in 1910 and 1911. *Poems (1909–1911)* was progressively enlarged by the addition of earlier and later poems, becoming, finally, in 1930, *Poems (1905–1915)*. This series of thematic collections had now absorbed all the post-1904 poems of *Poems 1910*, with one apparent exception, 'The funeral of Sarpedon'. A radically revised form of this poem had been published in 1908, but Cavafy, it seems, continued to regard it as a poem of 1898 (the year the original version was first published). In 1929 a separate thematic collection, *Poems (1916–1918)*, was put into circulation, leaving only the post-1918 poems in the current chronological collection.

In the last months of his life Cavafy had in circulation two bound thematic collections, *Poems (1905–1915)* and *Poems (1916–1918)*, and

[1] The use of brackets around the dates in the titles of this and the later thematic collections, but not in the titles of the chronological collections, follows Cavafy's own practice.

the chronological collection *Poems 1919–1932* (a folder of unbound sheets). To this last collection we have added 'In the outskirts of Antioch', which Cavafy was working on in the last weeks of his life, and which he is said to have prepared for the printers shortly before his death; and we have renamed the collection *Poems 1919–1933*, as Cavafy would undoubtedly have done had he lived long enough to add the printed text of this poem to copies of the chronological collection.

It was certainly not Cavafy's intention to abandon the fifteen pre-1905 poems of *Poems 1910* which he did not incorporate into the later thematic collections. All of them were republished, at Cavafy's instigation, in periodicals receptive to his work between 1924 and 1929. 'Walls', a poem of 1897 which had not been included in *Poems 1904* or *Poems 1910*, was also republished at this time; and when, in 1927, Cavafy produced, at the request of Alekos Sengopoulos, a manuscript version of the poems of the 1910 collection (known as the 'Sengopoulos Notebook'), he included 'Walls', inserting it in the established thematic sequence between 'Monotony' and 'Waiting for the barbarians'. Consequently 'Walls' has always been regarded as part of the Cavafy canon, and will be found as an integral part of *Poems 1910* in the present volume.

The principal posthumous editions

The canon was defined by the first commercial edition of Cavafy's poetry, entitled simply *Poiemata* (*Poems*), edited by Rika Sengopoulou. Printed in Athens and published in Alexandria in 1935, this edition included 'Walls' and 'In the outskirts of Antioch', along with the 152 poems found in the collections described above. Sengopoulou, however, completely ignored Cavafy's thematic arrangements and his division of the poems into distinct collections, and presented the 154 poems in a single—and inaccurate—chronological sequence, which was reproduced in the second, third, and fourth editions (1948, 1952, and 1958) from the Athenian publishing house Ikaros, with no named editor.

George Savidis's two-volume edition of 1963 restored the division into four collections, the thematic arrangements of the poems in the first three collections, and the proper chronological sequence of the post-1918 poems. The first volume contained the thematic collections, *Poems (1905–1915)*, *Poems (1916–1918)*, and *Poems 1910*, in that order. *Poems 1910* was, of course, incomplete, with only sixteen poems: it included 'Walls' but omitted the six poems which had been incorporated in *Poems (1905–1915)*. Savidis's 'new edition' of 1991 presents, instead of this defective version of *Poems 1910*, the complete thematic sequence of the fourteen poems of *Poems 1904*, but headed 'Appendix I, 1897–1904', with 'Walls' and 'The funeral of Sarpedon' as 'Appendix II, 1897, 1908'. Similarly, while in the second volume of Savidis's 1963 edition 'In the outskirts of Antioch' was presented as the final poem of the period '1919–1933', in his 1991 edition it is relegated to 'Appendix [1933?]', with the main sequence retitled '1919–1932'.

The arrangement of the present edition

To the bibliographical niceties and the implicit downgrading of certain poems represented by Savidis's appendices, we have preferred to present all four collections in their integral forms and in the chronological order of the periods they represent, beginning with *Poems 1910 [1897–1909]*.[2] This is the first time the Greek texts have been presented in this way. In each of the four collections the thematic or chronological sequence established by Cavafy has been scrupulously followed.

Although the *texts* of only sixteen poems are included here in *Poems 1910*, the six poems of the period 1905–9 whose texts will be found later in the volume are represented by their titles, inserted at the appropriate points in the thematic sequence of *Poems 1910*, with cross reference to the pages where the texts may be found in *Poems (1905–1915)*. This means that the reader who wishes to follow the complete thematic sequence of *Poems 1910*, in Greek or in English, can easily do so. *Poems 1910* is followed by the two later thematic collections, *Poems (1905–1915)* and *Poems (1916–1918)*, and then the chronological collection *Poems 1919–1933*, including, as its final poem, 'In the outskirts of Antioch'.

The copy texts and editorial principles

For the first sixteen poems (that is, those whose texts will be found here in *Poems 1910*) I have used the published facsimile of the

[2] We have added in square brackets the dates of first publication of the earliest and latest poems in *Poems 1910* for comparison with the titles of the other collections in this volume, which all show the date-range of the poems included, rather than the date of publication of the collection.

'Sengopoulos Notebook' as the copy text;[3] and for the last poem, 'In the outskirts of Antioch', I have used the facsimile of the manuscript which appeared in the journal *Nea Estia* in 1963.[4] These manuscript sources contain quite a number of obvious errors, such as missing or incorrect accents, and missing punctuation marks. Such errors, which are significantly more frequent than in the author's printings referred to below, have been corrected.

For the 137 poems of the period 1905–32, I have used wherever possible the final printing of the poem as the copy text. There are two short poems, 'Monotony' and 'That they come—', and parts of two longer ones, the first folio of 'Ithaca' (lines 1–21) and the second folio of 'Caesarion' (lines 21–30), for which I have not been able to find a copy of the final printing. In these cases I used the penultimate printing as the copy text.[5]

The final printings range in date from 1926 to 1932, and it would be difficult to argue that these do not represent Cavafy's final intentions for the poems, except where obvious printers' errors can be identified. Such errors are relatively few, and most of any significance were corrected by hand by Cavafy. Manuscripts are often taken to override the authority of published texts, but in Cavafy's case, given his close control over the printing of his poems, his final printings can be taken to override any manuscripts, including the many fair-copy manuscripts he presented to friends.

My intention in editing the Greek texts of the 154 poems of the Cavafy canon has been to present as nearly as possible the orthography and punctuation of the copy texts. I have deviated from the copy texts only where they contain indubitable errors. This means that the texts presented here frequently differ in detail from the current standard texts, that is, those found in the reprints of Savidis's 'new edition' of 1991. In many respects the present texts are closer to Savidis's original edition of 1963, and to Sengopoulou's edition of 1935. Sengopoulou (evidently) and Savidis (explicitly, in 1963) based their editions chiefly on the final printings of the poems, though in practice they often preferred the readings of earlier printings, especially

[3] *Autographa poiemata (1896–1910): To Tetradio Senkopoulou se panomoiotype ekdose*, ed. G. P. Savvides (Athens: Technographike, 1968).

[4] No. 875, 1 Nov. 1963, pp. 1486–7.

[5] A number of Cavafy's later poems were printed only once, but the others were reprinted every two to three years, and a number of poems were printed twelve, thirteen, or even fourteen times in total.

in the matter of punctuation; and, beginning with Sengopoulou, and continuing through the three Ikaros editions and Savidis's editions of 1963 and 1991, we see the progressive standardization and modernization of Cavafy's orthography. With this, and with the recent proliferation of editions of the Greek texts based, usually, on Savidis's 1991 edition, including editions employing the current single-accent system, there is now a pressing need to re-establish the texts as Cavafy left them. This is what the present edition seeks to do.

Readers familiar with other editions of the Greek text may be surprised by what they find here. No attempt has been made to render Cavafy's orthography any more consistent than *he* chose to make it. All variants in spelling and accentuation are retained, provided they had some currency in his day. In some cases the choice of a non-standard spelling may have poetic significance, as for example in 'Come back', where the Greek for 'take hold', in the repeated phrase 'take hold of me', is spelt *pérne* in all nine printings of this poem, instead of the standard and 'correct' *paírne*. In all other poems where this verb occurs the normal spelling is found, but here *pérne* with two *epsilons* forms a fitting counterpart to the other imperative with which it is paired, *epéstrephe* ('come back') with four *epsilons*, and also invokes the comparable imperative *pérna* from a different verb, meaning 'pass by or through'.

Perhaps the most surprising (and in this case unprecedented) spelling is to be found in 'A town in Osroene'. The word at the end of the third line, which rhymes with *mesánychta* ('midnight') in the second, is spelled correctly in the first four printings of this poem: *olánoichta* ('wide open'). In the last two printings, however, it appears as *olánychta*. This misspelling is conceivably a printers' error (but, if so, one which remained uncorrected by Cavafy); on the other hand it may represent a deliberate amendment on Cavafy's part, a playful and modernist touch: a wilful misspelling, creating a visual as well as auditory consonance with *mesánychta*, and suggesting a double meaning—'wide open' and 'all night', hinting at the adverb *olonychtís* ('all night long'). I have left it as found, so that readers can consider the matter for themselves.

The late printings of many poems are distinguished by punctuation changes, usually the removal or addition of a comma, changes which have in most cases been rejected by previous editors in favour of the punctuation of earlier printings. While a few of these changes could be printers' errors, the sheer number of them and their nature suggests that in his last years Cavafy was moving towards a more poetic—and less strictly grammatical—approach to punctuation. The punctuation of the copy texts is always followed, except in the rare cases where it is obviously defective.

My research into Cavafy's own printings of his poems and collections which underlies the present edition of the Greek text, and the extensive travelling involved in the research, were materially supported by the Leverhulme Trust through a Special Research Fellowship (2002–4) and by the Friends of Princeton University Library through a Short-Term Visiting Fellowship (2002). The ultimate aim of this research is the production of a critical edition, and I am very grateful to Oxford University Press for this opportunity to publish the restored Greek texts of Cavafy's poems in the interim, without prejudice to their eventual republication elsewhere with critical apparatus.

I am grateful too to the staff of the Rare Books and Special Collections in the Firestone Library at Princeton University, the staff of the Houghton Library at Harvard University, and of the Rare Book and Manuscript department in the Butler Library at Columbia University; of the Taylor Institution Slavonic and Modern Greek Library in the University of Oxford, of the Special Collections in the library of King's College London, and of the Archive of King's College Cambridge; of the National Library of Greece, the Gennadius Library, the Benakeios Library, the Library of the Benaki Museum, the Benaki Archive, and the Rare Books and Special Collections Library of the American College of Greece, all in Athens; and of the Cavafy Museum in Alexandria. All of these institutions hold copies of Cavafy's self-published collections, and their staff were most helpful in providing me with photo-reproductions of large quantities of material or, in some cases, allowing me to photograph the material myself. Special thanks are due to Dimitri Gondicas, Executive Director of the Program in Hellenic Studies at Princeton University, who has taken a keen interest in my research from the outset, and to Manos Haritatos, Director of the Greek Literary and Historical Archive (ELIA) in Athens, who not only gave me access to all the materials housed in ELIA, but also allowed me to inspect more than twenty examples of Cavafy's self-published collections from his private library.

The advice of the other contributors to the present volume, Evangelos Sachperoglou and Peter Mackridge, has been invaluable.

Anthony Hirst

NOTE ON THE TRANSLATION

W. H. Auden once made the notable distinction between separable (i.e. translatable) and inseparable (non-translatable) linguistic elements in poetry. This distinction is a useful point of departure when referring to the problems inherent in the translation of Cavafy's works. Thus, Auden maintains, internal alliteration, similes, and metaphors can be accordingly preserved in the new language, while lyrical components, homophonic associations, and rhyme are destined to be lost.

In addition to the above inseparable elements, other particular aspects of the Greek language, like Cavafy's admixture of puristic and demotic Greek, are destined to be lost also. And yet in English Cavafy attains his distinct and alluring tone of voice, potent enough to captivate the poetic imagination of English-speakers ever since the earliest translations.

The mode in which his tone of voice is interpreted and conveyed can determine the effectiveness of the translation: a literary endeavour that has been rightly labelled a frustrating charade after endless and relentless choices. In translating Cavafy, these choices will affect the specific poetic transmutation of the reflective or erotic moods of the original, not to speak of the dreamlike imagery or the irony inherent in his artistry.

The current viewpoint which assumes that translations ought to emulate some established kind of contemporary poetry also presupposes that the translator is bound to dispense with the aesthetic equivalents that seek to maximize the poetic effect of the original. In Cavafy's case these include the loose, free, and relaxed iambic metre, the length of his verses, the repetitions, and the rhythm of the accented syllables within a line. And yet some of these features may indeed be approximated in the English language.

Translatable too, up to a point, is what Cavafy himself defines as 'his fastidiousness of style that verges on the laconic', concision being the chief method by which he projects the ironic stance in so many of his poems. Yet the English language is well suited to expressing the laconic, just as it is to expressing the ironic.

But Cavafy the critic of men and deeds is also the master conjurer of imagery and suggestiveness. In a large number of compositions he revisits memories of youth, love, and beauty, or he stages entire tableaux of dissipation and languorous abandonment. Interspersed with these themes, Cavafy introduces reflections—unmediated by facile simile or metaphor—on the symbolism of shadow and light, the facets of the large city, the cycles of nepotism, greed, and personal ambition.

Cavafy's work, world, and art deal directly with our personal experience of loss over time as well as with the concept of time itself in art. It may be proven true, he seems to be saying, that as with the extracts distilled from magical herbs by Syro-Phoenician sages, the remedy to hopelessly irretrievable experiences and personal loss may be poetry itself; it provides us with the means by which we may survive, dream, and even creatively refashion the past and, perhaps, ourselves; poetry as well as beauty, the ultimate redeeming catalysts of grace in our lives.

These aspects of Cavafy's poetic and intellectual persona are indispensable ingredients of his art and allure, and I have deemed it my duty to respect and pattern my translation upon them. I loved Cavafy's poetry long before attempting to translate it; and often pondered on the image that can be created, once these pieces of the literary jigsaw-puzzle have been put together. I am still unsure of the answer. Yet again, the ultimate judge is time—time and the reader.

I am deeply grateful to all the members of my family who had to endure my lengthy preoccupation with the present endeavour. I am particularly indebted to Peter Mackridge for his expert advice on a great number of issues, to Anthony Hirst, and to Mrs Alexandra Doumas.

I would like to thank Matti and Nicholas Egon and Stamatia Cottakis for their extreme kindness and support.

And finally I would like to thank the following friends who contributed, each in their own way, to this work: Ann Blassingham, Kiki Birtaka, Paris Tacopoulos, Stephanos Tassopoulos, David and Jan Jordan, Stavros Deligiorgis, John Philipson, Leo Cottakis, Nicos Biniaris, Judith Binder, Carl Henrik Svenstedt, Manos Haritatos, Artemis Leontis.

Evangelos Sachperoglou

SELECT BIBLIOGRAPHY

The principal Greek editions of the Cavafy canon

Kavaphes, K. P., *Poiemata* [*Poems*], ed. Rika Senkopoulou (Alexandria: Alexandrine Techne, 1935; repr. Athens: Eridanos, n.d. [1980s]).

—— *Poiemata* [*Poems*], 2 vols. (vol. 1: *1896–1918*; vol. 2, *1919–1933*), ed. G. P. Savvides (Athens: Ikaros, 1963).

—— *Ta poiemata: nea ekdose* [*The Poems: A New Edition*], 2 vols. (vol. 1: *1897–1918*; vol. 2, *1919–1933*), ed. G. P. Savvides (Athens: Ikaros, 1991).

Editions of Cavafy's other works,
including works in the original English

Haas, Diana, 'Cavafy's Reading Notes on Gibbon's "Decline and Fall"', *Folia Neohellenica*, 4 (Amsterdam, 1982), 25–96; the notes are in English.

Kavaphes, K. P., *Apokerygmena poiemata kai metaphraseis 1886–1898* [*Repudiated Poems, and Translations*], ed. G. P. Savvides (Athens: Ikaros, 1983).

—— 'Anekdota semeiomata poietikes kai ethikes' ['Unpublished Notes on Poetics and Ethics'], in G. P. Savvides, *Mikra Kavaphika* [*Short Cavafian Studies*], vol. 2 (Athens: Hermes, 1987), 87–146; includes several notes in English (see pp. 128–33).

—— *Krymmena poiemata 1877?–1923* [*Hidden* (i.e. unpublished) *Poems*], ed. G. P. Savvides (Athens: Ikaros, 1993); includes three early poems (juvenilia) in English (see pp. 131–6).

—— *Atele poiemata 1918–1932* [*Unfinished Poems*], ed. Renata Lavagnini (Athens: Ikaros, 1994).

—— *Hapanta ta peza* [*Complete Prose*], vol. 1, ed. G. P. Phexes and G. Papoutsakes (Athens: Ekdoseis Mermenka, n.d. ['1963' in printers' colophon, but this is a recent reprint]); includes Cavafy's English journal of his first visit to Greece in 1901 (see pp. 259–302), in addition to several of the English texts in *Ta peza (1882?–1931)* (see below).

—— *Ta peza (1882?–1931)* [*Prose Works*], ed. Michales Pieres (Athens: Ikaros, 2003); includes the following prose texts in English: 'Give back the Elgin Marbles', 'What I Remember of my Essay on Christopulus', '[Fragment on Lycanthropy]', 'Woman and the Ancients [unfinished]', '[Fragment on Beliefs Concerning the Soul]', 'Misplaced Tenderness',

'Romaïc Folk-lore of Enchanted Animals', 'Persian Manners', 'Masks', and '[Philosophical Scrutiny]' (see pp. 31–3, 187–203, 256–60).

—— 'Constantinopoliad: An Epic', in Lena Savvide (ed.), *Leukoma Kavaphe 1836–1910* [*A Cavafy Album*] (Athens: Hermes, 1983), 43–9; a youthful journal of the Cavafy family's move to Constantinople in 1882; the *Album* contains other texts in English, including correspondence.

English translations of Cavafy's prose and of poems outside the canon

Cavafy, C. P., *The Complete Poems of Cavafy*, tr. Rae Dalven, expanded edn. (New York, San Diego, and London: Harcourt, 1976); includes most of the 'repudiated' poems and a selection of the 'unpublished' poems.

—— *The Greek Poems of C. P. Cavafy*, vol. 2: *The Unissued and 'Repudiated' Poems*, tr. Memas Kolaitis (New Rochelle, NY: Aristide D. Caratzas, 1989).

—— *Collected poems*, tr. Edmund Keeley and Philip Sherrard, ed. George Savidis, rev. edn. (Princeton: Princeton University Press, 1992); includes a selection of the unpublished poems.

—— 'King Claudius' [a 'repudiated' poem], 'Shakespeare on Life' and 'Greek Traces in Shakespeare' [critical articles], tr. Martin McKinsey, *In-Between,* 6.1 (New Delhi, March 1997), 3–18.

—— *Before Time Could Change Them: The Complete Poems of C. P. Cavafy*, tr. Theoharis Constantine Theoharis (New York, San Diego, and London: Harcourt, 2001); includes all of the 'repudiated' and 'unpublished' poems.

—— 'In the light of day' [a short story] in *The Dedalus Book of Greek Fantasy*, tr. David Connolly (Sawtry, Cambs.: Dedalus, 2004), 41–50.

Hirst, Anthony, 'C. P. Cavafy: Fourteen Byzantine Texts and Translations', in *Metaphrastes, or, Gained in Translation: Essays and Translations in Honour of Robert H. Jordan*, ed. Margaret Mullett, Belfast Byzantine Texts and Translations, 9 (Belfast: Belfast Byzantine Enterprises, 2004), 296–313; includes translations of five of the 'unfinished' poems.

Critical works in English

Beaton, Roderick, 'The History Man', *Journal of the Hellenic Diaspora,* 10.1–2, special issue on Cavafy (New York, 1983), 23–44.

Harvey, Denise (ed.), *The Mind and Art of C. P. Cavafy*, The Romiosyni Series, 6 (Athens: Denise Harvey & Co., 1983).

Hirst, Anthony, 'Philosophical, Historical and Sensual: An Examination of Cavafy's Thematic Collections', *Byzantine and Modern Greek Studies,* 19 (Birmingham, 1995), 33–93.

Jusdanis, Gregory, *The Poetics of Cavafy: Textuality, Eroticism, History* (Princeton: Princeton University Press, 1987).

Keeley, Edmund, *Cavafy's Alexandria*, 2nd edn. (Princeton: Princeton University Press, 1996).

Liddell, Robert, *Cavafy: A Critical Biography*, 2nd edn. (London: Duckworth, 2000).

Pinchin, Jane Lagoudis, *Alexandria Still: Forster, Durrell and Cavafy* (Princeton: Princeton University Press, 1977).

Ricks, David, 'Modes of Misquotation' and 'Ancient Days', chs. 7 and 8 of *The Shade of Homer: A Study in Modern Greek Poetry* (Cambridge: Cambridge University Press, 1989).

Robinson, Christopher, *C. P. Cavafy*, Studies in Modern Greek (Bristol: Bristol Classical Press, 1988).

Further reading in Oxford World's Classics

Apollodorus, *The Library of Greek Mythology*, tr. Robin Hard.

Greek Lyric Poetry, tr. M. L. West.

Homer, *The Iliad*, tr. Robert Fitzgerald.

—— *The Odyssey*, tr. Walter Shewring.

The Homeric Hymns, tr. Michael Crudden.

Lucian, *Selected Dialogues*, tr. C. D. N. Costa.

Theocritus, *Idylls*, tr. Anthony Verity and Richard Hunter.

A CHRONOLOGY OF C. P. CAVAFY

1863 17/29 April: Constantine born in Alexandria, Egypt, last of nine children of Petros I. Cavafy (b. 1814) and Charikleia Photiades. At the time the family of the wealthy Greek merchant resides in the exclusive part of Alexandria. A two-storey edifice houses the offices of the commercial enterprise Cavafy & Co. as well as the large Cavafy family.

1864 28 May: Constantine baptized in the Greek Orthodox Church.

1870 Sudden death of father at the age of 56.

1872 The family faces its first financial difficulties. They move to Liverpool (12 Balmoral Road, Fairfield) and stay in England for six years.

1874 The family moves to London (15 Queensborough Terrace, Hyde Park). In the following years the poet develops his considerable skills in the English language.

1876 The firm Cavafy & Co. goes out of business in the wake of a severe economic crisis in Egypt; the family faces ever-greater financial difficulties.

1877 Cavafy family returns to Alexandria. Older son George stays behind in London.

1879 Cavafy family rents a house at Ramli Street.

1881 Constantine attends the Hermes School of Commerce in Alexandria.

1882 Serious nationalist uprising provokes the British bombardment of Alexandria. The Cavafy residence severely damaged. June: Cavafy family moves to Constantinople for three years.

1884 Begins to write poetry in Greek and prose essays in English.

1885 Cavafy family returns to Alexandria. Constantine relinquishes his British citizenship, taking up Greek nationality instead. Tries out diverse professions as a journalist, a broker, an employee in the Cotton Stock Exchange, and finally an apprentice in the Irrigation Service, where he is later offered permanent employment.

1886 First publication of an article by Constantine in a Constantinople newspaper.

1889 Close friend Mikes Rallis dies at the age of 23 in Alexandria.

1891 Brother Peter-John dies, aged 40. His uncle, George Cavafy, once partner in the family business, dies in London.

1892 Hired as an office clerk at the Irrigation Service, a position he will keep till his retirement.

1894 Visits Cairo. Receives commendation by his superiors for his efficient work at the office.

1896 The first modern Olympic Games take place in Athens. Cavafy contributes to the newspaper *Phare d'Alexandrie*.

1897 The Greek–Turkish War ends with a disastrous defeat for the Greeks. Cavafy describes in diary form his desperate but futile efforts to rid himself of his erotic passions. Goes on an extended vacation, with brother John, to Paris and London.

1898 Anglo-Egyptian army occupies Sudan.

1899 Death of mother (b. 1834) in February.

1900 Visits Cairo. Brother George (b. 1850) dies in Alexandria.

1901 Visits Athens with brother Alexander. Keeps a detailed diary of that visit. Meets Greek intellectuals in Athens, with some of whom he later corresponds.

1902 Death of brother Aristeides.

1903 Another visit to Athens. Begins to be noticed and admired by some of the important literary figures of Greece. Gregorios Xenopoulos writes the first laudatory article on Cavafy's poetry ever published, in the Athens magazine *Panathenaia*.

1904 First uses the form of his name that he keeps for the rest of his life: C. P. Cavafy. Towards the end of that year moves into a rented apartment which he shares with his brother Paul.

1905 Makes the acquaintance of Ion Dragoumis, an important figure in Greek society and politics, with whom he later corresponds. Travels to Athens, where his brother Alexander has fallen ill with typhoid fever. Alexander dies in August.

1906 In the Athens literary magazine *Noumas* the novelist and critic Gregorios Xenopoulos once more defends Cavafy's poetry from its many critics.

1907 Moves with brother Paul to an apartment at 10 Lepsius Street, where he lives till the end of his life.

1908 Brother Paul moves to France.

1909 Starts writing his 'Genealogy'. In Greece a military coup alters the old political balance in the country.

1912 Signs a five-year contract with the Irrigation Service. First Balkan War: Greek army occupies Salonika.

1913 Assassination of King George of Greece. Second Balkan War.

1914 First World War. Egypt on the side of the Allies. Many European intellectuals find their way to Egypt because of the war. Cavafy makes the acquaintance of E. M. Forster, who introduces him to the English public.

1915 Makes the acquaintance of Timos Malanos and M. Perides (his future biographers). Attends lectures organized by the literary magazine *Grammata*.

1917 Signs another five-year contract with the Irrigation Service. Makes the acquaintance of Alekos Sengopoulos.

1918 End of the First World War. Sengopoulos delivers a lecture (authorized by the poet himself) on Cavafy's poetry.

1919 Greek army occupies Smyrna. E. M. Forster writes an article on the poetry of Cavafy in the London magazine *The Athenaeum*.

1920 Death of brother Paul in France.

1922 Defeat of the Greek forces by Turkey; expulsion of all Greeks from Asia Minor (about 1.5 million people). Cavafy resigns from his office job and proclaims: 'I have been liberated at last from this hateful thing.' E. M. Forster's book *Alexandria: A History and a Guide* published. The second edition (1938) is dedicated to: 'C. P. Cavafy, Greek by birth, Alexandrian by spirit, and a great poet.'

1923 Brother John (b. 1861) dies. E. M. Forster's book *Pharos and Pharillon* published, including an important essay on Cavafy. Cavafy writes his will, naming Alekos Sengopoulos as principal heir and executor.

1924 A year of intense debates and discussions in Alexandria and in Athens about Cavafy's poetic work. A group of sixty Greek intellectuals publish a manifesto in defence of the poet. T. S. Eliot publishes 'Ithaca' in the London magazine *Criterion*.

1926 Awarded a medal of honour by the Greek State. Greek composer and conductor Dimitri Mitropoulos sets ten of Cavafy's poems to music.

1927 Makes the acquaintance of the Greek thinker, poet, and novelist Nikos Kazantzakis.

1928 'I was capable of two things, writing Poetry and writing History. I didn't manage to write History and now it is too late.' Greek lyric poet Kostas Karyotakis commits suicide. Many articles, essays, and studies dedicated to Cavafy's work published. Visited by the Futurist poet F. T. Marinetti (born in Alexandria in 1876), who includes a description of their meeting in his book *Il fascino dell'Egitto* (*The Allure of Egypt*), published five years later.

1929 E. M. Forster revisits Egypt and meets Cavafy. Forster gives an interview to Rika Sengopoulou, published in the magazine *Tachydromos*, in which he describes his great admiration for Cavafy, as a thinker and a poet.

1930 Interest in and admiration for Cavafy's poetry continues unabated. The number of lectures, articles, and publications about his work grows steadily.

1932 Diagnosed with throat cancer, he tries to smoke and talk less. Persuaded to see a doctor in Athens. Hospitalized and a tracheotomy performed; loses the capacity to speak. Returns to Alexandria.

1933 While bedridden he works on his last poem, 'In the outskirts of Antioch'. Enters the Greek Hospital of Alexandria. He is administered the last rites. At two o'clock in the morning, on the day of his birthday, 29 April, he suffers a stroke and dies.

POEMS 1910

ΠΟΙΗΜΑΤΑ 1910

[1897–1909]

ΦΩΝΕΣ

Ἰδανικὲς φωνὲς κι ἀγαπημένες
ἐκείνων ποῦ πεθάναν ἢ ἐκείνων ποῦ εἶναι
γιὰ μᾶς χαμένοι σὰν τοὺς πεθαμένους.

Κάποτε μὲς τὰ ὄνειρά μας ὁμιλοῦνε·
κάποτε μὲς τὴν σκέψι τὲς ἀκούει τὸ μυαλό.

Καὶ μὲ τὸν ἦχο των γιὰ μιὰ στιγμὴ ἐπιστρέφουν
ἦχοι ἀπὸ τὴν πρώτη ποίησι τῆς ζωῆς μας—
σὰ μουσική, τὴν νύχτα, μακρυνή, ποῦ σβύνει.

ΕΠΙΘΥΜΙΕΣ

Σὰν σώματα ὡραῖα νεκρῶν ποῦ δὲν ἐγέρασαν
καὶ τἄκλεισαν, μὲ δάκρυα, σὲ μαυσωλεῖο λαμπρό,
μὲ ρόδα στὸ κεφάλι καὶ στὰ πόδια γιασεμιὰ—
ἔτσ' ἡ ἐπιθυμίες μοιάζουν ποῦ ἐπέρασαν
χωρὶς νὰ ἐκπληρωθοῦν· χωρὶς ν' ἀξιωθεῖ καμιὰ
τῆς ἡδονῆς μιὰ νύχτα, ἢ ἕνα πρωΐ της φεγγερό.

ΚΕΡΙΑ

Τοῦ μέλλοντος ἡ μέρες στέκοντ' ἐμπροστά μας
σὰ μιὰ σειρὰ κεράκια ἀναμένα—
χρυσά, ζεστά, καὶ ζωηρὰ κεράκια.

Ἡ περασμένες μέρες πίσω μένουν,
μιὰ θλιβερὴ γραμμὴ κεριῶν σβυσμένων·
τὰ πιὸ κοντὰ βγάζουν καπνὸν ἀκόμη,
κρύα κεριά, λυωμένα, καὶ κυρτά.

*

VOICES

Ideal voices and beloved
of those who have died, or of those
who are lost to us like the dead.

Sometimes, within our dreams, they speak;
sometimes the mind can hear them in our thoughts.

And with their sound for an instant return
sounds from the early poetry of our life—
like music in the night, faraway, that fades.

DESIRES

Like beautiful bodies of the dead who did not grow old,
and were shut away with tears in a splendid mausoleum,
with roses at their head and jasmine at their feet—
that is what those desires are like, which have passed
without fulfilment; not one of them ever granted
a pleasure's night, or a pleasure's radiant morn.

CANDLES

The days to come are standing right before us,
like a row of little lighted candles—
golden, warm, and lively little candles.

The bygone days are left behind,
a dismal row of burned-out candles;
those that are nearest smoking still,
cold candles, melted and bent.

*

Δὲν θέλω νὰ τὰ βλέπω· μὲ λυπεῖ ἡ μορφή των,
καὶ μὲ λυπεῖ τὸ πρῶτο φῶς των νὰ θυμοῦμαι.
Ἐμπρὸς κυττάζω τ' ἀναμένα μου κεριά.

Δὲν θέλω νὰ γυρίσω νὰ μὴ διῶ καὶ φρίξω
τὶ γρήγορα ποῦ ἡ σκοτεινὴ γραμμὴ μακραίνει,
τὶ γρήγορα ποῦ τὰ σβυστὰ κεριὰ πληθαίνουν.

ΕΝΑΣ ΓΕΡΟΣ

Στοῦ καφενείου τοῦ βοεροῦ τὸ μέσα μέρος
σκυμένος στὸ τραπέζι κάθετ' ἕνας γέρος·
μὲ μιὰν ἐφημερίδα ἐμπρός του, χωρὶς συντροφιά.

Καὶ μὲς στῶν ἄθλιων γηρατειῶν τὴν καταφρόνεια
σκέπτεται πόσο λίγο χάρηκε τὰ χρόνια
ποῦ εἶχε καὶ δύναμι, καὶ λόγο, κ' ἐμορφιά.

Ξέρει ποῦ γέρασε πολύ· τὸ νοιώθει, τὸ κυττάζει.
Κ' ἐν τούτοις ὁ καιρὸς ποῦ ἦταν νέος μοιάζει
σὰν χθές. Τὶ διάστημα μικρό, τὶ διάστημα μικρό.

Καὶ συλλογιέται ἡ Φρόνησις πῶς τὸν ἐγέλα·
καὶ πῶς τὴν ἐμπιστεύονταν πάντα — τὶ τρέλλα! —
τὴν ψεύτρα ποῦ ἔλεγε· «Αὔριο. Ἔχεις πολὺν καιρό.»

Θυμᾶται ὁρμὲς ποῦ βάσταγε· καὶ πόση
χαρὰ θυσίαζε. Τὴν ἄμυαλή του γνῶσι
κάθ' εὐκαιρία χαμένη τώρα τὴν ἐμπαίζει.

. . . Μὰ ἀπ' τὸ πολὺ νὰ σκέπτεται καὶ νὰ θυμᾶται
ὁ γέρος ἐξαλίσθηκε. Κι ἀποκοιμᾶται
στοῦ καφενείου ἀκουμπισμένος τὸ τραπέζι.

I don't want to see them; their sight saddens me,
and it saddens me to recall their former glow.
I look ahead at my still lighted candles.

I don't want to turn around, lest I see and shudder
how fast the darksome line grows longer,
how fast the burned-out candles multiply.

AN OLD MAN

Deep inside the noisy café,
huddled over the table sits an old man,
with a newspaper in front of him, all alone.

And in the indignity of his miserable old age
he ponders on how little he enjoyed the years
when he had vigour, eloquence, and looks.

He knows that he has aged a lot; he senses it, he sees it.
And yet the time when he was young seems like
yesterday. What a short span of time, what a short span.

And he reflects on how Prudence deceived him;
and how he always trusted her—what folly!—
that liar who used to say: 'Tomorrow. You still have plenty of time.'

He recalls impulses that he restrained; and how much
joy he sacrificed. Every lost opportunity
now mocks his mindless wisdom.

. . . But from too much reflection and reminiscence
the old man becomes dizzy. And he falls asleep
leaning upon the table of the café.

ΔΕΗΣΙΣ

Ἡ θάλασσα στὰ βάθη της πῆρ' ἕναν ναύτη.—
Ἡ μάνα του, ἀνήξερη, πιαίνει κι ἀνάφτει

στὴν Παναγία μπροστὰ ἕνα ὑψηλὸ κερὶ
γιὰ νὰ ἐπιστρέψει γρήγορα καὶ νἆν καλοὶ καιροὶ—

καὶ ὅλο πρὸς τὸν ἄνεμο στήνει τ' αὐτί.
Ἀλλὰ ἐνῶ προσεύχεται καὶ δέεται αὐτή,

ἡ εἰκὼν ἀκούει, σοβαρὴ καὶ λυπημένη,
ξεύροντας πῶς δὲν θἄλθει πιὰ ὁ υἱὸς ποῦ περιμένει.

Η ΨΥΧΕΣ ΤΩΝ ΓΕΡΟΝΤΩΝ

Μὲς στὰ παληὰ τὰ σώματά των τὰ φθαρμένα
κάθονται τῶν γερόντων ἡ ψυχές.
Τί θλιβερὲς ποῦ εἶναι ἡ πτωχὲς
καὶ πῶς βαρυοῦνται τὴν ζωὴ τὴν ἄθλια ποῦ τραβοῦνε.
Πῶς τρέμουν μὴν τὴν χάσουνε καὶ πῶς τὴν ἀγαποῦνε
ἡ σαστισμένες κι ἀντιφατικὲς
ψυχές, ποῦ κάθονται—κωμικοτραγικὲς—
μὲς στὰ παληά των τὰ πετσιὰ τ' ἀφανισμένα.

ΤΟ ΠΡΩΤΟ ΣΚΑΛΙ

Εἰς τὸν Θεόκριτο παραπονιοῦνταν
μιὰ μέρα ὁ νέος ποιητὴς Εὐμένης·
«Τώρα δυὸ χρόνια πέρασαν ποῦ γράφω
κ' ἕνα εἰδύλλιο ἔκαμα μονάχα.
Τὸ μόνον ἄρτιόν μου ἔργον εἶναι.
Ἀλλοίμονον, εἶν' ὑψηλὴ τὸ βλέπω,
πολὺ ὑψηλὴ τῆς Ποιήσεως ἡ σκάλα·

SUPPLICATION

The sea took a sailor into its depths.—
His mother, unaware, goes to light

a tall candle before the Virgin Mary,
that he return soon and meet with fine weather—

all the while turning windward her ear.
But as she prays and supplicates,

the icon listens, solemn and sad, well aware
that he'll never come back, the son she awaits.

THE SOULS OF OLD MEN

Within their aged, worn-out bodies
dwell the souls of old men.
How pathetic they are, poor souls,
and how weary of the miserable life they must endure.
How they tremble lest they lose it, and how they cherish it,
the confused and contradictory
souls that dwell—tragicomically—
within their aged, ravaged hides.

THE FIRST STEP

The young poet Eumenes complained
to Theocritus* one day:
'Two years have passed since I began to write,
and all I've composed is just one idyll.
It is my only completed work.
Alas, it's high, so I see,
the stairway of Poetry is so very high;

κι ἀπ' τὸ σκαλὶ τὸ πρῶτο ἐδῶ ποῦ εἶμαι
ποτὲ δὲν θ' ἀναιβῶ ὁ δυστυχισμένος.»
Εἶπ' ὁ Θεόκριτος· «Αὐτὰ τὰ λόγια
ἀνάρμοστα καὶ βλασφημίες εἶναι.
Κι ἂν εἶσαι στὸ σκαλὶ τὸ πρῶτο, πρέπει
νἆσαι ὑπερήφανος κι εὐτυχισμένος.
Ἐδῶ ποῦ ἔφθασες, λίγο δὲν εἶναι·
τόσο ποῦ ἔκαμες, μεγάλη δόξα.
Κι αὐτὸ ἀκόμη τὸ σκαλὶ τὸ πρῶτο
πολὺ ἀπὸ τὸν κοινὸ τὸν κόσμο ἀπέχει.
Εἰς τὸ σκαλὶ γιὰ νὰ πατήσεις τοῦτο
πρέπει μὲ τὸ δικαίωμά σου νἆσαι
πολίτης εἰς τῶν ἰδεῶν τὴν πόλι.
Καὶ δύσκολο στὴν πόλι ἐκείνην εἶναι
καὶ σπάνιο νὰ σὲ πολιτογραφήσουν.
Στὴν ἀγορά της βρίσκεις Νομοθέτας
ποῦ δὲν γελᾶ κανένας τυχοδιώκτης.
Ἐδῶ ποῦ ἔφθασες, λίγο δὲν εἶναι·
τόσο ποῦ ἔκαμες, μεγάλη δόξα.»

ΔΙΑΚΟΠΗ

Τὸ ἔργον τῶν θεῶν διακόπτομεν ἐμεῖς,
τὰ βιαστικὰ κι ἄπειρα ὄντα τῆς στιγμῆς.
Στῆς Ἐλευσῖνος καὶ στῆς Φθίας τὰ παλάτια
ἡ Δήμητρα κ' ἡ Θέτις ἀρχινοῦν ἔργα καλὰ
μὲς σὲ μεγάλες φλόγες καὶ βαθὺν καπνόν. Ἀλλὰ
πάντοτε ὁρμᾶ ἡ Μετάνειρα ἀπὸ τὰ δωμάτια
τοῦ βασιλέως, ξέπλεγη καὶ τρομαγμένη,
καὶ πάντοτε ὁ Πηλεὺς φοβᾶται κ' ἐπεμβαίνει.

and from the first step, where I stand,
miserable me, I'll never climb higher.'
Theocritus said: 'These words
are blasphemous and unbecoming.
Even though you stand on the first step,
you still ought to be proud and happy.
To have come so far is no small matter;
to have done so much is great glory.
For even this first step is still
by far above the common people.
In order to set foot upon this step,
you must be in your own right
a citizen in the city of ideas.
It is both difficult and rare
to be made a citizen of that city.
In its agora you come across Lawgivers
that cannot be deceived by any opportunist.
To have come so far is no small matter;
to have done so much is great glory.'

INTERRUPTION

We interrupt the work of the gods,
we hasty and naive ephemeral beings.
In the palaces of Eleusis and of Phthia
Demeter and Thetis begin righteous works
amid tall flames and dense smoke. But
always Metaneira* rushes out of the king's
chambers dishevelled and terrified,
and always Peleus gets scared and intervenes.

ΘΕΡΜΟΠΥΛΕΣ

Τιμὴ σ' ἐκείνους ὅπου στὴν ζωή των
ὥρισαν καὶ φυλάγουν Θερμοπύλες.
Ποτὲ ἀπὸ τὸ χρέος μὴ κινοῦντες·
δίκαιοι κ' ἴσιοι σ' ὅλες των τὲς πράξεις,
ἀλλὰ μὲ λύπη κιόλας κ' εὐσπλαχνία·
γενναῖοι ὁσάκις εἶναι πλούσιοι, κι ὅταν
εἶναι πτωχοί, πάλ' εἰς μικρὸν γενναῖοι,
πάλι συντρέχοντες ὅσο μποροῦνε·
πάντοτε τὴν ἀλήθεια ὁμιλοῦντες,
πλὴν χωρὶς μῖσος γιὰ τοὺς ψευδομένους.

Καὶ περισσότερη τιμὴ τοὺς πρέπει
ὅταν προβλέπουν (καὶ πολλοὶ προβλέπουν)
πῶς ὁ Ἐφιάλτης θὰ φανεῖ στὸ τέλος,
κ' οἱ Μῆδοι ἐπὶ τέλους θὰ διαβοῦνε.

CHE FECE . . . IL GRAN RIFIUTO

Σὲ μερικοὺς ἀνθρώπους ἔρχεται μιὰ μέρα
ποῦ πρέπει τὸ μεγάλο Ναὶ ἢ τὸ μεγάλο τὸ Ὄχι
νὰ ποῦνε. Φανερώνεται ἀμέσως ὅποιος τὄχει
ἕτοιμο μέσα του τὸ Ναί, καὶ λέγοντάς το πέρα

πηγαίνει στὴν τιμὴ καὶ στὴν πεποίθησί του.
Ὁ ἀρνηθεὶς δὲν μετανοιώνει. Ἂν ρωτιούνταν πάλι,
ὄχι θὰ ξαναέλεγε. Κι ὅμως τὸν καταβάλλει
ἐκεῖνο τ' ὄχι — τὸ σωστὸ — εἰς ὅλην τὴν ζωή του.

THERMOPYLAE

Honour to those who in their life
set out and guard Thermopylae.*
Never wavering from duty;
just and forthright in all their actions,
though yet with mercy and compassion;
generous when rich, and when
poor, still in small measure generous,
helping again, as they can;
always speaking forth the truth,
yet without malice for the deceitful.

A higher honour indeed is due
when they foresee (as many do)
that Ephialtes will in the end appear,
and the Medes will eventually break through.

CHE FECE . . . IL GRAN RIFIUTO

For some people, there comes a day
when they have to say the great Yes or the great No.
It becomes at once apparent who has
the Yes ready within him, and in saying it

he crosses over to his honour and conviction.
He who refused does not repent. If asked again
he would once more say No. And yet that No—
the right one—weighs him down for all his life.

ΤΑ ΠΑΡΑΘΥΡΑ

Σ' αὐτὲς τὲς σκοτεινὲς κάμαρες ποῦ περνῶ
μέρες βαρυές, ἐπάνω κάτω τριγυρνῶ
γιὰ νἄβρω τὰ παράθυρα.—Ὅταν ἀνοίξει
ἕνα παράθυρο θἄναι παρηγορία.—
Μὰ τὰ παράθυρα δὲν βρίσκονται, ἢ δὲν μπορῶ
νὰ τἄβρω. Καὶ καλλίτερα ἴσως νὰ μὴν τὰ βρῶ.
Ἴσως τὸ φῶς θἄναι μιὰ νέα τυραννία.
Ποιὸς ξέρει τί καινούρια πράγματα θὰ δείξει.

[ΤΡΩΕΣ]

βλ. *Ποιήματα (1905–1915)*, σελ. 40.

ΤΕΙΧΗ

Χωρὶς περίσκεψιν, χωρὶς λύπην, χωρὶς αἰδὼ
μεγάλα κ' ὑψηλὰ τριγύρω μου ἔκτισαν τείχη.

Καὶ κάθομαι καὶ ἀπελπίζομαι τώρα ἐδῶ.
Ἄλλο δὲν σκέπτομαι: τὸν νοῦν μου τρώγει αὐτὴ ἡ τύχη·

διότι πράγματα πολλὰ ἔξω νὰ κάμω εἶχον.
Ἅ, ὅταν ἔκτιζαν τὰ τείχη πῶς νὰ μὴν προσέξω.

Ἀλλὰ δὲν ἄκουσα ποτὲ κρότον κτιστῶν ἢ ἦχον.
Ἀνεπαισθήτως μ' ἔκλεισαν ἀπὸ τὸν κόσμον ἔξω.

THE WINDOWS

Within these dark chambers, where I live through
oppressive days, I pace up and down,
trying to find the windows.—When a window
opens, it will be a consolation.—
But the windows are not to be found, or I am unable
to find them. And perhaps it's better that I don't.
Perhaps the light will be a new tyranny.
Who knows what novel things it will reveal.

[TROJANS]

For the text, see *Poems (1905–1915)*, p. 41.

WALLS

Without consideration, without pity, without shame,
they built around me great and towering walls.

And now I am sitting and despairing here.
I think of nothing else: this fate is gnawing at my mind;

for I had many things to do out there.
When they were building the walls, how could I not be aware?

Yet never did I hear clatter of builders, or any sound.
Imperceptibly, they shut me off from the world outside.

ΠΕΡΙΜΕΝΟΝΤΑΣ ΤΟΥΣ ΒΑΡΒΑΡΟΥΣ

—Τί περιμένουμε στὴν ἀγορὰ συναθροισμένοι;

Εἶναι οἱ βάρβαροι νὰ φθάσουν σήμερα.

—Γιατί μέσα στὴν Σύγκλητο μιὰ τέτοια ἀπραξία;
Τί κάθοντ' οἱ Συγκλητικοὶ καὶ δὲν νομοθετοῦνε;

Γιατί οἱ βάρβαροι θὰ φθάσουν σήμερα.
Τί νόμους πιὰ θὰ κάμουν οἱ Συγκλητικοί;
Οἱ βάρβαροι σὰν ἔλθουν θὰ νομοθετήσουν.

—Γιατί ὁ αὐτοκράτωρ μας τόσο πρωῒ σηκώθη,
καὶ κάθεται στῆς πόλεως τὴν πιὸ μεγάλη πύλη
στὸν θρόνο ἐπάνω, ἐπίσημος, φορῶντας τὴν κορώνα;

Γιατί οἱ βάρβαροι θὰ φθάσουν σήμερα.
Κι ὁ αὐτοκράτωρ περιμένει νὰ δεχθεῖ
τὸν ἀρχηγό τους. Μάλιστα ἑτοίμασε
γιὰ νὰ τὸν δώσει μιὰ περγαμηνή. Ἐκεῖ
τὸν ἔγραψε τίτλους πολλοὺς κι ὀνόματα.

—Γιατί οἱ δυό μας ὕπατοι κ' οἱ πραίτορες ἐβγῆκαν
σήμερα μὲ τὲς κόκκινες, τὲς κεντημένες τόγες·
γιατί βραχιόλια φόρεσαν μὲ τόσους ἀμεθύστους,
καὶ δαχτυλίδια μὲ λαμπρά, γυαλιστερὰ σμαράγδια·
γιατί νὰ πιάσουν σήμερα πολύτιμα μπαστούνια
μ' ἀσήμια καὶ μαλάματα ἔκτακτα σκαλιγμένα;

Γιατί οἱ βάρβαροι θὰ φθάσουν σήμερα·
καὶ τέτοια πράγματα θαμπόνουν τοὺς βαρβάρους.

*

WAITING FOR THE BARBARIANS

—What are we waiting for, assembled in the Forum?

The barbarians are to arrive today.

—Why then such inactivity in the Senate?
Why do the Senators sit back and do not legislate?

Because the barbarians will arrive today.
What sort of laws now can Senators enact?
When the barbarians come, they'll do the legislating.

—Why is our emperor up and about so early,
and seated at the grandest gate of our city,
upon the throne, in state, wearing the crown?

Because the barbarians will arrive today.
And the emperor expects to receive their leader.
Indeed, he has prepared to present him
with a parchment scroll. Thereon he has
invested him with many names and titles.

—Why have our two consuls and the praetors come out
today in their purple, embroidered togas;
why did they put on bracelets studded with amethysts,
and rings with resplendent, glittering emeralds;
why are they carrying today precious staves
carved exquisitely in gold and silver?

Because the barbarians will arrive today;
and such things dazzle the barbarians.

*

—Γιατὶ κ' οἱ ἄξιοι ρήτορες δὲν ἔρχονται σὰν πάντα
νὰ βγάλλουνε τοὺς λόγους τους, νὰ ποῦνε τὰ δικά τους;

Γιατὶ οἱ βάρβαροι θὰ φθάσουν σήμερα·
κι αὐτοὶ βαρυοῦντ' εὐφράδειες καὶ δημηγορίες.

—Γιατὶ ν' ἀρχίσει μονομιᾶς αὐτὴ ἡ ἀνησυχία
κ' ἡ σύγχυσις. (Τὰ πρόσωπα τὶ σοβαρὰ ποῦ ἐγίναν).
Γιατὶ ἀδειάζουν γρήγορα οἱ δρόμοι κ' ἡ πλατέες,
κι ὅλοι γυρνοῦν στὰ σπίτια τους πολὺ συλλογισμένοι;

Γιατὶ ἐνύχτωσε κ' οἱ βάρβαροι δὲν ἦλθαν.
Καὶ μερικοὶ ἔφθασαν ἀπ' τὰ σύνορα,
καὶ εἴπανε πῶς βάρβαροι πιὰ δὲν ὑπάρχουν.

Καὶ τώρα τὶ θὰ γένουμε χωρὶς βαρβάρους.
Οἱ ἄνθρωποι αὐτοὶ ἦσαν μιὰ κάποια λύσις.

[ΜΟΝΟΤΟΝΙΑ]

βλ. *Ποιήματα (1905–1915)*, σελ. 36.

— And why don't our worthy orators, as always, come out
to deliver their speeches, to have their usual say?

Because the barbarians will arrive today;
and they get bored with eloquence and orations.

— Why has there suddenly begun all this commotion,
and this confusion? (How solemn people's faces have become).
Why are the streets and the squares emptying so swiftly,
and everyone is returning home in deep preoccupation?

Because night has fallen and the barbarians have not come.
And some people have arrived from the frontiers,
and said that there are no barbarians anymore.

And now, what will become of us without barbarians?
Those people were some sort of a solution.

[MONOTONY]

For the text, see *Poems (1905–1915)*, p. 37.

ΑΠΙΣΤΙΑ

«Πολλὰ ἄρα Ὁμήρου ἐπαινοῦντες ἄλλα τοῦτο οὐκ
«ἐπαινεσόμεθα . . . οὐδὲ Αἰσχύλου, ὅταν φῇ ἡ Θέτις τὸν
«Ἀπόλλω ἐν τοῖς αὐτῆς γάμοις ᾄδοντα

«ἐνδατεῖσθαι τὰς ἑὰς εὐπαιδίας,
«νόσων τ' ἀπείρους καὶ μακραίωνας βίους.
«Ξύμπαντά τ' εἰπὼν θεοφιλεῖς ἐμὰς τύχας
«παιῶν' ἐπευφήμησεν, εὐθυμῶν ἐμέ.
«Κἀγὼ τὸ Φοίβου θεῖον ἀψευδὲς στόμα
«ἤλπιζον εἶναι, μαντικῇ βρύον τέχνῃ.
«Ὁ δ', αὐτὸς ὑμνῶν, . . .
«. . . . . αὐτός ἐστιν ὁ κτανὼν
«τὸν παῖδα τὸν ἐμόν».

Πλάτων, Πολιτείας Β'.

Σὰν πάντρευαν τὴν Θέτιδα μὲ τὸν Πηλέα
σηκώθηκε ὁ Ἀπόλλων στὸ λαμπρὸ τραπέζι
τοῦ γάμου, καὶ μακάρισε τοὺς νεονύμφους
γιὰ τὸν βλαστὸ ποῦ θἄβγαινε ἀπ' τὴν ἕνωσί των.
Εἶπε· Ποτὲ αὐτὸν ἀρρώστια δὲν θἀγγίξει
καὶ θἄχει μακρυνὴ ζωή. —Αὐτὰ σὰν εἶπε
ἡ Θέτις χάρηκε πολύ, γιατὶ τὰ λόγια
τοῦ Ἀπόλλωνος ποῦ γνώριζε ἀπὸ προφητεῖες
τὴν φάνηκαν ἐγγύησις γιὰ τὸ παιδί της.
Κι ὅταν μεγάλωνεν ὁ Ἀχιλλεύς, και ἦταν
τῆς Θεσσαλίας ἔπαινος ἡ ἐμορφιά του,
ἡ Θέτις τοῦ θεοῦ τὰ λόγια ἐνθυμοῦνταν.
Ἀλλὰ μιὰ μέρα ἦλθαν γέροι μὲ εἰδήσεις,
κ' εἶπαν τὸν σκοτωμὸ τοῦ Ἀχιλλέως στὴν Τροία.
Κ' ἡ Θέτις ξέσχιζε τὰ πορφυρά της ροῦχα,
κ' ἔβγαζεν ἀπὸ πάνω της καὶ ξεπετοῦσε
στὸ χῶμα τὰ βραχιόλια καὶ τὰ δαχτυλίδια.
Καὶ μὲς στὸν ὀδυρμό της τὰ παληὰ θυμήθη·
καὶ ρώτησε τί ἔκαμνε ὁ σοφὸς Ἀπόλλων,
ποῦ γύριζεν ὁ ποιητὴς ποῦ στὰ τραπέζια
ἔξοχα ὁμιλεῖ, ποῦ γύριζε ὁ προφήτης
ὅταν τὸν υἱό της σκότωναν στὰ πρῶτα νειάτα.
Κ' οἱ γέροι τὴν ἀπήντησαν πῶς ὁ Ἀπόλλων
αὐτὸς ὁ ἴδιος ἐκατέβηκε στὴν Τροία,
καὶ μὲ τοὺς Τρῶας σκότωσε τὸν Ἀχιλλέα.

PERFIDY

Then, though there are many other things that we praise in Homer, this we will not applaud . . . nor shall we approve of Aeschylus when his Thetis owns that Apollo, singing at her wedding, foretold the happy fortunes of her issue:

> 'Their days prolonged,
> from pain and sickness free;
> and rounding out the tale of heaven's blessings
> raised the proud paean, making glad my heart;
> and I believed that Phoebus' mouth divine,
> filled with the breath of prophecy, could not lie.
> But he himself, the singer . . .
> is now the slayer of my son.'

Plato, *Republic*, II (tr. Paul Shorey)

When Thetis was given in marriage to Peleus,
Apollo stood up at the splendid wedding banquet
and gave his blessings to the newlyweds
for the offspring that would be born of their union.
He said: 'Never will he be touched by illness,
and he'll enjoy a long life.' When he said this
Thetis was very pleased, because the words
of Apollo—who knew all about prophecies—
seemed to her an assurance for her child.
And as Achilles was growing up and his
good looks were the praise of Thessaly,
Thetis used to think back on the god's words.
One day, however, some elders came with news
and told that Achilles was slain at Troy.
And Thetis rent her purple robes,
and pulled off and hurled onto
the ground her bracelets and her rings.
And in her deep lament, she recalled the past
and asked what was he doing, the wise Apollo,
where was the poet wandering who at banquets
eloquently speaks, where was the prophet wandering,
when they were killing her son, in the prime of life.
And the elders replied that it was Apollo
himself who had descended to the city of Troy
and along with the Trojans killed Achilles.

Η ΚΗΔΕΙΑ ΤΟΥ ΣΑΡΠΗΔΟΝΟΣ

Βαρυὰν ὀδύνην ἔχει ὁ Ζεύς. Τὸν Σαρπηδόνα
ἐσκότωσεν ὁ Πάτροκλος· καὶ τώρα ὁρμοῦν
ὁ Μενοιτιάδης κ' οἱ Ἀχαιοὶ τὸ σῶμα
ν' ἁρπάξουνε καὶ νὰ τὸ ἐξευτελίσουν.

Ἀλλὰ ὁ Ζεὺς διόλου δὲν στέργει αὐτά.
Τὸ ἀγαπημένο του παιδὶ — ποῦ τὸ ἄφισε
καὶ χάθηκεν· ὁ Νόμος ἦταν ἔτσι —
τουλάχιστον θὰ τὸ τιμήσει πεθαμένο.
Καὶ στέλνει, ἰδού, τὸν Φοῖβο κάτω στὴν πεδιάδα
ἑρμηνευμένο πῶς τὸ σῶμα νὰ νοιασθεῖ.

Τοῦ ἥρωος τὸν νεκρὸ μ' εὐλάβεια καὶ μὲ λύπη
σηκώνει ὁ Φοῖβος καὶ τὸν πάει στὸν ποταμό.
Τὸν πλένει ἀπὸ τὲς σκόνες κι ἀπ' τὰ αἵματα·
κλείει τὲς φοβερὲς πληγές, μὴ ἀφίνοντας
κανένα ἴχνος νὰ φανεῖ· τῆς ἀμβροσίας
τ' ἀρώματα χύνει ἐπάνω του· καὶ μὲ λαμπρὰ
Ὀλύμπια φορέματα τὸν ντύνει.
Τὸ δέρμα του ἀσπρίζει καὶ μὲ μαργαριταρένιο
χτένι κτενίζει τὰ κατάμαυρα μαλλιά.
Τὰ ὡραῖα μέλη σχηματίζει καὶ πλαγιάζει.

Τώρα σὰν νέος μοιάζει βασιλεὺς ἁρματηλάτης —
στὰ εἰκοσιπέντε χρόνια του, στὰ εἰκοσιέξι —
ἀναπαυόμενος μετὰ ποῦ ἐκέρδισε,
μ' ἅρμα ὁλόχρυσο καὶ ταχυτάτους ἵππους,
σὲ ξακουστὸν ἀγῶνα τὸ βραβεῖον.

Ἔτσι σὰν ποῦ τελείωσεν ὁ Φοῖβος
τὴν ἐντολή του, κάλεσε τοὺς δυὸ ἀδελφοὺς
τὸν Ὕπνο καὶ τὸν Θάνατο, προστάζοντάς τους
νὰ πᾶν τὸ σῶμα στὴν Λυκία, τὸν πλούσιο τόπο.

Καὶ κατὰ ἐκεῖ τὸν πλούσιο τόπο, τὴν Λυκία
τοῦτοι ὁδοιπόρησαν οἱ δυὸ ἀδελφοὶ
Ὕπνος καὶ Θάνατος, κι ὅταν πιὰ ἔφθασαν

THE FUNERAL OF SARPEDON

Zeus is in deep sorrow. Sarpedon*
has been slain by Patroclus; and
now he—the son of Menoetius—and the Achaeans
rush forward to seize and to desecrate the body.

But Zeus does not agree to this at all.
His beloved child—whom he left
to perish; such was the Law—
he will, at least, honour in death.
And behold, he sends Phoebus down to the plain
with instructions on how to tend the body.

Phoebus lifts the hero's corpse with reverence
and sorrow, and carries it to the river.
He washes away the dust and blood;
he closes the frightful wounds, leaving
not a trace to show; he pours on him
ambrosial perfumes and attires
the body in splendid Olympian robes.
He blanches the skin and with a pearly
comb grooms the raven hair.
He arranges the lovely limbs, and lays them down.

Now the dead man resembles a young king, a royal charioteer—
about twenty-five or twenty-six years old—
resting after he has won,
with a golden chariot and the swiftest horses,
the prize in a famous race.

Having thus carried out his assignment,
Phoebus summoned the two brothers,
Sleep and Death, ordering them
to take the body to Lycia, the wealthy land.

And toward the wealthy land of Lycia,
journeyed on foot the two brothers,
Sleep and Death, and when they at last

στὴν πόρτα τοῦ βασιλικοῦ σπιτιοῦ
παρέδοσαν τὸ δοξασμένο σῶμα,
καὶ γύρισαν στὲς ἄλλες τους φροντίδες καὶ δουλειές.

Κι ὡς τὄλαβαν αὐτοῦ στὸ σπίτι, ἀρχίνησε
μὲ συνοδεῖες, καὶ τιμές, καὶ θρήνους,
καὶ μ' ἄφθονες σπονδὲς ἀπὸ ἱεροὺς κρατῆρας,
καὶ μ' ὅλα τὰ πρεπὰ ἡ θλιβερὴ ταφή·
κ' ἔπειτα ἔμπειροι ἀπ' τὴν πολιτείαν ἐργάται,
καὶ φημισμένοι δουλευταὶ τῆς πέτρας
ἦλθανε κ' ἔκαμαν τὸ μνῆμα καὶ τὴν στήλη.

ΤΑ ΑΛΟΓΑ ΤΟΥ ΑΧΙΛΛΕΩΣ

Τὸν Πάτροκλο σὰν εἶδαν σκοτωμένο,
ποῦ ἦταν τόσο ἀνδρεῖος, καὶ δυνατός, καὶ νέος,
ἄρχισαν τ' ἄλογα νὰ κλαῖνε τοῦ Ἀχιλλέως·
ἡ φύσις των ἡ ἀθάνατη ἀγανακτοῦσε
γιὰ τοῦ θανάτου αὐτὸ τὸ ἔργον ποῦ θωροῦσε.
Τίναζαν τὰ κεφάλια των καὶ τὲς μακρυὲς χαῖτες κουνοῦσαν,
τὴν γῆ χτυποῦσαν μὲ τὰ πόδια, καὶ θρηνοῦσαν
τὸν Πάτροκλο ποῦ ἐνοιώθανε ἄψυχο — ἀφανισμένο —
μιὰ σάρκα τώρα ποταπὴ — τὸ πνεῦμα του χαμένο —
ἀνυπεράσπιστο — χωρὶς πνοὴ —
εἰς τὸ μεγάλο Τίποτε ἐπιστραμένο ἀπ' τὴν ζωή.

Τὰ δάκρυα εἶδε ὁ Ζεὺς τῶν ἀθανάτων
ἀλόγων καὶ λυπήθη. «Στοῦ Πηλέως τὸν γάμο»
εἶπε «δὲν ἔπρεπ' ἔτσι ἄσκεπτα νὰ κάμω·
καλλίτερα νὰ μὴ σᾶς δείναμε ἄλογά μου
δυστυχισμένα! Τί γυρεύατ' ἐκεῖ χάμου
στὴν ἄθλια ἀνθρωπότητα ποῦ εἶναι τὸ παίγνιον τῆς μοίρας.
Σεῖς ποῦ οὐδὲ ὁ θάνατος φυλάγει, οὐδὲ τὸ γῆρας
πρόσκαιρες συμφορὲς σᾶς τυραννοῦν. Στὰ βάσανά των
σᾶς ἔμπλεξαν οἱ ἄνθρωποι.» — Ὅμως τὰ δάκρυά των
γιὰ τοῦ θανάτου τὴν παντοτινὴ
τὴν συμφορὰν ἐχύνανε τὰ δυὸ τὰ ζῶα τὰ εὐγενῆ.

arrived at the gate of the royal house,
they delivered the glorified body,
and returned to their other cares and labours.

And once the body was received there, at the house,
the mournful funeral began, with processions,
honours, and lamentations, with copious libations
poured from sacred craters, and all the proper rites;
afterwards, skilled workers from the city,
and renowned craftsmen in stone,
came and built the sepulchre and the stele.

THE HORSES OF ACHILLES

When they saw Patroclus slain,
who was so brave, and strong, and young,
the horses of Achilles* started to weep;
their immortal nature grew indignant
at witnessing this work of death.
They kept tossing their heads, and shaking their long manes,
striking the earth with their hooves, and lamenting
for Patroclus, whom they sensed to be lifeless—annihilated—
a base piece of flesh now—his spirit vanished—
defenceless—his breath gone—
rendered by life back to the great Void.

Zeus saw the tears of the immortal horses
and was saddened. 'At the wedding of Peleus',
he said, 'I should not have acted so rashly;
my poor horses, better that we had not
given you away! What were you to do down there,
among the wretched race of men, that is the plaything of fate.
You, whom neither death nor old age awaits,
are tormented by ephemeral misfortunes. Mortals
have embroiled you in their troubles.'—Yet
the two noble creatures went on
shedding their tears for the everlasting tragedy of death.

[Η ΣΥΝΟΔΕΙΑ ΤΟΥ ΔΙΟΝΥΣΟΥ]

[Ο ΒΑΣΙΛΕΥΣ ΔΗΜΗΤΡΙΟΣ]

[ΤΑ ΒΗΜΑΤΑ]

[ΟΥΤΟΣ ΕΚΕΙΝΟΣ]

βλ. *Ποιήματα (1905–1915)*, σελ. 44, 42, 56, καὶ 62.

[THE RETINUE OF DIONYSUS]

[KING DEMETRIUS]

[THE FOOTSTEPS]

[THAT IS THE MAN]

For the texts, see *Poems (1905–1915)*, pp. 45, 43, 57, and 63.

POEMS (1905–1915)

ΠΟΙΗΜΑΤΑ (1905–1915)

Η ΠΟΛΙΣ

Εἶπες· «Θὰ πάγω σ' ἄλλη γῆ, θὰ πάγω σ' ἄλλη θάλασσα.
Μιὰ πόλις ἄλλη θὰ βρεθεῖ καλλίτερη ἀπὸ αὐτή.
Κάθε προσπάθεια μου μιὰ καταδίκη εἶναι γραφτή·
κ' εἶν' ἡ καρδιά μου—σὰν νεκρὸς—θαμένη.
Ὁ νοῦς μου ὡς πότε μὲς στὸν μαρασμὸν αὐτὸν θὰ μένει.
Ὅπου τὸ μάτι μου γυρίσω, ὅπου κι ἂν δῶ
ἐρείπια μαῦρα τῆς ζωῆς μου βλέπω ἐδῶ,
ποῦ τόσα χρόνια πέρασα καὶ ρήμαξα καὶ χάλασα.»

Καινούριους τόπους δὲν θὰ βρεῖς, δὲν θἄβρεις ἄλλες θάλασσες.
Ἡ πόλις θὰ σὲ ἀκολουθεῖ. Στοὺς δρόμους θὰ γυρνᾶς
τοὺς ἴδιους. Καὶ στὲς γειτονιὲς τὲς ἴδιες θὰ γερνᾶς·
καὶ μὲς στὰ ἴδια σπίτια αὐτὰ θ' ἀσπρίζεις.
Πάντα στὴν πόλι αὐτὴ θὰ φθάνεις. Γιὰ τὰ ἀλλοῦ—μὴ
    ἐλπίζεις—
δὲν ἔχει πλοῖο γιὰ σέ, δὲν ἔχει ὁδό.
Ἔτσι ποῦ τὴ ζωή σου ρήμαξες ἐδῶ
στὴν κώχη τούτη τὴν μικρή, σ' ὅλην τὴν γῆ τὴν χάλασες.

Η ΣΑΤΡΑΠΕΙΑ

Τὶ συμφορά, ἐνῶ εἶσαι καμωμένος
γιὰ τὰ ὡραῖα καὶ μεγάλα ἔργα
ἡ ἄδικη αὐτή σου ἡ τύχη πάντα
ἐνθάρρυνσι κ' ἐπιτυχία νὰ σὲ ἀρνεῖται·
νὰ σ' ἐμποδίζουν εὐτελεῖς συνήθειες,
καὶ μικροπρέπειες, κι ἀδιαφορίες.
Καὶ τὶ φρικτὴ ἡ μέρα ποῦ ἐνδίδεις
(ἡ μέρα ποῦ ἀφέθηκες κ' ἐνδίδεις),
καὶ φεύγεις ὁδοιπόρος γιὰ τὰ Σοῦσα,
καὶ πιαίνεις στὸν μονάρχην Ἀρταξέρξη
ποῦ εὐνοϊκὰ σὲ βάζει στὴν αὐλή του,
καὶ σὲ προσφέρει σατραπεῖες καὶ τέτοια.

THE CITY

You said: 'I'll go to another land, I'll go to another sea.
Another city will be found, a better one than this.
My every effort is doomed by destiny
and my heart—like a dead man—lies buried.
How long will my mind languish in such decay?
Wherever I turn my eyes, wherever I look,
the blackened ruins of my life I see here,
where so many years I've lived and wasted and ruined.'

Any new lands you will not find; you'll find no other seas.
The city will be following you. In the same streets
you'll wander. And in the same neighbourhoods you'll age,
and in these same houses you will grow grey.
Always in this same city you'll arrive. For elsewhere—do not hope—
there is no ship for you, there is no road.
Just as you've wasted your life here,
in this tiny niche, in the entire world you've ruined it.

SATRAPY

What a misfortune, though you're made
for noble and prodigious deeds,
this unjust fate of yours always
denies you encouragement and success;
and you're encumbered by base habits,
and by pettiness and by indifference.
And what a frightful day when you give in,
(the day when you let go and give in)
and you depart, a wayfarer, for Susa,*
and you go to the monarch Artaxerxes,
who favourably places you in his court
and offers you satrapies and the like.

Καὶ σὺ τὰ δέχεσαι μὲ ἀπελπισία
αὐτὰ τὰ πράγματα ποῦ δὲν τὰ θέλεις.
Ἄλλα ζητεῖ ἡ ψυχή σου, γι' ἄλλα κλαίει·
τὸν ἔπαινο τοῦ Δήμου καὶ τῶν Σοφιστῶν,
τὰ δύσκολα καὶ τ' ἀνεκτίμητα Εὖγε·
τὴν Ἀγορά, τὸ Θέατρο, καὶ τοὺς Στεφάνους.
Αὐτὰ ποῦ θὰ στὰ δώσει ὁ Ἀρταξέρξης,
αὐτὰ ποῦ θὰ τὰ βρεῖς στὴ σατραπεία·
καὶ τὶ ζωὴ χωρὶς αὐτὰ θὰ κάμεις.

ΣΟΦΟΙ ΔΕ ΠΡΟΣΙΟΝΤΩΝ

«Θεοὶ μὲν γὰρ μελλόντων, ἄνθρωποι δὲ γιγνομένων, σοφοὶ
«δὲ προσιόντων αἰσθάνονται.»

Φιλόστρατος, Τὰ ἐς τὸν Τυανέα Ἀπολλώνιον, VIII, 7.

Οἱ ἄνθρωποι γνωρίζουν τὰ γινόμενα.
Τὰ μέλλοντα γνωρίζουν οἱ θεοί,
πλήρεις καὶ μόνοι κάτοχοι πάντων τῶν φώτων.
Ἐκ τῶν μελλόντων οἱ σοφοὶ τὰ προσερχόμενα
ἀντιλαμβάνονται. Ἡ ἀκοὴ

αὐτῶν κάποτε ἐν ὥραις σοβαρῶν σπουδῶν
ταράττεται. Ἡ μυστικὴ βοὴ
τοὺς ἔρχεται τῶν πλησιαζόντων γεγονότων.
Καὶ τὴν προσέχουν εὐλαβεῖς. Ἐνῷ εἰς τὴν ὁδὸν
ἔξω, οὐδὲν ἀκούουν οἱ λαοί.

And you accept them in despair,
those things you do not want.
Your soul craves other things, for other things it weeps:
the praise of the Demos and the Sophists,
the hard-won and priceless acclaim;
the Agora, the Theatre, the Laurel Wreaths.
How can you get any of these from Artaxerxes?
Where in a satrapy can any of these be found;
and what a life, without them, will you live?

WISE MEN

For gods perceive future things, mortals present things and wise men things about to happen.

Philostratus, *Life of Apollonius of Tyana*, viii. 7

Mortals are aware of present things.
The gods, full and sole possessors
of all Knowledge, are aware of things to come.
Of things to come, wise men perceive
the imminent. Their hearing

at times, in hours of serious contemplation,
is disturbed. The secret sound
of approaching events reaches them.
And they pay it reverent attention. While out in the street
the people hear nothing at all.

ΜΑΡΤΙΑΙ ΕΙΔΟΙ

Τὰ μεγαλεῖα νὰ φοβᾶσαι, ὦ ψυχή.
Καὶ τὲς φιλοδοξίες σου νὰ ὑπερνικήσεις
ἂν δὲν μπορεῖς, μὲ δισταγμὸ καὶ προφυλάξεις
νὰ τὲς ἀκολουθεῖς. Κι ὅσο ἐμπροστὰ προβαίνεις,
τόσο ἐξεταστική, προσεκτικὴ νὰ εἶσαι.

Κι ὅταν θὰ φθάσεις στὴν ἀκμή σου, Καῖσαρ πιά·
ἔτσι περιωνύμου ἀνθρώπου σχῆμα ὅταν λάβεις,
τότε κυρίως πρόσεξε σὰν βγεῖς στὸν δρόμον ἔξω,
ἐξουσιαστὴς περίβλεπτος μὲ συνοδεία,
ἂν τύχει καὶ πλησιάσει ἀπὸ τὸν ὄχλο
κανένας Ἀρτεμίδωρος, ποῦ φέρνει γράμμα,
καὶ λέγει βιαστικὰ «Διάβασε ἀμέσως τοῦτα,
«εἶναι μεγάλα πράγματα ποῦ σ' ἐνδιαφέρουν»,
μὴ λείψεις νὰ σταθεῖς· μὴ λείψεις ν' ἀναβάλλεις
κάθε ὁμιλίαν ἢ δουλειά· μὴ λείψεις τοὺς διαφόρους
ποῦ χαιρετοῦν καὶ προσκυνοῦν νὰ τοὺς παραμερίσεις
(τοὺς βλέπεις πιὸ ἀργά)· ἂς περιμένει ἀκόμη
κ' ἡ Σύγκλητος αὐτή, κ' εὐθὺς νὰ τὰ γνωρίσεις
τὰ σοβαρὰ γραφόμενα τοῦ Ἀρτεμιδώρου.

ΤΕΛΕΙΩΜΕΝΑ

Μέσα στὸν φόβο καὶ στὲς ὑποψίες,
μὲ ταραγμένο νοῦ καὶ τρομαγμένα μάτια,
λυώνουμε καὶ σχεδιάζουμε τὸ πῶς νὰ κάμουμε
γιὰ ν' ἀποφύγουμε τὸν βέβαιο
τὸν κίνδυνο ποῦ ἔτσι φρικτὰ μᾶς ἀπειλεῖ.
Κι ὅμως λανθάνουμε, δὲν εἶν' αὐτὸς στὸν δρόμο·
ψεύτικα ἦσαν τὰ μηνύματα
(ἢ δὲν τ' ἀκούσαμε, ἢ δὲν τὰ νοιώσαμε καλά).
Ἄλλη καταστροφή, ποῦ δὲν τὴν φανταζόμεθαν,
ἐξαφνική, ραγδαία πέφτει ἐπάνω μας,
κι ἀνέτοιμους — ποῦ πιὰ καιρὸς — μᾶς συνεπαίρνει.

THE IDES OF MARCH

Beware of grandeurs, oh my soul,
and if you cannot overcome your own
ambitions, pursue them, at least, with hesitancy
and circumspection. The more you advance,
the more questioning, more careful you must be.

And when you reach your zenith, Caesar at last,
invested with the authority of such a famous man,
then be particularly careful, as you go out
into the street, a prominent ruler with a retinue,
if out of the crowd some Artemidorus*
chances to approach bearing a letter,
and hurriedly says: 'Read this right now,
these are important matters that concern you,'
don't fail to halt; don't fail to postpone
any discussion or business; don't fail to brush
aside all those who salute or bow
(see to them later), let even the Senate itself
wait, and immediately pay heed
to the serious missive of Artemidorus.

FINISHED

Deep in fear and in suspicions,
with troubled mind and frightened eyes,
we sweat away and scheme at what to do
in order to avoid the certain
danger that so frightfully threatens us.
And yet we err—that danger is not in our path;
false were the portents
(either we didn't hear them, or didn't fully understand them).
A different disaster, which we never imagined,
unexpected, rapidly falls upon us,
and unprepared—no time left—we're swept away.

ΑΠΟΛΕΙΠΕΙΝ Ο ΘΕΟΣ ΑΝΤΩΝΙΟΝ

Σὰν ἔξαφνα ὥρα μεσάνυχτ᾽ ἀκουσθεῖ
ἀόρατος θίασος νὰ περνᾶ
μὲ μουσικὲς ἐξαίσιες, μὲ φωνὲς—
τὴν τύχη σου ποῦ ἐνδίδει πιά, τὰ ἔργα σου
ποῦ ἀπέτυχαν, τὰ σχέδια τῆς ζωῆς σου
ποῦ βγῆκαν ὅλα πλάνες μὴ ἀνοφέλετα θρηνήσεις.
Σὰν ἕτοιμος ἀπὸ καιρό, σὰ θαρραλέος,
ἀποχαιρέτα την, τὴν Ἀλεξάνδρεια ποῦ φεύγει.
Πρὸ πάντων νὰ μὴ γελασθεῖς, μὴν πεῖς πῶς ἦταν
ἕνα ὄνειρο, πῶς ἀπατήθηκεν ἡ ἀκοή σου·
μάταιες ἐλπίδες τέτοιες μὴν καταδεχθεῖς.
Σὰν ἕτοιμος ἀπὸ καιρό, σὰ θαρραλέος,
σὰν ποῦ ταιριάζει σε ποῦ ἀξιώθηκες μιὰ τέτοια πόλι,
πλησίασε σταθερὰ πρὸς τὸ παράθυρο,
κι ἄκουσε μὲ συγκίνησιν, ἀλλ᾽ ὄχι
μὲ τῶν δειλῶν τὰ παρακάλια καὶ παράπονα,
ὡς τελευταία ἀπόλαυσι τοὺς ἤχους,
τὰ ἐξαίσια ὄργανα τοῦ μυστικοῦ θιάσου,
κι ἀποχαιρέτα την, τὴν Ἀλεξάνδρεια ποῦ χάνεις.

Ο ΘΕΟΔΟΤΟΣ

Ἂν εἶσαι ἀπ᾽ τοὺς ἀληθινὰ ἐκλεκτούς,
τὴν ἐπικράτησί σου κύταζε πῶς ἀποκτᾶς.
Ὅσο κι ἂν δοξασθεῖς, τὰ κατορθώματά σου
στὴν Ἰταλία καὶ στὴν Θεσσαλία
ὅσο κι ἂν διαλαλοῦν ἡ πολιτεῖες,
ὅσα ψηφίσματα τιμητικὰ
κι ἂν σ᾽ ἔβγαλαν στὴ Ρώμη οἱ θαυμασταί σου,
μήτε ἡ χαρά σου, μήτε ὁ θρίαμβος θὰ μείνουν,
μήτε ἀνώτερος—τὶ ἀνώτερος;—ἄνθρωπος θὰ αἰσθανθεῖς,
ὅταν, στὴν Ἀλεξάνδρεια, ὁ Θεόδοτος σὲ φέρει,
ἐπάνω σὲ σινὶ αἱματωμένο,
τοῦ ἀθλίου Πομπηΐου τὸ κεφάλι.

*

THE GOD FORSAKES ANTONY

When suddenly, at the midnight hour
an invisible company is heard going past,
with exquisite music, with voices—
your fate that's giving in now, your deeds
that failed, your life's plans that proved to be
all illusions, do not needlessly lament.
As one long since prepared, as one courageous,
bid farewell to the Alexandria that's leaving.
Above all, don't be misled, don't say it was
a dream, that your ears deceived you;
don't deign to foster such vain hopes.
As one long since prepared, as one courageous,
as befits you who were deemed worthy of such a city,
move with steady steps toward the window
and listen with deepest feeling, yet not
with a coward's entreaties and complaints,
listen as an ultimate delight to the sounds,
to the exquisite instruments of the mystical company,
and bid farewell to the Alexandria you are losing.

THEODOTUS

If you are one of the truly elect,
be careful how you attain your dominance.
No matter how much you are glorified, how much
your Italian and Thessalian exploits
are acclaimed by the city-states,
how many honorific decrees
are issued for you in Rome by your admirers,
neither your happiness nor your triumph will last,
nor will you feel like a superior being—superior indeed—
when, in Alexandria, Theodotus brings you
upon a bloodstained tray
the wretched Pompey's head.

*

Καὶ μὴ ἐπαναπαύεσαι ποῦ στὴν ζωή σου
περιωρισμένη, τακτοποιημένη, καὶ πεζή,
τέτοια θεαματικὰ καὶ φοβερὰ δὲν ἔχει.
Ἴσως αὐτὴν τὴν ὥρα εἰς κανενὸς γειτόνου σου
τὸ νοικοκερεμένο σπίτι μπαίνει—
ἀόρατος, ἄϋλος—ὁ Θεόδοτος,
φέρνοντας τέτοιο ἕνα φρικτὸ κεφάλι.

ΜΟΝΟΤΟΝΙΑ

Τὴν μιὰ μονότονην ἡμέραν ἄλλη
μονότονη, ἀπαράλλακτη ἀκολουθεῖ. Θὰ γίνουν
τὰ ἴδια πράγματα, θὰ ξαναγίνουν πάλι—
ἡ ὅμοιες στιγμὲς μᾶς βρίσκουνε καὶ μᾶς ἀφίνουν.

Μῆνας περνᾶ καὶ φέρνει ἄλλον μῆνα.
Αὐτὰ ποῦ ἔρχονται κανεὶς εὔκολα τὰ εἰκάζει·
εἶναι τὰ χθεσινὰ τὰ βαρετὰ ἐκεῖνα.
Καὶ καταντᾶ τὸ αὔριο πιὰ σὰν αὔριο νὰ μὴ μοιάζει.

ΙΘΑΚΗ

Σὰ βγεῖς στὸν πηγαιμὸ γιὰ τὴν Ἰθάκη,
νὰ εὔχεσαι νἆναι μακρὺς ὁ δρόμος,
γεμάτος περιπέτειες, γεμάτος γνώσεις.
Τοὺς Λαιστρυγόνας καὶ τοὺς Κύκλωπας,
τὸν θυμωμένο Ποσειδῶνα μὴ φοβᾶσαι,
τέτοια στὸν δρόμο σου ποτέ σου δὲν θὰ βρεῖς,
ἂν μέν' ἡ σκέψις σου ὑψηλή, ἂν ἐκλεκτὴ
συγκίνησις τὸ πνεῦμα καὶ τὸ σῶμα σου ἀγγίζει.
Τοὺς Λαιστρυγόνας καὶ τοὺς Κύκλωπας,
τὸν ἄγριο Ποσειδῶνα δὲν θὰ συναντήσεις,
ἂν δὲν τοὺς κουβανεῖς μὲς στὴν ψυχή σου,
ἂν ἡ ψυχή σου δὲν τοὺς στήνει ἐμπρός σου.

*

And do not rest assured that in your life,
circumscribed, settled, and mundane,
such spectacular and dreadful things do not exist.
Perhaps at this very hour, in some neighbour's
neat and tidy home, enters—
invisible, incorporeal—Theodotus,
bearing just such a ghastly head.

MONOTONY

One monotonous day follows another
identically monotonous. The selfsame
things will happen again and again—
similar moments find us and leave us.

A month goes by and brings another month.
The things about to come, one can readily surmise:
they are those boring ones of yesterday.
And the morrow resembles a morrow no more.

ITHACA

When you set out on the journey to Ithaca,*
pray that the road be long,
full of adventures, full of knowledge.
The Laestrygonians and the Cyclopes,*
the raging Poseidon do not fear:
you'll never find the likes of these on your way,
if lofty be your thoughts, if rare emotion
touches your spirit and your body.
The Laestrygonians and the Cyclopes,
the fierce Poseidon you'll not encounter,
unless you carry them along within your soul,
unless your soul raises them before you.

*

Νὰ εὔχεσαι νἆναι μακρὺς ὁ δρόμος.
Πολλὰ τὰ καλοκαιρινὰ πρωϊὰ νὰ εἶναι
ποῦ μὲ τί εὐχαρίστηση, μὲ τί χαρὰ
θὰ μπαίνεις σὲ λιμένας πρωτοειδωμένους·
νὰ σταματήσεις σ' ἐμπορεῖα Φοινικικά,
καὶ τὲς καλὲς πραγμάτειες ν' ἀποκτήσεις,
σεντέφια καὶ κοράλλια, κεχριμπάρια κ' ἔβενους,
καὶ ἡδονικὰ μυρωδικὰ κάθε λογῆς,
ὅσο μπορεῖς πιὸ ἄφθονα ἡδονικὰ μυρωδικά·
σὲ πόλεις Αἰγυπτιακὲς πολλὲς νὰ πᾶς,
νὰ μάθεις καὶ νὰ μάθεις ἀπ' τοὺς σπουδασμένους.

Πάντα στὸν νοῦ σου νἄχεις τὴν Ἰθάκη.
Τὸ φθάσιμον ἐκεῖ εἶν' ὁ προορισμός σου.
Ἀλλὰ μὴ βιάζεις τὸ ταξεῖδι διόλου.
Καλλίτερα χρόνια πολλὰ νὰ διαρκέσει·
καὶ γέρος πιὰ ν' ἀράξεις στὸ νησί,
πλούσιος μὲ ὅσα κέρδισες στὸν δρόμο,
μὴ προσδοκῶντας πλούτη νὰ σὲ δώσει ἡ Ἰθάκη.

Ἡ Ἰθάκη σ' ἔδωσε τ' ὡραῖο ταξεῖδι.
Χωρὶς αὐτὴν δὲν θἄβγαινες στὸν δρόμο.
Ἄλλα δὲν ἔχει νὰ σὲ δώσει πιά.

Κι ἂν πτωχικὴ τὴν βρεῖς, ἡ Ἰθάκη δὲν σὲ γέλασε.
Ἔτσι σοφὸς ποῦ ἔγινες, μὲ τόση πεῖρα,
ἤδη θὰ τὸ κατάλαβες ἡ Ἰθάκες τί σημαίνουν.

ΟΣΟ ΜΠΟΡΕΙΣ

Κι ἂν δὲν μπορεῖς νὰ κάμεις τὴν ζωή σου ὅπως τὴν θέλεις,
τοῦτο προσπάθησε τουλάχιστον
ὅσο μπορεῖς: μὴν τὴν ἐξευτελίζεις
μὲς στὴν πολλὴ συνάφεια τοῦ κόσμου,
μὲς στὲς πολλὲς κινήσεις κι ὁμιλίες.

*

Pray that the road be long;
that there be many a summer morning,
when with what delight, what joy,
you'll enter into harbours yet unseen;
that you may stop at Phoenician emporia
and acquire all the fine wares,
mother-of-pearl and coral, amber and ebony,
and sensuous perfumes of every kind,
as many sensuous perfumes as you can;
that you may visit many an Egyptian city,
to learn and learn again from lettered men.

Always keep Ithaca in your mind.
To arrive there is your final destination.
But do not rush the voyage in the least.
Better it last for many years;
and once you're old, cast anchor on the isle,
rich with all you've gained along the way,
expecting not that Ithaca will give you wealth.

Ithaca gave you the wondrous voyage:
without her you'd never have set out.
But she has nothing to give you any more.

If then you find her poor, Ithaca has not deceived you.
As wise as you've become, with such experience, by now
you will have come to know what Ithacas really mean.

AS BEST YOU CAN

Even if you cannot make your life the way you want,
try this, at least,
as best you can: do not demean it
by too much contact with the crowd,
by too much movement and idle talk.

*

Μὴν τὴν ἐξευτελίζεις πιαίνοντάς την,
γυρίζοντας συχνὰ κ' ἐκθέτοντάς την
στῶν σχέσεων καὶ τῶν συναναστροφῶν
τὴν καθημερινὴν ἀνοησία,
ὡς ποῦ νὰ γίνει σὰ μιὰ ξένη φορτική.

ΤΡΩΕΣ

Εἶν' ἡ προσπάθειές μας, τῶν συφοριασμένων·
εἶν' ἡ προσπάθειές μας σὰν τῶν Τρώων.
Κομμάτι κατορθώνουμε· κομμάτι
παίρνουμ' ἐπάνω μας· κι ἀρχίζουμε
νἄχουμε θάρρος καὶ καλὲς ἐλπίδες.

Μὰ πάντα κάτι βγαίνει καὶ μᾶς σταματᾶ.
Ὁ Ἀχιλλεὺς στὴν τάφρον ἐμπροστά μας
βγαίνει καὶ μὲ φωνὲς μεγάλες μᾶς τρομάζει.—

Εἶν' ἡ προσπάθειές μας σὰν τῶν Τρώων.
Θαρροῦμε πῶς μὲ ἀπόφασι καὶ τόλμη
θ' ἀλλάξουμε τῆς τύχης τὴν καταφορά,
κ' ἔξω στεκόμεθα ν' ἀγωνισθοῦμε.

Ἀλλ' ὅταν ἡ μεγάλη κρίσις ἔλθει,
ἡ τόλμη κ' ἡ ἀπόφασίς μας χάνονται·
ταράττεται ἡ ψυχή μας, παραλύει·
κι ὁλόγυρα ἀπ' τὰ τείχη τρέχουμε
ζητώντας νὰ γλυτώσουμε μὲ τὴν φυγή.

Ὅμως ἡ πτῶσις μας εἶναι βεβαία. Ἐπάνω,
στὰ τείχη, ἄρχισεν ἤδη ὁ θρῆνος.
Τῶν ἡμερῶν μας ἀναμνήσεις κλαῖν κ' αἰσθήματα.
Πικρὰ γιὰ μᾶς ὁ Πρίαμος κ' ἡ Ἑκάβη κλαῖνε.

Do not demean it by dragging it along,
by wandering all the time and exposing it
to the daily foolishness
of social relations and encounters,
until it becomes an importunate stranger.

TROJANS

Our efforts are those of ill-fated men;
our efforts are like those of the Trojans.
We succeed a little, we regain
our strength a little, and we start
to have courage and high hopes.

But always something comes along to stop us.
Achilles at the moat before us
comes forth and shouting violently scares us.—

Our efforts are like those of the Trojans.
We believe that with resolve and bravery
we'll alter our fate's malevolence,
and we stand outside ready to fight.

But when the great crisis comes,
our bravery and our resolve vanish;
our soul is troubled, paralysed;
and around the walls we run,
seeking to save ourselves in flight.

Yet our fall is certain. Already, up on
the walls the lamentation has started.
Memories and feelings of our days are weeping.
Bitterly for us Priam* and Hecuba wail.

Ο ΒΑΣΙΛΕΥΣ ΔΗΜΗΤΡΙΟΣ

«Ὥσπερ οὐ βασιλεύς, ἀλλ' ὑποκριτής, μεταμφιέννυται
«χλαμύδα φαιὰν ἀντὶ τῆς τραγικῆς ἐκείνης, καὶ διαλαθὼν
«ὑπεχώρησεν».

Πλούταρχος, Βίος Δημητρίου

Σὰν τὸν παραίτησαν οἱ Μακεδόνες
κι ἀπέδειξαν πῶς προτιμοῦν τὸν Πύρρο
ὁ βασιλεὺς Δημήτριος (μεγάλην
εἶχε ψυχὴ) καθόλου—ἔτσι εἶπαν—
δὲν φέρθηκε σὰν βασιλεύς. Ἐπῆγε
κ' ἔβγαλε τὰ χρυσὰ φορέματά του,
καὶ τὰ ποδήματά του πέταξε
τὰ ὁλοπόρφυρα. Μὲ ροῦχ' ἁπλὰ
ντύθηκε γρήγορα καὶ ξέφυγε.
Κάμνοντας ὅμοια σὰν ἠθοποιὸς
ποῦ ὅταν ἡ παράστασις τελειώσει,
ἀλλάζει φορεσιὰ κι ἀπέρχεται.

Η ΔΟΞΑ ΤΩΝ ΠΤΟΛΕΜΑΙΩΝ

Εἶμ' ὁ Λαγίδης, βασιλεύς. Ὁ κάτοχος τελείως
(μὲ τὴν ἰσχύ μου καὶ τὸν πλοῦτο μου) τῆς ἡδονῆς.
Ἢ Μακεδών, ἢ βάρβαρος δὲν βρίσκεται κανεὶς
ἴσος μου, ἢ νὰ μὲ πλησιάζει κάν. Εἶναι γελοῖος
ὁ Σελευκίδης μὲ τὴν ἀγοραία του τρυφή.
Ἂν ὅμως σεῖς ἄλλα ζητεῖτε, ἰδοὺ κι αὐτὰ σαφῆ.
Ἡ πόλις ἡ διδάσκαλος, ἡ πανελλήνια κορυφή,
εἰς κάθε λόγο, εἰς κάθε τέχνη ἡ πιὸ σοφή.

KING DEMETRIUS

Not like a king, but an actor, who put on a grey chlamys instead of the costume of tragedy, and stealthily departed.

Plutarch, *Life of Demetrius*

When the Macedonians abandoned him,
and displayed their preference for Pyrrhus,*
King Demetrius (a great soul he had)
did not—so they said—
behave like a king at all. He went ahead
and took off his golden garments
and threw away his royal-purple
shoes. He quickly dressed
in simple garb and fled;
emulating an actor who,
when the performance comes to an end,
changes costume and departs.

THE GLORY OF THE PTOLEMIES

I am the Lagid, king. The complete possessor
(by my power and wealth) of sensual pleasure.
No Macedonian or barbarian can be found
to be my equal or even to come close to me. He is ludicrous,
that Seleucid, so vulgarly effete.
If, however, you ask for more, here it is in plain words:
Alexandria is the educator, the pan-Hellenic pinnacle;
in every discipline, in every art the wisest.

Η ΣΥΝΟΔΕΙΑ ΤΟΥ ΔΙΟΝΥΣΟΥ

Ὁ Δάμων ὁ τεχνίτης (ἄλλον πιὸ ἱκανὸ
στὴν Πελοπόννησο δὲν ἔχει) εἰς παριανὸ
μάρμαρο ἐπεξεργάζεται τὴν συνοδεία
τοῦ Διονύσου. Ὁ θεὸς μὲ θεσπεσία
δόξαν ἐμπρός, μὲ δύναμι στὸ βάδισμά του.
Ὁ Ἄκρατος πίσω. Στὸ πλάγι τοῦ Ἀκράτου
ἡ Μέθη χύνει στοὺς Σατύρους τὸ κρασὶ
ἀπὸ ἀμφορέα ποῦ τὸν στέφουνε κισσοί.
Κοντά των ὁ Ἡδύοινος ὁ μαλθακός,
τὰ μάτια του μισοκλειστά, ὑπνωτικός.
Καὶ παρακάτω ἔρχοντ' οἱ τραγουδισταὶ
Μόλπος κ' Ἡδυμελής, κι ὁ Κῶμος ποῦ ποτὲ
νὰ σβύσει δὲν ἀφίνει τῆς πορείας τὴν σεπτὴ
λαμπάδα ποῦ βαστᾶ· καί, σεμνοτάτη, ἡ Τελετή.—
Αὐτὰ ὁ Δάμων κάμνει. Καὶ κοντὰ σ' αὐτὰ
ὁ λογισμός του κάθε τόσο μελετᾶ
τὴν ἀμοιβή του ἀπὸ τῶν Συρακουσῶν
τὸν βασιλέα, τρία τάλαντα, πολὺ ποσόν.
Μὲ τ' ἄλλα του τὰ χρήματα κι αὐτὰ μαζὺ
σὰν μποῦν, ὡς εὔπορος σπουδαῖα πιὰ θὰ ζεῖ,
καὶ θὰ μπορεῖ νὰ πολιτεύεται—χαρά!—
κι αὐτὸς μὲς στὴν βουλή, κι αὐτὸς στὴν ἀγορά.

Η ΜΑΧΗ ΤΗΣ ΜΑΓΝΗΣΙΑΣ

Ἔχασε τὴν παληά του ὁρμή, τὸ θάρρος του.
Τοῦ κουρασμένου σώματός του, τοῦ ἄρρωστου

σχεδόν, θἄχει κυρίως τὴν φροντίδα. Κι ὁ ἐπίλοιπος
βίος του θὰ διέλθει ἀμέριμνος. Αὐτὰ ὁ Φίλιππος

τουλάχιστον διατείνεται. Ἀπόψι κύβους παίζει·
ἔχει ὄρεξι νὰ διασκεδάσει. Στὸ τραπέζι

*

THE RETINUE OF DIONYSUS

Damon the craftsman (there is none more skilled
in the Peloponnese) is fashioning
in Parian marble the retinue of Dionysus.
The god, in sublime glory,
with vigorous stride to the fore.
Akratos* follows behind. At Akratos' side,
Methe pours for the satyrs wine
from an amphora wreathed with ivy-vine.
Near them the effete Hedyoinos soporific,
with his eyes half-closed.
And then follow the singers,
Molpos and Hedymeles, and Comus,
who never lets go out the procession's sacred torch
which he holds; and most modest Teleté.—
These Damon is elaborating. And while so doing,
his mind ponders now and then
on his remuneration from the King
of Syracuse, three talents, a goodly sum.
When this is added to the rest of his money,
he'll live grandly henceforth like a prosperous man,
and he'll be able to dabble in politics—what joy!—
he too in the Boule, he too in the Agora.

THE BATTLE OF MAGNESIA

He's lost his former ardour, his audacity.
To his tired, almost ailing body,

he'll mainly devote attention. And the remainder
of his life will pass without a care. So Philip

at least maintains. Tonight he plays dice;
he's eager for amusements. On the table

*

βάλτε πολλὰ τριαντάφυλλα. Τὶ ἂν στὴν Μαγνησία
ὁ Ἀντίοχος κατεστράφηκε. Λένε πανωλεθρία

ἔπεσ' ἐπάνω στοῦ λαμπροῦ στρατεύματος τὰ πλήθια.
Μπορεῖ νὰ τὰ μεγάλωσαν· ὅλα δὲν θἄναι ἀλήθεια.

Εἴθε. Γιατὶ ἀγκαλὰ κ' ἐχθρός, ἤσανε μιὰ φυλή.
Ὅμως ἕνα «εἴθε» εἶν' ἀρκετό. Ἴσως κιόλας πολύ.

Ὁ Φίλιππος τὴν ἑορτὴ βέβαια δὲν θ' ἀναβάλει.
Ὅσο κι ἂν στάθηκε τοῦ βίου του ἡ κόπωσις μεγάλη,

ἕνα καλὸ διατήρησεν, ἡ μνήμη διόλου δὲν τοῦ λείπει.
Θυμᾶται πόσο στὴν Συρία θρήνησαν, τὶ εἶδος λύπη

εἶχαν, σὰν ἔγινε σκουπίδι ἡ μάνα των Μακεδονία.—
Ν' ἀρχίσει τὸ τραπέζι. Δοῦλοι· τοὺς αὐλούς, τὴ φωταψία.

Η ΔΥΣΑΡΕΣΚΕΙΑ ΤΟΥ ΣΕΛΕΥΚΙΔΟΥ

Δυσαρεστήθηκεν ὁ Σελευκίδης
Δημήτριος νὰ μάθει ποὺ στὴν Ἰταλία
ἔφθασεν ἕνας Πτολεμαῖος σὲ τέτοιο χάλι.
Μὲ τρεῖς ἢ τέσσαρες δούλους μονάχα·
πτωχοντυμένος καὶ πεζός. Ἔτσι μιὰ εἰρωνία
θὰ καταντήσουν πιά, καὶ παίγνιο μὲς στὴν Ρώμη
τὰ γένη των. Ποὺ κατὰ βάθος ἔγιναν
σὰν ἕνα εἶδος ὑπηρέται τῶν Ρωμαίων
τὸ ξέρει ὁ Σελευκίδης, ποὺ αὐτοὶ τοὺς δίδουν
κι αὐτοὶ τοὺς παίρνουνε τοὺς θρόνους των
αὐθαίρετα, ὡς ἐπιθυμοῦν, τὸ ξέρει.
Ἀλλὰ τουλάχιστον στὸ παρουσιαστικό των
ἂς διατηροῦν κάποια μεγαλοπρέπεια·
νὰ μὴ ξεχνοῦν ποὺ εἶναι βασιλεῖς ἀκόμη,
ποὺ λέγονται (ἀλοίμονον!) ἀκόμη βασιλεῖς.

*

let's put a lot of roses! What of it, if Antiochus
met ruin in Magnesia. They say disaster

fell on the splendid army's multitudes.
They might have exaggerated; it cannot all be true.

Let's hope so; for though an enemy, they were of our race.
Well! One 'let's hope so' is enough. Maybe too much!

Philip, of course, will not postpone the feast.
No matter how intense has been his life's exhaustion,

one good thing he's retained: he hasn't lost his memory at all.
He recalls just how they wept in Syria, what sort of sorrow

they feigned when their mother Macedonia was humbled.—
Let the banquet begin. Slaves: the flutes, the lights.

THE DISPLEASURE OF THE SELEUCID

The Seleucid king Demetrius*
was displeased to hear that in Italy
a Ptolemy arrived in such a wretched state;
with three or four slaves only,
shabbily dressed and on foot. At this rate,
their dynasties will eventually become
the laughing-stock, the plaything of Rome.
Deep down the Seleucid knows that they've
become a sort of servant to the Romans;
that the Romans are those who give and take away
their thrones at will, as they please; that he knows!
But in their appearance they should
preserve at least some dignity,
and not forget that they are kings still,
that they (alas!) are still called kings.

★

Γι' αὐτὸ συγχίσθηκεν ὁ Σελευκίδης
Δημήτριος· κι ἀμέσως πρόσφερε στὸν Πτολεμαῖο
ἐνδύματα ὁλοπόρφυρα, διάδημα λαμπρό,
βαρύτιμα διαμαντικά, πολλοὺς
θεράποντας καὶ συνοδούς, τὰ πιὸ ἀκριβά του ἄλογα,
γιὰ νὰ παρουσιασθεῖ στὴν Ρώμη καθὼς πρέπει,
σὰν Ἀλεξανδρινὸς Γραικὸς μονάρχης.

Ἀλλ' ὁ Λαγίδης, ποὺ ἦλθε γιὰ τὴν ἐπαιτεία,
ἤξερε τὴν δουλειά του καὶ τ' ἀρνήθηκε ὅλα·
διόλου δὲν τοῦ χρειάζονταν αὐτὲς ἡ πολυτέλειες.
Παληοντυμένος, ταπεινὸς μπῆκε στὴν Ρώμη,
καὶ κόνεψε σ' ἑνὸς μικροῦ τεχνίτου σπίτι.
Κ' ἔπειτα παρουσιάσθηκε σὰν κακομοίρης
καὶ σὰν πτωχάνθρωπος στὴν Σύγκλητο,
ἔτσι μὲ πιὸ ἀποτέλεσμα νὰ ζητιανέψει.

ΟΡΟΦΕΡΝΗΣ

Αὐτὸς ποὺ εἰς τὸ τετράδραχμον ἐπάνω
μοιάζει σὰν νὰ χαμογελᾷ τὸ πρόσωπό του
τὸ ἔμορφο, λεπτό του πρόσωπο,
αὐτὸς εἶν' ὁ Ὀροφέρνης Ἀριαράθου.

Παιδὶ τὸν ἔδιωξαν ἀπ' τὴν Καππαδοκία,
ἀπ' τὸ μεγάλο πατρικὸ παλάτι,
καὶ τὸν ἐστείλανε νὰ μεγαλώσει
στὴν Ἰωνία, καὶ νὰ ξεχασθεῖ στοὺς ξένους.

Ἆ ἐξαίσιες τῆς Ἰωνίας νύχτες
ποὺ ἄφοβα, κ' ἑλληνικὰ ὅλως διόλου
ἐγνώρισε πλήρη τὴν ἡδονή.
Μὲς στὴν καρδιά του, πάντοτε Ἀσιανός·
ἀλλὰ στοὺς τρόπους του καὶ στὴν λαλιά του Ἕλλην,
μὲ περουζέδες στολισμένος, ἑλληνοντυμένος,

This is why the Seleucid King Demetrius
was upset. And offered Ptolemy at once
robes of royal purple, a splendid diadem,
precious diamonds, numerous
servants and attendants, his most expensive horses,
that he present himself properly in Rome,
as befits an Alexandrian Greek monarch.

But the Lagid, who had come intent on begging,
knew his business and refused it all;
he had no need at all of such luxuries.
Clad in old clothes, humble, he entered Rome,
and lodged in a simple artisan's home.
And later on he appeared before the Senate
as a wretched person and a pauper,
thus more effectively to beg.

OROPHERNES

He who appears upon the tetradrachm
with a hint of a smile on his face,
his beautiful, delicate face,
he is Orophernes,* son of Ariarathes.

Mere child he was when they drove him out of Cappadocia,
from the great ancestral palace
and they sent him away to grow up in Ionia
and be forgotten among strangers.

Ah, exquisite Ionian nights,
when in a fearless and entirely Greek way
he came to know of utter sensual bliss.
Deep in his heart, always an Asiatic;
but in his manners and his speech a Hellene,
adorned with turquoise gems, clad in Greek style,

τὸ σῶμα του μὲ μύρον ἰασεμιοῦ εὐωδιασμένο,
κι ἀπ' τοὺς ὡραίους τῆς Ἰωνίας νέους,
ὁ πιὸ ὡραῖος αὐτός, ὁ πιὸ ἰδανικός.

Κατόπι σὰν οἱ Σύροι στὴν Καππαδοκία
μπῆκαν, καὶ τὸν ἐκάμαν βασιλέα,
στὴν βασιλεία χύθηκεν ἐπάνω
γιὰ νὰ χαρεῖ μὲ νέον τρόπο κάθε μέρα,
γιὰ νὰ μαζεύει ἁρπαχτικὰ χρυσὸ κι ἀσῆμι,
καὶ γιὰ νὰ εὐφραίνεται καὶ νὰ κομπάζει
βλέποντας πλούτη στοιβαγμένα νὰ γυαλίζουν.
Ὅσο γιὰ μέριμνα τοῦ τόπου, γιὰ διοίκησι—
οὔτ' ἤξερε τὶ γένονταν τριγύρω του.

Οἱ Καππαδόκες γρήγορα τὸν βγάλαν·
καὶ στὴν Συρία ξέπεσε, μὲς στὸ παλάτι
τοῦ Δημητρίου νὰ διασκεδάζει καὶ νὰ ὀκνεύει.

Μιὰ μέρα ὡστόσο τὴν πολλὴν ἀργία του
συλλογισμοὶ ἀσυνείθιστοι διεκόψαν·
θυμήθηκε ποῦ ἀπ' τὴν μητέρα του Ἀντιοχίδα,
κι ἀπ' τὴν παληὰν ἐκείνη Στρατονίκη,
κι αὐτὸς βαστοῦσε ἀπ' τὴν κορώνα τῆς Συρίας,
καὶ Σελευκίδης ἤτανε σχεδόν.
Γιὰ λίγο βγῆκε ἀπ' τὴν λαγνεία κι ἀπ' τὴν μέθη,
κι ἀνίκανα, καὶ μισοζαλισμένος
κάτι ἐζήτησε νὰ ραδιουργήσει,
κάτι νὰ κάμει, κάτι νὰ σχεδιάσει,
κι ἀπέτυχεν οἰκτρὰ κ' ἐξουδενόθη.

Τὸ τέλος του κάπου θὰ γράφηκε κ' ἐχάθη·
ἢ ἴσως ἡ ἱστορία νὰ τὸ πέρασε,
καί, μὲ τὸ δίκιο της, τέτοιο ἀσήμαντο
πρᾶγμα δὲν καταδέχθηκε νὰ τὸ σημειώσει.

Αὐτὸς ποῦ εἰς τὸ τετράδραχμον ἐπάνω
μιὰ χάρι ἀφῆκε ἀπ' τὰ ὡραῖα του νειάτα,

his body scented with the perfume of jasmine oil,
of all the lovely Ionian youths,
he was the loveliest, the most ideal.

Later when the Syrians entered Cappadocia
and declared him king,
he flung himself into the kingship
to indulge each day in a new way,
rapaciously to gather gold and silver,
and to delight himself and boast,
watching his piled-up riches shine.
As for the cares of state and government—
he had no idea what went on around him.

The Cappadocians soon removed him;
and he ended up in Syria, in the palace
of Demetrius, basking in revelry and idleness.

One day, however, his great indolence
was interrupted by unusual thoughts;
he recalled how, through his mother Antiochis
and through that Stratonike of old,
he too was related to the Syrian crown
and was himself a Seleucid, almost.
For a while, he emerged from lechery and stupor,
and ineptly, and half-dazed,
he somehow endeavoured to engage in intrigue—
to do something, to plan something—
and he failed pitifully and was utterly overwhelmed.

His end was recorded somewhere and then lost;
or perhaps History passed it by,
and with good reason, a thing as trivial
as that she didn't deign to record.

He who upon the tetradrachm
left an allure of his lovely youth,

ἀπ' τὴν ποιητικὴ ἐμορφιά του ἕνα φῶς,
μιὰ μνήμη αἰσθητικὴ ἀγοριοῦ τῆς Ἰωνίας,
αὐτὸς εἶν' ὁ Ὀροφέρνης Ἀριαράθου.

ΑΛΕΞΑΝΔΡΙΝΟΙ ΒΑΣΙΛΕΙΣ

Μαζεύθηκαν οἱ Ἀλεξανδρινοὶ
νὰ δοῦν τῆς Κλεοπάτρας τὰ παιδιά,
τὸν Καισαρίωνα καὶ τὰ μικρά του ἀδέρφια,
Ἀλέξανδρο καὶ Πτολεμαῖο, ποὺ πρώτη
φορὰ τὰ βγάζαν ἔξω στὸ Γυμνάσιο,
ἐκεῖ νὰ τὰ κηρύξουν βασιλεῖς,
μὲς στὴ λαμπρὴ παράταξι τῶν στρατιωτῶν.

Ὁ Ἀλέξανδρος—τὸν εἶπαν βασιλέα
τῆς Ἀρμενίας, τῆς Μηδίας, καὶ τῶν Πάρθων.
Ὁ Πτολεμαῖος—τὸν εἶπαν βασιλέα
τῆς Κιλικίας, τῆς Συρίας, καὶ τῆς Φοινίκης.
Ὁ Καισαρίων στέκονταν πιὸ ἐμπροστά,
ντυμένος σὲ μετάξι τριανταφυλλί,
στὸ στῆθος του ἀνθοδέσμη ἀπὸ ὑακίνθους,
ἡ ζώνη του διπλὴ σειρὰ σαπφείρων κι ἀμεθύστων,
δεμένα τὰ ποδήματά του μ' ἄσπρες
κορδέλλες κεντημένες μὲ ροδόχροα μαργαριτάρια.
Αὐτὸν τὸν εἶπαν πιότερο ἀπὸ τοὺς μικρούς,
αὐτὸν τὸν εἶπαν Βασιλέα τῶν Βασιλέων.

Οἱ Ἀλεξανδρινοὶ ἔννοιωθαν βέβαια
ποὺ ἦσαν λόγια αὐτὰ καὶ θεατρικά.

Ἀλλὰ ἡ μέρα ἦτανε ζεστὴ καὶ ποιητική,
ὁ οὐρανὸς ἕνα γαλάζιο ἀνοιχτό,
τὸ Ἀλεξανδρινὸ Γυμνάσιον ἕνα
θριαμβικὸ κατόρθωμα τῆς τέχνης,
τῶν αὐλικῶν ἡ πολυτέλεια ἔκτακτη,
ὁ Καισαρίων ὅλο χάρις κ' ἐμορφιὰ
(τῆς Κλεοπάτρας υἱός, αἷμα τῶν Λαγιδῶν)·

a radiance of his poetic grace,
an aesthetic memory of a young Ionian man,
he is Orophernes, son of Ariarathes.

ALEXANDRIAN KINGS

The Alexandrians gathered together
to see Cleopatra's children,
Caesarion and his young brothers,
Alexander and Ptolemy, who for the first
time were brought out to the Gymnasium,
there to be proclaimed kings
amid the splendid array of the troops.

Alexander—they named him King of
Armenia, Media, and the Parthians.
Ptolemy—they named him King
of Cilicia, Syria, and Phoenicia.
Caesarion was standing more to the front,
dressed in rose-coloured silk,
a posy of hyacinths upon his chest,
his belt a double row of amethysts and sapphires,
his shoes fastened with white ribbons
embroidered with rose-coloured pearls.
Him they named above his younger brothers,
him they named King of Kings.

The Alexandrians sensed, of course,
that these were mere words and theatricals.

But the day was warm and poetical,
the sky a pale azure,
the Alexandrian Gymnasium
a triumphant accomplishment of art,
the extravagance of the courtiers exceptional,
Caesarion full of grace and beauty
(Cleopatra's son, Lagid blood);

κ᾽ οἱ Ἀλεξανδρινοὶ ἔτρεχαν πιὰ στὴν ἑορτή,
κ᾽ ἐνθουσιάζονταν, κ᾽ ἐπευφημοῦσαν
ἑλληνικά, κ᾽ αἰγυπτιακά, καὶ ποιοὶ ἑβραίικα,
γοητευμένοι μὲ τ᾽ ὡραῖο θέαμα—
μ᾽ ὅλο ποῦ βέβαια ἤξευραν τί ἄξιζαν αὐτά,
τί κούφια λόγια ἤσανε αὐτὲς ἡ βασιλεῖες.

ΦΙΛΕΛΛΗΝ

Τὴν χάραξι φρόντισε τεχνικὰ νὰ γίνει.
Ἔκφρασις σοβαρὴ καὶ μεγαλοπρεπής.
Τὸ διάδημα καλλίτερα μᾶλλον στενό·
ἐκεῖνα τὰ φαρδιὰ τῶν Πάρθων δὲν μὲ ἀρέσουν.
Ἡ ἐπιγραφή, ὡς σύνηθες, ἑλληνικά·
ὄχ᾽ ὑπερβολική, ὄχι πομπώδης—
μὴν τὰ παρεξηγήσει ὁ ἀνθύπατος
ποῦ ὅλο σκαλίζει καὶ μηνᾶ στὴν Ρώμη—
ἀλλ᾽ ὅμως βέβαια τιμητική.
Κάτι πολὺ ἐκλεκτὸ ἀπ᾽ τὸ ἄλλο μέρος·
κανένας δισκοβόλος ἔφηβος ὡραῖος.
Πρὸ πάντων σὲ συστείνω νὰ κυττάξεις
(Σιθάσπη, πρὸς θεοῦ, νὰ μὴ λησμονηθεῖ)
μετὰ τὸ Βασιλεὺς καὶ τὸ Σωτήρ,
νὰ χαραχθεῖ μὲ γράμματα κομψά, Φιλέλλην.
Καὶ τώρα μὴ μὲ ἀρχίζεις εὐφυολογίες,
τὰ «Ποῦ οἱ Ἕλληνες;» καὶ «Ποῦ τὰ Ἑλληνικὰ
«πίσω ἀπ᾽ τὸν Ζάγρο ἐδῶ, ἀπὸ τὰ Φράατα πέρα».
Τόσοι καὶ τόσοι βαρβαρότεροί μας ἄλλοι
ἀφοῦ τὸ γράφουν, θὰ τὸ γράψουμε κ᾽ ἐμεῖς.
Καὶ τέλος μὴ ξεχνᾶς ποῦ ἐνίοτε
μᾶς ἔρχοντ᾽ ἀπὸ τὴν Συρία σοφισταί,
καὶ στιχοπλόκοι, κι ἄλλοι ματαιόσπουδοι.
Ὥστε ἀνελλήνιστοι δὲν εἴμεθα, θαρρῶ.

and so the Alexandrians rushed to the festivities
and grew enthusiastic and kept cheering
in Greek and in Egyptian and some in Hebrew,
enchanted by the lovely spectacle—
though they knew full well what all this was worth,
what hollow words were those kingly titles.

PHILHELLENE

See to it the engraving be skilfully done.
The expression serious and dignified.
The diadem preferably rather narrow;
those broad Parthian ones are not to my liking.
The inscription, as usual in Greek;
nothing excessive, nothing pompous—
lest the proconsul, who always pokes around
and reports to Rome, take it the wrong way—
but nonetheless, of course, honorific.
Something very special on the other side;
some handsome youth, a discus-thrower.
Above all, I bid you pay attention
(Sithaspes, in god's name, don't let this be forgotten)
that after the words 'King' and 'Saviour'
be engraved in elegant lettering: 'Philhellene.'
And now don't start your witticisms on me,
like: 'where are the Greeks' and 'where is Greek used
around here, this side of Zagros, way beyond Fraata.'
Since so many others, more barbarous than we,
write it, we will write it too.
And finally, do not forget that on occasion
there come to us sophists from Syria,
and poetasters and other pretentious pedants.
Thus, we are not lacking in Greek culture, I do believe.

ΤΑ ΒΗΜΑΤΑ

Σ' ἐβένινο κρεββάτι στολισμένο
μὲ κοραλλένιους ἀετούς, βαθυὰ κοιμᾶται
ὁ Νέρων — ἀσυνείδητος, ἥσυχος, κ' εὐτυχής·
ἀκμαῖος μὲς στὴν εὐρωστία τῆς σαρκός,
καὶ στῆς νεότητος τ' ὡραῖο σφρῖγος.

Ἀλλὰ στὴν αἴθουσα τὴν ἀλαβάστρινη ποῦ κλείνει
τῶν Ἀηνοβάρβων τὸ ἀρχαῖο λαράριο
τὶ ἀνήσυχοι ποῦ εἶν' οἱ Λάρητές του.
Τρέμουν οἱ σπιτικοὶ μικροὶ θεοί,
καὶ προσπαθοῦν τ' ἀσήμαντά των σώματα νὰ κρύψουν.
Γιατὶ ἄκουσαν μιὰ ἀπαίσια βοή,
θανάσιμη βοὴ τὴν σκάλα ν' ἀνεβαίνει,
βήματα σιδερένια ποῦ τραντάζουν τὰ σκαλιά.
Καὶ λιγοθυμισμένοι τώρα οἱ ἄθλιοι Λάρητες,
μέσα στὸ βάθος τοῦ λαράριου χώνονται,
ὁ ἕνας τὸν ἄλλονα σκουντᾶ καὶ σκουντουφλᾶ,
ὁ ἕνας μικρὸς θεὸς πάνω στὸν ἄλλον πέφτει
γιατὶ κατάλαβαν τὶ εἶδος βοὴ εἶναι τούτη,
τἄνοιωσαν πιὰ τὰ βήματα τῶν Ἐριννύων.

ΗΡΩΔΗΣ ΑΤΤΙΚΟΣ

Ἆ τοῦ Ἡρώδη τοῦ Ἀττικοῦ τὶ δόξα εἶν' αὐτή.

Ὁ Ἀλέξανδρος τῆς Σελευκείας, ἀπ' τοὺς καλούς μας σοφιστάς,
φθάνοντας στὰς Ἀθήνας νὰ ὁμιλήσει,
βρίσκει τὴν πόλιν ἄδεια ἐπειδὴ ὁ Ἡρώδης
ἦταν στὴν ἐξοχή. Κ' ἡ νεολαία
ὅλη τὸν ἀκολούθησεν ἐκεῖ νὰ τὸν ἀκούει.
Ὁ σοφιστὴς Ἀλέξανδρος λοιπὸν
γράφει πρὸς τὸν Ἡρώδη ἐπιστολή,
καὶ τὸν παρακαλεῖ τοὺς Ἕλληνας νὰ στείλει.
Ὁ δὲ λεπτὸς Ἡρώδης ἀπαντᾶ εὐθύς,
«Ἔρχομαι μὲ τοὺς Ἕλληνας μαζὺ κ' ἐγώ.»—

*

THE FOOTSTEPS

Upon a bed of ebony adorned
with coral eagles, deeply asleep
lies Nero—oblivious, peaceful, and pleased;
robust in the ardour of his flesh
and in the handsome vigour of his youth.

But in the alabaster hall that shelters
the ancient shrine of the Aenobarbi,
how restless are its Lares.*
The little household gods are trembling
and trying to hide their paltry bodies.
For they've heard an inauspicious sound,
a deathly sound, ascending the staircase,
iron footsteps shaking the stairs.
And now in fearful faint, the wretched Lares
hide in the far end of the shrine,
shoving each other and stumbling,
one little god falling upon the other,
for they've understood what sort of sound this is,
they've sensed by now the footsteps of the Furies.*

HEROD ATTICUS

Ah, how great is the glory of Herod Atticus!*

Alexander of Seleucia,* one of our better sophists,
arriving in Athens to lecture,
finds the city empty, because Herod
was out in the country. And all the young men
had followed him there to hear him talk.
So Alexander the sophist
writes Herod a letter
entreating him to send the Greeks back.
And the tactful Herod immediately responds:
'Along with the Greeks, I'm coming myself.'—

*

Πόσα παιδιὰ στὴν Ἀλεξάνδρεια τώρα,
στὴν Ἀντιόχεια, ἢ στὴν Βηρυτὸ
(οἱ ρήτορές του οἱ αὔριανοὶ ποῦ ἑτοιμάζει ὁ ἑλληνισμός),
ὅταν μαζεύονται στὰ ἐκλεκτὰ τραπέζια
ποῦ πότε ἡ ὁμιλία εἶναι γιὰ τὰ ὡραῖα σοφιστικά,
καὶ πότε γιὰ τὰ ἐρωτικά των τὰ ἐξαίσια,
ἔξαφν' ἀφηρημένα σιωποῦν.
Ἄγγιχτα τὰ ποτήρια ἀφίνουνε κοντά των,
καὶ συλλογίζονται τὴν τύχη τοῦ Ἡρώδη—
ποιὸς ἄλλος σοφιστὴς τ' ἀξιώθηκεν αὐτά;—
κατὰ ποῦ θέλει καὶ κατὰ ποῦ κάμνει
οἱ Ἕλληνες (οἱ Ἕλληνες!) νὰ τὸν ἀκολουθοῦν,
μήτε νὰ κρίνουν ἢ νὰ συζητοῦν,
μήτε νὰ ἐκλέγουν πιά, ν' ἀκολουθοῦνε μόνο.

ΤΥΑΝΕΥΣ ΓΛΥΠΤΗΣ

Καθὼς ποῦ θὰ τὸ ἀκούσατε, δὲν εἶμ' ἀρχάριος.
Κάμποση πέτρα ἀπὸ τὰ χέρια μου περνᾶ.
Καὶ στὴν πατρίδα μου, τὰ Τύανα, καλὰ
μὲ ξέρουνε· κ' ἐδῶ ἀγάλματα πολλὰ
μὲ παραγγείλανε συγκλητικοί.

Καὶ νὰ σᾶς δείξω
ἀμέσως μερικά. Παρατηρεῖστ' αὐτὴν τὴν Ῥέα·
σεβάσμια, γεμάτη καρτερία, παναρχαία.
Παρατηρεῖστε τὸν Πομπήϊον. Ὁ Μάριος,
ὁ Αἰμίλιος Παῦλος, ὁ Ἀφρικανὸς Σκιπίων.
Ὁμοιώματα, ὅσο ποῦ μπόρεσα, πιστά.
Ὁ Πάτροκλος (ὀλίγο θὰ τὸν ξαναγγίξω).
Πλησίον στοῦ μαρμάρου τοῦ κιτρινωποῦ
ἐκεῖνα τὰ κομάτια, εἶν' ὁ Καισαρίων.

Καὶ τώρα καταγίνομαι ἀπὸ καιρὸ ἀρκετὸ
νὰ κάμω ἕναν Ποσειδῶνα. Μελετῶ
κυρίως γιὰ τ' ἄλογά του, πῶς νὰ πλάσσω αὐτά.
Πρέπει ἐλαφρὰ ἔτσι νὰ γίνουν ποῦ

How many young men now, in Alexandria,
in Antioch, or in Beirut
(tomorrow's orators that Hellenism is preparing),
when gathered at the select banquets—
where the talk at times is about fine sophistry
and at times about their exquisite love affairs—
suddenly distracted, they fall silent.
They leave their glasses on the side untouched,
and ponder on Herod's fortune:
what other sophist was ever deemed worthy of this?
In anything he wants, in anything he does,
the Greeks (the Greeks!) are following him,
neither judging nor discussing
nor choosing any more, just following.

SCULPTOR OF TYANA

As you might have heard, I am no novice.
Quite a lot of stone passes through my hands.
And in Tyana,* my country, they know me well;
here, too, I've been commissioned
for many a statue by senators.

And let me show you
a few right now. Look closely at this Rhea,*
venerable, all-forbearing, primeval.
Notice Pompey, Marius,
Aemilius Paulus, Scipio Africanus.*
Likenesses created as faithfully as I could.
Patroclus*—I'll retouch him a little.
Near those pieces of yellowish
marble, that's Caesarion.*

And for some time now, I've been busy
working on a Poseidon. I'm giving
particular thought to his horses, how to fashion them.
They ought to be made so light

τὰ σώματα, τὰ πόδια των νὰ δείχνουν φανερὰ
ποῦ δὲν πατοῦν τὴν γῆ, μὸν τρέχουν στὰ νερά.

Μὰ νὰ τὸ ἔργον μου τὸ πιὸ ἀγαπητὸ
ποῦ δούλεψα συγκινημένα καὶ τὸ πιὸ προσεκτικά·
αὐτόν, μιὰ μέρα τοῦ καλοκαιριοῦ θερμὴ
ποῦ ὁ νοῦς μου ἀνέβαινε στὰ ἰδανικά,
αὐτὸν ἐδῶ ὀνειρεύομουν τὸν νέον Ἑρμῆ.

ΛΥΣΙΟΥ ΓΡΑΜΜΑΤΙΚΟΥ ΤΑΦΟΣ

Πλησιέστατα, δεξιὰ ποῦ μπαίνεις, στὴν βιβλιοθήκη
τῆς Βηρυτοῦ θάψαμε τὸν σοφὸ Λυσία,
γραμματικόν. Ὁ χῶρος κάλλιστα προσήκει.
Τὸν θέσαμε κοντὰ σ' αὐτά του ποῦ θυμᾶται
ἴσως κ' ἐκεῖ—σχόλια, κείμενα, τεχνολογία,
γραφές, εἰς τεύχη ἑλληνισμῶν πολλὴ ἑρμηνεία.
Κ' ἐπίσης ἔτσι ἀπὸ μᾶς θὰ βλέπεται καὶ θὰ τιμᾶται
ὁ τάφος του, ὅταν ποῦ περνοῦμε στὰ βιβλία.

ΕΥΡΙΩΝΟΣ ΤΑΦΟΣ

Εἰς τὸ περίτεχνον αὐτὸ μνημεῖον,
ὁλόκληρον ἐκ λίθου συηνίτου,
ποῦ τὸ σκεπάζουν τόσοι μενεξέδες, τόσοι κρίνοι,
εἶναι θαμένος ὁ ὡραῖος Εὐρίων.
Παιδὶ ἀλεξανδρινό, εἴκοσι πέντε χρόνων.
Ἀπ' τὸν πατέρα του, γενιὰ παληὰ τῶν Μακεδόνων·
ἀπὸ ἀλαβάρχας τῆς μητέρας του ἡ σειρά.
Ἔκαμε μαθητὴς τοῦ Ἀριστοκλείτου στὴν φιλοσοφία,
τοῦ Πάρου στὰ ρητορικά. Στὰς Θήβας τὰ ἱερὰ
γράμματα σπούδασε. Τοῦ Ἀρσινοΐτου
νομοῦ συνέγραψε ἱστορίαν. Αὐτὸ τουλάχιστον θὰ μείνει.
Χάσαμεν ὅμως τὸ πιὸ τίμιο—τὴν μορφή του,
ποῦ ἤτανε σὰν μιὰ ἀπολλώνια ὀπτασία.

that their bodies, their hooves, clearly appear
not to touch the ground, but to run upon the waters.

But here is the work that I love most,
on which I laboured with much emotion and the greatest care;
it's this one here—on a warm summer day,
when my mind was ascending towards the ideal—
it's this one here I was dreaming of, the young Hermes.

TOMB OF THE GRAMMARIAN LYSIAS

Nearby, on the right as you enter the library
of Beirut, we buried the learned Lysias
the grammarian. The location is most appropriate.
We placed him near those things of his he may
remember even there—annotations, texts, grammatical analyses,
writings, tomes of ample commentary on Greek idioms.
Thus his tomb will be seen and honoured by us,
each time we make our way towards the books.

TOMB OF EURION

In this most artfully ornate memorial—
entirely built of syenite stone,*
covered with so many violets, so many lilies—
the handsome Eurion is laid to rest.
An Alexandrian youth, aged twenty-five.
On his father's side, of old Macedonian stock;
from Jewish magistrates,* his mother's lineage.
He was a student of Aristocleitus in philosophy,
of Paros in rhetoric. The sacred scriptures
he studied at Thebes. He wrote a history
of the Arsinoïte nome.* That will, at least, survive.
But we have lost the most precious of all—his living image,
which had the semblance of an Apollonian vision.

ΟΥΤΟΣ ΕΚΕΙΝΟΣ

Ἄγνωστος—ξένος μὲς στὴν Ἀντιόχεια—Ἐδεσσηνὸς
γράφει πολλά. Καὶ τέλος πάντων, νά, ὁ λίνος
ὁ τελευταῖος ἔγινε. Μὲ αὐτὸν ὀγδόντα τρία

ποιήματα ἐν ὅλῳ. Πλὴν τὸν ποιητὴ
κούρασε τόσο γράψιμο, τόση στιχοποιΐα,
καὶ τόση ἔντασις σ' ἑλληνικὴ φρασιολογία,
καὶ τώρα τὸν βαραίνει πιὰ τὸ κάθε τί.—

Μιὰ σκέψις ὅμως παρευθὺς ἀπὸ τὴν ἀθυμία
τὸν βγάζει—τὸ ἐξαίσιον Οὗτος Ἐκεῖνος,
ποῦ ἄλλοτε στὸν ὕπνο του ἄκουσε ὁ Λουκιανός.

ΤΑ ΕΠΙΚΙΝΔΥΝΑ

Εἶπε ὁ Μυρτίας (Σύρος σπουδαστὴς
στὴν Ἀλεξάνδρεια· ἐπὶ βασιλείας
αὐγούστου Κώνσταντος καὶ αὐγούστου Κωνσταντίου·
ἐν μέρει ἐθνικός, κ' ἐν μέρει χριστιανίζων)·
«Δυναμωμένος μὲ θεωρία καὶ μελέτη,
ἐγὼ τὰ πάθη μου δὲν θὰ φοβοῦμαι σὰ δειλός.
Τὸ σῶμα μου στὲς ἡδονὲς θὰ δώσω,
στὲς ἀπολαύσεις τὲς ὀνειρεμένες,
στὲς τολμηρότερες ἐρωτικὲς ἐπιθυμίες,
στὲς λάγνες τοῦ αἵματός μου ὁρμές, χωρὶς
κανέναν φόβο, γιατὶ ὅταν θέλω—
καὶ θἄχω θέλησι, δυναμωμένος
ὡς θἄμαι μὲ θεωρία καὶ μελέτη—
στὲς κρίσιμες στιγμὲς θὰ ξαναβρίσκω
τὸ πνεῦμα μου, σὰν πρίν, ἀσκητικό.»

THAT IS THE MAN

An unknown—a stranger in Antioch—from Edessa*
writes copiously. And at long last, here it is,
the final hymn is ready. That makes eighty-three

poems in all. But the poet is tired
of so much writing, so much versifying
and so much strain in Greek phraseology,
that by now every small thing weighs him down.—

One thought, though, immediately takes him right out
of his despondency—the wonderful 'That is the Man',
which at one time Lucian heard in his sleep.

PERILOUS THINGS

Said Myrtias (a Syrian student
in Alexandria during the reign of
Augustus Constans* and Augustus Constantius;
in part pagan, in part with Christian leanings):
'Fortified by Theory and Study
I shall not fear my passions like a coward.
I shall abandon my body to sensual pleasures,
to dreamlike delights,
to the most daring erotic desires,
to the lascivious impulses of my blood,
without any fear, for when I wish—
and I'll possess the will, as I shall be
fortified by Theory and Study—
at critical moments I shall find again
my spiritual self, ascetic as before.'

ΜΑΝΟΥΗΛ ΚΟΜΝΗΝΟΣ

Ὁ βασιλεὺς κὺρ Μανουὴλ ὁ Κομνηνὸς
μιὰ μέρα μελαγχολικὴ τοῦ Σεπτεμβρίου
αἰσθάνθηκε τὸν θάνατο κοντά. Οἱ ἀστρολόγοι
(οἱ πληρωμένοι) τῆς αὐλῆς ἐφλυαροῦσαν
ποῦ ἄλλα πολλὰ χρόνια θὰ ζήσει ἀκόμη.
Ἐνῶ ὅμως ἔλεγαν αὐτοί, ἐκεῖνος
παληὲς συνήθειες εὐλαβεῖς θυμᾶται,
κι ἀπ' τὰ κελλιὰ τῶν μοναχῶν προστάζει
ἐνδύματα ἐκκλησιαστικὰ νὰ φέρουν,
καὶ τὰ φορεῖ κ' εὐφραίνεται ποῦ δείχνει
ὄψι σεμνὴν ἱερέως ἢ καλογήρου.

Εὐτυχισμένοι ὅλοι ποῦ πιστεύουν,
καὶ σὰν τὸν βασιλέα κὺρ Μανουὴλ τελειώνουν
ντυμένοι μὲς τὴν πίστι των σεμνότατα.

ΣΤΗΝ ΕΚΚΛΗΣΙΑ

Τὴν ἐκκλησίαν ἀγαπῶ—τὰ ἑξαπτέρυγά της,
τ' ἀσήμια τῶν σκευῶν, τὰ κηροπήγιά της,
τὰ φῶτα, τὲς εἰκόνες της, τὸν ἄμβωνά της.

Ἐκεῖ σὰν μπῶ, μὲς σ' ἐκκλησία τῶν Γραικῶν·
μὲ τῶν θυμιαμάτων της τὲς εὐωδίες,
μὲ τὲς λειτουργικὲς φωνὲς καὶ συμφωνίες,
τὲς μεγαλοπρεπεῖς τῶν ἱερέων παρουσίες
καὶ κάθε των κινήσεως τὸν σοβαρὸ ρυθμὸ—
λαμπρότατοι μὲς στῶν ἀμφίων τὸν στολισμὸ—
ὁ νοῦς μου πιαίνει σὲ τιμὲς μεγάλες τῆς φυλῆς μας,
στὸν ἔνδοξό μας Βυζαντινισμό.

MANUEL COMNENUS

King Manuel Comnenus,*
one melancholy day in September,
felt death to be near. The court astrologers
(the paid ones) went on prating
that he would live for many years more.
But while they kept on talking,
he calls to mind devout customs of the past,
and from the cells of monks he orders
ecclesiastical garments to be brought;
and he wears them, and delights in assuming
the modest aspect of a priest or monk.

Blessed are all who indeed believe
and, like King Manuel, end their days
vested most modestly in their faith.

IN CHURCH

I love the church—its liturgical fans,
the silver of the vessels, its candlesticks,
the lights, the icons, the pulpit.

When I enter there, in a church of the Greeks,
with its fragrances of incense,
amid the liturgical voices and harmonies,
the majestic presence of the priests
and the stately rhythm of their every move—
most resplendent in the finery of their vestments—
my mind travels to the great glories of our race,
to our illustrious Byzantine past.

ΠΟΛΥ ΣΠΑΝΙΩΣ

Εἶν' ἕνας γέροντας. Ἐξηντλημένος καὶ κυρτός,
σακατεμένος ἀπ' τὰ χρόνια, κι ἀπὸ καταχρήσεις,
σιγὰ βαδίζοντας διαβαίνει τὸ σοκάκι.
Κι ὅμως σὰν μπεῖ στὸ σπίτι του νὰ κρύψει
τὰ χάλια καὶ τὰ γηρατειά του, μελετᾶ
τὸ μερτικὸ ποῦ ἔχει ἀκόμη αὐτὸς στὰ νειάτα.

Ἔφηβοι τώρα τοὺς δικούς του στίχους λένε.
Στὰ μάτια των τὰ ζωηρὰ περνοῦν ἡ ὀπτασίες του.
Τὸ ὑγιές, ἡδονικὸ μυαλό των,
ἡ εὔγραμμη, σφιχτοδεμένη σάρκα των,
μὲ τὴν δική του ἔκφανσι τοῦ ὡραίου συγκινοῦνται.

ΤΟΥ ΜΑΓΑΖΙΟΥ

Τὰ ντύλιξε προσεκτικά, μὲ τάξι
σὲ πράσινο πολύτιμο μετάξι.

Ἀπὸ ρουμπίνια ρόδα, ἀπὸ μαργαριτάρια κρίνοι,
ἀπὸ ἀμεθύστους μενεξέδες. Ὡς αὐτὸς τὰ κρίνει,

τὰ θέλησε, τὰ βλέπει ὡραῖα· ὄχι ὅπως στὴν φύσι
τὰ εἶδεν ἢ τὰ σπούδασε. Μὲς στὸ ταμεῖον θὰ τ' ἀφίσει,

δεῖγμα τῆς τολμηρῆς δουλειᾶς του καὶ ἱκανῆς.
Στὸ μαγαζὶ σὰν μπεῖ ἀγοραστὴς κανεὶς

βγάζει ἀπ' τὲς θῆκες ἄλλα καὶ πουλεῖ—περίφημα στολίδια—
βραχιόλια, ἁλυσίδες, περιδέραια καὶ δαχτυλίδια.

VERY SELDOM

He is an old man. Worn out and stooped,
crippled by the years and by abuses,
walking slowly he crosses the narrow street.
But once he goes inside his home to hide
his wretchedness and his old age, he ponders on
the share of youth which still belongs to him.

Now, young men recite his own verses.
His visions pass before their lively eyes.
Their healthy, sensuous minds,
their elegant, firm bodies,
are stirred by his manifestation of Beauty.

OF THE SHOP

He wrapped them up carefully, neatly
in precious cloth of green silk.

Roses of rubies, lilies of pearls,
violets of amethysts. As he himself deems them,

wants them, sees them beautiful; not as he saw
or studied them in nature. He'll leave them in the safe;

samples of his more audacious and skilful work.
Yet, when a customer enters the shop,

he takes out of the cases and sells some other things—
fine ornaments—bracelets, chains, necklaces and rings.

ΖΩΓΡΑΦΙΣΜΕΝΑ

Τὴν ἐργασία μου τὴν προσέχω καὶ τὴν ἀγαπῶ.
Μὰ τῆς συνθέσεως μ' ἀποθαρρύνει σήμερα ἡ βραδύτης.
Ἡ μέρα μ' ἐπηρέασε. Ἡ μορφή της
ὅλο καὶ σκοτεινιάζει. Ὅλο φυσᾶ καὶ βρέχει.
Πιότερο ἐπιθυμῶ νὰ δῶ παρὰ νὰ πῶ.
Στὴ ζωγραφιὰν αὐτὴ κυττάζω τώρα
ἕνα ὡραῖο ἀγόρι ποῦ σιμὰ στὴ βρύσι
ἐπλάγιασεν, ἀφοῦ θ' ἀπέκαμε νὰ τρέχει.
Τί ὡραῖο παιδί· τί θεῖο μεσημέρι τὸ ἔχει
παρμένο πιὰ γιὰ νὰ τὸ ἀποκοιμίσει.—
Κάθομαι καὶ κυττάζω ἔτσι πολλὴν ὥρα.
Καὶ μὲς στὴν τέχνη πάλι, ξεκουράζομαι ἀπ' τὴν δούλεψή της.

ΘΑΛΑΣΣΑ ΤΟΥ ΠΡΩΪΟΥ

Ἐδῶ ἂς σταθῶ. Κι ἂς δῶ κ' ἐγὼ τὴν φύσι λίγο.
Θάλασσας τοῦ πρωϊοῦ κι ἀνέφελου οὐρανοῦ
λαμπρὰ μαβιά, καὶ κίτρινη ὄχθη· ὅλα
ὡραῖα καὶ μεγάλα φωτισμένα.

Ἐδῶ ἂς σταθῶ. Κι ἂς γελασθῶ πῶς βλέπω αὐτὰ
(τὰ εἶδ' ἀλήθεια μιὰ στιγμὴ σὰν πρωτοστάθηκα)·
κι ὄχι κ' ἐδῶ τὲς φαντασίες μου,
τὲς ἀναμνήσεις μου, τὰ ἰνδάλματα τῆς ἡδονῆς.

PAINTED

I'm careful about my work and I cherish it.
But today I'm disheartened by the slow pace of composition.
The day has affected me. Its aspect
keeps growing darker. All wind and rain.
I'd rather look at things than speak about them.
In this painting, I now observe
a lovely boy who near the fountain
lay down, having run to exhaustion.
What a lovely boy! What a divine midday
has taken hold of him to lull him now to sleep.—
I sit and I gaze like this for quite a while.
And immersed once more in art, I take a rest from its toil.

MORNING SEA

Let me stand here. And let me, too, look at nature a while.
The morning sea's and cloudless sky's
radiant violet hues and yellow shore; all
beautiful and brightly lit.

Let me stand here. And let me deceive myself that I see them
(indeed, I saw them for a moment when I first paused);
and that I don't see even here my fantasies,
my memories, the ideal visions of sensual bliss.

ΙΩΝΙΚΟΝ

Γιατὶ τὰ σπάσαμε τ' ἀγάλματά των,
γιατὶ τοὺς διώξαμεν ἀπ' τοὺς ναούς των,
διόλου δὲν πέθαναν γι' αὐτὸ οἱ θεοί.
Ὦ γῆ τῆς Ἰωνίας, σένα ἀγαποῦν ἀκόμη,
σένα ἡ ψυχές των ἐνθυμοῦνται ἀκόμη.
Σὰν ξημερώνει ἐπάνω σου πρωῒ αὐγουστιάτικο
τὴν ἀτμοσφαῖρα σου περνᾶ σφρῖγος ἀπ' τὴν ζωή των·
καὶ κάποτ' αἰθερία ἐφηβικὴ μορφή,
ἀόριστη μὲ διάβα γρήγορο,
ἐπάνω ἀπὸ τοὺς λόφους σου περνᾶ.

ΣΤΟΥ ΚΑΦΕΝΕΙΟΥ ΤΗΝ ΕΙΣΟΔΟ

Τὴν προσοχή μου κάτι ποῦ εἶπαν πλάγι μου
διεύθυνε στοῦ καφενείου τὴν εἴσοδο.
Κ' εἶδα τ' ὡραῖο σῶμα ποῦ ἔμοιαζε
σὰν ἀπ' τὴν ἄκρα πεῖρα του νὰ τὦκαμεν ὁ Ἔρως—
πλάττοντας τὰ συμμετρικά του μέλη μὲ χαρά·
ὑψώνοντας γλυπτὸ τὸ ἀνάστημα·
πλάττοντας μὲ συγκίνησι τὸ πρόσωπο
κι ἀφίνοντας ἀπ' τῶν χεριῶν του τὸ ἄγγιγμα
ἕνα αἴσθημα στὸ μέτωπο, στὰ μάτια, καὶ στὰ χείλη.

ΜΙΑ ΝΥΧΤΑ

Ἡ κάμαρα ἦταν πτωχικὴ καὶ πρόστυχη,
κρυμένη ἐπάνω ἀπὸ τὴν ὕποπτη ταβέρνα.
Ἀπ' τὸ παράθυρο φαίνονταν τὸ σοκάκι,
τὸ ἀκάθαρτο καὶ τὸ στενό. Ἀπὸ κάτω
ἤρχονταν ἡ φωνὲς κάτι ἐργατῶν
ποῦ ἔπαιζαν χαρτιὰ καὶ ποῦ γλεντοῦσαν.

*

IONIC

Even though we have broken their statues,
even though we drove them out of their temples,
in no wise did the gods die for all that.
O land of Ionia, it is you they love still,
it is you their souls still remember.
When upon you dawns an August morn,
some vigour of their life pervades your atmosphere,
and once in a while, an ethereal, youthful form,
indistinct, in rapid stride,
passes above your hills.

AT THE ENTRANCE OF THE CAFÉ

My attention was directed, by something said beside me,
toward the entrance of the café.
And I saw the lovely body that appeared
as if created by Eros in his consummate experience—
fashioning its well-proportioned limbs with joy;
raising a sculpted posture;
fashioning the face with deep emotion
and bestowing, by the touch of his hands,
a feeling upon the brow, the eyes, and the lips.

ONE NIGHT

The room was shabby and sordid,
concealed above the seedy tavern.
From the window you could see the alley,
squalid and narrow. From below
came the voices of some workmen
playing cards and revelling.

*

Κ' ἐκεῖ στὸ λαϊκό, τὸ ταπεινὸ κρεββάτι
εἶχα τὸ σῶμα τοῦ ἔρωτος, εἶχα τὰ χείλη
τὰ ἡδονικὰ καὶ ρόδινα τῆς μέθης—
τὰ ρόδινα μιᾶς τέτοιας μέθης, ποῦ καὶ τώρα
ποῦ γράφω, ἔπειτ' ἀπὸ τόσα χρόνια!,
μὲς στὸ μονῆρες σπίτι μου, μεθῶ ξανά.

ΕΠΕΣΤΡΕΦΕ

Ἐπέστρεφε συχνὰ καὶ πέρνε με,
ἀγαπημένη αἴσθησις ἐπέστρεφε καὶ πέρνε με—
ὅταν ξυπνᾶ τοῦ σώματος ἡ μνήμη,
κ' ἐπιθυμία παληὰ ξαναπερνᾶ στὸ αἷμα·
ὅταν τὰ χείλη καὶ τὸ δέρμα ἐνθυμοῦνται,
κ' αἰσθάνονται τὰ χέρια σὰν ν' ἀγγίζουν πάλι.

Ἐπέστρεφε συχνὰ καὶ πέρνε με τὴν νύχτα,
ὅταν τὰ χείλη καὶ τὸ δέρμα ἐνθυμοῦνται . . .

ΜΑΚΡΥΑ

Θἄθελα αὐτὴν τὴν μνήμη νὰ τὴν πῶ . . .
Μὰ ἔτσι ἐσβύσθη πιὰ . . . σὰν τίποτε δὲν ἀπομένει—
γιατὶ μακρυά, στὰ πρῶτα ἐφηβικά μου χρόνια κεῖται.

Δέρμα σὰν καμωμένο ἀπὸ ἰασεμί . . .
Ἐκείνη τοῦ Αὐγούστου—Αὔγουστος ἦταν;—ἡ βραδυά . . .
Μόλις θυμοῦμαι πιὰ τὰ μάτια· ἦσαν, θαρρῶ, μαβιά . . .
Ἆ ναί, μαβιά· ἕνα σαπφείρινο μαβί.

And there, upon the lowly, humble bed
I had the body of love, I had the lips,
the sensuous, rosy, intoxicating lips—
the rosy lips of such sensual ecstasy that even now,
as I am writing, after so many years,
in my lonely home, I feel drunk again.

COME BACK

Come back often and take hold of me,
beloved sensation, come back and take hold of me—
when the memory of the body is aroused,
and past desire flows into the blood again;
when the lips and the skin remember,
and the hands feel as if they are touching again.

Come back often, and take hold of me in the night,
when the lips and the skin remember . . .

FAR AWAY

I'd like to put this memory into words . . .
Yet it has faded so by now . . . as if but nothing remains—
for it lies far away, in the years of my earliest youth.

Skin as if made of jasmine . . .
In that August—was it August?—night . . .
Barely can I recall by now the eyes; they were, I think, deep
 blue . . .
Ah yes, deep blue; a sapphire blue.

ΟΜΝΥΕΙ

Ὀμνύει κάθε τόσο   ν' ἀρχίσει πιὸ καλὴ ζωή.
Ἀλλ' ὅταν ἔλθ' ἡ νύχτα   μὲ τὲς δικές της συμβουλές,
μὲ τοὺς συμβιβασμούς της,   καὶ μὲ τὲς ὑποσχέσεις της·
ἀλλ' ὅταν ἔλθ' ἡ νύχτα   μὲ τὴν δική της δύναμι
τοῦ σώματος ποῦ θέλει καὶ ζητεῖ, στὴν ἴδια
μοιραία χαρά, χαμένος, ξαναπιαίνει.

ΕΠΗΓΑ

Δὲν ἐδεσμεύθηκα. Τελείως ἀφέθηκα κ' ἐπῆγα.
Στὲς ἀπολαύσεις, ποῦ μισὸ πραγματικές,
μισὸ γυρνάμενες μὲς στὸ μυαλό μου ἦσαν,
ἐπῆγα μὲς στὴν φωτισμένη νύχτα.
Κ' ἤπια ἀπὸ δυνατὰ κρασιά, καθὼς
ποῦ πίνουν οἱ ἀνδρεῖοι τῆς ἡδονῆς.

ΠΟΛΥΕΛΑΙΟΣ

Σὲ κάμαρη ἄδεια καὶ μικρή, τέσσαρες τοῖχοι μόνοι,
καὶ σκεπασμένοι μὲ ὁλοπράσινα πανιά,
καίει ἕνας πολυέλαιος ὡραῖος καὶ κορόνει·
καὶ μὲς στὴ φλόγα του τὴν καθεμιὰ πυρόνει
μιὰ λάγνη πάθησις, μιὰ λάγνη ὁρμή.

Μὲς στὴν μικρὴ τὴν κάμαρη, ποῦ λάμπει ἀναμένη
ἀπὸ τοῦ πολυελαίου τὴν δυνατὴ φωτιά,
διόλου συνειθισμένο φῶς δὲν εἶν' αὐτὸ ποῦ βγαίνει.
Γι' ἄτολμα σώματα δὲν εἶναι καμωμένη
αὐτῆς τῆς ζέστης ἡ ἡδονή.

HE VOWS

He vows, every so often,   to start a better life.
But come the night   with its own counsel,
its own compromises,   its own promises;
but come the night   with its own potent allure
of the body that desires and demands, he returns
once more, lost, to the same fateful pleasure.

I WENT

I did not restrain myself. I let go completely and went.
To those pleasures that were partly real,
partly swirling in my mind,
I went, into the lighted night.
And drank of potent wines, such as
the fearless in their sensual pleasure drink.

CHANDELIER

In a chamber empty and small, four walls only
and draped with lengths of bright green cloth,
a lovely chandelier shines and glows,
and in its every single flame, simmering grows
a lustful passion, a lustful urge.

Within the small chamber, that gleams alight
from the fiery heat of the chandelier,
what emerges is no ordinary light.
It is not made for timid bodies,
the sensual rapture of this heat.

POEMS (1916–1918)

ΠΟΙΗΜΑΤΑ (1916–1918)

ΑΠ' ΤΕΣ ΕΝΝΙΑ —

Δώδεκα καὶ μισή. Γρήγορα πέρασεν ἡ ὥρα
ἀπ' τὲς ἐννιὰ ποῦ ἄναψα τὴν λάμπα,
καὶ κάθισα ἐδῶ. Κάθουμουν χωρὶς νὰ διαβάζω,
καὶ χωρὶς νὰ μιλῶ. Μὲ ποιόνα νὰ μιλήσω
κατάμονος μέσα στὸ σπίτι αὐτό.

Τὸ εἴδωλον τοῦ νέου σώματός μου,
ἀπ' τὲς ἐννιὰ ποῦ ἄναψα τὴν λάμπα,
ἦλθε καὶ μὲ ηὗρε καὶ μὲ θύμησε
κλειστὲς κάμαρες ἀρωματισμένες,
καὶ περασμένην ἡδονὴ — τί τολμηρὴ ἡδονή!
Κ' ἐπίσης μ' ἔφερε στὰ μάτια ἐμπρός,
δρόμους ποῦ τώρα ἔγιναν ἀγνώριστοι,
κέντρα γεμάτα κίνησι ποῦ τέλεψαν,
καὶ θέατρα καὶ καφενεῖα ποῦ ἦσαν μιὰ φορά.

Τὸ εἴδωλον τοῦ νέου σώματός μου
ἦλθε καὶ μ' ἔφερε καὶ τὰ λυπητερά·
πένθη τῆς οἰκογένειας, χωρισμοί,
αἰσθήματα δικῶν μου, αἰσθήματα
τῶν πεθαμένων τόσο λίγο ἐκτιμηθέντα.

Δώδεκα καὶ μισή. Πῶς πέρασεν ἡ ὥρα.
Δώδεκα καὶ μισή. Πῶς πέρασαν τὰ χρόνια.

ΝΟΗΣΙΣ

Τὰ χρόνια τῆς νεότητός μου, ὁ ἡδονικός μου βίος—
πῶς βλέπω τώρα καθαρὰ τὸ νόημά των.

Τί μεταμέλειες περιττές, τί μάταιες . . .

Ἀλλὰ δὲν ἔβλεπα τὸ νόημα τότε.

*

SINCE NINE O'CLOCK—

Half past twelve. The hours have passed quickly
since nine o'clock when I lit the lamp
and sat down here. I've been sitting without reading,
without talking. To whom could I talk,
all alone within this house!

The image of my young body,
since nine o'clock when I lit the lamp,
came and found me and reminded me
of closed, perfumed rooms
and past sensual pleasure—what audacious pleasure!
And also brought before my eyes
streets that have since become unrecognizable;
night clubs full of life that now are closed,
and theatres and cafés that once used to be.

The image of my young body
came back and brought to mind also sad memories;
family mournings, separations,
feelings of my dear ones, feelings
of the dead, so little appreciated.

Half past twelve. How the hours have passed.
Half past twelve. How have the years gone by.

PERCEPTION

The years of my youth, my sensuous life—
how clearly I see their meaning now!

What useless, what futile repentances . . .

But I couldn't see their meaning then.

*

Μέσα στὸν ἔκλυτο τῆς νεότητός μου βίο
μορφόνονταν βουλὲς τῆς ποιήσεώς μου,
σχεδιάζονταν τῆς τέχνης μου ἡ περιοχή.

Γι' αὐτὸ κ' ἡ μεταμέλειες σταθερὲς ποτὲ δὲν ἦσαν.
Κ' ἡ ἀποφάσεις μου νὰ κρατηθῶ, ν' ἀλλάξω
διαρκοῦσαν δυὸ ἑβδομάδες τὸ πολύ.

ΕΝΩΠΙΟΝ ΤΟΥ ΑΓΑΛΜΑΤΟΣ ΤΟΥ ΕΝΔΥΜΙΩΝΟΣ

Ἐπὶ ἅρματος λευκοῦ ποῦ τέσσαρες ἡμίονοι
πάλλευκοι σύρουν, μὲ κοσμήματ' ἀργυρᾶ,
φθάνω ἐκ Μιλήτου εἰς τὸν Λάτμον. Ἱερὰ
τελῶν — θυσίας καὶ σπονδὰς — τῷ Ἐνδυμίωνι,
ἀπὸ τὴν Ἀλεξάνδρειαν ἔπλευσα ἐν τριήρει πορφυρᾷ. —
Ἰδοὺ τὸ ἄγαλμα. Ἐν ἐκστάσει βλέπω νῦν
τοῦ Ἐνδυμίωνος τὴν φημισμένην καλλονήν.
Ἰάσμων κάνιστρα κενοῦν οἱ δοῦλοι μου· κ' εὐοίωνοι
ἐπευφημίαι ἐξύπνησαν ἀρχαίων χρόνων ἡδονήν.

ΠΡΕΣΒΕΙΣ ΑΠ' ΤΗΝ ΑΛΕΞΑΝΔΡΕΙΑ

Δὲν εἶδαν, ἐπὶ αἰῶνας, τέτοια ὡραῖα δῶρα στοὺς Δελφοὺς
σὰν τοῦτα ποῦ ἐστάλθηκαν ἀπὸ τοὺς δυὸ τοὺς ἀδελφούς,
τοὺς ἀντιζήλους Πτολεμαίους βασιλεῖς. Ἀφοῦ τὰ πῆραν
ὅμως, ἀνησυχῆσαν οἱ ἱερεῖς γιὰ τὸν χρησμό. Τὴν πεῖραν
ὅλην των θὰ χρειασθοῦν τὸ πῶς μὲ ὀξύνοιαν νὰ συνταχθεῖ,
ποιὸς ἀπ' τοὺς δυό, ποιὸς ἀπὸ τέτοιους δυὸ νὰ δυσαρεστηθεῖ.
Καὶ συνεδριάζουνε τὴν νύχτα μυστικὰ
καὶ συζητοῦν τῶν Λαγιδῶν τὰ οἰκογενειακά.

Ἀλλὰ ἰδοὺ οἱ πρέσβεις ἐπανῆλθαν. Χαιρετοῦν.
Στὴν Ἀλεξάνδρεια ἐπιστρέφουν, λέν. Καὶ δὲν ζητοῦν
χρησμὸ κανένα. Κ' οἱ ἱερεῖς τ' ἀκοῦνε μὲ χαρὰ
(ἐννοεῖται, ποῦ κρατοῦν τὰ δῶρα τὰ λαμπρά),

Within the wanton life of my youth
my poetic will was being shaped,
the territory of my art was being drawn.

And thus repentances were never steadfast.
And my resolutions to restrain myself, to change,
lasted no more than two weeks, at the most.

BEFORE THE STATUE OF ENDYMION

Upon a white chariot drawn by four
snow-white mules, adorned with silver ornaments,
I arrive at Latmos from Miletus. I sailed
in a purple trireme from Alexandria, in order to perform
sacred rites—sacrifices and libations—in honour of
Endymion.*—
Behold the statue! I now gaze in ecstasy
upon Endymion's renowned beauty. My servants
empty canisters of jasmine blossoms; and auspicious
acclaim awakens the pleasures of ancient times.

ENVOYS FROM ALEXANDRIA

They haven't seen for centuries such lovely gifts in Delphi
as those that had been sent to them by both of the two brothers,
the rival Ptolemaic kings. But after they'd received them,
the priests began worrying about the divination.
They'll need all their experience—how to compose astutely:
which of the two, of such as these two, will have to be offended.
So they hold a meeting secretly at night
to talk about the Lagids' family plight.

Lo and behold, though! The envoys are back. They bid goodbye.
They are returning—so they say—to Alexandria, and they
don't want an oracle at all. The priests listen with joy
(and as it is well understood, they keep the splendid presents),

ἀλλ' εἶναι καὶ στὸ ἔπακρον ἀπορημένοι,
μὴ νοιώθοντας τί ἡ ἐξαφνικὴ ἀδιαφορία αὐτὴ σημαίνει.
Γιατὶ ἀγνοοῦν ποῦ χθὲς στοὺς πρέσβεις ἦλθαν νέα βαρυά.
Στὴν Ρώμη δόθηκε ὁ χρησμός· ἔγειν' ἐκεῖ ἡ μοιρασιά.

ΑΡΙΣΤΟΒΟΥΛΟΣ

Κλαίει τὸ παλάτι, κλαίει ὁ βασιλεύς,
ἀπαρηγόρητος θρηνεῖ ὁ βασιλεὺς Ἡρώδης,
ἡ πολιτεία ὁλόκληρη κλαίει γιὰ τὸν Ἀριστόβουλο
ποῦ ἔτσι ἄδικα, τυχαίως πνίχθηκε
παίζοντας μὲ τοὺς φίλους του μὲς στὸ νερό.

Κι ὅταν τὸ μάθουνε καὶ στ' ἄλλα μέρη,
ὅταν ἐπάνω στὴν Συρία διαδοθεῖ,
κι ἀπὸ τοὺς Ἕλληνας πολλοὶ θὰ λυπηθοῦν·
ὅσοι ποιηταὶ καὶ γλύπται θὰ πενθήσουν,
γιατ' εἶχεν ἀκουσθεῖ σ' αὐτοὺς ὁ Ἀριστόβουλος,
καὶ ποιά τους φαντασία γιὰ ἔφηβο ποτὲ
ἔφθασε τέτοιαν ἐμορφιὰ σὰν τοῦ παιδιοῦ αὐτοῦ·
ποιὸ ἄγαλμα θεοῦ ἀξιώθηκεν ἡ Ἀντιόχεια
σὰν τὸ παιδὶ αὐτὸ τοῦ Ἰσραήλ.

Ὀδύρεται καὶ κλαίει ἡ Πρώτη Πριγκηπέσσα·
ἡ μάνα του, ἡ πιὸ μεγάλη Ἑβρέσσα.
Ὀδύρεται καὶ κλαίει ἡ Ἀλεξάνδρα γιὰ τὴν συμφορά.—
Μὰ σὰν βρεθεῖ μονάχη της ἀλλάζει ὁ καϋμός της.
Βογγᾶ· φρενιάζει· βρίζει· καταριέται.
Πῶς τὴν ἐγέλασαν! Πῶς τὴν φενάκισαν!
Πῶς ἐπὶ τέλους ἔγινε ὁ σκοπός των!
Τὸ ρήμαξαν τὸ σπίτι τῶν Ἀσαμωναίων.
Πῶς τὸ κατόρθωσε ὁ κακοῦργος βασιλεύς·
ὁ δόλιος, ὁ φαῦλος, ὁ ἀλιτήριος.
Πῶς τὸ κατόρθωσε. Τί καταχθόνιο σχέδιο
ποῦ νὰ μὴ νοιώσει κ' ἡ Μαριάμμη τίποτε.
Ἂν ἔνοιωθε ἡ Μαριάμμη, ἂν ὑποπτεύονταν,
θἄβρισκε τρόπο τὸ ἀδέρφι της νὰ σώσει·

but they are at the same time completely bewildered,
unable to perceive what this abrupt indifference means.
For they don't know that yesterday the envoys heard grave news.
The oracle was pronounced in Rome; it was there the deal was made.

ARISTOBOULOS

The palace is in tears, the king is in tears,
King Herod is inconsolably lamenting,
the entire State is crying for Aristoboulos,*
who drowned so unfairly by accident
while playing with his friends in the water.

And when they'll also hear of it in other places,
when the news will spread up to Syria,
many of the Greeks will be saddened, too.
So many poets and sculptors will mourn,
since the name of Aristoboulos was known to them,
and what fantasy of a youth could they have had
that might equal a beauty such as this boy's?
What statue of a god was Antioch proud to possess,
that could be compared to this child of Israel?

She wails and weeps, the First Princess,
his mother, the most prominent Hebrew Lady.
She, Alexandra, wails and weeps at the disaster.—
But as soon as she finds herself alone, her sorrow changes tone.
She moans, she raves, she swears, she curses.
How did they trick her! How did they deceive her!
How did they finally achieve their goal!
They have ruined the House of the Hasmoneans.*
How did he bring it about? That murderous king,
the perfidious, the wicked, the wretch.
How did he bring it about? What a fiendish plan,
that even Miriam should sense nothing.
Had Miriam sensed, had she suspected,
she would have found a way to save her brother;

βασίλισσα εἶναι τέλος, θὰ μποροῦσε κάτι.
Πῶς θὰ θριαμβεύουν τώρα καὶ θὰ χαίρονται κρυφὰ
ἡ μοχθηρὲς ἐκεῖνες, Κύπρος καὶ Σαλώμη·
ἡ πρόστυχες γυναῖκες, Κύπρος καὶ Σαλώμη.—
Καὶ νἆναι ἀνίσχυρη, κι ἀναγκασμένη
νὰ κάνει ποῦ πιστεύει τὲς ψευτιές των·
νὰ μὴ μπορεῖ πρὸς τὸν λαὸ νὰ πάγει,
νὰ βγεῖ καὶ νὰ φωνάξει στοὺς Ἑβραίους,
νὰ πεῖ, νὰ πεῖ πῶς ἔγινε τὸ φονικό.

ΚΑΙΣΑΡΙΩΝ

Ἐν μέρει γιὰ νὰ ἐξακριβώσω μιὰ ἐποχή,
ἐν μέρει καὶ τὴν ὥρα νὰ περάσω,
τὴν νύχτα χθὲς πῆρα μιὰ συλλογὴ
ἐπιγραφῶν τῶν Πτολεμαίων νὰ διαβάσω.
Οἱ ἄφθονοι ἔπαινοι κ' ἡ κολακεῖες
εἰς ὅλους μοιάζουν. Ὅλοι εἶναι λαμπροί,
ἔνδοξοι, κραταιοί, ἀγαθοεργοί·
καθ' ἐπιχείρησίς των σοφοτάτη.
Ἂν πεῖς γιὰ τὲς γυναῖκες τῆς γενιᾶς, κι αὐτές,
ὅλες ἡ Βερενίκες κ' ἡ Κλεοπάτρες θαυμαστές.

Ὅταν κατόρθωσα τὴν ἐποχὴ νὰ ἐξακριβώσω
θἄφινα τὸ βιβλίο ἂν μιὰ μνεία μικρή,
κι ἀσήμαντη, τοῦ βασιλέως Καισαρίωνος
δὲν εἴλκυε τὴν προσοχή μου ἀμέσως . . .

Ἄ, νά, ἦρθες σὺ μὲ τὴν ἀόριστη
γοητεία σου. Στὴν ἱστορία λίγες
γραμμὲς μονάχα βρίσκονται γιὰ σένα,
κ' ἔτσι πιὸ ἐλεύθερα σ' ἔπλασα μὲς στὸν νοῦ μου.
Σ' ἔπλασα ὡραῖο κ' αἰσθηματικό.
Ἡ τέχνη μου στὸ πρόσωπό σου δείνει
μιὰν ὀνειρώδη συμπαθητικὴ ἐμορφιά.
Καὶ τόσο πλήρως σὲ φαντάσθηκα,
ποῦ χθὲς τὴν νύχτα ἀργά, σὰν ἔσβυνεν
ἡ λάμπα μου—ἄφισα ἐπίτηδες νὰ σβύνει—

she's queen, after all, she could have done something.
How they will gloat now and secretly rejoice,
those wicked ones, Cyprus and Salome,*
those wanton sluts Cyprus and Salome.—
And she being powerless, and forced
to pretend she believes their lies;
being unable to turn to the people,
to come out and shout to the Hebrews
and tell, tell how the murder was done.

CAESARION

In part to examine an era,
and in part to while away the time,
last night I picked up to read
a collection of Ptolemaic inscriptions.
The copious praises and the flatteries
befit them all. All are illustrious,
glorious, mighty, beneficent;
their every endeavour most wise.
As for the females of that line, those too,
all the Berenices* and the Cleopatras are admirable.

When I'd managed to examine the era,
I would have put the book away, were it not
for a small, insignificant mention of King Caesarion
which at once attracted my attention . . .

And there you appeared with your indefinable
allure. In History only
a few lines are dedicated to you,
and thus I could form you more freely in my mind.
I made you beautiful and sentimental.
My art bestows upon your face
a dreamlike, genial grace.
And so fully I envisaged you
that late last night, as my lamp
died out—I deliberately let it die out—

ἐθάρεψα ποῦ μπῆκες μὲς στὴν κάμαρά μου,
μὲ φάνηκε ποῦ ἐμπρός μου στάθηκες ὡς θὰ ἦσουν
μὲς στὴν κατακτημένην Ἀλεξάνδρεια,
χλωμὸς καὶ κουρασμένος, ἰδεώδης ἐν τῇ λύπῃ σου,
ἐλπίζοντας ἀκόμη νὰ σὲ σπλαχνισθοῦν
οἱ φαῦλοι — ποῦ ψιθύριζαν τὸ «Πολυκαισαρίη».

Η ΔΙΟΡΙΑ ΤΟΥ ΝΕΡΩΝΟΣ

Δὲν ἀνησύχησεν ὁ Νέρων ὅταν ἄκουσε
τοῦ Δελφικοῦ Μαντείου τὸν χρησμό.
«Τὰ ἑβδομῆντα τρία χρόνια νὰ φοβᾶται.»
Εἶχε καιρὸν ἀκόμη νὰ χαρεῖ.
Τριάντα χρονῶ εἶναι. Πολὺ ἀρκετὴ
εἶν' ἡ διορία ποῦ ὁ θεὸς τὸν δίδει
γιὰ νὰ φροντίσει γιὰ τοὺς μέλλοντας κινδύνους.

Τώρα στὴν Ρώμη θὰ ἐπιστρέψει κουρασμένος λίγο,
ἀλλὰ ἐξαίσια κουρασμένος ἀπὸ τὸ ταξεῖδι αὐτό,
ποῦ ἦταν ὅλο μέρες ἀπολαύσεως —
στὰ θέατρα, στοὺς κήπους, στὰ γυμνάσια . . .
Τῶν πόλεων τῆς Ἀχαΐας ἑσπέρες . . .
Ἆ τῶν γυμνῶν σωμάτων ἡ ἡδονὴ πρὸ πάντων . . .

Αὐτὰ ὁ Νέρων. Καὶ στὴν Ἱσπανία ὁ Γάλβας
κρυφὰ τὸ στράτευμά του συναθροίζει καὶ τὸ ἀσκεῖ,
ὁ γέροντας ὁ ἑβδομῆντα τριῶ χρονῶ.

I imagined that you entered my room;
it seemed to me that you stood right before me;
pale and weary, as you would have been
in vanquished Alexandria, ideally beautiful in your sorrow,
still hoping they would show you mercy,
the villains who were whispering: 'Too Many Caesars!'*

NERO'S TERM

Nero was not alarmed when he heard
the prophecy of the Delphic Oracle:*
'He should beware the age of seventy-three.'
He still had plenty of time to enjoy himself.
He is only thirty. More than ample
is the time that the god has allotted him
to take care of future dangers.

Now, he'll go back to Rome a little tired,
but exquisitely so, from this journey
that was filled with days of pleasure—
in theatres, in gardens, in gymnasia . . .
Those evenings in the cities of Achaea . . .
The sensual bliss of naked bodies, above all . . .

That's what Nero thinks. And Galba in Spain
gathers and drills his army in secret;
that old man of seventy-three.

ΕΙΣ ΤΟ ΕΠΙΝΕΙΟΝ

Νέος, εἴκοσι ὀκτὼ ἐτῶν, μὲ πλοῖον τήνιον
ἔφθασε εἰς τοῦτο τὸ συριακὸν ἐπίνειον
ὁ Ἔμης, μὲ τὴν πρόθεσι νὰ μάθει μυροπώλης.
Ὅμως ἀρρώστησε εἰς τὸν πλοῦν. Καὶ μόλις
ἀπεβιβάσθη, πέθανε. Ἡ ταφή του, πτωχοτάτη,
ἔγιν' ἐδῶ. Ὀλίγες ὧρες πρὶν πεθάνει κάτι
ψιθύρισε γιὰ «οἰκίαν», γιὰ «πολὺ γέροντας γονεῖς».
Μὰ ποιοὶ ἦσαν τοῦτοι δὲν ἐγνώριζε κανείς,
μήτε ποιὰ ἡ πατρίς του μὲς στὸ μέγα πανελλήνιον.
Καλλίτερα. Γιατὶ ἔτσι ἐνῶ
κεῖται νεκρὸς σ' αὐτὸ τὸ ἐπίνειον,
θὰ τὸν ἐλπίζουν πάντα οἱ γονεῖς του ζωντανό.

ΕΝΑΣ ΘΕΟΣ ΤΩΝ

Ὅταν κανένας των περνοῦσεν ἀπ' τῆς Σελευκείας
τὴν ἀγορά, περὶ τὴν ὥρα ποῦ βραδυάζει,
σὰν ὑψηλὸς καὶ τέλεια ὡραῖος ἔφηβος,
μὲ τὴν χαρὰ τῆς ἀφθαρσίας μὲς στὰ μάτια,
μὲ τ' ἀρωματισμένα μαῦρα του μαλλιά,
οἱ διαβάται τὸν ἐκύτταζαν
κι ὁ ἕνας τὸν ἄλλονα ρωτοῦσεν ἂν τὸν γνώριζε,
κι ἂν ἦταν Ἕλλην τῆς Συρίας, ἢ ξένος. Ἀλλὰ μερικοί,
ποῦ μὲ περισσοτέρα προσοχὴ παρατηροῦσαν,
ἐκαταλάμβαναν καὶ παραμέριζαν·
κ' ἐνῶ ἐχάνετο κάτω ἀπ' τὲς στοές,
μὲς στὲς σκιὲς καὶ μὲς στὰ φῶτα τῆς βραδυᾶς,
πιαίνοντας πρὸς τὴν συνοικία ποῦ τὴν νύχτα
μονάχα ζεῖ, μὲ ὄργια καὶ κραιπάλη,
καὶ κάθε εἴδους μέθη καὶ λαγνεία,
ἐρέμβαζαν ποιὸς τάχα ἦταν ἐξ Αὐτῶν,
καὶ γιὰ ποιὰν ὕποπτην ἀπόλαυσί του
στῆς Σελευκείας τοὺς δρόμους ἐκατέβηκεν
ἀπ' τὰ Προσκυνητά, Πάνσεπτα Δώματα.

IN THE HARBOUR TOWN

Emes, a young man of twenty-eight, on a Tenian
boat, arrived in this Syrian harbour town,
with the intention of learning the incense trade.
But during the voyage, he fell ill; and as soon
as he disembarked, he died. His burial—the poorest—
took place here. A few hours before he died,
he whispered something about 'home' and 'very aged parents'.
But who they were, nobody knew,
or where his home was, within the great pan-Hellenic world.
It is better so. For in this way,
as he lies dead in this harbour town,
his parents will forever hope that he is alive.

ONE OF THEIR GODS

When one of them passed through Seleucia's
marketplace, about the hour of dusk,
like a tall and perfectly handsome ephebe—
with the joy of immortality in his eyes,
with his perfumed dark hair—
the passers-by kept looking at him
and asked each other if anyone knew him,
and whether he was a Syrian Greek, or a stranger.
But some, who observed with greater care
would understand and step aside;
and as he disappeared under the arcades,
into the shadows and the evening lights—
headed for that part of town that only at night
comes alive, with orgies and debauchery
and every sort of drunkenness and lust—
they wondered which of Them could he be,
and for what shady pleasure of his
he had descended to Seleucia's streets,
from the Hallowed, Most Venerated Halls.

ΛΑΝΗ ΤΑΦΟΣ

Ὁ Λάνης ποῦ ἀγάπησες ἐδῶ δὲν εἶναι, Μάρκε,
στὸν τάφο ποῦ ἔρχεσαι καὶ κλαῖς, καὶ μένεις ὧρες κι ὧρες.
Τὸν Λάνη ποῦ ἀγάπησες τὸν ἔχεις πιὸ κοντά σου
στὸ σπίτι σου ὅταν κλείεσαι καὶ βλέπεις τὴν εἰκόνα,
ποῦ αὐτὴ κάπως διατήρησεν ὅτ' εἶχε ποῦ ν' ἀξίζει,
ποῦ αὐτὴ κάπως διατήρησεν ὅτ' εἶχες ἀγαπήσει.

Θυμᾶσαι, Μάρκε, ποῦ ἔφερες ἀπὸ τοῦ ἀνθυπάτου
τὸ μέγαρον τὸν Κυρηναῖο περίφημο ζωγράφο,
καὶ μὲ τὶ καλλιτεχνικὴν ἐκεῖνος πανουργία
μόλις εἶδε τὸν φίλο σου κ' ἤθελε νὰ σᾶς πείσει
ποῦ ὡς Ὑάκινθον ἐξ ἅπαντος ἔπρεπε νὰ τὸν κάμει
(μ' αὐτὸν τὸν τρόπο πιὸ πολὺ θ' ἀκούονταν ἡ εἰκών του).

Μὰ ὁ Λάνης σου δὲν δάνειζε τὴν ἐμορφιά του ἔτσι·
καὶ σταθερὰ ἐναντιωθεὶς εἶπε νὰ παρουσιάσει
ὄχι διόλου τὸν Ὑάκινθον, ὄχι κανέναν ἄλλον,
ἀλλὰ τὸν Λάνη, υἱὸ τοῦ Ραμετίχου, Ἀλεξανδρέα.

ΙΑΣΗ ΤΑΦΟΣ

Κεῖμαι ὁ Ἰασῆς ἐνταῦθα. Τῆς μεγάλης ταύτης πόλεως
ὁ ἔφηβος ὁ φημισμένος γιὰ ἐμορφιά.
Μ' ἐθαύμασαν βαθεῖς σοφοί· κ' ἐπίσης ὁ ἐπιπόλαιος,
ὁ ἁπλοῦς λαός. Καὶ χαίρομουν ἴσα καὶ γιὰ

τὰ δυό. Μὰ ἀπ' τὸ πολὺ νὰ μ' ἔχει ὁ κόσμος Νάρκισσο
κ' Ἑρμῆ,
ἡ καταχρήσεις μ' ἔφθειραν, μ' ἐσκότωσαν. Διαβάτη,
ἂν εἶσαι Ἀλεξανδρεύς, δὲν θὰ ἐπικρίνεις. Ξέρεις τὴν ὁρμὴ
τοῦ βίου μας· τὶ θέρμην ἔχει· τὶ ἡδονὴ ὑπερτάτη.

TOMB OF LANES

Marcus! The Lanes whom you loved is no more in this place,
within the tomb near which you come and weep and stay long hours.
The Lanes whom you so much loved, you have him closer to you
when you shut yourself at home and gaze upon his portrait
that somehow has preserved alive what of him was of value,
that somehow has preserved alive what of him you so cherished.

Remember, Marcus, when you brought from the Proconsul's palace
the Cyrenian painter who was of great renown,
and with what guileful artistry immediately he endeavoured,
as soon as he had seen your friend, to persuade you both
that by all means he must portray him as Hyacinthus*
(since this way his painting would be much better known).

Your Lanes, though, did not lend out his beauty in this manner
and steadfastly opposing this, he bade to be portrayed
not in the least as Hyacinthus, or indeed as any other,
but only as Lanes, Rhametichos' son, of Alexandria.

TOMB OF IASES

I, Iases, lie here. Of this great city,
the young man most renowned for beauty.
Profound sages admired me, as well as the shallow,
the simple folk. And I delighted equally in both.

But for so long people considered me both Narcissus* and
Hermes,
that excesses wore me out, killed me. You passer-by,
if an Alexandrian, you will not reproach. You know the pace
of our lives; what fervour it has; what utter sensual bliss.

ΕΝ ΠΟΛΕΙ ΤΗΣ ΟΣΡΟΗΝΗΣ

Ἀπ' τῆς ταβέρνας τὸν καυγᾶ μᾶς φέραν πληγωμένο
τὸν φίλον Ρέμωνα χθὲς περὶ τὰ μεσάνυχτα.
Ἀπ' τὰ παράθυρα ποῦ ἀφίσαμεν ὁλάνυχτα,
τ' ὡραῖο του σῶμα στὸ κρεββάτι φώτιζε ἡ σελήνη.
Εἴμεθα ἕνα κρᾶμα ἐδῶ· Σύροι, Γραικοί, Ἀρμένιοι, Μῆδοι.
Τέτοιος κι ὁ Ρέμων εἶναι. Ὅμως χθὲς σὰν φώτιζε
τὸ ἐρωτικό του πρόσωπο ἡ σελήνη,
ὁ νοῦς μας πῆγε στὸν πλατωνικὸ Χαρμίδη.

ΙΓΝΑΤΙΟΥ ΤΑΦΟΣ

Ἐδῶ δὲν εἶμαι ὁ Κλέων ποῦ ἀκούσθηκα
στὴν Ἀλεξάνδρεια (ὅπου δύσκολα ξιπάζονται)
γιὰ τὰ λαμπρά μου σπίτια, γιὰ τοὺς κήπους,
γιὰ τ' ἄλογα καὶ γιὰ τ' ἁμάξια μου,
γιὰ τὰ διαμαντικὰ καὶ τὰ μετάξια ποῦ φοροῦσα.
Ἄπαγε· ἐδῶ δὲν εἶμαι ὁ Κλέων ἐκεῖνος·
τὰ εἰκοσιοκτώ του χρόνια νὰ σβυσθοῦν.
Εἶμ' ὁ Ἰγνάτιος, ἀναγνώστης, ποῦ πολὺ ἀργὰ
συνῆλθα· ἀλλ' ὅμως κ' ἔτσι δέκα μῆνες ἔζησα εὐτυχεῖς
μὲς στὴν γαλήνη καὶ μὲς στὴν ἀσφάλεια τοῦ Χριστοῦ.

ΕΝ ΤΩι ΜΗΝΙ ΑΘΥΡ

Μὲ δυσκολία διαβάζω   στὴν πέτρα τὴν ἀρχαία.
«Κύ[ρι]ε Ἰησοῦ Χριστέ».   Ἕνα «Ψυ[χ]ὴν» διακρίνω.
«Ἐν τῷ μη[νὶ] Ἀθὺρ»   «Ὁ Λεύκιο[ς] ἐ[κοιμ]ήθη».
Στὴ μνεία τῆς ἡλικίας   «Ἐβί[ωσ]εν ἐτῶν»,
τὸ Κάππα Ζῆτα δείχνει   ποῦ νέος ἐκοιμήθη.
Μὲς στὰ φθαρμένα βλέπω   «Αὐτὸ[ν] . . . Ἀλεξανδρέα».
Μετὰ ἔχει τρεῖς γραμμὲς   πολὺ ἀκρωτηριασμένες·
μὰ κάτι λέξεις βγάζω —   σὰν «δ[ά]κρυα ἡμῶν», «ὀδύνην»,

A TOWN IN OSROENE

Yesterday about midnight, they brought to us
our friend Rhemon, wounded in a tavern brawl.
Through the windows that we left wide open,
his handsome body upon the bed was illumined by the moon.
We are a mixture of races here: Syrians, Greeks, Armenians,
Medes.
Such is Rhemon, too. Last night, though, when
his sensuous face was illumined by the moon,
our mind went to Plato's Charmides.*

TOMB OF IGNATIUS

Here, I'm not that Cleon who was famous
in Alexandria (where it's hard to boast)
for my splendid houses, for my gardens,
for my horses and my chariots,
for the diamonds and the silken robes I wore.
Be it far from me! Here, I'm not that Cleon;
let his twenty-eight years be erased.
I am Ignatius, lay-reader, who very late
came to my senses; yet even so, I lived ten happy months
in the serenity and the security of Christ.

IN THE MONTH OF ATHYR

With difficulty I read   upon the ancient stone:
'LO[R]D JESUS CHRIST.'   I discern a 'SO[U]L'
'IN THE MON[TH] OF ATHYR'*   'LEUCIUS WAS LAID TO SL[EE]P.'
Where age is mentioned   'HE LI[VE]D TO THE AGE OF'
the Kappa Zeta* shows   he was laid to sleep so young.
In the abraded part I see   'HI[M] . . . ALEXANDRIAN.'
There follow three lines   quite mutilated;
but I make out some words   like 'OUR T[EA]RS' and 'SUFFERING'

κατόπιν πάλι «δάκρυα», καὶ «[ἡμ]ῖν τοῖς [φ]ίλοις πένθος».
Μὲ φαίνεται ποῦ ὁ Λεύκιος μεγάλως θ' ἀγαπήθη.
Ἐν τῷ μηνὶ Ἀθὺρ ὁ Λεύκιος ἐκοιμήθη.

ΓΙΑ ΤΟΝ ΑΜΜΟΝΗ, ΠΟΥ ΠΕΘΑΝΕ 29 ΕΤΩΝ, ΣΤΑ 610

Ραφαήλ, ὀλίγους στίχους σὲ ζητοῦν
γιὰ ἐπιτύμβιον τοῦ ποιητοῦ Ἀμμόνη νὰ συνθέσεις.
Κάτι πολὺ καλαίσθητον καὶ λεῖον. Σὺ θὰ μπορέσεις,
εἶσαι ὁ κατάλληλος, νὰ γράψεις ὡς ἁρμόζει
γιὰ τὸν ποιητὴν Ἀμμόνη, τὸν δικό μας.

Βέβαια θὰ πεῖς γιὰ τὰ ποιήματά του —
ἀλλὰ νὰ πεῖς καὶ γιὰ τὴν ἐμορφιά του,
γιὰ τὴν λεπτὴ ἐμορφιά του ποῦ ἀγαπήσαμε.

Πάντοτε ὡραῖα καὶ μουσικὰ τὰ ἑλληνικά σου εἶναι.
Ὅμως τὴν μαστοριά σου ὅληνα τὴ θέμε τώρα.
Σὲ ξένη γλῶσσα ἡ λύπη μας κ' ἡ ἀγάπη μας περνοῦν.
Τὸ αἰγυπτιακό σου αἴσθημα χύσε στὴν ξένη γλῶσσα.

Ραφαήλ, οἱ στίχοι σου ἔτσι νὰ γραφοῦν
ποῦ νἄχουν ξέρεις, ἀπὸ τὴν ζωή μας μέσα των,
ποῦ κι ὁ ρυθμὸς κ' ἡ κάθε φράσις νὰ δηλοῦν
ποῦ γι' Ἀλεξανδρινὸ γράφει Ἀλεξανδρινός.

and then once more 'TEARS', and 'TO [U]S HIS FRIENDS BEREAVEMENT.'
It seems to me the love for Leucius was deep.
During the month of Athyr Leucius was laid to sleep.

FOR AMMONES, WHO DIED AGED 29, IN 610

Raphael, they want you to compose a few verses
as an epitaph for the poet Ammones.
Something polished and in good taste. You
can do it, you are the appropriate person to write
as befits the poet Ammones, our very own.

You must, of course, mention his poems—
but you should also speak about his beauty,
his delicate beauty that we loved.

Your Greek has always been elegant and musical.
But we're in need of your entire skill now.
Our love and our sorrow pass into a foreign tongue.
Pour your Egyptian feeling into the foreign tongue.

Raphael, your verses must be written in such a way
that they contain, you know, something in them of our lives,
that both cadence as well as every phrase denote,
that an Alexandrian is writing about an Alexandrian.

ΑΙΜΙΛΙΑΝΟΣ ΜΟΝΑΗ, ΑΛΕΞΑΝΔΡΕΥΣ, 628–655 Μ.Χ.

Μὲ λόγια, μὲ φυσιογνωμία, καὶ μὲ τρόπους
μιὰ ἐξαίρετη θὰ κάμω πανοπλία·
καὶ θ' ἀντικρύζω ἔτσι τοὺς κακοὺς ἀνθρώπους
χωρὶς νὰ ἔχω φόβον ἢ ἀδυναμία.

Θὰ θέλουν νὰ μὲ βλάψουν. Ἀλλὰ δὲν θὰ ξέρει
κανεὶς ἀπ' ὅσους θὰ μὲ πλησιάζουν
ποῦ κεῖνται ἡ πληγές μου, τὰ τρωτά μου μέρη,
κάτω ἀπὸ τὰ ψεύδη ποῦ θὰ μὲ σκεπάζουν.—

Ῥήματα τῆς καυχήσεως τοῦ Αἰμιλιανοῦ Μονάη.
Ἄραγε νἄκαμε ποτὲ τὴν πανοπλία αὐτή;
Ἐν πάσῃ περιπτώσει, δὲν τὴν φόρεσε πολύ.
Εἴκοσι ἑπτὰ χρονῶ, στὴν Σικελία πέθανε.

ΟΤΑΝ ΔΙΕΓΕΙΡΟΝΤΑΙ

Προσπάθησε νὰ τὰ φυλάξεις, ποιητή,
ὅσο κι ἂν εἶναι λίγα αὐτὰ ποῦ σταματιοῦνται.
Τοῦ ἐρωτισμοῦ σου τὰ ὁράματα.
Βάλ' τα, μισοκρυμένα, μὲς τὲς φράσεις σου.
Προσπάθησε νὰ τὰ κρατήσεις, ποιητή,
ὅταν διεγείρονται μὲς τὸ μυαλό σου
τὴν νύχτα ἢ μὲς τὴν λάμψι τοῦ μεσημεριοῦ.

AEMILIANUS MONAË, ALEXANDRIAN, A.D. 628–655

With words, appearance, and demeanour,
an excellent suit of armour I shall fashion;
and thus I'll face the wicked,
having no fear or weakness.

They'll want to harm me, but none of those
who approach me will ever know
where my wounds lie, my vulnerable parts,
under the falsehoods that will cloak me.—

Boastful dicta of Aemilianus Monaë.
I wonder, did he ever fashion that suit of armour?
Be that as it may, he did not wear it long.
At the age of twenty-seven, in Sicily, he died.

WHEN THEY ARE ROUSED

Try to keep them, O poet,
however few of them can be contained:
the visions of your eroticism.
Put them, half-hidden, in your phrases.
Try to hold them back, O poet,
when they are roused within your mind,
at night, or in the blaze of noon.

ΗΔΟΝΗι

Χαρὰ καὶ μύρο τῆς ζωῆς μου ἡ μνήμη τῶν ὡρῶν
ποὺ ηὗρα καὶ ποὺ κράτηξα τὴν ἡδονὴ ὡς τὴν ἤθελα.
Χαρὰ καὶ μύρο τῆς ζωῆς μου ἐμένα, ποὺ ἀποστράφηκα
τὴν κάθε ἀπόλαυσιν ἐρώτων τῆς ρουτίνας.

ΕΤΣΙ ΠΟΛΥ ΑΤΕΝΙΣΑ —

Τὴν ἐμορφιὰ ἔτσι πολὺ ἀτένισα,
ποὺ πλήρης εἶναι αὐτῆς ἡ ὅρασίς μου.

Γραμμὲς τοῦ σώματος. Κόκκινα χείλη. Μέλη ἡδονικά.
Μαλλιὰ σὰν ἀπὸ ἀγάλματα ἑλληνικὰ παρμένα·
πάντα ἔμορφα, κι ἀχτένιστα σὰν εἶναι,
καὶ πέφτουν, λίγο, ἐπάνω στ' ἄσπρα μέτωπα.
Πρόσωπα τῆς ἀγάπης, ὅπως τἄθελεν
ἡ ποίησίς μου . . . μὲς στὲς νύχτες τῆς νεότητός μου,
μέσα στὲς νύχτες μου, κρυφά, συναντημένα . . .

ΕΝ ΤΗ ΟΔΩ

Τὸ συμπαθητικό του πρόσωπο, κομάτι ὠχρό·
τὰ καστανά του μάτια, σὰν κομένα·
εἴκοσι πέντ' ἐτῶν, πλὴν μοιάζει μᾶλλον εἴκοσι·
μὲ κάτι καλλιτεχνικὸ στὸ ντύσιμό του
— τίποτε χρῶμα τῆς κραβάτας, σχῆμα τοῦ κολλάρου —
ἀσκόπως περπατεῖ μὲς στὴν ὁδό,
ἀκόμη σὰν ὑπνωτισμένος ἀπ' τὴν ἄνομη ἡδονή,
ἀπὸ τὴν πολὺ ἄνομη ἡδονὴ ποὺ ἀπέκτησε.

TO SENSUAL PLEASURE

Joy and balm of my life: the memory of the hours
when I found and held onto sensual pleasure as I wished.
Joy and balm of my life: for me who spurned
every delight of routine amours.

SO LONG I GAZED—

So long I gazed on beauty,
that it completely fills my vision.

Lines of the body. Red lips. Sensuous limbs.
Hair as if taken from Grecian statues,
always lovely, even when uncombed
and falling a little over the white temples.
Faces of love, as my poetry
fancied them . . . within the nights of my youth,
within my own nights, secretly encountered . . .

IN THE STREET

His appealing face somewhat wan,
his chestnut eyes seem drawn;
twenty-five years old, but could pass for twenty;
with an artistic flair in his mode of dress
—in the tint of the tie, in the shape of the collar—
he is walking aimlessly down the street,
still as if in a trance, from the deviant pleasure,
from so much deviant pleasure he'd possessed.

Η ΠΡΟΘΗΚΗ ΤΟΥ ΚΑΠΝΟΠΩΛΕΙΟΥ

Κοντὰ σὲ μιὰ κατάφωτη προθήκη
καπνοπωλείου ἐστέκονταν, ἀνάμεσα σ' ἄλλους πολλούς.
Τυχαίως τὰ βλέμματά των συναντήθηκαν,
καὶ τὴν παράνομην ἐπιθυμία τῆς σαρκός των
ἐξέφρασαν δειλά, διστακτικά.
Ἔπειτα, ὀλίγα βήματα στὸ πεζοδρόμιο ἀνήσυχα—
ὡς ποῦ ἐμειδίασαν, κ' ἔνευσαν ἐλαφρῶς.

Καὶ τότε πιὰ τὸ ἁμάξι τὸ κλεισμένο . . .
τὸ αἰσθητικὸ πλησίασμα τῶν σωμάτων·
τὰ ἑνωμένα χέρια, τὰ ἑνωμένα χείλη.

ΠΕΡΑΣΜΑ

Ἐκεῖνα ποῦ δειλὰ φαντάσθη μαθητής, εἶν' ἀνοιχτά,
φανερωμένα ἐμπρός του. Καὶ γυρνᾶ, καὶ ξενυχτᾶ,
καὶ παρασύρεται. Κι ὡς εἶναι (γιὰ τὴν τέχνη μας) σωστό,
τὸ αἷμα του, καινούριο καὶ ζεστό,
ἡ ἡδονὴ τὸ χαίρεται. Τὸ σῶμα του νικᾶ
ἔκνομη ἐρωτικὴ μέθη· καὶ τὰ νεανικὰ
μέλη ἐνδίδουνε σ' αὐτήν.
Κ' ἔτσι ἕνα παιδὶ ἁπλὸ
γίνεται ἄξιο νὰ τὸ δοῦμε, κι ἀπ' τὸν Ὑψηλὸ
τῆς Ποιήσεως Κόσμο μιὰ στιγμὴ περνᾶ κι αὐτὸ—
τὸ αἰσθητικὸ παιδὶ μὲ τὸ αἷμα του καινούριο καὶ ζεστό.

THE TOBACCONIST'S WINDOW

Near a tobacconist's brightly-lit window,
they were standing among a crowd of people.
Their eyes met by chance,
and expressed timidly, hesitantly,
the deviant desire of their flesh.
Then, a few uneasy steps on the sidewalk—
until they smiled and slightly nodded.

And after that, the closed carriage . . .
the sensuous closeness of the bodies;
the joined hands, the joined lips.

PASSAGE

Those things he timidly imagined as a schoolboy are now in the open,
exposed before him. And he roams around and stays up nights,
and yields to temptation. And as is right (for our Art)
sensuality relishes his blood,
so young and hot. His body is overwhelmed
by deviant erotic rapture; and his youthful limbs
succumb to it.
And thus a simple boy
becomes worthy of our attention, and for an instant,
he too passes through the Exalted Realm of Poetry—
the sensuous boy, with his blood so young and hot.

ΕΝ ΕΣΠΕΡΑ

Πάντως δὲν θὰ διαρκούσανε πολύ. Ἡ πεῖρα
τῶν χρόνων μὲ τὸ δείχνει. Ἀλλ' ὅμως κάπως βιαστικὰ
ἦλθε καὶ τὰ σταμάτησεν ἡ Μοῖρα.
Ἦτανε σύντομος ὁ ὡραῖος βίος.
Ἀλλὰ τὶ δυνατὰ ποὺ ἦσαν τὰ μύρα,
σὲ τὶ ἐξαίσια κλίνην ἐπλαγιάσαμε,
σὲ τὶ ἡδονὴ τὰ σώματά μας δώσαμε.

Μιὰ ἀπήχησις τῶν ἡμερῶν τῆς ἡδονῆς,
μιὰ ἀπήχησις τῶν ἡμερῶν κοντά μου ἦλθε,
κάτι ἀπ' τῆς νεότητός μας τῶν δυονῶ τὴν πύρα·
στὰ χέρια μου ἕνα γράμμα ξαναπῆρα,
καὶ διάβαζα πάλι καὶ πάλι ὡς ποὺ ἔλειψε τὸ φῶς.

Καὶ βγῆκα στὸ μπαλκόνι μελαγχολικὰ—
βγῆκα ν' ἀλλάξω σκέψεις βλέποντας τουλάχιστον
ὀλίγη ἀγαπημένη πολιτεία,
ὀλίγη κίνησι τοῦ δρόμου καὶ τῶν μαγαζιῶν.

ΓΚΡΙΖΑ

Κυττάζοντας ἕνα ὀπάλλιο μισὸ γκρίζο
θυμήθηκα δυὸ ὡραῖα γκρίζα μάτια
ποὺ εἶδα· θἆναι εἴκοσι χρόνια πρὶν . . .

. . . .

Γιὰ ἕναν μῆνα ἀγαπηθήκαμε.
Ἔπειτα ἔφυγε, θαρρῶ στὴν Σμύρνη,
γιὰ νὰ ἐργασθεῖ ἐκεῖ, καὶ πιὰ δὲν ἰδωθήκαμε.

Θ' ἀσχήμισαν—ἂν ζεῖ—τὰ γκρίζα μάτια·
θὰ χάλασε τ' ὡραῖο πρόσωπο.

*

IN THE EVENING

In any case, they couldn't have lasted long. The experience
of years shows me that. Yet even so, Destiny
came along and put an end to them, rather in haste.
Brief indeed was the lovely life.
And yet, how potent were the fragrances,
upon what exquisite bed we lay,
and to what pleasure we gave our bodies.

A faint echo of the days of sensual pleasure,
a faint echo of those days neared me;
some of the fervour of our youth that we both shared;
I took once more a letter in my hands,
and read it again and again, till the light was gone.

And I came out onto the balcony, in melancholy—
came out to change my thoughts by seeing at least
a little of the beloved city,
a little movement in the street and shops.

GREY

While looking at a pale grey opal,
I brought to mind two pretty grey eyes
that I saw; must be twenty years ago . . .

. . . .

We loved each other for a month.
Then he left, I think for Smyrna,
to work there, and we never saw each other again.

The grey eyes—if he's still alive—will have lost their beauty;
the pretty face will have blemished.

★

Μνήμη μου, φύλαξέ τα σὺ ὡς ἦσαν.
Καί, μνήμη, ὅτι μπορεῖς ἀπὸ τὸν ἔρωτά μου αὐτόν,
ὅτι μπορεῖς φέρε με πίσω ἀπόψι.

ΚΑΤΩ ΑΠ' ΤΟ ΣΠΙΤΙ

Χθὲς περπατῶντας σὲ μιὰ συνοικία
ἀπόκεντρη, πέρασα κάτω ἀπὸ τὸ σπίτι
ποῦ ἔμπαινα σὰν ἤμουν νέος πολύ.
Ἐκεῖ τὸ σῶμα μου εἶχε λάβει ὁ Ἔρως
μὲ τὴν ἐξαίσια του ἰσχύν.

Καὶ χθὲς
σὰν πέρασ' ἀπ' τὸν δρόμο τὸν παληό,
ἀμέσως ὡραΐσθηκαν ἀπ' τὴν γοητεία τοῦ ἔρωτος
τὰ μαγαζιά, τὰ πεζοδρόμια, ἡ πέτρες,
καὶ τοῖχοι, καὶ μπαλκόνια, καὶ παράθυρα·
τίποτε ἄσχημο δὲν ἔμεινεν ἐκεῖ.

Καὶ καθὼς στέκομουν, κ' ἐκύτταζα τὴν πόρτα,
καὶ στέκομουν, κ' ἐβράδυνα κάτω ἀπ' τὸ σπίτι,
ἡ ὑπόστασίς μου ὅλη ἀπέδιδε
τὴν φυλαχθεῖσα ἡδονικὴ συγκίνησι.

ΤΟ ΔΙΠΛΑΝΟ ΤΡΑΠΕΖΙ

Θἆναι μόλις εἴκοσι δυὸ ἐτῶν.
Κι ὅμως ἐγὼ εἶμαι βέβαιος ποῦ, σχεδὸν τὰ ἴσα
χρόνια προτήτερα, τὸ ἴδιο σῶμα αὐτὸ τὸ ἀπήλαυσα.

Δὲν εἶναι διόλου ἔξαψις ἐρωτισμοῦ.
Καὶ μοναχὰ πρὸ ὀλίγου μπῆκα στὸ καζίνο·
δὲν εἶχα οὔτε ὥρα γιὰ νὰ πιῶ πολύ.
Τὸ ἴδιο σῶμα ἐγὼ τὸ ἀπήλαυσα.

*

Memory of mine, keep them as they were.
And, Memory, whatever you can of that love of mine,
whatever you can, bring back to me tonight.

OUTSIDE THE HOUSE

Yesterday, while walking in an outlying
neighbourhood, I passed outside the house
that I used to visit when I was very young.
There, Eros had possessed my body,
with his exquisite sway.
And yesterday,
as I crossed that street of long ago,
the shops, the sidewalks, the stones
were immediately enhanced by the allure of love,
and the walls, balconies, and windows too;
nothing unsightly lingered there.

And while I stood and gazed at the door,
and stood and tarried outside the house,
my entire being exuded
the pent-up sensual emotion.

THE NEXT TABLE

He must be barely twenty-two.
And yet I am convinced that nearly as many
years ago, I enjoyed that selfsame body.

It is not at all a matter of erotic excitation.
I entered the gambling house just a little while ago;
I didn't even have the time to drink a lot.
That selfsame body did I enjoy.

*

Κι ἂν δὲν θυμοῦμαι, ποῦ—ἕνα ξέχασμά μου δὲν σημαίνει.

Ἆ τώρα, νά, ποῦ κάθησε στὸ διπλανὸ τραπέζι
γνωρίζω κάθε κίνησι ποῦ κάμνει—κι ἀπ' τὰ ροῦχα κάτω
γυμνὰ τ' ἀγαπημένα μέλη ξαναβλέπω.

ΘΥΜΗΣΟΥ, ΣΩΜΑ . . . .

Σῶμα, θυμήσου ὄχι μόνο τὸ πόσο ἀγαπήθηκες,
ὄχι μονάχα τὰ κρεββάτια ὅπου πλάγιασες,
ἀλλὰ κ' ἐκεῖνες τὲς ἐπιθυμίες ποῦ γιὰ σένα
γυάλιζαν μὲς στὰ μάτια φανερά,
κ' ἐτρέμανε μὲς στὴν φωνὴ—καὶ κάποιο
τυχαῖον ἐμπόδιο τὲς ματαίωσε.
Τώρα ποῦ εἶναι ὅλα πιὰ μέσα στὸ παρελθόν,
μοιάζει σχεδὸν καὶ στὲς ἐπιθυμίες
ἐκεῖνες σὰν νὰ δόθηκες—πῶς γυάλιζαν,
θυμήσου, μὲς στὰ μάτια ποῦ σὲ κύτταζαν·
πῶς ἔτρεμαν μὲς στὴν φωνή, γιὰ σέ, θυμήσου, σῶμα.

ΜΕΡΕΣ ΤΟΥ 1903

Δὲν τὰ ηὗρα πιὰ ξανὰ—τὰ τόσο γρήγορα χαμένα . . .
τὰ ποιητικὰ τὰ μάτια, τὸ χλωμὸ
τὸ πρόσωπο . . . στὸ νύχτωμα τοῦ δρόμου . . .

Δὲν τὰ ηὗρα πιὰ—τ' ἀποκτηθέντα κατὰ τύχην ὅλως,
ποῦ ἔτσι εὔκολα παραίτησα·
καὶ ποῦ κατόπι μὲ ἀγωνίαν ἤθελα.
Τὰ ποιητικὰ τὰ μάτια, τὸ χλωμὸ τὸ πρόσωπο,
τὰ χείλη ἐκεῖνα δὲν τὰ ηὗρα πιά.

And if I don't remember where—a memory lapse means nothing.

There now, as he sat down at the next table
I recognize every single move he makes—and under his clothes,
naked the beloved limbs I see once more.

BODY, REMEMBER . . .

Body, remember not only how much you were loved,
not only the beds upon which you have lain,
but also those desires that
glistened for you openly in the eyes,
and trembled in the voice—and some
chance obstacle frustrated them.
Now that all this belongs to the past,
it seems as if you gave yourself also
to those desires—how they glistened,
remember, in the eyes that gazed at you,
how they trembled in the voice for you, remember, body!

DAYS OF 1903

I never found them again—those things so swiftly vanished . . .
the poetic eyes, the pale
face . . . in the nightfall of the road . . .

I never found them again—those that I gained entirely by chance,
that I so readily abandoned;
and that afterwards, in agony, I craved.
The poetic eyes, the pale face,
those lips, I never found them again.

POEMS 1919–1933

ΠΟΙΗΜΑΤΑ 1919–1933

Ο ΗΛΙΟΣ ΤΟΥ ΑΠΟΓΕΥΜΑΤΟΣ

Τὴν κάμαρην αὐτή, πόσο καλὰ τὴν ξέρω.
Τώρα νοικιάζονται κι αὐτὴ κ' ἡ πλαγινὴ
γιὰ ἐμπορικὰ γραφεῖα. Ὅλο τὸ σπίτι ἔγινε
γραφεῖα μεσιτῶν, κ' ἐμπόρων, κ' Ἑταιρεῖες.

Ἄ ἡ κάμαρη αὐτή, τὶ γνώριμη ποῦ εἶναι.

Κοντὰ στὴν πόρτα ἐδῶ ἦταν ὁ καναπές,
κ' ἐμπρός του ἕνα τουρκικὸ χαλί·
σιμὰ τὸ ράφι μὲ δυὸ βάζα κίτρινα.
Δεξιά· ὄχι, ἀντικρύ, ἕνα ντολάπι μὲ καθρέπτη.
Στὴ μέση τὸ τραπέζι ὅπου ἔγραφε·
κ' ἡ τρεῖς μεγάλες ψάθινες καρέγλες.
Πλάϊ στὸ παράθυρο ἦταν τὸ κρεββάτι
ποῦ ἀγαπηθήκαμε τόσες φορές.

Θὰ βρίσκονται ἀκόμη τὰ καϋμένα πουθενά.

Πλάϊ στὸ παράθυρο ἦταν τὸ κρεββάτι·
ὁ ἥλιος τοῦ ἀπογεύματος τὤφθανε ὡς τὰ μισά.

. . . Ἀπόγευμα ἡ ὥρα τέσσερες, εἴχαμε χωρισθεῖ
γιὰ μιὰ ἑβδομάδα μόνο . . . Ἀλλοίμονον,
ἡ ἑβδομὰς ἐκείνη ἔγινε παντοτινή.

ΝΑ ΜΕΙΝΕΙ

Ἡ ὥρα μιὰ τὴν νύχτα θἄτανε,
ἢ μιάμισυ.

Σὲ μιὰ γωνιὰ τοῦ καπηλειοῦ·
πίσω ἀπ' τὸ ξύλινο τὸ χώρισμα.
Ἐκτὸς ἡμῶν τῶν δυὸ τὸ μαγαζὶ ὅλως διόλου ἄδειο.
Μιὰ λάμπα πετρελαίου μόλις τὸ φώτιζε.
Κοιμούντανε, στὴν πόρτα, ὁ ἀγρυπνισμένος ὑπηρέτης.

*

THE AFTERNOON SUN

This room, how well I know it.
Now this one and the one next door are rented
as commercial offices. The entire house has become
offices of agents, merchants, and Companies.

Ah! This room, how familiar it is.

Over here, near the door, was the couch,
and in front of it a Turkish rug;
nearby, the shelf with two yellow vases.
To the right; no opposite, a wardrobe with a mirror.
In the centre, the table where he used to write;
and the three large wicker chairs.
Next to the window was the bed,
where we made love so many times.

Those poor old things must still be around somewhere.

Next to the window was the bed;
the afternoon sun would reach the middle.

. . . One afternoon, at four o'clock, we parted
just for a week . . . Alas,
that week was to last forever.

HAS COME TO REST

It must have been one o'clock at night,
or half past one.

In a corner of the wine tavern;
behind the wooden partition;
except for the two of us, the shop completely empty.
A kerosene lantern barely lit it;
the heavy-eyed servant was dozing by the door.

*

Δὲν θὰ μᾶς ἔβλεπε κανείς. Μὰ κιόλας
εἴχαμεν ἐξαφθεῖ τόσο πολύ,
ποῦ γίναμε ἀκατάλληλοι γιὰ προφυλάξεις.

Τὰ ἐνδύματα μισοανοίχθηκαν—πολλὰ δὲν ἦσαν
γιατὶ ἐπύρωνε θεῖος Ἰούλιος μῆνας.

Σάρκας ἀπόλαυσις ἀνάμεσα
στὰ μισοανοιγμένα ἐνδύματα·
γρήγορο σάρκας γύμνωμα—ποῦ τὸ ἴνδαλμά του
εἴκοσι ἕξη χρόνους διάβηκε· καὶ τώρα ἦλθε
νὰ μείνει μὲς στὴν ποίησιν αὐτή.

ΤΩΝ ΕΒΡΑΙΩΝ (50 Μ.Χ.)

Ζωγράφος καὶ ποιητής, δρομεὺς καὶ δισκοβόλος,
σὰν Ἐνδυμίων ἔμορφος, ὁ Ἰάνθης Ἀντωνίου.
Ἀπὸ οἰκογένειαν φίλην τῆς συναγωγῆς.

«Ἡ τιμιότερές μου μέρες εἶν' ἐκεῖνες
ποῦ τὴν αἰσθητικὴ ἀναζήτησιν ἀφίνω,
ποῦ ἐγκαταλείπω τὸν ὡραῖο καὶ σκληρὸν ἑλληνισμό,
μὲ τὴν κυρίαρχη προσήλωσι
σὲ τέλεια καμωμένα καὶ φθαρτὰ ἄσπρα μέλη.
Καὶ γένομαι αὐτὸς ποῦ θὰ ἤθελα
πάντα νὰ μένω· τῶν Ἑβραίων, τῶν ἱερῶν Ἑβραίων, ὁ υἱός.»

Ἔνθερμη λίαν ἡ δήλωσίς του. «Πάντα
νὰ μένω τῶν Ἑβραίων, τῶν ἱερῶν Ἑβραίων—»

Ὅμως δὲν ἔμενε τοιοῦτος διόλου.
Ὁ Ἡδονισμὸς κ' ἡ Τέχνη τῆς Ἀλεξανδρείας
ἀφοσιωμένο τους παιδὶ τὸν εἶχαν.

No one would have seen us. But already
we were so aroused,
that we became unsuited for precautions.

Clothes just undone—not that there were many,
for an exquisite July was blazing.

Delight of the flesh, between
half-opened clothes;
quick baring of the body—whose image
traversed twenty-six years; and now
has come to rest within this verse.

OF THE HEBREWS (A.D. 50)

Painter and poet, runner and discus-thrower,
handsome as Endymion: Ianthes, son of Antony.
From a family friendly to the Synagogue.

'My most precious days are those
when I leave behind the aesthetic quest,
when I abandon the beautiful and demanding Hellenism,
with its prevailing attachment
to perfectly constructed and perishable white limbs.
And I become the one I should always wish
to remain: son of the Hebrews, son of the holy Hebrews.'

Most ardent is his statement: 'Always
to remain of the Hebrews, the holy Hebrews—'

But he did not remain such a man at all.
The Hedonism and Art of Alexandria
kept him their own devoted child.

ΙΜΕΝΟΣ

«. . . Ν' ἀγαπηθεῖ ἀκόμη περισσότερον
ἡ ἡδονὴ ποῦ νοσηρῶς καὶ μὲ φθορὰ ἀποκτᾶται·
σπάνια τὸ σῶμα βρίσκοντας ποῦ αἰσθάνεται ὅπως θέλει αὐτή—
ποῦ νοσηρῶς καὶ μὲ φθορά, παρέχει
μιὰν ἔντασιν ἐρωτική, ποῦ δὲν γνωρίζει ἡ ὑγεία . . .»

Ἀπόσπασμα ἀπὸ μιὰν ἐπιστολὴ
τοῦ νέου Ἰμένου (ἐκ πατρικίων) διαβοήτου
ἐν Συρακούσαις ἐπὶ ἀσωτία,
στοὺς ἄσωτους καιροὺς τοῦ τρίτου Μιχαήλ.

ΤΟΥ ΠΛΟΙΟΥ

Τὸν μοιάζει βέβαια ἡ μικρὴ αὐτή,
μὲ τὸ μολύβι ἀπεικόνισίς του.

Γρήγορα καμωμένη, στὸ κατάστρωμα τοῦ πλοίου·
ἕνα μαγευτικὸ ἀπόγευμα.
Τὸ Ἰόνιον πέλαγος ὁλόγυρά μας.

Τὸν μοιάζει. Ὅμως τὸν θυμοῦμαι σὰν πιὸ ἔμορφο.
Μέχρι παθήσεως ἦταν αἰσθητικός,
κι αὐτὸ ἐφώτιζε τὴν ἔκφρασί του.
Πιὸ ἔμορφος μὲ φανερώνεται
τώρα ποῦ ἡ ψυχή μου τὸν ἀνακαλεῖ, ἀπ' τὸν Καιρό.

Ἀπ' τὸν Καιρό. Εἶν' ὅλ' αὐτὰ τὰ πράγματα πολὺ παληὰ—
τὸ σκίτσο, καὶ τὸ πλοῖο, καὶ τὸ ἀπόγευμα.

IMENOS

'. . . It should be cherished even more, the sensual
pleasure, which in an unhealthy and wasteful way is gained;
rarely finding a body that feels as that pleasure would wish—
a body offering in an unhealthy and wasteful way,
an erotic intensity that healthy love does not experience . . .'

Extract from a letter
of young Imenos (of a patrician family),
notorious in Syracuse for debauchery,
during the debauched times of Michael III.*

ON THE SHIP

It's a good likeness,
this small pencil sketch of him.

Done in a hurry, on the deck of the ship;
one enchanting afternoon.
All around us the Ionian Sea.

It's a good likeness. Yet I remember him as more handsome.
He was appealing to the point of passion,
and that illumined his expression.
He appears to me more handsome
now that my soul evokes him out of Time.

Out of Time. These things are all so very old—
the sketch, and the ship, and the afternoon.

ΔΗΜΗΤΡΙΟΥ ΣΩΤΗΡΟΣ (162–150 Π.Χ.)

Κάθε του προσδοκία βγῆκε λανθασμένη!

Φαντάζονταν ἔργα νὰ κάμει ξακουστά,
νὰ παύσει τὴν ταπείνωσι ποῦ ἀπ' τὸν καιρὸ τῆς μάχης
τῆς Μαγνησίας τὴν πατρίδα του πιέζει.
Νὰ γίνει πάλι κράτος δυνατὸ ἡ Συρία,
μὲ τοὺς στρατούς της, μὲ τοὺς στόλους της,
μὲ τὰ μεγάλα κάστρα, μὲ τὰ πλούτη.

Ὑπέφερε, πικραίνονταν στὴν Ρώμη
σὰν ἔνοιωθε στὲς ὁμιλίες τῶν φίλων του,
τῆς νεολαίας τῶν μεγάλων οἴκων,
μὲς σ' ὅλην τὴν λεπτότητα καὶ τὴν εὐγένεια
ποῦ ἔδειχναν σ' αὐτόν, τοῦ βασιλέως
Σελεύκου Φιλοπάτορος τὸν υἱὸ —
σὰν ἔνοιωθε ποῦ ὅμως πάντα ὑπῆρχε μιὰ κρυφὴ
ὀλιγωρία γιὰ τὲς δυναστεῖες τὲς ἑλληνίζουσες·
ποῦ ξέπεσαν, ποῦ γιὰ τὰ σοβαρὰ ἔργα δὲν εἶναι,
γιὰ τῶν λαῶν τὴν ἀρχηγία πολὺ ἀκατάλληλες.
Τραβιούνταν μόνος του, κι ἀγανακτοῦσε, κι ὄμνυε
ποῦ ὅπως τὰ θαρροῦν διόλου δὲν θἆναι·
ἰδοὺ ποῦ ἔχει θέλησιν αὐτός·
θ' ἀγωνισθεῖ, θὰ κάμει, θ' ἀνυψώσει.

Ἀρκεῖ νὰ βρεῖ ἕναν τρόπο στὴν Ἀνατολὴ νὰ φθάσει,
νὰ κατορθώσει νὰ ξεφύγει ἀπὸ τὴν Ἰταλία —
κι ὅλην αὐτὴν τὴν δύναμι ποῦ ἔχει
μὲς στὴν ψυχή του, ὅλην τὴν ὁρμὴν
αὐτὴ θὰ μεταδώσει στὸν λαό.

Ἆ στὴν Συρία μονάχα νὰ βρεθεῖ!
Ἔτσι μικρὸς ἀπ' τὴν πατρίδα ἔφυγε
ποῦ ἀμυδρῶς θυμοὺνταν τὴν μορφή της.
Μὰ μὲς στὴν σκέψι του τὴν μελετοῦσε πάντα

OF DEMETRIUS SOTER (162–150 B.C.)

His every expectation turned out wrong!

He imagined himself doing famous deeds,
putting an end to the humiliation that since the Battle
of Magnesia, was weighing down his country.
Turning Syria again into a strong state,
with her armies, her navies,
with great fortresses and wealth.

In Rome, he suffered, he felt embittered
when he sensed, in speaking with his friends,
the young men of noble families,
in all the delicacy and civility
they displayed towards him,
the son of King Seleucus Philopator,
when he sensed that nonetheless there was always
a latent apprehension about those Hellenizing dynasties;
which were in decline, incapable of any serious endeavour,
for the leadership of peoples highly unsuitable.
He would retire alone, and grow indignant and swear
that things won't be at all as they believe;
behold, he has resolve;
he'll strive, he'll accomplish, he'll raise all back.

If only he could devise a way to get himself to the East,
to manage an escape from Italy—
and all that strength he carries
within his soul, all this vigour,
he'll pass it on to the people.

If only he could get himself to Syria!
So very young he was, when he left home,
that he vaguely remembered what home looked like.
In his thoughts, though, he pondered always on it

σὰν κάτι ἱερὸ ποῦ προσκυνώντας τὸ πλησιάζεις,
σὰν ὀπτασία τόπου ὡραίου, σὰν ὅραμα
ἑλληνικῶν πόλεων καὶ λιμένων.—

Καὶ τώρα;
Τώρα ἀπελπισία καὶ καϋμός.
Εἴχανε δίκιο τὰ παιδιὰ στὴν Ρώμη.
Δὲν εἶναι δυνατὸν νὰ βασταχθοῦν ἡ δυναστεῖες
ποῦ ἔβγαλε ἡ Κατάκτησις τῶν Μακεδόνων.

Ἀδιάφορον: ἐπάσχισεν αὐτός,
ὅσο μποροῦσεν ἀγωνίσθηκε.
Καὶ μὲς στὴν μαύρη ἀπογοήτευσί του,
ἕνα μονάχα λογαριάζει πιὰ
μὲ ὑπερηφάνειαν· ποῦ, κ' ἐν τῇ ἀποτυχίᾳ του,
τὴν ἴδιαν ἀκατάβλητην ἀνδρεία στὸν κόσμο δείχνει.

Τ' ἄλλα—ἦσαν ὄνειρα καὶ ματαιοπονίες.
Αὐτὴ ἡ Συρία—σχεδὸν δὲν μοιάζει σὰν πατρίς του,
αὐτὴ εἶν' ἡ χώρα τοῦ Ἡρακλείδη καὶ τοῦ Βάλα.

ΕΙΓΕ ΕΤΕΛΕΥΤΑ

«Ποῦ ἀπεσύρθηκε, ποῦ ἐχάθηκε ὁ Σοφός;
Ἔπειτ' ἀπὸ τὰ θαύματά του τὰ πολλά,
τὴν φήμη τῆς διδασκαλίας του
ποῦ διεδόθηκεν εἰς τόσα ἔθνη
ἐκρύφθηκ' αἴφνης καὶ δὲν ἔμαθε κανεὶς
μὲ θετικότητα τί ἔγινε
(οὐδὲ κανεὶς ποτὲ εἶδε τάφον του).
Ἔβγαλαν μερικοὶ πῶς πέθανε στὴν Ἔφεσο.
Δὲν τὄγραψεν ὁ Δάμις ὅμως· τίποτε
γιὰ θάνατο τοῦ Ἀπολλωνίου δὲν ἔγραψεν ὁ Δάμις.
Ἄλλοι εἴπανε πῶς ἔγινε ἄφαντος στὴν Λίνδο.
Ἢ μήπως εἶν' ἐκείν' ἡ ἱστορία
ἀληθινή, ποῦ ἀνελήφθηκε στὴν Κρήτη,

as something sacrosanct that you approach reverently,
as an illusion of a wondrous land, a vision
of Hellenic cities and harbours.—

And now?
Now despair and longing.
They were right, those young men in Rome.
It is not possible to sustain the dynasties
that emerged from the Macedonian Conquest.

All the same: he himself tried,
fought all he could.
And in his dismal disappointment,
there is but one thing he still considers
with pride; that even in his failure,
he displays to the world the same indomitable valour.

As for the rest, they were dreams and futile efforts.
This Syria now barely resembles his native land;
this is the country of Heracleides and Balas.

IF DEAD INDEED

'Where did he retire to, where did he disappear, the Sage?*
Following his numerous miracles
and the fame of his teaching
which spread to many a nation,
he went suddenly into hiding, and no one ever learnt
with any certainty what had happened
(nor did anyone ever see his grave).
Some spread the rumour that he died at Ephesus.
But Damis did not record it;
about the death of Apollonius Damis wrote down nothing.
Others said that he vanished into thin air at Lindos.
Or perhaps that other story is true,
that he ascended to the skies in Crete,

στὸ ἀρχαῖο τῆς Δικτύννης ἱερόν.—
Ἀλλ᾿ ὅμως ἔχουμε τὴν θαυμασία,
τὴν ὑπερφυσικὴν ἐμφάνισί του
εἰς ἕναν νέον σπουδαστὴ στὰ Τύανα.—
Ἴσως δὲν ἦλθεν ὁ καιρὸς γιὰ νὰ ἐπιστρέψει
γιὰ νὰ φανερωθεῖ στὸν κόσμο πάλι·
ἢ μεταμορφωμένος, ἴσως, μεταξύ μας
γυρίζει ἀγνώριστος.—Μὰ θὰ ξαναφανερωθεῖ
ὡς ἤτανε, διδάσκοντας τὰ ὀρθά· καὶ τότε βέβαια
θὰ ἐπαναφέρει τὴν λατρεία τῶν θεῶν μας,
καὶ τὲς καλαίσθητες ἑλληνικές μας τελετές».

Ἔτσι ἐρέμβαζε στὴν πενιχρή του κατοικία—
μετὰ μιὰ ἀνάγνωσι τοῦ Φιλοστράτου
«Τὰ ἐς τὸν Τυανέα Ἀπολλώνιον»—
ἕνας ἀπὸ τοὺς λίγους ἐθνικούς,
τοὺς πολὺ λίγους ποῦ εἶχαν μείνει. Ἄλλωστε—ἀσήμαντος
ἄνθρωπος καὶ δειλὸς—στὸ φανερὸν
ἔκανε τὸν Χριστιανὸ κι αὐτὸς κ᾿ ἐκκλησιάζονταν.
Ἦταν ἡ ἐποχὴ καθ᾿ ἣν βασίλευεν,
ἐν ἄκρᾳ εὐλαβείᾳ, ὁ γέρων Ἰουστῖνος
κ᾿ ἡ Ἀλεξάνδρεια, πόλις θεοσεβής,
ἀθλίους εἰδωλολάτρας ἀποστρέφονταν.

ΝΕΟΙ ΤΗΣ ΣΙΔΩΝΟΣ (400 Μ.Χ.)

Ὁ ἠθοποιὸς ποῦ ἔφεραν γιὰ νὰ τοὺς διασκεδάσει
ἀπήγγειλε καὶ μερικὰ ἐπιγράμματα ἐκλεκτά.

Ἡ αἴθουσα ἄνοιγε στὸν κῆπο ἐπάνω·
κ᾿ εἶχε μιὰν ἐλαφρὰ εὐωδία ἀνθέων
ποῦ ἑνώνονταν μὲ τὰ μυρωδικὰ
τῶν πέντε ἀρωματισμένων Σιδωνίων νέων.

Διαβάσθηκαν Μελέαγρος, καὶ Κριναγόρας, καὶ Ριανός.
Μὰ σὰν ἀπήγγειλεν ὁ ἠθοποιός,
«Αἰσχύλον Εὐφορίωνος Ἀθηναῖον τόδε κεύθει»—

at the ancient sanctuary of Dictynna.—
On the other hand, we have that wondrous,
that supernatural appearance of his
to a young student at Tyana.—
Maybe the time's not come for him to return
and to manifest himself to the world again;
or perhaps, transfigured, he goes about
among us, unrecognized.—But he will reappear,
just as he was, teaching what is right: and then,
of course, he'll restore the worship of our gods,
and our elegant Hellenic rituals.'

So he mused in his simple dwelling—
following a reading of Philostratus'
On Apollonius of Tyana—
one of the few, very few pagans
who still remained. Besides—an insignificant
and cowardly man—he posed in public
as a Christian and attended church.
It was in those days when the aged Justin*
reigned in utter piety,
and Alexandria, a god-fearing city,
wretched idolaters abhorred.

YOUNG MEN OF SIDON (A.D. 400)

The actor they had brought in to entertain them
also recited a few choice epigrams.

The room opened directly onto the garden
and held a faint fragrance of blossoms
that blended with the perfumes
of the five scented Sidonian youths.

They read from Meleager and Crinagoras and Rhianos.*
But when the actor recited:
'Aeschylus, son of Euphorion, the Athenian, lies here—'

(τονίζοντας ἴσως ὑπὲρ τὸ δέον
τὸ «ἀλκὴν δ' εὐδόκιμον», τὸ «Μαραθώνιον ἄλσος»),
πετάχθηκεν εὐθὺς ἕνα παιδὶ ζωηρό,
φανατικὸ γιὰ γράμματα, καὶ φώναξε·

«Ἆ δὲν μ' ἀρέσει τὸ τετράστιχον αὐτό.
Ἐκφράσεις τοιούτου εἴδους μοιάζουν κάπως σὰν λειποψυχίες.
Δόσε — κηρύττω — στὸ ἔργον σου ὅλην τὴν δύναμί σου,
ὅλην τὴν μέριμνα, καὶ πάλι τὸ ἔργον σου θυμήσου
μὲς στὴν δοκιμασίαν, ἢ ὅταν ἡ ὥρα σου πιὰ γέρνει.
Ἔτσι ἀπὸ σένα περιμένω κι ἀπαιτῶ.
Κι ὄχι ἀπ' τὸν νοῦ σου ὁλότελα νὰ βγάλεις
τῆς Τραγωδίας τὸν Λόγο τὸν λαμπρὸ —
τὶ Ἀγαμέμνονα, τὶ Προμηθέα θαυμαστό,
τὶ Ὀρέστου, τὶ Κασσάνδρας παρουσίες,
τὶ Ἑπτὰ ἐπὶ Θήβας — καὶ γιὰ μνήμη σου νὰ βάλεις
μ ό ν ο ποῦ μὲς στῶν στρατιωτῶν τὲς τάξεις, τὸν σωρὸ
πολέμησες καὶ σὺ τὸν Δᾶτι καὶ τὸν Ἀρταφέρνη».

ΓΙΑ ΝΑΡΘΟΥΝ —

Ἕνα κερὶ ἀρκεῖ.   Τὸ φῶς του τὸ ἀμυδρὸ
ἁρμόζει πιὸ καλά,   θἆναι πιὸ συμπαθὲς
σὰν ἔρθουν τῆς Ἀγάπης,   σὰν ἔρθουν ἡ Σκιές.

Ἕνα κερὶ ἀρκεῖ.   Ἡ κάμαρη ἀπόψι
νὰ μὴ ἔχει φῶς πολύ.   Μέσα στὴν ρέμβην ὅλως
καὶ τὴν ὑποβολή,   καὶ μὲ τὸ λίγο φῶς —
μέσα στὴν ρέμβην ἔτσι   θὰ ὁραματισθῶ
γιὰ νἄρθουν τῆς Ἀγάπης,   γιὰ νἄρθουν ἡ Σκιές.

(stressing perhaps more than was necessary
the 'distinguished valour', and the 'Marathonian grove'),
a spirited young man, zealot of letters,
interrupted at once and shouted:

'I do not like that quatrain at all.
Such expressions seem rather like faintness of spirit.
Give—I declare—to your work all your vigour,
all your attention, and again think back on it
in time of trial, or when your hour is near.
That is what I expect and demand of you.
And not that you should dispel entirely from your mind
the brilliant Word of Tragedy—
an *Agamemnon*, a wonderful *Prometheus*,
the presence of an Orestes, a Cassandra,
the *Seven Against Thebes*—and place as your memorial
only that amid the ranks of soldiers, in the host,
you too fought against Datis* and Artaphernes.'

THAT THEY COME—

One candle is enough.   Its light, ever so faint,
is suited all the more,   more genial it will be
when they come, the Shadows;   when Love's Shadows come.

One candle is enough.   The room tonight should not
be lighted in excess.   Utterly in reverie
and in suggestive rapture,   and with the scanty light—
deep thus in reverie,   I'll drift into my visions,
so that they come, the Shadows;   so that Love's Shadows come.

Ο ΔΑΡΕΙΟΣ

Ὁ ποιητὴς Φερνάζης τὸ σπουδαῖον μέρος
τοῦ ἐπικοῦ ποιήματός του κάμνει.
Τὸ πῶς τὴν βασιλεία τῶν Περσῶν
παρέλαβε ὁ Δαρεῖος Ὑστάσπου. (Ἀπὸ αὐτὸν
κατάγεται ὁ ἔνδοξός μας βασιλεύς,
ὁ Μιθριδάτης, Διόνυσος κ' Εὐπάτωρ). Ἀλλ' ἐδῶ
χρειάζεται φιλοσοφία· πρέπει ν' ἀναλύσει
τὰ αἰσθήματα ποῦ θὰ εἶχεν ὁ Δαρεῖος:
ἴσως ὑπεροψίαν καὶ μέθην· ὄχι ὅμως — μᾶλλον
σὰν κατανόησι τῆς ματαιότητος τῶν μεγαλείων.
Βαθέως σκέπτεται τὸ πρᾶγμα ὁ ποιητής.

Ἀλλὰ τὸν διακόπτει ὁ ὑπηρέτης του ποῦ μπαίνει
τρέχοντας, καὶ τὴν βαρυσήμαντην εἴδησι ἀγγέλλει.
Ἄρχισε ὁ πόλεμος μὲ τοὺς Ρωμαίους.
Τὸ πλεῖστον τοῦ στρατοῦ μας πέρασε τὰ σύνορα.

Ὁ ποιητὴς μένει ἐνεός. Τί συμφορά!
Ποῦ τώρα ὁ ἔνδοξός μας βασιλεύς,
ὁ Μιθριδάτης, Διόνυσος κ' Εὐπάτωρ,
μ' ἑλληνικὰ ποιήματα ν' ἀσχοληθεῖ.
Μέσα σὲ πόλεμο — φαντάσου, ἑλληνικὰ ποιήματα.

Ἀδημονεῖ ὁ Φερνάζης. Ἀτυχία!
Ἐκεῖ ποῦ τὸ εἶχε θετικὸ μὲ τὸν «Δαρεῖο»
ν' ἀναδειχθεῖ, καὶ τοὺς ἐπικριτάς του,
τοὺς φθονερούς, τελειωτικὰ ν' ἀποστομώσει.
Τί ἀναβολή, τί ἀναβολὴ στὰ σχέδιά του.

Καὶ νἆταν μόνο ἀναβολή, πάλι καλά.
Ἀλλὰ νὰ δοῦμε ἂν ἔχουμε κι ἀσφάλεια
στὴν Ἀμισό. Δὲν εἶναι πολιτεία ἐκτάκτως ὀχυρή.
Εἶναι φρικτότατοι ἐχθροὶ οἱ Ρωμαῖοι.
Μποροῦμε νὰ τὰ βγάλουμε μ' αὐτούς,
οἱ Καππαδόκες; Γένεται ποτέ;
Εἶναι νὰ μετρηθοῦμε τώρα μὲ τὲς λεγεῶνες;
Θεοὶ μεγάλοι, τῆς Ἀσίας προστάται, βοηθῆστε μας. —

*

DARIUS

The poet Phernazes is composing
the important part of his epic work.
The way in which Darius, son of Hystaspes,*
assumed the kingship of the Persians.
(It is from him that our glorious king,
Mithridates Dionysus and Eupator,* descends.)
Here, though, one needs to reflect; to analyse
the emotions that Darius might have felt:
arrogance, maybe, and exhilaration; but no—
rather an awareness of the vanity of grandeur.
The poet ponders profoundly on the matter.

But he is interrupted by his servant, who enters
in a rush, and announces the momentous news:
the war with the Romans has begun.
The bulk of our army has crossed the border.

The poet is speechless. What a disaster!
How can our glorious king,
Mithridates Dionysus and Eupator,
concern himself now with Greek poems.
In the middle of a war—imagine, Greek poems.

Phernazes is impatient. What bad luck!
Just as he felt certain that with his 'Darius'
he would distinguish himself and silence at last,
once and for all, his envious critics.
What a setback, what a setback to his plans.

And if it were just a setback, that wouldn't be so bad.
But let us see if we are indeed safe at Amisos.*
It's not a particularly well-fortified city.
They are most dreadful enemies, the Romans.
Are we a match for them,
we Cappadocians? Is it ever possible?
Are we to measure ourselves against the legions now?
Great gods, patrons of Asia, help us.—

*

Ὅμως μὲς σ' ὅλη του τὴν ταραχὴ καὶ τὸ κακό,
ἐπίμονα κ' ἡ ποιητικὴ ἰδέα πάει κ' ἔρχεται—
τὸ πιθανότερο εἶναι, βέβαια, ὑπεροψίαν καὶ μέθην·
ὑπεροψίαν καὶ μέθην θὰ εἶχεν ὁ Δαρεῖος.

ΑΝΝΑ ΚΟΜΝΗΝΗ

Στὸν πρόλογο τῆς Ἀλεξιάδος της θρηνεῖ,
γιὰ τὴν χηρεία της ἡ Ἄννα Κομνηνή.

Εἰς ἴλιγγον εἶν' ἡ ψυχή της. «Καὶ
«ρείθροις δακρύων» μᾶς λέγει «περιτέγγω
«τοὺς ὀφθαλμούς . . . Φεῦ τῶν κυμάτων» τῆς ζωῆς της,
«φεῦ τῶν ἐπαναστάσεων». Τὴν καίει ἡ ὀδύνη
«μέχρις ὀστέων καὶ μυελῶν καὶ μερισμοῦ ψυχῆς».

Ὅμως ἡ ἀλήθεια μοιάζει ποῦ μιὰ λύπη μόνην
καιρίαν ἐγνώρισεν ἡ φίλαρχη γυναῖκα·
ἕναν καϋμὸ βαθὺ μονάχα εἶχε
(κι ἂς μὴν τ' ὁμολογεῖ) ἡ ἀγέρωχη αὐτὴ Γραικιά,
ποῦ δὲν κατάφερε, μ' ὅλην τὴν δεξιότητά της,
τὴν Βασιλείαν ν' ἀποκτήσει· μὰ τὴν πῆρε
σχεδὸν μέσ' ἀπ' τὰ χέρια της ὁ προπετὴς Ἰωάννης.

ΒΥΖΑΝΤΙΝΟΣ ΑΡΧΩΝ, ΕΞΟΡΙΣΤΟΣ, ΣΤΙΧΟΥΡΓΩΝ

Οἱ ἐλαφροὶ ἂς μὲ λέγουν ἐλαφρόν.
Στὰ σοβαρὰ πράγματα ἤμουν πάντοτε
ἐπιμελέστατος. Καὶ θὰ ἐπιμείνω,
ὅτι κανεὶς καλλίτερά μου δὲν γνωρίζει
Πατέρας ἢ Γραφάς, ἢ τοὺς Κανόνας τῶν Συνόδων.
Εἰς κάθε ἀμφιβολίαν του ὁ Βοτανειάτης,
εἰς κάθε δυσκολίαν στὰ ἐκκλησιαστικά,
ἐμένα συμβουλεύονταν, ἐμένα πρῶτον.
Ἀλλὰ ἐξόριστος ἐδῶ (νὰ ὄψεται ἡ κακεντρεχὴς

But yet, amid all his excitement and the tumult,
persistently the poetic idea comes and goes—
most likely, of course, it is arrogance and exhilaration;
arrogance and exhilaration Darius must have felt.

ANNA COMNENA

In the prologue to her *Alexiad*,
Anna Comnena* laments her widowhood.

Her soul is in a daze. 'And I wet
my eyes', she tells us, 'with rivers of
tears . . . Alas for the wavering fortunes' of her life,
'alas for the revolutions'. She is consumed by pain,
'to the bones and marrow and to the rending of her soul'.

But, truth is, it seems that this power-loving woman
experienced just one cardinal grief;
she had but one consuming passion
(whether she admits it or not), this haughty Greek woman:
that she never managed, despite all her dexterity,
to obtain the kingship; for it was snatched,
practically out of her hands, by that impudent John.

A BYZANTINE NOBLEMAN, IN EXILE, COMPOSING VERSES

Let the frivolous call me frivolous.
In serious matters, I have always been
most diligent. And I'll insist
that no one is better acquainted than I
with Church Fathers, or Scriptures, or the Canons of the Councils.
Whenever Botaneiates* was in doubt,
whenever in difficulty on ecclesiastic issues,
it is to me he would come for advice, to me before anyone else.
But being in exile here (no thanks to that malicious

Εἰρήνη Δούκαινα), καὶ δεινῶς ἀνιῶν,
οὐδόλως ἄτοπον εἶναι νὰ διασκεδάζω
ἑξάστιχα κι ὀκτάστιχα ποιῶν—
νὰ διασκεδάζω μὲ μυθολογήματα
Ἑρμοῦ, καὶ Ἀπόλλωνος, καὶ Διονύσου,
ἢ ἡρώων τῆς Θεσσαλίας καὶ τῆς Πελοποννήσου·
καὶ νὰ συνθέτω ἰάμβους ὀρθοτάτους,
ὅπως—θὰ μ' ἐπιτρέψετε νὰ πῶ—οἱ λόγιοι
τῆς Κωνσταντινουπόλεως δὲν ξέρουν νὰ συνθέσουν.
Αὐτὴ ἡ ὀρθότης, πιθανόν, εἶν' ἡ αἰτία τῆς μομφῆς.

Η ΑΡΧΗ ΤΩΝ

Ἡ ἐκπλήρωσις τῆς ἔκνομής των ἡδονῆς
ἔγινεν. Ἀπ' τὸ στρῶμα σηκωθῆκαν,
καὶ βιαστικὰ ντύνονται χωρὶς νὰ μιλοῦν.
Βγαίνουνε χωριστά, κρυφὰ ἀπ' τὸ σπίτι· καὶ καθὼς
βαδίζουνε κάπως ἀνήσυχα στὸν δρόμο, μοιάζει
σὰν νὰ ὑποψιάζονται ποῦ κάτι ἐπάνω των προδίδει
σὲ τὶ εἴδους κλίνην ἔπεσαν πρὸ ὀλίγου.

Πλὴν τοῦ τεχνίτου πῶς ἐκέρδισε ἡ ζωή.
Αὔριο, μεθαύριο, ἢ μετὰ χρόνια θὰ γραφοῦν
οἱ στίχ' οἱ δυνατοὶ ποῦ ἐδῶ ἦταν ἡ ἀρχή των.

ΕΥΝΟΙΑ ΤΟΥ ΑΛΕΞΑΝΔΡΟΥ ΒΑΛΑ

Ἂ δὲν συγχίζομαι ποῦ ἔσπασε μιὰ ρόδα
τοῦ ἁμαξιοῦ, καὶ ποῦ ἔχασα μιὰ ἀστεία νίκη.
Μὲ τὰ καλὰ κρασιά, καὶ μὲς στὰ ὡραῖα ρόδα
τὴν νύχτα θὰ περάσω. Ἡ Ἀντιόχεια μὲ ἀνήκει.
Εἶμαι ὁ νέος ὁ πιὸ δοξαστός.
Τοῦ Βάλα εἶμ' ἐγὼ ἡ ἀδυναμία, ὁ λατρευτός.
Αὔριο, νὰ δεῖς, θὰ ποῦν πῶς ὁ ἀγὼν δὲν ἔγινε σωστός.
(Μὰ ἂν ἤμουν ἀκαλαίσθητος, κι ἂν μυστικὰ τὸ εἶχα
προστάξει—
θἄβγαζαν πρῶτο, οἱ κόλακες, καὶ τὸ κουτσό μου ἁμάξι).

Irene Doukaina), and terribly bored,
it is not in the least unseemly to entertain myself
by composing six- and eight-line verses;
to amuse myself with mythological tales
about Hermes and Apollo and Dionysus,
or about the heroes of Thessaly and the Peloponnese;
and to compose perfect iambic verses,
the likes of which—allow me to say—the scholars
in Constantinople do not know how to compose.
That perfection, probably, is the reason behind the reproach.

THEIR ORIGIN

The fulfilment of their deviant pleasure
is complete. They rise from the mattress
and put on their clothes hurriedly, in silence.
They leave the house separately, furtively; and
as they walk somewhat uneasily in the street, it seems
as if they suspect something about them betrays
upon what sort of bed they had just lain.

But how the artist's life has profited.
Tomorrow, the day after, or years later the fervent
lines will be composed that had right here their origin.

THE FAVOUR OF ALEXANDER BALAS

Well, I'm not upset that a wheel
of my chariot broke, and I lost an easy victory.
With the fine wines, amid the lovely roses,
I'll spend the night. Antioch is mine,
I'm the most acclaimed young man,
I'm Balas' weakness, his adored one.
You'll see, tomorrow they'll say the contest was not fair.
If though I had no elegance and ordered it in secret—
the flatterers
would've awarded first prize even to my crippled chariot.

ΜΕΛΑΓΧΟΛΙΑ ΤΟΥ ΙΑΣΩΝΟΣ ΚΛΕΑΝΔΡΟΥ· ΠΟΙΗΤΟΥ ΕΝ ΚΟΜΜΑΓΗΝΗ· 595 Μ.Χ.

Τὸ γήρασμα τοῦ σώματος καὶ τῆς μορφῆς μου
εἶναι πληγὴ ἀπὸ φρικτὸ μαχαῖρι.
Δὲν ἔχω ἐγκαρτέρησι καμιά.
Εἰς σὲ προστρέχω Τέχνη τῆς Ποιήσεως,
ποὺ κάπως ξέρεις ἀπὸ φάρμακα·
νάρκης τοῦ ἄλγους δοκιμές, ἐν Φαντασίᾳ καὶ Λόγῳ.

Εἶναι πληγὴ ἀπὸ φρικτὸ μαχαῖρι.—
Τὰ φάρμακά σου φέρε Τέχνη τῆς Ποιήσεως,
ποὺ κάμνουνε—γιὰ λίγο—νὰ μὴ νοιώθεται ἡ πληγή.

Ο ΔΗΜΑΡΑΤΟΣ

Τὸ θέμα, ὁ Χαρακτὴρ τοῦ Δημαράτου,
ποὺ τὸν ἐπρότεινε ὁ Πορφύριος, ἐν συνομιλίᾳ,
ἔτσι τὸ ἐξέφρασεν ὁ νέος σοφιστὴς
(σκοπεύοντας, μετά, ρητορικῶς νὰ τὸ ἀναπτύξει).

«Πρῶτα τοῦ βασιλέως Δαρείου, κ' ἔπειτα
τοῦ βασιλέως Ξέρξη ὁ αὐλικός·
καὶ τώρα μὲ τὸν Ξέρξη καὶ τὸ στράτευμά του,
νὰ ἐπὶ τέλους θὰ δικαιωθεῖ ὁ Δημάρατος.

«Μεγάλη ἀδικία τὸν ἔγινε.
Ἦταν τοῦ Ἀρίστωνος ὁ υἱός. Ἀναίσχυντα
ἐδωροδόκησαν οἱ ἐχθροί του τὸ μαντεῖον.
Καὶ δὲν τοὺς ἔφθασε ποὺ τὸν ἐστέρησαν τὴν βασιλεία,
ἀλλ' ὅταν πιὰ ὑπέκυψε, καὶ τὸ ἀπεφάσισε
νὰ ζήσει μ' ἐγκαρτέρησιν ὡς ἰδιώτης,
ἔπρεπ' ἐμπρὸς καὶ στὸν λαὸ νὰ τὸν προσβάλουν,
ἔπρεπε δημοσίᾳ νὰ τὸν ταπεινώσουν στὴν γιορτή.

*

MELANCHOLY OF JASON, SON OF KLEANDER, POET IN COMMAGENE, A.D. 595

The aging of my body and of my face:
it's a wound from an atrocious knife.
I can endure it no more.
I appeal to you, Art of Poetry,
since you know something about soothing drugs;
attempts to numb the pain, in Imagery and Word.

It is a wound from an atrocious knife.—
Art of Poetry, bring forth your soothing drugs
that manage—for a little while—to benumb the wound.

DEMARATUS

The subject: 'The Character of Demaratus',
suggested to him by Porphyry in conversation,
was rendered by the young sophist
(intending to develop it rhetorically later) as follows:

'A courtier to King Darius, at first,
and then to King Xerxes,
and now with Xerxes and his armies,
at long last, Demaratus will be vindicated.

'Great injustice has befallen him.
He *was* Ariston's son. Shamelessly
his enemies bribed the oracle.
And if it weren't enough for them to deprive him of the kingship,
when he finally relented and made up his mind
to live, with stoic resignation, as a private citizen,
they had to insult him as well before the people;
they had to humiliate him publicly at the feast.

*

«Ὅθεν τὸν Ξέρξη μὲ πολὺν ζῆλον ὑπηρετεῖ.
Μὲ τὸν μεγάλο Περσικὸ στρατό,
κι αὐτὸς στὴν Σπάρτη θὰ ξαναγυρίσει·
καὶ βασιλεὺς σὰν πρίν, πῶς θὰ τὸν διώξει
ἀμέσως, πῶς θὰ τὸν ἐξευτελίσει
ἐκεῖνον τὸν ραδιοῦργον Λεωτυχίδη.

«Κ' ἡ μέρες του περνοῦν γεμάτες μέριμνα·
νὰ δίδει συμβουλὲς στοὺς Πέρσας, νὰ τοὺς ἐξηγεῖ
τὸ πῶς νὰ κάμουν γιὰ νὰ κατακτήσουν τὴν Ἑλλάδα.

«Πολλὲς φροντίδες, πολλὴ σκέψις καὶ γιὰ τοῦτο
εἶν' ἔτσι ἀνιαρὲς τοῦ Δημαράτου ἡ μέρες·
πολλὲς φροντίδες, πολλὴ σκέψις καὶ γιὰ τοῦτο
καμιὰ στιγμὴ χαρᾶς δὲν ἔχει ὁ Δημάρατος·
γιατὶ χαρὰ δὲν εἶν' αὐτὸ ποῦ αἰσθάνεται
(δὲν εἶναι· δὲν τὸ παραδέχεται·
πῶς νὰ τὸ πεῖ χαρά; ἐκορυφώθ' ἡ δυστυχία του)
ὅταν τὰ πράγματα τὸν δείχνουν φανερὰ
ποῦ οἱ Ἕλληνες θὰ βγοῦνε νικηταί.»

ΕΚΟΜΙΣΑ ΕΙΣ ΤΗΝ ΤΕΧΝΗ

Κάθομαι καὶ ρεμβάζω. Ἐπιθυμίες κ' αἰσθήσεις
ἐκόμισα εἰς τὴν Τέχνην— κάτι μισοειδωμένα,
πρόσωπα ἢ γραμμές· ἐρώτων ἀτελῶν
κάτι ἀβέβαιες μνῆμες. Ἂς ἀφεθῶ σ' αὐτήν.
Ξέρει νὰ σχηματίσει Μορφὴν τῆς Καλλονῆς·
σχεδὸν ἀνεπαισθήτως τὸν βίον συμπληροῦσα,
συνδυάζουσα ἐντυπώσεις, συνδυάζουσα τὲς μέρες.

'Therefore, he serves Xerxes with much zeal.
Along with the great Persian army,
he too will return to Sparta,
and king again, as before, how he'll expel
at once, how he'll disgrace
that scheming intriguer, Leotychides.

'And his days go by, full of care;
giving advice to the Persians, explaining to them
how to go about conquering Greece.

'Many concerns, a lot of thought; and for this reason
so tedious are Demaratus' days;
many concerns, a lot of thought, and for this reason
Demaratus has not a moment of joy;
it is not joy that he feels
(it is not; he won't admit it;
how can he call this joy? His misery has come to a head);
since circumstances show him clearly
that the Greeks will emerge victorious.'

I BROUGHT TO ART

I sit and muse in reverie. I brought to Art
desires and sensations— some dimly envisaged
faces and features; some vague memories
of unfulfilled affairs. Let me surrender myself to Art;
Art knows how to shape the Likeness of Beauty,
barely perceptibly enhancing life,
blending impressions, blending the days.

ΑΠΟ ΤΗΝ ΣΧΟΛΗΝ ΤΟΥ ΠΕΡΙΩΝΥΜΟΥ ΦΙΛΟΣΟΦΟΥ

Ἔμεινε μαθητὴς τοῦ Ἀμμωνίου Σακκᾶ δυὸ χρόνια·
ἀλλὰ βαρέθηκε καὶ τὴν φιλοσοφία καὶ τὸν Σακκᾶ.

Κατόπι μπῆκε στὰ πολιτικά.
Μὰ τὰ παραίτησεν. Ἦταν ὁ Ἔπαρχος μωρός·
κ' οἱ πέριξ του ξόανα ἐπίσημα καὶ σοβαροφανῆ·
τρισβάρβαρα τὰ ἑλληνικά των, οἱ ἄθλιοι.

Τὴν περιέργειάν του εἵλκυσε
κομμάτ' ἡ Ἐκκλησία· νὰ βαπτισθεῖ
καὶ νὰ περάσει Χριστιανός. Μὰ γρήγορα
τὴν γνώμη του ἄλλαξε. Θὰ κάκιωνε ἀσφαλῶς
μὲ τοὺς γονεῖς του, ἐπιδεικτικὰ ἐθνικούς·
καὶ θὰ τοῦ ἔπαυαν — πρᾶγμα φρικτὸν —
εὐθὺς τὰ λίαν γενναῖα δοσίματα.

Ἔπρεπεν ὅμως καὶ νὰ κάμει κάτι. Ἔγινε ὁ θαμὼν
τῶν διεφθαρμένων οἴκων τῆς Ἀλεξανδρείας,
κάθε κρυφοῦ καταγωγίου κραιπάλης.

Ἡ τύχη τοῦ ἐφάν' εἰς τοῦτο εὐμενής·
τὸν ἔδοσε μορφὴν εἰς ἄκρον εὐειδῆ.
Καὶ χαίρονταν τὴν θείαν δωρεάν.

Τουλάχιστον γιὰ δέκα χρόνια ἀκόμη
ἡ καλλονή του θὰ διαρκοῦσεν. Ἔπειτα —
ἴσως ἐκ νέου στὸν Σακκᾶ νὰ πήγαινε.
Κι ἂν ἐν τῷ μεταξὺ ἀπέθνησκεν ὁ γέρος,
πήγαινε σ' ἄλλου φιλοσόφου ἢ σοφιστοῦ·
πάντοτε βρίσκεται κατάλληλος κανείς.

Ἢ τέλος, δυνατὸν καὶ στὰ πολιτικὰ
νὰ ἐπέστρεφεν — ἀξιεπαίνως ἐνθυμούμενος
τὲς οἰκογενειακές του παραδόσεις,
τὸ χρέος πρὸς τὴν πατρίδα, κι ἄλλα ἠχηρὰ παρόμοια.

FROM THE SCHOOL OF THE RENOWNED PHILOSOPHER

He was a student of Ammonius Saccas* for two years;
but he grew tired of both philosophy and Saccas.

Then he went into politics,
but gave it up. The Eparch was an idiot;
and those around him pompous, officious numbskulls;
thrice-barbarous their Greek, the miserable wretches.

The Church attracted his interest
for a while; to be baptized,
and pass as a Christian. But quickly he
changed his mind. He'd surely embitter
his ostentatiously pagan parents;
and—perish the thought—they would suspend
at once their most generous allowance.

And yet he ought to do something. He became
a regular customer of Alexandria's corrupt houses,
of every clandestine den of debauchery.

Fate appeared to him in this benevolent,
endowing him with most attractive looks.
And he delighted in the god-sent gift.

His beauty would endure at least
another ten more years. And after that
perhaps, once more, he'd go to Saccas.
And if in the meantime, the old man were to die,
he would go to some other philosopher or sophist;
there is always a suitable one around.

Or in the end, he might well
go back to politics—in commendable remembrance
of his family traditions, his duty to his country,
and other such resounding platitudes.

ΤΕΧΝΟΥΡΓΟΣ ΚΡΑΤΗΡΩΝ

Εἰς τὸν κρατῆρα αὐτὸν ἀπὸ ἁγνὸν ἀσῆμι—
ποῦ γιὰ τοῦ Ἡρακλείδη ἔγινε τὴν οἰκία,
ἔνθα καλαισθησία πολλὴ ἐπικρατεῖ—
ἰδοὺ ἄνθη κομψά, καὶ ρύακες καὶ θύμοι,
κ' ἔθεσα ἐν τῷ μέσῳ ἕναν ὡραῖον νέον,
γυμνόν, ἐρωτικόν· μὲς στὸ νερὸ τὴν κνήμη
τὴν μιά του ἔχει ἀκόμη.— Ἱκέτευσα, ὦ μνήμη,
νὰ σ' εὕρω βοηθὸν ἀρίστην, γιὰ νὰ κάμω
τοῦ νέου ποῦ ἀγαποῦσα τὸ πρόσωπον ὡς ἦταν.
Μεγάλη ἡ δυσκολία ἀπέβη ἐπειδὴ
ὡς δέκα πέντε χρόνια πέρασαν ἀπ' τὴν μέρα
ποῦ ἔπεσε, στρατιώτης, στῆς Μαγνησίας τὴν ἧτταν.

ΥΠΕΡ ΤΗΣ ΑΧΑΪΚΗΣ ΣΥΜΠΟΛΙΤΕΙΑΣ ΠΟΛΕΜΗΣΑΝΤΕΣ

Ἀνδρεῖοι σεῖς ποῦ πολεμήσατε καὶ πέσατ' εὐκλεῶς·
τοὺς πανταχοῦ νικήσαντας μὴ φοβηθέντες.
Ἄμωμοι σεῖς, ἂν ἔπταισαν ὁ Δίαιος κι ὁ Κριτόλαος.
Ὅταν θὰ θέλουν οἱ Ἕλληνες νὰ καυχηθοῦν,
«Τέτοιους βγάζει τὸ ἔθνος μας» θὰ λένε
γιὰ σᾶς. Ἔτσι θαυμάσιος θἆναι ὁ ἔπαινός σας.—

Ἐγράφη ἐν Ἀλεξανδρείᾳ ὑπὸ Ἀχαιοῦ·
ἕβδομον ἔτος Πτολεμαίου, Λαθύρου.

CRAFTSMAN OF CRATERS

Upon this very crater   out of the purest silver—
that's crafted for the house   of Heracleides where
delicacy of taste   is highly prevalent—
behold: elegant blossoms   and rivulets and thyme
and right there in the middle   I put a handsome youth,
naked and erotic;   one of his legs immersed
still knee-deep in the water.—   I begged of you, O Memory,
to be my best assistant,   so that I might fashion
just as it was the face   of the young man I loved.
The difficulty proved   considerable, because
as many as fifteen years   have gone by since that day
when he fell, a soldier   in the Magnesian defeat.*

THOSE WHO FOUGHT FOR THE ACHAEAN LEAGUE

Valiant are you, who fought and fell in glory;
undaunted by those victorious everywhere.
Unblemished are you, if Diaeus and Critolaus* were to blame.
Whenever the Greeks will want to vaunt,
'It's such as these that our nation breeds', they'll say
of you. So marvellous will be your praise.—

Written in Alexandria by an Achaean;
seventh year of Ptolemy Lathyros.*

ΠΡΟΣ ΤΟΝ ΑΝΤΙΟΧΟΝ ΕΠΙΦΑΝΗ

Ὁ νέος Ἀντιοχεὺς εἶπε στὸν βασιλέα,
«Μὲς τὴν καρδιά μου πάλλει μιὰ προσφιλὴς ἐλπίς·
οἱ Μακεδόνες πάλι, Ἀντίοχε Ἐπιφανῆ,
οἱ Μακεδόνες εἶναι μὲς στὴν μεγάλη πάλη.
Ἂς ἦταν νὰ νικήσουν— καὶ σ' ὅποιον θέλει δίδω
τὸν λέοντα καὶ τοὺς ἵππους, τὸν Πᾶνα ἀπὸ κοράλλι,
καὶ τὸ κομψὸ παλάτι, καὶ τοὺς ἐν Τύρῳ κήπους,
κι ὅσ' ἄλλα μ' ἔχεις δώσει, Ἀντίοχε Ἐπιφανῆ.»

Ἴσως νὰ συγκινήθη κομάτι ὁ βασιλεύς.
Μὰ πάραυτα θυμήθη πατέρα κι ἀδελφόν,
καὶ μήτε ἀπεκρίθη. Μποροῦσε ὠτακουστὴς
νὰ ἐπαναλάβει κάτι.— Ἄλλωστε, ὡς φυσικόν,
ταχέως ἐπῆλθε εἰς Πύδναν ἡ ἀπαισία λῆξις.

Σ' ΕΝΑ ΒΙΒΛΙΟ ΠΑΛΗΟ—

Σ' ἕνα βιβλίο παληὸ—περίπου ἑκατὸ ἐτῶν—
ἀνάμεσα στὰ φύλλα του λησμονημένη,
ηὗρα μιὰν ὑδατογραφία ἄνευ ὑπογραφῆς.
Θἄταν τὸ ἔργον καλλιτέχνου λίαν δυνατοῦ.
Ἔφερ' ὡς τίτλον, «Παρουσίασις τοῦ Ἔρωτος».

Πλὴν μᾶλλον ἥρμοζε, «—τοῦ ἔρωτος τῶν ἄκρως
αἰσθητῶν».

Γιατὶ ἦταν φανερὸ σὰν ἔβλεπες τὸ ἔργον
(εὔκολα νοιώθονταν ἡ ἰδέα τοῦ καλλιτέχνου)
ποῦ γιὰ ὅσους ἀγαποῦνε κάπως ὑγιεινά,
μὲς στ' ὁπωσδήποτε ἐπιτετραμμένον μένοντες,
δὲν ἦταν προωρισμένος ὁ ἔφηβος
τῆς ζωγραφιᾶς—μὲ καστανά, βαθύχροα μάτια·
μὲ τοῦ προσώπου του τὴν ἐκλεκτὴ ἐμορφιά,
τὴν ἐμορφιὰ τῶν ἀνωμάλων ἕλξεων·

TO ANTIOCHUS EPIPHANES

The young Antiochian announced to the king:
'There pulses in my heart a deeply cherished hope;
once more the Macedonians, O Antiochus Epiphanes,
the Macedonians are involved in the great conflict.
If only they would prevail— and I'd grant to any taker
the lion and the horses, the Pan made out of coral,
as well as the elegant palace, and the gardens at Tyre,*
and all else you have given me, O Antiochus Epiphanes.'

Perhaps in some small way, the king might have been moved.
But at once he remembered his father and his brother
and didn't even answer; for an eavesdropper
could well repeat something.— In any case, as expected
swiftly came at Pydna the abominable end.

IN AN OLD BOOK—

In an old book—about a hundred years old—
I discovered, forgotten between the pages,
an unsigned watercolour painting.
It must have been the work of quite a powerful artist.
It bore the title, 'Presentation of Love.'

Though more befitting it would be: 'love of the extreme
aesthetes.'

Because it was obvious, when looking at the work
(one could readily perceive the idea of the artist),
that the young man in the painting was not intended
for those who engage in healthful love,
remaining, by all means, within sanctioned bounds—
with his deep-hued chestnut eyes;
with the exquisite beauty of his face,
a beauty of deviant appeal;

μὲ τὰ ἰδεώδη χείλη του ποῦ φέρνουνε
τὴν ἡδονὴ εἰς ἀγαπημένο σῶμα·
μὲ τὰ ἰδεώδη μέλη του πλασμένα γιὰ κρεββάτια
ποῦ ἀναίσχυντα τ' ἀποκαλεῖ ἡ τρεχάμενη ἠθική.

ΕΝ ΑΠΟΓΝΩΣΕΙ

Τὸν ἔχασ' ἐντελῶς. Καὶ τώρα πιὰ ζητεῖ
στὰ χείλη καθενὸς καινούριου ἐραστῆ
τὰ χείλη τὰ δικά του· στὴν ἕνωσι μὲ κάθε
καινούριον ἐραστὴ ζητεῖ νὰ πλανηθεῖ
πῶς εἶναι ὁ ἴδιος νέος, πῶς δίδεται σ' ἐκεῖνον.

Τὸν ἔχασ' ἐντελῶς, σὰν νὰ μὴ ὑπῆρχε κάν.
Γιατὶ ἤθελε — εἶπ' ἐκεῖνος — ἤθελε νὰ σωθεῖ
ἀπ' τὴν στιγματισμένη, τὴν νοσηρὰ ἡδονή·
ἀπ' τὴν στιγματισμένη, τοῦ αἴσχους ἡδονή.
Ἦταν καιρὸς ἀκόμη — ὡς εἶπε — νὰ σωθεῖ.

Τὸν ἔχασ' ἐντελῶς, σὰν νὰ μὴ ὑπῆρχε κάν.
Ἀπὸ τὴν φαντασίαν, ἀπὸ τὲς παραισθήσεις
στὰ χείλη ἄλλων νέων τὰ χείλη του ζητεῖ·
γυρεύει νὰ αἰσθανθεῖ ξανὰ τὸν ἔρωτά του.

Ο ΙΟΥΛΙΑΝΟΣ, ΟΡΩΝ ΟΛΙΓΩΡΙΑΝ

«Ὁρῶν οὖν πολλὴν μὲν ὀλιγωρίαν οὖσαν
«ἡμῖν πρὸς τοὺς θεοὺς» — λέγει μὲ ὕφος σοβαρόν.
Ὀλιγωρίαν. Μὰ τί περίμενε λοιπόν;
Ὅσο ἤθελεν ἂς ἔκαμνεν ὀργάνωσι θρησκευτική,
ὅσο ἤθελεν ἂς ἔγραφε στὸν ἀχιερέα Γαλατίας,
ἢ εἰς ἄλλους τοιούτους, παροτρύνων κι ὁδηγῶν.
Οἱ φίλοι του δὲν ἦσαν Χριστιανοί·

with his ideal lips that bring
sensual delight to the beloved body;
with his ideal limbs, created for beds
that everyday morality labels shameless.

IN DESPAIR

He lost his friend completely.   And now he tries to find
upon the lips of every   other new paramour
his former lover's lips.   He tries in the union
with each new paramour   to make himself believe
he's found that same young lover,   and that he yields to him.

He lost his friend completely,   as if he ceased to exist.
Because he wanted—so he said—   he wanted to be saved
from such a stigmatized,   wasteful carnal pleasure,
from such a stigmatized,   carnal pleasure of shame.
There was still time—so he said—   for him to save himself.

He lost his friend completely,   as if he ceased to exist.
Through his imagination,   through his hallucinations,
upon the lips of other youths   he seeks his lover's lips;
endeavouring to experience   his lover's love once more.

JULIAN, NOTICING NEGLIGENCE

'Noticing, therefore, that there is much negligence
among us towards the gods'—he states in a solemn manner.
Negligence. What did he expect then?
Let him undertake religious organization, as much as he liked;
or write, as much as he liked, to the High Priest of Galatia,
or to others such as he, encouraging and counselling.
His friends were not Christians;

αὐτὸ ἦταν θετικόν. Μὰ δὲν μποροῦσαν κιόλας
νὰ παίζουν σὰν κι αὐτόνα (τὸν Χριστιανομαθημένο)
μὲ σύστημα καινούριας ἐκκλησίας,
ἀστεῖον καὶ στὴν σύλληψι καὶ στὴν ἐφαρμογή.
Ἕλληνες ἦσαν ἐπὶ τέλους. Μηδὲν ἄγαν, Αὔγουστε.

ΕΠΙΤΥΜΒΙΟΝ ΑΝΤΙΟΧΟΥ, ΒΑΣΙΛΕΩΣ ΚΟΜΜΑΓΗΝΗΣ

Μετὰ ποῦ ἐπέστρεψε, περίλυπη, ἀπ' τὴν κηδεία του,
ἡ ἀδελφὴ τοῦ ἐγκρατῶς καὶ πράως ζήσαντος,
τοῦ λίαν ἐγγραμμάτου Ἀντιόχου, βασιλέως
Κομμαγηνῆς, ἤθελ' ἕνα ἐπιτύμβιον γι' αὐτόν.
Κι ὁ Ἐφέσιος σοφιστὴς Καλλίστρατος—ὁ κατοικῶν
συχνὰ ἐν τῷ κρατιδίῳ τῆς Κομμαγηνῆς,
κι ἀπὸ τὸν οἶκον τὸν βασιλικὸν
ἀσμένως κ' ἐπανειλημμένως φιλοξενηθεὶς—
τὸ ἔγραψε, τῇ ὑποδείξει Σύρων αὐλικῶν,
καὶ τὸ ἔστειλε εἰς τὴν γραῖαν δέσποιναν.

«Τοῦ Ἀντιόχου τοῦ εὐεργέτου βασιλέως
νὰ ὑμνηθεῖ ἐπαξίως, ὦ Κομμαγηνοί, τὸ κλέος.
Ἦταν τῆς χώρας κυβερνήτης προνοητικός.
Ὑπῆρξε δίκαιος, σοφός, γενναῖος.
Ὑπῆρξεν ἔτι τὸ ἄριστον ἐκεῖνο, Ἑλληνικὸς—
ἰδιότητα δὲν ἔχ' ἡ ἀνθρωπότης τιμιοτέραν·
εἰς τοὺς θεοὺς εὑρίσκονται τὰ πέραν.»

that much was certain. But even so, they couldn't
fool around as he (brought up a Christian) could,
with a novel religious system,
ludicrous both in concept and application.
They were Greeks, after all! Nothing in excess,* Augustus.

EPITAPH OF ANTIOCHUS, KING OF COMMAGENE

Upon returning, sorrowful, from his funeral,
the sister of the highly cultured King Antiochus of Commagene—
a man who'd led an abstemious and quiet life—
she wanted an epitaph for him.
And the Ephesian sophist Kallistratos—who often
was a visiting resident in the small state of Commagene
and had been readily and repeatedly accommodated
by the royal household—composed it
on the advice of Syrian court officials,
and had it sent to the elderly lady.

'The glory of King Antiochus the beneficent
must be praised as befits, O Commagenes.
He was a provident governor of the land.
He has been just, wise, brave.
He has been, also, that best of all things: Greek-cultured—
humanity does not possess a quality more precious;
beyond that lies the realm of gods.'

ΘΕΑΤΡΟΝ ΤΗΣ ΣΙΔΩΝΟΣ (400 Μ.Χ.)

Πολίτου ἐντίμου υἱός— πρὸ πάντων, εὐειδὴς
ἔφηβος τοῦ θεάτρου, ποικίλως ἀρεστός,
ἐνίοτε συνθέτω ἐν γλώσση ἑλληνικῆ
λίαν εὐτόλμους στίχους, ποῦ τοὺς κυκλοφορῶ
πολὺ κρυφά, ἐννοεῖται— θεοί! νὰ μὴν τοὺς δοῦν
οἱ τὰ φαιὰ φοροῦντες, περὶ ἠθικῆς λαλοῦντες—
στίχους τῆς ἡδονῆς τῆς ἐκλεκτῆς, ποῦ πιαίνει
πρὸς ἄγονην ἀγάπη κι ἀποδοκιμασμένη.

Ο ΙΟΥΛΙΑΝΟΣ ΕΝ ΝΙΚΟΜΗΔΕΙΑ

Ἄστοχα πράγματα καὶ κινδυνώδη.
Οἱ ἔπαινοι γιὰ τῶν Ἑλλήνων τὰ ἰδεώδη.

Ἡ θεουργίες κ' ἡ ἐπισκέψεις στοὺς ναοὺς
τῶν ἐθνικῶν. Οἱ ἐνθουσιασμοὶ γιὰ τοὺς ἀρχαίους θεούς.

Μὲ τὸν Χρυσάνθιον ἡ συχνὲς συνομιλίες.
Τοῦ φιλοσόφου—τοῦ ἄλλωστε δεινοῦ—Μαξίμου ἡ θεωρίες.

Καὶ νὰ τὸ ἀποτέλεσμα. Ὁ Γάλλος δείχνει ἀνησυχία
μεγάλην. Ὁ Κωνστάντιος ἔχει κάποιαν ὑποψία.

Ἆ οἱ συμβουλεύσαντες δὲν ἦσαν διόλου συνετοί.
Παρέγινε—λέγει ὁ Μαρδόνιος—ἡ ἱστορία αὐτή,

καὶ πρέπει ἐξ ἅπαντος νὰ παύσει ὁ θόρυβός της.—
Ὁ Ἰουλιανὸς πηγαίνει πάλιν ἀναγνώστης

στὴν ἐκκλησία τῆς Νικομηδείας,
ὅπου μεγαλοφώνως καὶ μετ' εὐλαβείας

πολλῆς τὲς ἱερὲς Γραφὲς διαβάζει,
καὶ τὴν χριστιανική του εὐσέβεια ὁ λαὸς θαυμάζει.

THEATRE OF SIDON (A.D. 400)

An honest citizen's son— above all a good-looking
young man of the theatre, cherished in many ways,
at times I compose in the Hellenic tongue
rather audacious verses, which I circulate,
clandestinely of course— O gods! lest they be seen
by those who dress in grey and prate about morality—
verses of sensual pleasure, of choice sensual pleasure
that leads toward a barren and deprecated love.

JULIAN IN NICOMEDIA

Misguided and perilous things:
those praises for the Greek ideals;

participation in rituals and mysteries, visits to
pagan temples. Enthusiasm for the ancient gods,

frequent discussions with Chrysanthius;
the theories of the—admittedly accomplished—philosopher
Maximus.*

And here is the outcome. Gallus displays considerable
concern; Constantius entertains suspicions.

Well, the advisers were not prudent at all!
This affair—Mardonius* insists—has gone too far,

and the commotion must, at any cost, be allayed.—
Julian goes back again as a lay-reader

to the church of Nicomedia,*
where in a loud voice and with deep

reverence he reads out of the Holy Scriptures,
and the people admire his Christian piety.

ΠΡΙΝ ΤΟΥΣ ΑΛΛΑΞΕΙ Ο ΧΡΟΝΟΣ

Λυπήθηκαν μεγάλως στὸν ἀποχωρισμό των.
Δὲν τὄθελαν αὐτοί· ἦταν ἡ περιστάσεις.
Βιοτικὲς ἀνάγκες ἐκάμνανε τὸν ἕνα
νὰ φύγει μακρυὰ — Νέα Ὑόρκη ἢ Καναδᾶ.
Ἡ ἀγάπη των βεβαίως δὲν ἦταν ἴδια ὡς πρίν·
εἶχεν ἐλαττωθεῖ ἡ ἕλξις βαθμηδόν,
εἶχεν ἐλαττωθεῖ ἡ ἕλξις της πολύ.
Ὅμως νὰ χωρισθοῦν, δὲν τὄθελαν αὐτοί.
Ἦταν ἡ περιστάσεις. — Ἢ μήπως καλλιτέχνις
ἐφάνηκεν ἡ Τύχη χωρίζοντάς τους τώρα
πρὶν σβύσει τὸ αἴσθημά των, πρὶν τοὺς ἀλλάξει ὁ Χρόνος·
ὁ ἕνας γιὰ τὸν ἄλλον θὰ εἶναι ὡς νὰ μένει πάντα
τῶν εἴκοσι τεσσάρων ἐτῶν τ' ὡραῖο παιδί.

ΗΛΘΕ ΓΙΑ ΝΑ ΔΙΑΒΑΣΕΙ —

Ἦλθε γιὰ νὰ διαβάσει. Εἶν' ἀνοιχτὰ
δυό, τρία βιβλία· ἱστορικοὶ καὶ ποιηταί.
Μὰ μόλις διάβασε δέκα λεπτά,
καὶ τὰ παραίτησε. Στὸν καναπὲ
μισοκοιμᾶται. Ἀνήκει πλήρως στὰ βιβλία —
ἀλλ' εἶναι εἴκοσι τριῶ ἐτῶν, κ' εἶν' ἔμορφος πολύ·
καὶ σήμερα τὸ ἀπόγευμα πέρασ' ὁ ἔρως
στὴν ἰδεώδη σάρκα του, στὰ χείλη.
Στὴ σάρκα του ποῦ εἶναι ὅλο καλλονὴ
ἡ θέρμη πέρασεν ἡ ἐρωτική·
χωρὶς ἀστείαν αἰδὼ γιὰ τὴν μορφὴ τῆς ἀπολαύσεως . . .

BEFORE THEY ARE CHANGED BY TIME

They were so very sad   during their separation.
It was not what they wanted;   it was circumstances.
Necessities of life   forced one of them to leave
and travel far away—   New York or Canada.
Their love for sure was not   what it once used to be;
the sexual attraction   had gradually waned,
the sexual attraction   had been reduced a lot.
Yet to be separated   was not what they wanted.
It was circumstances.—   Or perhaps Destiny
appeared like an artist,   separating them now,
before their feeling fades,   before they are changed by Time;
each of them for the other   will then remain forever
a twenty-four-year-old   and beautiful young man.

HE CAME TO READ—

He came to read. Two or three books
are open; historians and poets.
But he didn't read more than ten minutes
and gave it up. He is dozing
on the couch. He is entirely devoted to books—
but he's only twenty-three years old, and very handsome;
and this afternoon Love passed through
his ideal flesh, his lips.
Through his flesh that is so full of beauty
passed the erotic fever;
with no silly modesty about the nature of the pleasure . . .

ΤΟ 31 Π.Χ. ΣΤΗΝ ΑΛΕΞΑΝΔΡΕΙΑ

Ἀπ' τὴν μικρή του, στὰ περίχωρα πλησίον, κώμη,
καὶ σκονισμένος ἀπὸ τὸ ταξεῖδι ἀκόμη

ἔφθασεν ὁ πραγματευτής. Καὶ «Λίβανον!» και «Κόμμι!»
«Ἄριστον Ἔλαιον!» «Ἄρωμα γιὰ τὴν κόμη!»

στοὺς δρόμους διαλαλεῖ. Ἀλλ' ἡ μεγάλη ὀχλοβοή,
κ' ἡ μουσικές, κ' ἡ παρελάσεις ποῦ ἀφίνουν ν' ἀκουσθεῖ.

Τὸ πλῆθος τὸν σκουντᾶ, τὸν σέρνει, τὸν βροντᾶ.
Κι ὅταν πιὰ τέλεια σαστισμένος, Τί εἶναι ἡ τρέλλα αὐτή; ρωτᾶ,

ἕνας τοῦ ρίχνει κι αὐτουνοῦ τὴν γιγαντιαία ψευτιὰ
τοῦ παλατιοῦ—ποῦ στὴν Ἑλλάδα ὁ Ἀντώνιος νικᾶ.

Ο ΙΩΑΝΝΗΣ ΚΑΝΤΑΚΟΥΖΗΝΟΣ ΥΠΕΡΙΣΧΥΕΙ

Τοὺς κάμπους βλέπει ποῦ ἀκόμη ὁρίζει
μὲ τὸ σιτάρι, μὲ τὰ ζῶα, μὲ τὰ καρποφόρα
δένδρα. Καὶ πιὸ μακρυὰ τὸ σπίτι του τὸ πατρικό,
γεμάτο ροῦχα κ' ἔπιπλα πολύτιμα, κι ἀσημικό.

Θὰ τοῦ τὰ πάρουν—Ἰησοῦ Χριστέ!—θὰ τοῦ τὰ πάρουν τώρα.

Ἄραγε νὰ τὸν λυπηθεῖ ὁ Καντακουζηνὸς
ἂν πάει στὰ πόδια του νὰ πέσει. Λὲν πῶς εἶν' ἐπιεικής,
λίαν ἐπιεικής. Ἀλλ' οἱ περὶ αὐτόν; ἀλλ' ὁ στρατός;—
Ἤ, στὴν κυρία Εἰρήνη νὰ προσπέσει, νὰ κλαυθεῖ;

Κουτός! στὸ κόμμα νὰ μπλεχθεῖ τῆς Ἄννας—
ποῦ νὰ μὴν ἔσωνε νὰ τὴν στεφανωθεῖ
ὁ κὺρ Ἀνδρόνικος ποτέ. Εἴδαμε προκοπὴ
ἀπὸ τὸ φέρσιμό της, εἴδαμε ἀνθρωπιά;
Μὰ ὡς κ' οἱ Φράγκοι δὲν τὴν ἐκτιμοῦνε πιά.

IN ALEXANDRIA, 31 B.C.

From his little village near the outskirts
and still covered with the journey's dust,

arrived the peddler. 'Incense' and 'Gum!'
'Excellent Oil!' 'Perfume for the hair!'

he cries through the city streets. But amid the great hustle,
the music and the parades, how can he be heard?

The crowd jostles him, carries him along, jolts him violently
and when, in total bewilderment, he asks: 'What's all this
madness?'

someone hurls at him too the monstrous lie
of the palace—that Antony is victorious in Greece.

JOHN CANTACUZENUS PREVAILS

He looks upon the fields that he still calls his own,
with the wheat, the livestock, the fruit-bearing
trees. And far yonder, his paternal house,
full of clothes, expensive furniture and silverware.

They'll be taken from him—Jesus Christ!—they'll be taken from
him now.

Would Cantacuzenus take pity on him,
were he to throw himself at his feet? They say he is merciful,
quite merciful. But what about those around him? Or the army?
Or should he fall at Lady Irene's* feet, should he entreat her?

How stupid of him! To get mixed up with Anna's party—
damn the moment Lord Andronicus ever
married her! Did we benefit at all
from her behaviour, did we see any compassion?
Even the Franks do not respect her any more.

Γελοῖα τὰ σχέδια της, μωρὰ ἡ ἑτοιμασία της ὅλη.
Ἐνῶ φοβέριζαν τὸν κόσμο ἀπὸ τὴν Πόλι,
τοὺς ρήμαξεν ὁ Καντακουζηνός, τοὺς ρήμαξε ὁ κὺρ Γιάννης.

Καὶ ποῦ τὸ εἶχε σκοπὸ νὰ πάει μὲ τοῦ κὺρ Γιάννη
τὸ μέρος! Καὶ θὰ τὄκαμνε. Καὶ θἆταν τώρα εὐτυχισμένος,
μεγάλος ἄρχοντας πάντα, καὶ στεριωμένος,
ἂν ὁ δεσπότης δὲν τὸν ἔπειθε τὴν τελευταία στιγμή,
μὲ τὴν ἱερατική του ἐπιβολή,
μὲ τὲς ἀπὸ ἄκρου εἰς ἄκρον ἐσφαλμένες του πληροφορίες,
καὶ μὲ τὲς ὑποσχέσεις του, καὶ τὲς βλακεῖες.

ΤΕΜΕΘΟΣ, ΑΝΤΙΟΧΕΥΣ· 400 Μ.Χ.

Στίχοι τοῦ νέου Τεμέθου   τοῦ ἐρωτοπαθοῦς.
Μὲ τίτλον «Ὁ Ἐμονίδης» —   τοῦ Ἀντιόχου Ἐπιφανοῦς
ὁ προσφιλὴς ἑταῖρος·   ἕνας περικαλλὴς
νέος ἐκ Σαμοσάτων.   Μὰ ἂν ἔγιναν οἱ στίχοι
θερμοί, συγκινημένοι   εἶναι ποῦ ὁ Ἐμονίδης
(ἀπὸ τὴν παλαιὰν   ἐκείνην ἐποχή·
τὸ ἑκατὸν τριάντα ἑπτὰ   τῆς βασιλείας Ἑλλήνων! —
ἴσως καὶ λίγο πρὶν)   στὸ ποίημα ἐτέθη
ὡς ὄνομα ψιλόν·   εὐάρμοστον ἐν τούτοις.
Μιὰ ἀγάπη τοῦ Τεμέθου   τὸ ποίημα ἐκφράζει,
ὡραίαν κι ἀξίαν αὐτοῦ.   Ἐμεῖς οἱ μυημένοι
οἱ φίλοι του οἱ στενοί·   ἐμεῖς οἱ μυημένοι
γνωρίζουμε γιὰ ποιόνα   ἐγράφησαν οἱ στίχοι.
Οἱ ἀνίδεοι Ἀντιοχεῖς   διαβάζουν, Ἐμονίδην.

Ludicrous were her plans, idiotic all her arrangements.
While they were threatening everybody from Constantinople,
Cantacuzenus destroyed them; Lord John destroyed them.

And to think he had intended to take Lord John's
side! And he could have done so. And now he'd be happy,
always a great nobleman, and firmly established,
had the bishop not swayed him at the very last moment,
with his hieratic authority,
with his utterly erroneous information,
and with his promises, and his stupidities.

TEMETHOS, ANTIOCHIAN, A.D. 400

Verses composed by the young   Temethos, the lovelorn.
Entitled: 'Emonides'—   beloved companion
of Antiochus Epiphanes;   a divinely beautiful
youth from Samosata.*   Yet if the verses were composed
with ardour and emotion,   it is because Emonides
(from that bygone age,   the hundred-and-thirty-seventh
year in the dynastic   succession of the Greeks!*—
or maybe just before)   was put into the poem
as merely another name;   nevertheless well-suited.
The poem intimates   a certain love of Temethos,
worthy of him and handsome.   We the initiated,
his most intimate friends;   we the initiated
are well aware for whom   the verses were composed.
The clueless Antiochians   read only: Emonides.

ΑΠΟ ΥΑΛΙ ΧΡΩΜΑΤΙΣΤΟ

Πολὺ μὲ συγκινεῖ μιὰ λεπτομέρεια
στὴν στέψιν, ἐν Βλαχέρναις, τοῦ Ἰωάννη Καντακουζηνοῦ
καὶ τῆς Εἰρήνης Ἀνδρονίκου Ἀσάν.
Ὅπως δὲν εἶχαν παρὰ λίγους πολυτίμους λίθους
(τοῦ ταλαιπώρου κράτους μας ἦταν μεγάλ' ἡ πτώχεια)
φόρεσαν τεχνητούς. Ἕνα σωρὸ κομάτια ἀπὸ ὑαλί,
κόκκινα, πράσινα ἢ γαλάζια. Τίποτε
τὸ ταπεινὸν ἢ τὸ ἀναξιοπρεπὲς
δὲν ἔχουν κατ' ἐμὲ τὰ κοματάκια αὐτὰ
ἀπὸ ὑαλὶ χρωματιστό. Μοιάζουνε τουναντίον
σὰν μιὰ διαμαρτυρία θλιβερὴ
κατὰ τῆς ἄδικης κακομοιριᾶς τῶν στεφομένων.
Εἶναι τὰ σύμβολα τοῦ τὶ ἥρμοζε νὰ ἔχουν,
τοῦ τὶ ἐξ ἅπαντος ἦταν ὀρθὸν νὰ ἔχουν
στὴν στέψι των ἕνας Κὺρ Ἰωάννης Καντακουζηνός,
μιὰ Κυρία Εἰρήνη Ἀνδρονίκου Ἀσάν.

ΤΟ 25ον ΕΤΟΣ ΤΟΥ ΒΙΟΥ ΤΟΥ

Πηγαίνει στὴν ταβέρνα τακτικὰ
ποῦ εἶχανε γνωρισθεῖ τὸν περασμένο μῆνα.
Ρώτησε· μὰ δὲν ἤξεραν τίποτε νὰ τὸν ποῦν.
Ἀπὸ τὰ λόγια των, κατάλαβε πῶς εἶχε γνωρισθεῖ
μ' ἕνα ὅλως ἄγνωστο ὑποκείμενον·
μιὰ ἀπ' τὲς πολλὲς ἄγνωστες κ' ὕποπτες
νεανικὲς μορφὲς ποῦ ἀπ' ἐκεῖ περνοῦσαν.
Πηγαίνει ὅμως στὴν ταβέρνα τακτικά, τὴν νύχτα,
καὶ κάθεται καὶ βλέπει πρὸς τὴν εἴσοδο·
μέχρι κοπώσεως βλέπει πρὸς τὴν εἴσοδο.
Ἴσως νὰ μπεῖ. Ἀπόψ' ἴσως νἄρθεῖ.

Κοντὰ τρεῖς ἑβδομάδες ἔτσι κάμνει.
Ἀρρώστησεν ὁ νοῦς του ἀπὸ λαγνεία.
Στὸ στόμα του μείνανε τὰ φιλιά.

OF COLOURED GLASS

I'm deeply touched by a certain detail
in the coronation, at Blachernae, of John Cantacuzenus*
and Irene, daughter of Andronicus Asan.*
Since they possessed but a few precious stones
(so great was the poverty of our wretched State)
they put on false ones. A lot of pieces made of glass,
red, green, or blue. There is
nothing humble or undignified,
I believe, about those pieces
of coloured glass. On the contrary,
they seem to be a pitiful protest
against the unjust misery of those being crowned.
They're symbols of what it befitted them to have,
of what, by all means, was proper for them to have
at their coronation, a Lord such as John Cantacuzenus
and a Lady such as Irene, daughter of Andronicus Asan.

THE 25TH YEAR OF HIS LIFE

He visits regularly the tavern
where they had met each other the previous month.
He asked around; but they had nothing to tell him.
From what they said, he gathered that his friend
got to know a totally unknown individual,
one of several unknown and shady
young faces that came in and out of the place.
But he visits the tavern regularly at night,
and sits and gazes towards the doorway,
and gazes till he tires, towards the doorway.
His friend might come in. Tonight, he might come.

That's what he's been doing for almost three weeks.
His mind is suffering from lovesickness.
The kisses linger on his mouth.

Παθαίνεται ἀπ' τὸν διαρκῆ πόθον ἡ σάρκα του ὅλη.
Τοῦ σώματος ἐκείνου ἡ ἁφὴ εἶν' ἐπάνω του.
Θέλει τὴν ἕνωσι μαζύ του πάλι.

Νὰ μὴν προδίδεται, τὸ προσπαθεῖ ἐννοεῖται.
Μὰ κάποτε σχεδὸν ἀδιαφορεῖ.—
Ἐξ ἄλλου, σὲ τὶ ἐκτίθεται τὸ ξέρει,
τὸ πῆρε ἀπόφασι. Δὲν εἶν' ἀπίθανον ἡ ζωή του αὐτὴ
σὲ σκάνδαλον ὀλέθριο νὰ τὸν φέρει.

ΕΙΣ ΙΤΑΛΙΚΗΝ ΠΑΡΑΛΙΑΝ

Ὁ Κῆμος Μενεδώρου, Ἰταλιώτης νέος,
τὸν βίον του περνᾶ μέσα στὲς διασκεδάσεις·
ὡς συνειθίζουν τοῦτοι οἱ ἀπ' τὴν Μεγάλη Ἑλλάδα
μὲς στὰ πολλὰ τὰ πλούτη ἀναθρεμένοι νέοι.

Μὰ σήμερα εἶναι λίαν, παρὰ τὸ φυσικό του,
σύννους καὶ κατηφής. Κοντὰ στὴν παραλίαν,
μὲ ἄκραν μελαγχολίαν βλέπει ποῦ ἐκφορτώνουν
τὰ πλοῖα μὲ τὴν λείαν ἐκ τῆς Πελοποννήσου.

Λάφυρα ἑλληνικά· ἡ λεία τῆς Κορίνθου.

Ἄ σήμερα βεβαίως δὲν εἶναι θεμιτόν,
δὲν εἶναι δυνατὸν ὁ Ἰταλιώτης νέος
νἄχει γιὰ διασκεδάσεις καμιὰν ἐπιθυμίαν.

ΣΤΟ ΠΛΗΚΤΙΚΟ ΧΩΡΙΟ

Στὸ πληκτικὸ χωριὸ ποῦ ἐργάζεται—
ὑπάλληλος σ' ἕνα κατάστημα
ἐμπορικό· νεότατος—καὶ ποῦ ἀναμένει
ἀκόμη δυὸ τρεῖς μῆνες νὰ περάσουν,
ἀκόμη δυὸ τρεῖς μῆνες γιὰ νὰ λιγοστέψουν ἡ δουλειές,

All of his flesh aches from endless need.
That body's touch is still upon him.
He craves to be united with him again.

He tries not to betray himself, of course.
At times, though, he becomes almost indifferent.—
Anyway, he knows what he's exposed to;
he's resigned to it. Quite possibly this life of his
will lead him to a ruinous scandal.

ON AN ITALIAN SHORE

Kemos, son of Menedoros, a young Italiote Greek,
goes through his life amid amusements,
as these young men from Magna Graecia
raised in great wealth are so accustomed.

But on this day he is —against his very nature—
pensive and despondent. Nearby, upon the shore,
he looks in utter sadness as they are unloading
the vessels with the spoils from the Peloponnese.

Greek booty; the spoils of Corinth.

Alas, today, of course, it's not permissible;
it is not possible that the Italiote youth
should have any desire for entertainment.

IN THE DREARY VILLAGE

In the dreary village where he works—
assistant in a drapery store,
so very young a man—and where he awaits
two, three more months to go by,
two, three more months for business to slow down,

κ' ἔτσι νὰ μεταβεῖ στὴν πόλιν νὰ ριχθεῖ
στὴν κίνησι καὶ στὴν διασκέδασιν εὐθύς·
στὸ πληκτικὸ χωριὸ ὅπου ἀναμένει—
ἔπεσε στὸ κρεββάτι ἀπόψι ἐρωτοπαθής,
ὅλ' ἡ νεότης του στὸν σαρκικὸ πόθο ἀναμένη,
εἰς ἔντασιν ὡραίαν ὅλ' ἡ ὡραία νεότης του.
Καὶ μὲς στὸν ὕπνον ἡ ἡδονὴ προσῆλθε· μέσα
στὸν ὕπνο βλέπει κ' ἔχει τὴν μορφή, τὴν σάρκα ποὺ ἤθελε . . .

ΑΠΟΛΛΩΝΙΟΣ Ο ΤΥΑΝΕΥΣ ΕΝ ΡΟΔΩ

Γιὰ τὴν ἁρμόζουσα παίδευσι κι ἀγωγὴ
ὁ Ἀπολλώνιος ὁμιλοῦσε μ' ἕναν
νέον ποὺ ἔκτιζε πολυτελῆ
οἰκίαν ἐν Ρόδῳ. «Ἐγὼ δὲ ἐς ἱερὸν»
εἶπεν ὁ Τυανεὺς στὸ τέλος «παρελθὼν
πολλῷ ἂν ἥδιον ἐν αὐτῷ μικρῷ
ὄντι ἄγαλμα ἐλέφαντός τε καὶ χρυσοῦ
ἴδοιμι ἢ ἐν μεγάλῳ κεραμεοῦν τε καὶ φαῦλον.»

Τὸ «κεραμεοῦν» καὶ «φαῦλον»· τὸ σιχαμερό:
ποὺ κιόλας μερικοὺς (χωρὶς προπόνησι ἀρκετὴ)
ἀγυρτικῶς ἐξαπατᾶ. Τὸ κεραμεοῦν καὶ φαῦλον.

Η ΑΡΡΩΣΤΙΑ ΤΟΥ ΚΛΕΙΤΟΥ

Ὁ Κλεῖτος, ἕνα συμπαθητικὸ
παιδί, περίπου εἴκοσι τριῶ ἐτῶν—
μὲ ἀρίστην ἀγωγή, μὲ σπάνια ἑλληνομάθεια—
εἶν' ἄρρωστος βαρειά. Τὸν ηὗρε ὁ πυρετὸς
ποὺ φέτος θέρισε στὴν Ἀλεξάνδρεια.

Τὸν ηὗρε ὁ πυρετὸς ἐξαντλημένο κιόλας ἠθικῶς
ἀπ' τὸν καϋμὸ ποὺ ὁ ἑταῖρος του, ἕνας νέος ἠθοποιός,
ἔπαυσε νὰ τὸν ἀγαπᾶ καὶ νὰ τὸν θέλει.

*

so he can travel to the city and fling himself
at once into all the activities and amusements;
in the dreary village where he awaits—
he fell in bed tonight longing for love,
all of his youth inflamed by carnal need,
all of his lovely youth in exquisite fervour.
And in his sleep the sensual pleasure came; he sees,
and he possesses, in his sleep, the face, the flesh he craved . . .

APOLLONIUS OF TYANA IN RHODES

Apollonius was discussing
suitable education and upbringing
with a young man who was constructing
a luxurious residence in Rhodes. 'When I come
to a temple,' concluded the Tyanian,
'be it a small one, I'd rather see in it
a statue of gold and ivory, than see
in a big temple, one of clay and worthless.'

The 'one of clay' and 'worthless'; the vile one:
that still insidiously beguiles some (not adequately trained)
people. The 'one of clay' and 'worthless'.

KLEITOS' ILLNESS

Kleitos, a likeable young man,
about twenty-three years old—
with excellent upbringing and rare Greek learning—
is gravely ill. He caught the fever
that swept through Alexandria this year.

The fever found him also morally exhausted
from pining for his companion, a young actor,
who ceased to love and want him.

*

Εἶν' ἄρρωστος βαρειά, καὶ τρέμουν οἱ γονεῖς του.

Καὶ μιὰ γρηὰ ὑπηρέτρια ποῦ τὸν μεγάλωσε,
τρέμει κι αὐτὴ γιὰ τὴν ζωὴ τοῦ Κλείτου.
Μὲς στὴν δεινὴν ἀνησυχία της
στὸν νοῦ της ἔρχεται ἕνα εἴδωλο
ποῦ λάτρευε μικρή, πρὶν μπεῖ αὐτοῦ, ὑπηρέτρια,
σὲ σπίτι Χριστιανῶν ἐπιφανῶν, καὶ χριστιανέψει.
Παίρνει κρυφὰ κάτι πλακούντια, καὶ κρασί, καὶ μέλι.
Τὰ πάει στὸ εἴδωλο μπροστά. Ὅσα θυμᾶται μέλη
τῆς ἱκεσίας ψάλλει· ἄκρες, μέσες. Ἡ κουτὴ
δὲν νοιώθει ποῦ τὸν μαῦρον δαίμονα λίγο τὸν μέλει
ἂν γιάνει ἢ ἂν δὲν γιάνει ἕνας Χριστιανός.

ΕΝ ΔΗΜΩι ΤΗΣ ΜΙΚΡΑΣ ΑΣΙΑΣ

Ἡ εἰδήσεις γιὰ τὴν ἔκβασι τῆς ναυμαχίας, στὸ Ἄκτιον,
ἦσαν βεβαίως ἀπροσδόκητες.
Ἀλλὰ δὲν εἶναι ἀνάγκη νὰ συντάξουμε νέον ἔγγραφον.
Τ' ὄνομα μόνον ν' ἀλλαχθεῖ. Ἀντίς, ἐκεῖ
στὲς τελευταῖες γραμμές, «Λυτρώσας τοὺς Ρωμαίους
ἀπ' τὸν ὀλέθριον Ὀκτάβιον,
τὸν δίκην παρωδίας Καίσαρα,»
τώρα θὰ βάλουμε «Λυτρώσας τοὺς Ρωμαίους
ἀπ' τὸν ὀλέθριον Ἀντώνιον».
Ὅλο τὸ κείμενον ταιριάζει ὡραῖα.

«Στὸν νικητήν, τὸν ἐνδοξότατον,
τὸν ἐν παντὶ πολεμικῷ ἔργῳ ἀνυπέρβλητον,
τὸν θαυμαστὸν ἐπὶ μεγαλουργίᾳ πολιτικῇ,
ὑπὲρ τοῦ ὁποίου ἐνθέρμως εὔχονταν ὁ δῆμος
τὴν ἐπικράτησι τοῦ Ἀντωνίου»
ἐδῶ, ὅπως εἴπαμεν, ἡ ἀλλαγή: «τοῦ Καίσαρος
ὡς δῶρον τοῦ Διὸς κάλλιστον θεωρῶν—
στὸν κραταιὸ προστάτη τῶν Ἑλλήνων,
τὸν ἔθη ἑλληνικὰ εὐμενῶς γεραίροντα,
τὸν προσφιλῆ ἐν πάσῃ χώρᾳ ἑλληνικῇ,

He's gravely ill and his parents are trembling.

And an old servant woman who had raised him
is trembling too for the life of Kleitos.
Deep in her terrible distress,
an idol comes to her mind, which she worshipped
as a girl, before she entered there, a servant
in the home of prominent Christians, and converted.
She secretly takes some unleavened cakes, wine and honey.
She puts them before the idol, intoning those chants
of supplication she still remembers: bits and pieces. The fool!
She doesn't realize that the dark demon couldn't care less
whether a Christian were to get well or not.

IN A TOWNSHIP OF ASIA MINOR

The news about the outcome of the naval battle at Actium*
was to be sure unexpected.
But there is no need to draft a new document.
Only the name needs changing. There,
in the last lines, instead of 'Having delivered
the Romans from that disastrous Octavian,
that travesty of a Caesar',
now we can insert 'Having delivered the Romans
from that disastrous Antony'.
The entire text fits quite nicely.

'To the victor, the most glorious,
the unsurpassed in every military endeavour,
admirable for his great political achievement,
on whose behalf the Demos fervently
prayed for victory: to Antony.'
Here, as we said, comes the substitution: 'to Caesar—
considering his victory the finest gift from Zeus—
the mighty protector of the Greeks,
who graciously pays honour to Greek customs;
beloved in every Hellenic land;

τὸν λίαν ἐνδεδειγμένον γιὰ ἔπαινο περιφανῆ,
καὶ γιὰ ἐξιστόρησι τῶν πράξεών του ἐκτενῆ
ἐν λόγῳ ἑλληνικῷ κ' ἐμμέτρῳ καὶ πεζῷ·
ἐν λόγῳ ἑλληνικῷ ποῦ εἶν' ὁ φορεὺς τῆς φήμης,»
καὶ τὰ λοιπά, καὶ τὰ λοιπά. Λαμπρὰ ταιριάζουν ὅλα.

ΙΕΡΕΥΣ ΤΟΥ ΣΕΡΑΠΙΟΥ

Τὸν γέροντα καλὸν πατέρα μου,
τὸν ἀγαπῶντα με τὸ ἴδιο πάντα·
τὸν γέροντα καλὸν πατέρα μου θρηνῶ
ποῦ πέθανε προχθές, ὀλίγο πρὶν χαράξει.

Ἰησοῦ Χριστέ, τὰ παραγγέλματα
τῆς ἱεροτάτης ἐκκλησίας σου νὰ τηρῶ
εἰς κάθε πρᾶξιν μου, εἰς κάθε λόγον,
εἰς κάθε σκέψι εἶν' ἡ προσπάθεια μου
ἡ καθημερινή. Κι ὅσους σὲ ἀρνοῦνται
τοὺς ἀποστρέφομαι.—Ἀλλὰ τώρα θρηνῶ·
ὀδύρομαι, Χριστέ, γιὰ τὸν πατέρα μου
μ' ὅλο ποῦ ἦτανε—φρικτὸν εἰπεῖν—
στὸ ἐπικατάρατον Σεράπιον ἱερεύς.

ΜΕΣΑ ΣΤΑ ΚΑΠΗΛΕΙΑ—

Μέσα στὰ καπηλειὰ   καὶ τὰ χαμαιτυπεῖα
τῆς Βηρυτοῦ κυλιέμαι.   Δὲν ἤθελα νὰ μένω
στὴν Ἀλεξάνδρεια ἐγώ.   Μ' ἄφισεν ὁ Ταμίδης·
κ' ἐπῆγε μὲ τοῦ Ἐπάρχου   τὸν υἱὸ γιὰ ν' ἀποκτήσει
μιὰ ἔπαυλι στὸν Νεῖλο,   ἕνα μέγαρον στὴν πόλιν.
Δὲν ἔκανε νὰ μένω   στὴν Ἀλεξάνδρεια ἐγώ.—
Μέσα στὰ καπηλειὰ   καὶ τὰ χαμαιτυπεῖα
τῆς Βηρυτοῦ κυλιέμαι.   Μὲς σ' εὐτελῆ κραιπάλη
διάγω ποταπῶς.   Τὸ μόνο ποῦ μὲ σώζει
σὰν ἐμορφιὰ διαρκής,   σὰν ἄρωμα ποῦ ἐπάνω

well-deserving of exalted praise
and a detailed account of his exploits,
in the Greek language, both in verse and prose;
in the *Greek language*, which is the vehicle of fame,'
and so on and so on. Everything fits splendidly.

A PRIEST OF THE SERAPEUM

My kind old father
who always loved me the same;
my kind old father I mourn,
who died two days ago, just before dawn.

Jesus Christ, the ordinances
of your most holy church I uphold
in everything I do, in every word,
in every thought it is my daily
endeavour. And I abhor
all those who deny you.—But now I mourn;
I lament, O Christ, for my father
though he was—dreadful to say—
a priest at the accursed Serapeum.

IN THE WINE TAVERNS—

I wallow in Beirut's   wine taverns and dens
of wantonness.   I didn't want to stay
in Alexandria.   Tamides has left me;
and followed the Eparch's   son so he'd acquire
a villa on the Nile,   a mansion in the city.
It was not right for me   to stay in Alexandria.—
I wallow in Beirut's   wine taverns and dens
of wantonness. In cheap   debauchery, I lead
a sordid life. Just one   thing comes to my rescue,
like a lasting grace,   like a fragrance that lingers

στὴν σάρκα μου ἔχει μείνει, εἶναι ποῦ εἶχα δυὸ χρόνια
δικό μου τὸν Ταμίδη, τὸν πιὸ ἐξαίσιο νέο,
δικό μου ὄχι γιὰ σπίτι ἢ γιὰ ἔπαυλι στὸν Νεῖλο.

ΜΕΓΑΛΗ ΣΥΝΟΔΕΙΑ ΕΞ ΙΕΡΕΩΝ ΚΑΙ ΛΑΪΚΩΝ

Ἐξ ἱερέων καὶ λαϊκῶν μιὰ συνοδεία,
ἀντιπροσωπευμένα πάντα τὰ ἐπαγγέλματα,
διέρχεται ὁδούς, πλατέες, καὶ πύλες
τῆς περιωνύμου πόλεως Ἀντιοχείας.
Στῆς ἐπιβλητικῆς, μεγάλης συνοδείας τὴν ἀρχὴ
ὡραῖος, λευκοντυμένος ἔφηβος βαστᾶ
μὲ ἀνυψωμένα χέρια τὸν Σταυρόν,
τὴν δύναμιν καὶ τὴν ἐλπίδα μας, τὸν ἅγιον Σταυρόν.
Οἱ ἐθνικοί, οἱ πρὶν τοσοῦτον ὑπερφίαλοι,
συνεσταλμένοι τώρα καὶ δειλοὶ μὲ βίαν
ἀπομακρύνονται ἀπὸ τὴν συνοδείαν.
Μακρὰν ἡμῶν, μακρὰν ἡμῶν νὰ μένουν πάντα
(ὅσο τὴν πλάνη τους δὲν ἀπαρνοῦνται). Προχωρεῖ
ὁ ἅγιος Σταυρός. Εἰς κάθε συνοικίαν
ὅπου ἐν θεοσεβείᾳ ζοῦν οἱ Χριστιανοὶ
φέρει παρηγορίαν καὶ χαρά:
βγαίνουν, οἱ εὐλαβεῖς, στὲς πόρτες τῶν σπιτιῶν τους
καὶ πλήρεις ἀγαλλιάσεως τὸν προσκυνοῦν—
τὴν δύναμιν, τὴν σωτηρίαν τῆς οἰκουμένης, τὸν Σταυρόν.—

Εἶνε μιὰ ἐτήσια ἑορτὴ Χριστιανική.
Μὰ σήμερα τελεῖται, ἰδού, πιὸ ἐπιφανῶς.
Λυτρώθηκε τὸ κράτος ἐπὶ τέλους.
Ὁ μιαρότατος, ὁ ἀποτρόπαιος
Ἰουλιανὸς δὲν βασιλεύει πιά.

Ὑπὲρ τοῦ εὐσεβεστάτου Ἰοβιανοῦ εὐχηθῶμεν.

redolent on my skin: it is that for two years
Tamides was all mine, the most exquisite youth,
all mine not for a house or a villa on the Nile.

A GREAT PROCESSION OF PRIESTS AND LAYMEN

A procession of priests and laymen,
representing professions from every walk of life,
passes through the streets, squares, and gates
of the renowned city of Antioch.
At the head of this great, imposing procession
a handsome, white-clad young man
carries with uplifted arms the Cross:
our strength and our hope, the Holy Cross.
The pagans, so arrogant a while ago,
cowed now and timorous, hurriedly
walk away from the procession.
Far from us, may they always stay far from us
(as long as they do not renounce their fallacy).
The Holy Cross moves on. In every district
where Christians live in piety,
it brings comfort and joy:
the pious come out, at the doorways of their homes,
and filled with elation, they kneel to worship—
the strength and the salvation of the world: the Cross.—

This is an annual religious festival of the Christians.
Today, though, behold, performed more prominently.
At last, the State has been delivered.
The most sacrilegious, the abhorrent
Julian reigns no more.

For the most pious Jovian, let us pray.

ΣΟΦΙΣΤΗΣ ΑΠΕΡΧΟΜΕΝΟΣ ΕΚ ΣΥΡΙΑΣ

Δόκιμε σοφιστὴ   ποῦ ἀπέρχεσαι ἐκ Συρίας
καὶ περὶ Ἀντιοχείας   σκοπεύεις νὰ συγγράψεις,
ἐν τῷ ἔργῳ σου τὸν Μέβη   ἀξίζει ν' ἀναφέρεις.
Τὸν φημισμένο Μέβη   ποῦ ἀναντιρρήτως εἶναι
ὁ νέος ὁ πιὸ εὐειδής,   κι ὁ πιὸ ἀγαπηθεὶς
σ' ὅλην τὴν Ἀντιόχεια.   Κανέν' ἀπὸ τοὺς ἄλλους
τοῦ ἰδίου βίου νέους,   κανένα δὲν πληρώνουν
τόσο ἀκριβὰ ὡς αὐτόν.   Γιὰ νἄχουνε τὸν Μέβη
μονάχα δυό, τρεῖς μέρες   πολὺ συχνὰ τὸν δείνουν
ὡς ἑκατὸ στατῆρας.—   Εἶπα, Στὴν Ἀντιόχεια·
μὰ καὶ στὴν Ἀλεξάνδρεια,   μὰ καὶ στὴν Ρώμη ἀκόμη,
δὲν βρίσκετ' ἕνας νέος   ἐράσμιος σὰν τὸν Μέβη.

Ο ΙΟΥΛΙΑΝΟΣ ΚΑΙ ΟΙ ΑΝΤΙΟΧΕΙΣ

«Τὸ Χῖ, φασίν, οὐδὲν ἠδίκησε τὴν πόλιν οὐδὲ τὸ Κάππα.
«. . . Τυχόντες δ' ἡμεῖς ἐξηγητῶν . . . ἐδιδάχθημεν
«ἀρχὰς ὀνομάτων εἶναι τὰ γράμματα, δηλοῦν δ' ἐθέλειν
«τὸ μὲν Χριστόν, τὸ δὲ Κωνστάντιον.»

Ἰουλιανοῦ Μισοπώγων.

Ἤτανε δυνατὸν ποτὲ ν' ἀπαρνηθοῦν
τὴν ἔμορφή τους διαβίωσι· τὴν ποικιλία
τῶν καθημερινῶν τους διασκεδάσεων· τὸ λαμπρό τους
θέατρον ὅπου μιὰ ἕνωσις ἐγένονταν τῆς Τέχνης
μὲ τὲς ἐρωτικὲς τῆς σάρκας τάσεις!

Ἀνήθικοι μέχρι τινὸς—καὶ πιθανὸν μέχρι πολλοῦ—
ἦσαν. Ἀλλ' εἶχαν τὴν ἱκανοποίησι ποῦ ὁ βίος τους
ἦταν ὁ περιλάλητος βίος τῆς Ἀντιοχείας,
ὁ ἐνήδονος, ὁ ἀπόλυτα καλαίσθητος.

Νὰ τ' ἀρνηθοῦν αὐτά, γιὰ νὰ προσέξουν κιόλας τί;

*

SOPHIST LEAVING SYRIA

Distinguished sophist, as you depart from Syria
and want to write about the city of Antioch,
Mebes in your work is well worth a mention;
the celebrated Mebes, who is without doubt
the most beautiful youth, as well as the most cherished
in all of Antioch. Not one of the other youths
that lead this kind of life, not one of them gets paid
as highly as he does. In order to have Mebes
for just two or three days, quite often they offer him
up to a hundred staters.— Did I say in Antioch?
But also in Alexandria, and even so in Rome,
no young man can be found as lovable as Mebes.

JULIAN AND THE ANTIOCHIANS

They maintain that the CHI never harmed their city and neither did KAPPA. We came across interpreters and found out that these represent initial letters of names, the former Christ and the latter Konstantios.

Julian, *Misopogon*

Was it ever possible that they should relinquish
their beautiful way of life; the variety
of their daily amusements; their splendid
theatre, where a union took place between Art
and the erotic inclinations of the flesh!

Immoral to a point—perhaps even to excess—indeed
they were. But they relished the satisfaction that theirs
was the *much talked about* life of Antioch,
so full of pleasures, so perfectly elegant in taste.

Deny all this and devote their attention to what?

*

Τὲς περὶ τῶν ψευδῶν θεῶν ἀερολογίες του,
τὲς ἀνιαρὲς περιαυτολογίες·
τὴν παιδαριώδη του θεατροφοβία·
τὴν ἄχαρι σεμνοτυφία του· τὰ γελοῖα του γένεια.

Ἆ βέβαια προτιμούσανε τὸ Χῖ,
ἆ βέβαια προτιμούσανε τὸ Κάππα· ἑκατὸ φορές.

ΑΝΝΑ ΔΑΛΑΣΣΗΝΗ

Εἰς τὸ χρυσόβουλλον ποῦ ἔβγαλ' ὁ Ἀλέξιος Κομνηνὸς
γιὰ νὰ τιμήσει τὴν μητέρα του ἐπιφανῶς,
τὴν λίαν νοήμονα Κυρίαν Ἄννα Δαλασσηνὴ—
τὴν ἀξιόλογη στὰ ἔργα της, στὰ ἤθη—
ὑπάρχουν διάφορα ἐγκωμιαστικά:
ἐδῶ ἂς μεταφέρουμε ἀπὸ αὐτὰ
μιὰ φράσιν ἔμορφην, εὐγενικὴ
«Οὐ τὸ ἐμὸν ἢ τὸ σόν, τὸ ψυχρὸν τοῦτο ῥῆμα, ἐρρήθη».

ΜΕΡΕΣ ΤΟΥ 1896

Ἐξευτελίσθη πλήρως.   Μιὰ ἐρωτικὴ ῥοπή του
λίαν ἀπαγορευμένη   καὶ περιφρονημένη
(ἔμφυτη μολοντοῦτο)   ὑπῆρξεν ἡ αἰτία:
ἦταν ἡ κοινωνία   σεμνότυφη πολύ.
Ἔχασε βαθμηδὸν   τὸ λιγοστό του χρῆμα·
κατόπι τὴ σειρά,   καὶ τὴν ὑπόληψί του.
Πλησίαζε τὰ τριάντα   χωρὶς ποτὲ ἕναν χρόνο
νὰ βγάλει σὲ δουλειά,   τουλάχιστον γνωστή.
Ἐνίοτε τὰ ἔξοδά του   τὰ κέρδιζεν ἀπὸ
μεσολαβήσεις ποῦ   θεωροῦνται ντροπιασμένες.
Κατήντησ' ἕνας τύπος   ποῦ ἂν σ' ἔβλεπαν μαζύ του
συχνά, ἦταν πιθανὸν   μεγάλως νὰ ἐκτεθεῖς.

*

To his hot-air utterances about false gods,
to his tedious self-glorification;
his childish phobia of the theatre;
his awkward prudery; his ridiculous beard.

Well, of course they preferred the CHI,
of course, they preferred the KAPPA; a hundred times over.

ANNA DALASSENE

In the chrysobull issued by Alexius Comnenus,
to honour his mother eminently,
that highly intelligent Lady Anna Dalassene—
noteworthy for her deeds and her morality—
there are several expressions of praise:
let us relate one of them here,
a nice and courteous phrase:
'"mine" or "thine": those cold words she never uttered.'

DAYS OF 1896

He was disgraced completely.   A sexual inclination
of his, strongly forbidden,   and much despised
(nevertheless innate)   happened to be the reason:
society was indeed   prudish to the extreme.
He gradually lost   his meagre capital
and then his social standing,   and then his reputation.
He was nearing thirty   without having lasted
a year in any job,   at least an honest one.
From time to time he earned   his living by acting as
a go-between in deals   which are considered shameful.
He ended up a type   that were you seen with him
too often, you'd no doubt be   most greatly compromised.

*

Ἀλλ' ὄχι μόνον τοῦτα.   Δὲν θἄτανε σωστό.
Ἀξίζει παραπάνω   τῆς ἐμορφιᾶς του ἡ μνήμη.
Μιὰ ἄποψις ἄλλη ὑπάρχει   ποῦ ἂν ἰδωθεῖ ἀπὸ αὐτὴν
φαντάζει, συμπαθής·   φαντάζει, ἁπλὸ καὶ γνήσιο
τοῦ ἔρωτος παιδί,   ποῦ ἄνω ἀπ' τὴν τιμή,
καὶ τὴν ὑπόληψί του   ἔθεσε ἀνεξετάστως
τῆς καθαρῆς σαρκός του   τὴν καθαρὴ ἡδονή.

Ἀπ' τὴν ὑπόληψί του;   Μὰ ἡ κοινωνία ποῦ ἦταν
σεμνότυφη πολὺ   συσχέτιζε κουτά.

ΔΥΟ ΝΕΟΙ, 23 ΕΩΣ 24 ΕΤΩΝ

Ἀπ' τὲς δεκάμισυ ἤτανε στὸ καφενεῖον,
καὶ τὸν περίμενε σὲ λίγο νὰ φανεῖ.
Πῆγαν μεσάνυχτα—καὶ τὸν περίμενεν ἀκόμη.
Πῆγεν ἡ ὥρα μιάμισυ· εἶχε ἀδειάσει
τὸ καφενεῖον ὁλοτελῶς σχεδόν.
Βαρέθηκεν ἐφημερίδες νὰ διαβάζει
μηχανικῶς. Ἀπ' τὰ ἔρημα, τὰ τρία σελίνια του
ἔμεινε μόνον ἕνα: τόση ὥρα ποῦ περίμενε
ξόδιασε τ' ἄλλα σὲ καφέδες καὶ κονιάκ.
Κάπνισεν ὅλα του τὰ σιγαρέτα.
Τὸν ἐξαντλοῦσε ἡ τόση ἀναμονή. Γιατὶ
κιόλας μονάχος ὅπως ἦταν γιὰ ὧρες, ἄρχισαν
νὰ τὸν καταλαμβάνουν σκέψεις ὀχληρὲς
τῆς παραστρατημένης του ζωῆς.

Μὰ σὰν εἶδε τὸν φίλο του νὰ μπαίνει—εὐθὺς
ἡ κούρασις, ἡ ἀνία, ἡ σκέψεις φύγανε.

Ὁ φίλος του ἔφερε μιὰ ἀνέλπιστη εἴδησι.
Εἶχε κερδίσει στὸ χαρτοπαικτεῖον ἑξήντα λίρες.

Τὰ ἔμορφά τους πρόσωπα, τὰ ἐξαίσιά τους νειάτα,
ἡ αἰσθητικὴ ἀγάπη ποῦ εἶχαν μεταξύ τους,

But this, though, is not everything; else it would not be fair.
The memory of his beauty indeed is worth much more.
There is a different aspect; seen from that point of view,
he would appear as likeable; he would appear a simple
and genuine child of Eros, who without hesitation,
has placed above his honour, above his reputation,
the pure sensual pleasure of his pure sensual flesh.

Above his reputation? Well, society that was
prudish to the extreme, made stupid correlations.

TWO YOUNG MEN, 23 TO 24 YEARS OLD

He'd been in the café since ten-thirty
waiting for him to show up soon.
Midnight came and he was waiting still.
It was nearing one-thirty; the café
had emptied almost completely.
He got tired of reading newspapers
absentmindedly. Of his paltry three shillings,
a single one was left; whilst waiting all this time,
he'd spent the rest on coffee and cognac.
He smoked all his cigarettes.
He was exhausted by such lengthy anticipation. Because,
as he was alone for hours, he began
to be seized by disturbing thoughts
about his life, which had gone astray.

But as soon as he saw his friend come in—
fatigue, boredom, and ill thoughts vanished at once.

His friend brought unexpected news.
He had won sixty pounds in a card game.

Their lovely faces, their exquisite youth,
the sensitive affection they held for each other

δροσίσθηκαν, ζωντάνεψαν, τονώθηκαν
ἀπ' τὲς ἑξήντα λίρες τοῦ χαρτοπαικτείου.

Κι ὅλο χαρὰ καὶ δύναμις, αἴσθημα κι ὡραιότης
πῆγαν—ὄχι στὰ σπίτια τῶν τιμίων οἰκογενειῶν τους
(ὅπου, ἄλλωστε, μήτε τοὺς θέλαν πιά):
σ' ἕνα γνωστό τους, καὶ λίαν εἰδικό,
σπίτι τῆς διαφθορᾶς πήγανε καὶ ζητῆσαν
δωμάτιον ὕπνου, κι ἀκριβὰ πιοτά, καὶ ξαναήπιαν.

Καὶ σὰν σωθῆκαν τ' ἀκριβὰ πιοτά,
καὶ σὰν πλησίαζε πιὰ ἡ ὥρα τέσσερες,
στὸν ἔρωτα δοθῆκαν εὐτυχεῖς.

ΠΑΛΑΙΟΘΕΝ ΕΛΛΗΝΙΣ

Καυχιέται ἡ Ἀντιόχεια   γιὰ τὰ λαμπρά της κτίρια,
καὶ τοὺς ὡραίους της δρόμους·   γιὰ τὴν περὶ αὐτὴν
θαυμάσιαν ἐξοχήν,   καὶ γιὰ τὸ μέγα πλῆθος
τῶν ἐν αὐτῇ κατοίκων.   Καυχιέται ποῦ εἶν' ἡ ἕδρα
ἐνδόξων βασιλέων·   καὶ γιὰ τοὺς καλλιτέχνας
καὶ τοὺς σοφοὺς ποῦ ἔχει,   καὶ γιὰ τοὺς βαθυπλούτους
καὶ γνωστικοὺς ἐμπόρους.   Μὰ πιὸ πολὺ ἀσυγκρίτως
ἀπ' ὅλα, ἡ Ἀντιόχεια   καυχιέται ποῦ εἶναι πόλις
παλαιόθεν ἑλληνίς·   τοῦ Ἄργους συγγενής:
ἀπ' τὴν Ἰώνη ποῦ   ἱδρύθη ὑπὸ Ἀργείων
ἀποίκων πρὸς τιμὴν   τῆς κόρης τοῦ Ἰνάχου.

were refreshed, rejuvenated, invigorated
by the sixty pounds of the card game.

And full of joy and vigour, feeling and loveliness,
they went—not to the homes of their righteous families
(where anyway, they were not wanted any more):
they went to a familiar and quite particular
house of vice, they asked for a bedroom
and for expensive drinks, and drank again.

And once they'd run out of expensive drinks,
and since, by then, it was nearing four o'clock,
they abandoned themselves blissfully to love.

GREEK SINCE ANCIENT TIMES

Antioch* prides herself   on her splendid edifices
and well-paved streets;   her wonderful
surrounding countryside   and the great host
of her inhabitants,   she prides herself on being
the seat of glorious kings;   as well as on her artists
and her wise men, and   on her fabulously wealthy
and prudent merchants.   But well above all else
Antioch prides herself   on being a Greek city
since days of old;   a relative of Argos
through Ione, which   was founded by Argive
settlers, in honour of   the daughter of Inachus.*

ΜΕΡΕΣ ΤΟΥ 1901

Τοῦτο εἰς αὐτὸν ὑπῆρχε τὸ ξεχωριστό,
ποῦ μέσα σ' ὅλην του τὴν ἔκλυσι
καὶ τὴν πολλήν του πεῖραν ἔρωτος,
παρ' ὅλην τὴν συνειθισμένη του
στάσεως καὶ ἡλικίας ἐναρμόνισιν,
ἐτύχαιναν στιγμὲς — πλὴν βέβαια
σπανιότατες — ποῦ τὴν ἐντύπωσιν
ἔδιδε σάρκας σχεδὸν ἄθικτης.

Τῶν εἴκοσι ἐννιά του χρόνων ἡ ἐμορφιά,
ἡ τόσο ἀπὸ τὴν ἡδονὴ δοκιμασμένη,
ἦταν στιγμὲς ποῦ θύμιζε παράδοξα
ἔφηβο ποῦ — κάπως ἀδέξια — στὴν ἀγάπη
πρώτη φορὰ τὸ ἁγνό του σῶμα παραδίδει.

ΟΥΚ ΕΓΝΩΣ

Γιὰ τὲς θρησκευτικές μας δοξασίες —
ὁ κοῦφος Ἰουλιανὸς εἶπεν «Ἀνέγνων, ἔγνων,
κατέγνων». Τάχατες μᾶς ἐκμηδένισε
μὲ τὸ «κατέγνων» του, ὁ γελοιωδέστατος.

Τέτοιες ξυπνάδες ὅμως πέρασι δὲν ἔχουνε σ' ἐμᾶς
τοὺς Χριστιανούς. «Ἀνέγνως, ἀλλ' οὐκ ἔγνως· εἰ γὰρ ἔγνως,
οὐκ ἂν κατέγνως» ἀπαντήσαμεν ἀμέσως.

DAYS OF 1901

This is what was exceptional about him:
that in all his wantonness
and extensive sexual experience,
and in spite of the fact that he was wont
to reconcile harmoniously attitude to age,
there were instances—quite rare,
to be sure—when he conveyed
the impression of an almost untarnished body.

The beauty of his twenty-nine years,
so tested by sensual pleasure,
at times, strange to say, brought to mind
a young man who—rather awkwardly—surrenders
his chaste body to love for the first time.

YOU DIDN'T UNDERSTAND

Regarding our religious doctrines—
the vacuous Julian stated: 'I read, I understood,
I condemned.' As though he wiped us out
with his 'I condemned', that most ludicrous of men.

Such witticisms cannot fool us Christians.
'You read, but didn't understand; had you understood,
you wouldn't have condemned', we replied immediately.

ΕΝΑΣ ΝΕΟΣ, ΤΗΣ ΤΕΧΝΗΣ ΤΟΥ ΛΟΓΟΥ — ΣΤΟ 24ον ΕΤΟΣ ΤΟΥ

Ὅπως μπορεῖς πιὰ δούλεψε, μυαλό.—
Τὸν φθείρει αὐτὸν μιὰ ἀπόλαυσις μισή.
Εἶναι σὲ μιὰ κατάστασι ἐκνευριστική.
Φιλεῖ τὸ πρόσωπο τὸ ἀγαπημένο κάθε μέρα,
τὰ χέρια του εἶναι πάνω στὰ πιὸ ἐξαίσια μέλη.
Ποτέ του δὲν ἀγάπησε μὲ τόσο μέγα
πάθος. Μὰ λείπει ἡ ὡραία πραγμάτωσις
τοῦ ἔρωτος· λείπει ἡ πραγμάτωσις
ποῦ πρέπει νἆναι κι ἀπ' τοὺς δυὸ μ' ἔντασιν ἐπιθυμητή.

(Δὲν εἶν' ὁμοίως δοσμένοι στὴν ἀνώμαλη ἡδονὴ κ' οἱ δυό.
Μονάχ' αὐτὸν κυρίεψε ἀπολύτως).

Καὶ φθείρεται, καὶ νεύριασε ἐντελῶς.
Ἐξ ἄλλου εἶναι κι ἄεργος· κι αὐτὸ πολὺ συντείνει.
Κάτι μικρὰ χρηματικὰ ποσὰ
μὲ δυσκολία δανείζεται (σχεδὸν
τὰ ζητιανεύει κάποτε) καὶ ψευτοσυντηρεῖται.
Φιλεῖ τὰ λατρεμένα χείλη· πάνω
στὸ ἐξαίσιο σῶμα—ποῦ ὅμως τώρα νοιώθει
πῶς στέργει μόνον—ἡδονίζεται.
Κ' ἔπειτα πίνει καὶ καπνίζει· πίνει καὶ καπνίζει·
καὶ σέρνεται στὰ καφενεῖα ὁλημερίς,
σέρνει μὲ ἀνία τῆς ἐμορφιᾶς του τὸ μαράζι.—
Ὅπως μπορεῖς πιὰ δούλεψε, μυαλό.

ΕΝ ΣΠΑΡΤΗ

Δὲν ἤξερεν ὁ βασιλεὺς Κλεομένης, δὲν τολμοῦσε—
δὲν ἤξερε ἕναν τέτοιον λόγο πῶς νὰ πεῖ
πρὸς τὴν μητέρα του: ὅτι ἀπαιτοῦσε ὁ Πτολεμαῖος
γιὰ ἐγγύησιν τῆς συμφωνίας των ν' ἀποσταλεῖ κι αὐτὴ
εἰς Αἴγυπτον καὶ νὰ φυλάττεται·

A YOUNG MAN OF LETTERS— IN HIS 24TH YEAR

Mind, henceforth work as best you can.—
He is consumed by half-fulfilled erotic pleasure.
He is in a nerve-racked state.
He kisses the beloved face each day,
his hands caress the most exquisite limbs.
Never has he been in love with such fervent
passion. But the wondrous consummation of love
is missing; that consummation is missing
which ought to be desired intensely by both of them.

(They are not both equally given to aberrant pleasure.
Only he has been obsessed by it absolutely.)

So he wears himself down and he's completely unnerved.
Moreover he is jobless, and this makes it worse.
He borrows with difficulty
some petty sums of money (at times
he almost begs for them) and ekes out a living.
He kisses the beloved lips; upon
that exquisite body—which though, he senses,
is only just consenting now—he takes his pleasure.
And afterwards, he drinks and smokes; drinks and smokes.
And trails all day in and out of cafés,
wearily dragging along the dissipation of his beauty.—
Mind, henceforth work as best you can.

IN SPARTA

King Cleomenes* didn't know, he didn't dare—
he didn't know how to say this
to his mother: that Ptolemy demanded
she too be sent to Egypt and kept
a hostage, as security for their agreement,

λίαν ταπεινωτικόν, ἀνοίκειον πρᾶγμα.
Κι ὅλο ἤρχονταν γιὰ νὰ μιλήσει· κι ὅλο δίσταζε.
Κι ὅλο ἄρχιζε νὰ λέγει· κι ὅλο σταματοῦσε.

Μὰ ἡ ὑπέροχη γυναῖκα τὸν κατάλαβε
(εἶχεν ἀκούσει κιόλα κάτι διαδόσεις σχετικές),
καὶ τὸν ἐνθάρρυνε νὰ ἐξηγηθεῖ.
Καὶ γέλασε· κ' εἶπε βεβαίως πιαίνει.
Καὶ μάλιστα χαίρονταν ποῦ μποροῦσε νἆναι
στὸ γῆρας της ὀφέλιμη στὴν Σπάρτη ἀκόμη.

Ὅσο γιὰ τὴν ταπείνωσι — μὰ ἀδιαφοροῦσε.
Τὸ φρόνημα τῆς Σπάρτης ἀσφαλῶς δὲν ἦταν ἱκανὸς
νὰ νοιώσει ἕνας Λαγίδης χθεσινός·
ὅθεν κ' ἡ ἀπαίτησίς του δὲν μποροῦσε
πραγματικῶς νὰ ταπεινώσει Δέσποιναν
Ἐπιφανῆ ὡς αὐτήν· Σπαρτιάτου βασιλέως μητέρα.

ΕΙΚΩΝ ΕΙΚΟΣΙΤΡΙΕΤΟΥΣ ΝΕΟΥ ΚΑΜΩΜΕΝΗ ΑΠΟ ΦΙΛΟΝ ΤΟΥ ΟΜΗΛΙΚΑ, ΕΡΑΣΙΤΕΧΝΗΝ

Τελείωσε τὴν εικόνα   χθὲς μεσημέρι. Τώρα
λεπτομερῶς τὴν βλέπει.   Τὸν ἔκαμε μὲ γκρίζο
ροῦχο ξεκουμπωμένο,   γκρίζο βαθύ· χωρὶς
γελέκι καὶ κραβάτα.   Μ' ἕνα τριανταφυλλὶ
πουκάμισο· ἀνοιγμένο,   γιὰ νὰ φανεῖ καὶ κάτι
ἀπὸ τὴν ἐμορφιὰ   τοῦ στήθους, τοῦ λαιμοῦ.
Τὸ μέτωπο δεξιὰ   ὁλόκληρο σχεδὸν
σκεπάζουν τὰ μαλλιά του,   τὰ ὡραῖα του μαλλιὰ
(ὡς εἶναι ἡ χτενισιὰ   ποῦ προτιμᾶ ἐφέτος).
Ὑπάρχει ὁ τόνος πλήρως   ὁ ἡδονιστικὸς
ποῦ θέλησε νὰ βάλει   σὰν ἔκανε τὰ μάτια,
σὰν ἔκανε τὰ χείλη . . .   Τὸ στόμα του, τὰ χείλη
ποῦ γιὰ ἐκπληρώσεις εἶναι   ἐρωτισμοῦ ἐκλεκτοῦ.

a highly humiliating, unbecoming thing.
And he kept visiting her; and always wavered.
And always started to say something; and always stopped.

But that wonderful lady saw through him
(some rumours about it had reached her as well),
and she encouraged him to speak out.
And she laughed and said, of course she'd go,
and as a matter of fact, she was glad to be
still useful to Sparta in her old age.

As for the humiliation—well, she couldn't care less.
A Lagid, a king of only yesterday, was of course
unable to grasp the Spartan spirit;
wherefore his demand could not truly
humble such a Distinguished Lady
as she; mother of a Spartan king.

PORTRAIT OF A 23-YEAR-OLD MAN, PAINTED BY A FRIEND OF THE SAME AGE, AN AMATEUR ARTIST

He finished the portrait   yesterday at noon. And now
he examines it in detail.   He painted him wearing
a grey unbuttoned coat,   dark grey; without any
waistcoat or necktie;   with a rose-pink shirt
partly undone so that   a little could be glimpsed
of his beautiful chest,   of his beautiful neck.
The right side of the forehead   is for the most part
covered by his hair,   his truly lovely hair
(done in the fashion   that he prefers this year).
The whole thing is pervaded   by the hedonistic tone
he intended to convey   in painting the eyes,
in painting the lips . . .   His mouth and his lips,
made for consummations   of choice eroticism.

ΕΝ ΜΕΓΑΛΗ ΕΛΛΗΝΙΚΗ ΑΠΟΙΚΙΑ, 200 Π.Χ.

Ὅτι τὰ πράγματα δὲν βαίνουν κατ' εὐχὴν στὴν Ἀποικία
δὲν μέν' ἡ ἐλαχίστη ἀμφιβολία,
καὶ μ' ὅλο ποῦ ὁπωσοῦν τραβοῦμ' ἐμπρός,
ἴσως, καθὼς νομίζουν οὐκ ὀλίγοι, νὰ ἔφθασε ὁ καιρὸς
νὰ φέρουμε Πολιτικὸ Ἀναμορφωτή.

Ὅμως τὸ πρόσκομμα κ' ἡ δυσκολία
εἶναι ποῦ κάμνουνε μιὰ ἱστορία
μεγάλη κάθε πρᾶγμα οἱ Ἀναμορφωταὶ
αὐτοί. (Εὐτύχημα θὰ ἦταν ἂν ποτὲ
δὲν τοὺς χρειάζονταν κανείς). Γιὰ κάθε τί,
γιὰ τὸ παραμικρὸ ρωτοῦνε κ' ἐξετάζουν,
κ' εὐθὺς στὸν νοῦ τους ριζικὲς μεταρρυθμίσεις βάζουν,
μὲ τὴν ἀπαίτησι νὰ ἐκτελεσθοῦν ἄνευ ἀναβολῆς.

Ἔχουνε καὶ μιὰ κλίσι στὲς θυσίες.
Παραιτηθεῖτε ἀπὸ τὴν κτῆσιν σας ἐκείνη·
ἡ κατοχή σας εἶν' ἐπισφαλής:
ἡ τέτοιες κτήσεις ἀκριβῶς βλάπτουν τὲς Ἀποικίες.
Παραιτηθεῖτε ἀπὸ τὴν πρόσοδον αὐτή,
κι ἀπὸ τὴν ἄλληνα τὴν συναφῆ,
κι ἀπὸ τὴν τρίτη τούτην: ὡς συνέπεια φυσική·
εἶναι μὲν οὐσιώδεις, ἀλλὰ τί νὰ γίνει;
σᾶς δημιουργοῦν μιὰ ἐπιβλαβῆ εὐθύνη.

Κι ὅσο στὸν ἔλεγχό τους προχωροῦνε,
βρίσκουν και βρίσκουν περιττά, καὶ νὰ παυθοῦν ζητοῦνε·
πράγματα ποῦ ὅμως δύσκολα τὰ καταργεῖ κανείς.

Κι ὅταν, μὲ τὸ καλό, τελειώσουνε τὴν ἐργασία,
κι ὁρίσαντες καὶ περικόψαντες τὸ πᾶν λεπτομερῶς,
ἀπέλθουν, παίρνοντας καὶ τὴν δικαία μισθοδοσία,
νὰ δοῦμε τί ἀπομένει πιά, μετὰ
τόση δεινότητα χειρουργική.—

*

IN A LARGE GREEK COLONY, 200 B.C.

That the affairs in the Colony are not going well
not the slightest doubt remains,
and though somehow or other we are moving along,
perhaps, as many believe, the time has come
to bring in a Political Reformer.

But the obstacle and the difficulty is,
that these Reformers make
a great issue out of everything.
(A blessing it would be if nobody
ever needed them.) They examine
and inquire about the slightest little thing,
and they set their mind immediately on radical reforms,
demanding that these be executed without delay.

They also have an inclination toward sacrifices:
Give up that possession of yours;
your control over it is precarious:
it is precisely such possessions that are detrimental to the Colonies.
Give up this revenue
and that other similar one,
and this third, as a natural consequence;
they are indeed substantial, but what can you do?
They create for you a harmful liability.

And as they continue with their investigation,
they find more and more redundant things and they ask for their
    suspension;
things, however, that one can not readily relinquish.

And when, in good time, they complete their assignment,
and having specified and reduced everything down to the last detail,
they depart taking away their rightful wages,
then let us see what else is left
after such surgical dexterity.

*

Ἴσως δὲν ἔφθασεν ἀκόμη ὁ καιρός.
Νὰ μὴ βιαζόμεθα· εἶν' ἐπικίνδυνον πρᾶγμα ἡ βία.
Τὰ πρόωρα μέτρα φέρνουν μεταμέλεια.
Ἔχει ἄτοπα πολλά, βεβαίως καὶ δυστυχῶς, ἡ Ἀποικία.
Ὅμως ὑπάρχει τὶ τὸ ἀνθρώπινον χωρὶς ἀτέλεια;
Καὶ τέλος πάντων, νά, τραβοῦμ' ἐμπρός.

ΗΓΕΜΩΝ ΕΚ ΔΥΤΙΚΗΣ ΛΙΒΥΗΣ

Ἄρεσε γενικῶς στὴν Ἀλεξάνδρεια,
τὲς δέκα μέρες ποῦ διέμεινεν αὐτοῦ,
ὁ ἡγεμὼν ἐκ Δυτικῆς Λιβύης
Ἀριστομένης, υἱὸς τοῦ Μενελάου.
Ὡς τ' ὄνομά του, κ' ἡ περιβολή, κοσμίως, ἑλληνική.
Δέχονταν εὐχαρίστως τὲς τιμές, ἀλλὰ
δὲν τὲς ἐπιζητοῦσεν· ἦταν μετριόφρων.
Ἀγόραζε βιβλία ἑλληνικά,
ἰδίως ἱστορικὰ καὶ φιλοσοφικά.
Πρὸ πάντων δὲ ἄνθρωπος λιγομίλητος.
Θἆταν βαθὺς στὲς σκέψεις, διεδίδετο,
κ' οἱ τέτοιοι τὄχουν φυσικὸ νὰ μὴ μιλοῦν πολλά.

Μήτε βαθὺς στὲς σκέψεις ἦταν, μήτε τίποτε.
Ἕνας τυχαῖος, ἀστεῖος ἄνθρωπος.
Πῆρε ὄνομα ἑλληνικό, ντύθηκε σὰν τοὺς Ἕλληνας,
ἔμαθ' ἐπάνω, κάτω σὰν τοὺς Ἕλληνας νὰ φέρεται·
κ' ἔτρεμεν ἡ ψυχή του μὴ τυχὸν
χαλάσει τὴν καλούτσικην ἐντύπωσι
μιλώντας μὲ βαρβαρισμοὺς δεινοὺς τὰ ἑλληνικά,
κ' οἱ Ἀλεξανδρινοὶ τὸν πάρουν στὸ ψιλό,
ὡς εἶναι τὸ συνήθειο τους, οἱ ἀπαίσιοι.

Γι' αὐτὸ καὶ περιορίζονταν σὲ λίγες λέξεις,
προσέχοντας μὲ δέος τὲς κλίσεις καὶ τὴν προφορά·
κ' ἔπληττεν οὐκ ὀλίγον ἔχοντας
κουβέντες στοιβαγμένες μέσα του.

Well, possibly the time may not, as yet, be ripe.
Let's not be hasty; rashness is a hazardous thing.
Untimely measures foster regrets. To be sure,
there is, unfortunately, a lot that's out of place in the Colony.
But is there anything human devoid of imperfection?
And, well, one way or another we are moving along.

THE POTENTATE FROM WESTERN LIBYA

He was generally liked in Alexandria
during the ten days he sojourned there,
the potentate from Western Libya,
Aristomenes, son of Menelaus.
As with his name, his dress properly Greek.
He gladly accepted the honours, but
didn't solicit them; he was modest.
He bought books in Greek,
particularly on history and philosophy.
But above all, he was a man of few words.
He must be profound of thought, it was rumoured,
and such people have it in their nature not to say much.

He was neither profound of thought, nor anything.
Just an ordinary, silly man.
He assumed a Greek name, he dressed like a Greek,
taught himself to behave—more or less—like a Greek;
and trembled in his soul lest
he mar the tolerable impression
by speaking Greek with dreadful barbarisms,
and have the Alexandrians poke fun at him,
as is their habit—awful people.

And for this reason, he confined himself to a few words,
fearfully paying attention to the declensions and the accent;
and he got bored no end, having
so many things to say piled up inside him.

ΚΙΜΩΝ ΛΕΑΡΧΟΥ, 22 ΕΤΩΝ, ΣΠΟΥΔΑΣΤΗΣ ΕΛΛΗΝΙΚΩΝ ΓΡΑΜΜΑΤΩΝ (ΕΝ ΚΥΡΗΝΗι)

«Τὸ τέλος μου ἐπῆλθε   ὅτε ἤμουν εὐτυχής.
Ὁ Ἑρμοτέλης μὲ εἶχε   ἀχώριστόν του φίλον.
Τὲς ὕστατές μου μέρες,   μ' ὅλο ποῦ προσποιούνταν
πῶς δὲν ἀνησυχοῦσε,   ἔνοιωνα ἐγὼ συχνὰ
τὰ μάτια του κλαμένα.   Σὰν νόμιζε ποῦ λίγο
εἶχ' ἀποκοιμηθεῖ,   ἔπεφτεν ὡς ἀλλόφρων
στῆς κλίνης μου τὸ ἄκρον.   Ἀλλ' ἤμεθαν κ' οἱ δυὸ
νέοι μιᾶς ἡλικίας,   εἴκοσι τριῶ ἐτῶν.
Προδότις εἶναι ἡ Μοῖρα.   Ἴσως κανένα πάθος
ἄλλο τὸν Ἑρμοτέλη   νἄπαιρνεν ἀπὸ μένα.
Τελείωσα καλῶς· ἐν τῇ ἀμερίστῳ ἀγάπῃ».—

Τὸ ἐπιτύμβιον τοῦτο   Μαρύλου Ἀριστοδήμου
ἀποθανόντος πρὸ   μηνὸς στὴν Ἀλεξάνδρεια,
ἔλαβα ἐγὼ πενθῶν,   ὁ ἐξάδελφός του Κίμων.
Μὲ τὸ ἔστειλεν ὁ γράψας,   γνωστός μου ποιητής.
Μὲ τὸ ἔστειλ' ἐπειδὴ   ἤξερε συγγενὴς
ὅτ' ἤμουν τοῦ Μαρύλου: δὲν ἤξερε ἄλλο τί.
Εἶν' ἡ ψυχή μου πλήρης   λύπης γιὰ τὸν Μαρύλο.
Εἴχαμε μεγαλώσει   μαζύ, σὰν ἀδελφοί.
Βαθυὰ μελαγχολῶ.   Ὁ πρόωρος θάνατός του
κάθε μνησικακίαν   μοῦ ἔσβυσ' ἐντελῶς . . .
κάθε μνησικακίαν   γιὰ τὸν Μαρύλο — μ' ὅλο
ποῦ μὲ εἶχε κλέψει τὴν   ἀγάπη τοῦ Ἑρμοτέλη,
ποῦ κι ἂν μὲ θέλει τώρα   ὁ Ἑρμοτέλης πάλι
δὲν θἆναι διόλου τὸ ἴδιο.   Ξέρω τὸν χαρακτῆρα
τὸν εὐπαθῆ ποῦ ἔχω.   Τὸ ἴνδαλμα τοῦ Μαρύλου
θἄρχεται ἀνάμεσό μας,   καὶ θὰ νομίζω ποῦ
μὲ λέγει, Ἰδοὺ εἶσαι τώρα   ἱκανοποιημένος·
Ἰδοὺ τὸν ξαναπῆρες   ὡς ἐποθοῦσες, Κίμων·
Ἰδοὺ δὲν ἔχεις πιὰ   ἀφορμὴ νὰ μὲ διαβάλεις.

KIMON, SON OF LEARCHOS, 22 YEARS OLD, STUDENT OF GREEK LETTERS (IN CYRENE)

'The end of my life has come   while in a state of joy.
Hermoteles had me as his   inseparable companion.
During my final days,   although he pretended
that he did not worry,   I quite often sensed
his eyes reddened with tears.   When he believed I was
asleep for a little while,   he threw himself distraught
upon the edge of my bed.   We were both young men
of the very same age,   three and twenty years old.
Destiny is perfidious.   Possibly another passionate
love-affair might have taken   Hermoteles away from me.
I ended my days well,   amid undivided affection.'—

This epitaph for Marylos   son of Aristodemos,
who died one month ago   in Alexandria,
was delivered to me   his grieving cousin Kimon;
sent to me by the writer: a poet I once used to know.
It was sent to me because   he knew that I was
a relative of Marylos;   he didn't know anything else.
My soul is full of   sorrow for Marylos.
We grew up together,   as if we were brothers.
I am deeply saddened.   His untimely death
blotted out completely   any feelings of malice . . .
any feelings of malice   against Marylos—even though
he took away from me   the love of Hermoteles;
so that if now Hermoteles   should want me back again,
it just would not be the same.   I know full well what a sensitive
nature I possess.   The image of Marylos
will always come between us,   and I shall imagine him
saying to me: well then,   are you satisfied now?
There, he's all yours again,   as you had wanted, Kimon.
There, you no longer have   a reason to malign me.

ΕΝ ΠΟΡΕΙΑι ΠΡΟΣ ΤΗΝ ΣΙΝΩΠΗΝ

Ὁ Μιθριδάτης, ἔνδοξος καὶ κραταιός,
μεγάλων πόλεων ὁ κύριος,
κάτοχος ἰσχυρῶν στρατῶν καὶ στόλων,
πηγαίνοντας πρὸς τὴν Σινώπην πέρασε ἀπὸ δρόμον
ἐξοχικὸν πολὺ ἀπόκεντρον
ὅπου ἕνας μάντις εἶχε κατοικίαν.

Ἔστειλεν ἀξιωματικό του ὁ Μιθριδάτης
τὸν μάντι νὰ ρωτήσει πόσα θ' ἀποκτήσει ἀκόμη
στὸ μέλλον ἀγαθά, πόσες δυνάμεις ἄλλες.

Ἔστειλεν ἀξιωματικό του, καὶ μετὰ
πρὸς τὴν Σινώπην τὴν πορεία του ξακολούθησε.

Ὁ μάντις ἀποσύρθηκε σ' ἕνα δωμάτιο μυστικό.
Μετὰ περίπου μισὴν ὥρα βγῆκε
περίφροντις, κ' εἶπε στὸν ἀξιωματικό,
«Ἱκανοποιητικῶς δὲν μπόρεσα νὰ διευκρινίσω.
Κατάλληλη δὲν εἶν' ἡ μέρα σήμερα.
Κάτι σκιώδη πράγματα εἶδα. Δὲν κατάλαβα καλά.—
Μὰ ν' ἀρκεσθεῖ, φρονῶ, μὲ τόσα ποὺ ἔχει ὁ βασιλεύς.
Τὰ περισσότερα εἰς κινδύνους θὰ τὸν φέρουν.
Θυμήσου νὰ τὸν πεῖς αὐτὸ ἀξιωματικέ:
μὲ τόσα ποὺ ἔχει, πρὸς θεοῦ, ν' ἀρκεῖται!
Ἡ τύχη ξαφνικὲς ἔχει μεταβολές.
Νὰ πεῖς στὸν βασιλέα Μιθριδάτη:
λίαν σπανίως βρίσκεται ὁ ἑταῖρος τοῦ προγόνου του
ὁ εὐγενής, ποὺ ἐγκαίρως μὲ τὴν λόγχην γράφει
στὸ χῶμα ἐπάνω τὸ σωτήριον *Φεῦγε Μιθριδάτα*».

ON THE MARCH TO SINOPE

Mithridates,* glorious and powerful,
lord of great cities,
master of mighty armies and navies,
on his way to Sinope passed along
a very remote country road
where a seer had his dwelling.

Mithridates dispatched one of his officers
to ask the seer how much more wealth
he'd acquire in the future, how much more power.

He dispatched his officer and then
continued his march to Sinope.

The seer withdrew into a secret room.
About half an hour later he emerged
preoccupied, and said to the officer:
'I could discern nothing to my satisfaction.
It is not a suitable day today.
A few shadowy things I made out, I didn't understand well.—
But in my opinion, the king ought to content himself
with what he has; anything more will lead him into danger.
Remember to tell him this, officer:
for god's sake, he should content himself with all he has!
Fate is fraught with sudden twists.
Tell King Mithridates:
there rarely comes along someone like the noble companion
of his ancestor, who in the nick of time traced in the dust
of the road, with his spear, the life-saving words: *Flee, Mithridates.*'

ΜΕΡΕΣ ΤΟΥ 1909, '10 ΚΑΙ '11

Ἑνὸς τυραννισμένου, πτωχοτάτου ναυτικοῦ
(ἀπὸ νησὶ τοῦ Αἰγαίου Πελάγους) ἦταν υἱός.
Ἐργάζονταν σὲ σιδερᾶ. Παληόρουχα φοροῦσε.
Σχισμένα τὰ ποδήματά του τῆς δουλειᾶς κ' ἐλεεινά.
Τὰ χέρια του ἦσαν λερωμένα ἀπὸ σκουριὲς καὶ λάδια.

Τὸ βραδυνό, σὰν ἔκλειε τὸ μαγαζί,
ἂν ἦταν τίποτε νὰ ἐπιθυμεῖ πολύ,
καμιὰ κραβάτα κάπως ἀκριβή,
καμιὰ κραβάτα γιὰ τὴν Κυριακή,
ἢ σὲ βιτρίνα ἂν εἶχε δεῖ καὶ λαχταροῦσε
κανένα ὡραῖο πουκάμισο μαβί,
τὸ σῶμα του γιὰ ἕνα τάλληρο ἢ δυὸ πουλοῦσε.

Διερωτῶμαι ἂν στοὺς ἀρχαίους καιροὺς
εἶχεν ἡ ἔνδοξη Ἀλεξάνδρεια νέον πιὸ περικαλλῆ,
πιὸ τέλειο ἀγόρι ἀπὸ αὐτὸν—ποῦ πῆε χαμένος:
δὲν ἔγινε, ἐννοεῖται, ἄγαλμά του ἢ ζωγραφιά·
στὸ παληομάγαζο ἑνὸς σιδερᾶ ριχμένος,
γρήγορ' ἀπ' τὴν ἐπίπονη δουλειά,
κι ἀπὸ λαϊκὴ κραιπάλη, ταλαιπωρημένη, εἶχε φθαρεῖ.

ΜΥΡΗΣ· ΑΛΕΞΑΝΔΡΕΙΑ ΤΟΥ 340 Μ.Χ.

Τὴν συμφορὰ ὅταν ἔμαθα, ποῦ ὁ Μύρης πέθανε,
πῆγα στὸ σπίτι του, μ' ὅλο ποῦ τὸ ἀποφεύγω
νὰ εἰσέρχομαι στῶν Χριστιανῶν τὰ σπίτια,
πρὸ πάντων ὅταν ἔχουν θλίψεις ἢ γιορτές.

Στάθηκα σὲ διάδρομο. Δὲν θέλησα
νὰ προχωρήσω πιὸ ἐντός, γιατὶ ἀντελήφθην
ποῦ οἱ συγγενεῖς τοῦ πεθαμένου μ' ἔβλεπαν
μὲ προφανῆ ἀπορίαν καὶ μὲ δυσαρέσκεια.

*

DAYS OF 1909, '10 AND '11

He was the son of a much-tormented, destitute
seaman (from one of the Aegean islands).
He worked for a blacksmith. He wore shabby clothes.
His working shoes were torn and shoddy.
His hands were grimed with rust and oil.

In the evenings, when they closed shop,
if there was something he fancied a lot,
a rather expensive tie,
a tie to be worn on Sundays,
or if he'd seen in a shop window and yearned
for a nice lavender shirt,
he would sell his body for a few shillings.

I wonder whether in times of old,
glorious Alexandria could boast of a lovelier youth,
a lad more exquisite than he—who went to waste:
needless to say, no statue or painting of him was ever made;
thrown into a blacksmith's run-down shop,
he quickly wore himself out
with strenuous labour and cheap, wretched debauchery.

MYRES: ALEXANDRIA, A.D. 340

When I heard the tragic news that Myres was dead,
I went to his house, even though I avoid
entering Christian homes, particularly
during their sorrows or celebrations.

I stood in a hallway. I did not want
to proceed further inside, because I sensed
that the dead man's relatives kept looking at me,
with obvious perplexity and displeasure.

*

Τὸν εἶχανε σὲ μιὰ μεγάλη κάμαρη
ποῦ ἀπὸ τὴν ἄκρην ὅπου στάθηκα
εἶδα κομάτι· ὅλο τάπητες πολύτιμοι,
καὶ σκεύη ἐξ ἀργύρου καὶ χρυσοῦ.

Στέκομουν κ' ἔκλαια σὲ μιὰ ἄκρη τοῦ διαδρόμου.
Καὶ σκέπτομουν ποῦ ἡ συγκεντρώσεις μας κ' ἡ ἐκδρομὲς
χωρὶς τὸν Μύρη δὲν θ' ἀξίζουν πιά·
καὶ σκέπτομουν ποῦ πιὰ δὲν θὰ τὸν δῶ
στὰ ὡραῖα κι ἄσεμνα ξενύχτια μας
νὰ χαίρεται, καὶ νὰ γελᾶ, καὶ ν' ἀπαγγέλλει στίχους
μὲ τὴν τελεία του αἴσθησι τοῦ ἑλληνικοῦ ρυθμοῦ·
καὶ σκέπτομουν ποῦ ἔχασα γιὰ πάντα
τὴν ἐμορφιά του, ποῦ ἔχασα γιὰ πάντα
τὸν νέον ποῦ λάτρευα παράφορα.

Κάτι γρηές, κοντά μου, χαμηλὰ μιλοῦσαν γιὰ
τὴν τελευταία μέρα ποῦ ἔζησε—
στὰ χείλη του διαρκῶς τ' ὄνομα τοῦ Χριστοῦ,
στὰ χέρια του βαστοῦσ' ἕναν σταυρό.—
Μπῆκαν κατόπι μὲς στὴν κάμαρη
τέσσαρες Χριστιανοὶ ἱερεῖς, κ' ἔλεγαν προσευχὲς
ἐνθέρμως καὶ δεήσεις στὸν Ἰησοῦν,
ἢ στὴν Μαρίαν (δὲν ξέρω τὴν θρησκεία τους καλά).

Γνωρίζαμε, βεβαίως, ποῦ ὁ Μύρης ἦταν Χριστιανός.
Ἀπὸ τὴν πρώτην ὥρα τὸ γνωρίζαμε, ὅταν
πρόπερσι στὴν παρέα μας εἶχε μπεῖ.
Μὰ ζοῦσεν ἀπολύτως σὰν κ' ἐμᾶς.
Ἀπ' ὅλους μας πιὸ ἔκδοτος στὲς ἡδονές·
σκορπώντας ἀφειδῶς τὸ χρῆμα του στὲς διασκεδάσεις.
Γιὰ τὴν ὑπόληψι τοῦ κόσμου ξένοιαστος,
ρίχνονταν πρόθυμα σὲ νύχτιες ρήξεις στὲς ὁδοὺς
ὅταν ἐτύχαινε ἡ παρέα μας
νὰ συναντήσει ἀντίθετη παρέα.
Ποτὲ γιὰ τὴν θρησκεία του δὲν μιλοῦσε.
Μάλιστα μιὰ φορὰ τὸν εἴπαμε
πῶς θὰ τὸν πάρουμε μαζύ μας στὸ Σεράπιον.
Ὅμως σὰν νὰ δυσαρεστήθηκε
μ' αὐτόν μας τὸν ἀστεϊσμό: θυμοῦμαι τώρα.

They had placed him in a large room,
part of which I could see from the corner
where I stood; full of precious carpets
and vessels made of silver and gold.

I was standing and crying at one end of the hallway.
And I kept thinking how our gatherings and excursions,
without Myres, won't be as worthwhile any more;
and I kept thinking that I wouldn't see him again
at our lovely, brazen night-long parties,
revelling and laughing and reciting verses,
with his perfect sense of Greek rhythm;
and I kept thinking that I'd lost forever
his beauty, that I'd lost forever
the young man I ardently adored.

Some old women near me spoke in subdued voices
about the last day of his life—
upon his lips constantly the name of Christ,
in his hands, clasping a cross.—
Then, four Christian priests
entered the room, reciting fervent
prayers and supplications to Jesus
or to Mary (I don't know their religion that well).

We knew, of course, that Myres was a Christian.
We knew it right from the start, when
he joined our group of friends two years ago.
But he led his life exactly as we did.
More given to sensual pleasures than any of us,
squandering his money lavishly on amusements.
Oblivious of his reputation in society,
he threw himself readily into nocturnal street-brawls,
when our group of friends chanced
to encounter a hostile company.
He never spoke about his religion.
As a matter of fact, we told him once
that we'd take him with us to the Serapeum,
but he appeared displeased
with this little joke of ours: I remember now.

Ἆ κι ἄλλες δυὸ φορὲς τώρα στὸν νοῦ μου ἔρχονται.
Ὅταν στὸν Ποσειδῶνα κάμναμε σπονδές,
τραβήχθηκε ἀπ' τὸν κύκλο μας, κ' ἔστρεψε ἀλλοῦ
τὸ βλέμμα.
Ὅταν ἐνθουσιασμένος ἕνας μας
εἶπεν, Ἡ συντροφιά μας νἆναι ὑπὸ
τὴν εὔνοιαν καὶ τὴν προστασίαν τοῦ μεγάλου,
τοῦ πανωραίου Ἀπόλλωνος—ψιθύρισεν ὁ Μύρης
(οἱ ἄλλοι δὲν ἄκουσαν) «τῇ ἐξαιρέσει ἐμοῦ».

Οἱ Χριστιανοὶ ἱερεῖς μεγαλοφώνως
γιὰ τὴν ψυχὴ τοῦ νέου δέονταν.—
Παρατηροῦσα μὲ πόση ἐπιμέλεια,
καὶ μὲ τί προσοχὴν ἐντατικὴ
στοὺς τύπους τῆς θρησκείας τους, ἑτοιμάζονταν
ὅλα γιὰ τὴν χριστιανικὴ κηδεία.
Κ' ἐξαίφνης μὲ κυρίευσε μιὰ ἀλλόκοτη
ἐντύπωσις. Ἀόριστα, αἰσθάνομουν
σὰν νἄφευγεν ἀπὸ κοντά μου ὁ Μύρης·
αἰσθάνομουν ποῦ ἑνώθη, Χριστιανός,
μὲ τοὺς δικούς του, καὶ ποῦ γένομουν
ξ έ ν ο ς ἐγώ, ξ έ ν ο ς π ο λ ύ· ἔνοιωθα κιόλα
μιὰ ἀμφιβολία νὰ μὲ σιμόνει: μήπως κ' εἶχα γελασθεῖ
ἀπὸ τὸ πάθος μου, καὶ π ά ν τ α τοῦ ἤμουν ξένος.—
Πετάχθηκα ἔξω ἀπ' τὸ φρικτό τους σπίτι,
ἔφυγα γρήγορα πρὶν ἁρπαχθεῖ, πρὶν ἀλλοιωθεῖ
ἀπ' τὴν χριστιανοσύνη τους ἡ θύμηση τοῦ Μύρη.

ΑΛΕΞΑΝΔΡΟΣ ΙΑΝΝΑΙΟΣ, ΚΑΙ ΑΛΕΞΑΝΔΡΑ

Ἐπιτυχεῖς καὶ πλήρως ἱκανοποιημένοι,
ὁ βασιλεὺς Ἀλέξανδρος Ἰανναῖος,
κ' ἡ σύζυγός του ἡ βασίλισσα Ἀλεξάνδρα
περνοῦν μὲ προπορευομένην μουσικὴν
καὶ μὲ παντοίαν μεγαλοπρέπειαν καὶ χλιδήν,
περνοῦν ἀπ' τὲς ὁδοὺς τῆς Ἱερουσαλήμ.

Oh yes! Two more occasions come now to mind.
When we were offering libations to Poseidon,
he withdrew from our circle, and turned his eyes elsewhere.
When one of us, in his excitement,
said: 'May our company be under
the auspices and protection of the great,
the sublimely beautiful Apollo'—Myres whispered
(the others didn't hear), 'except for me.'

The Christian priests were praying in loud voices
for the young man's soul.—
I was noticing with what meticulous care
and intense attention to the rituals
of their religion they were preparing
everything for the Christian funeral.
And suddenly I was overwhelmed by an eerie
awareness. Vaguely, I felt
as if Myres was drifting away from me;
I felt that he, a Christian, was being united
with his own kind, and I was becoming
a stranger, a total stranger; I could already feel
a certain ambivalence closing in: was it possible I'd been misled
by my passion, that I had *always* been a stranger to him?—
I hastened out of their dreadful house;
I left in a hurry, before their Christianity could snatch away,
before it could distort the memory of Myres.

ALEXANDER JANNAEUS, AND ALEXANDRA

Successful and utterly content,
King Alexander Jannaeus*
and his wife, Queen Alexandra,
parade with a band in the lead,
and every kind of majesty and opulence,
through the streets of Jerusalem.

Ἐτελεσφόρησε λαμπρῶς τὸ ἔργον
ποῦ ἄρχισαν ὁ μέγας Ἰούδας Μακκαβαῖος
κ' οἱ τέσσαρες περιώνυμοι ἀδελφοί του·
καὶ ποῦ μετὰ ἀνενδότως συνεχίσθη ἐν μέσῳ
πολλῶν κινδύνων καὶ πολλῶν δυσχερειῶν.
Τώρα δὲν ἔμεινε τίποτε τὸ ἀνοίκειον.
Ἔπαυσε κάθε ὑποταγὴ στοὺς ἀλαζόνας
μονάρχας τῆς Ἀντιοχείας. Ἰδοὺ
ὁ βασιλεὺς Ἀλέξανδρος Ἰανναῖος,
κ' ἡ σύζυγός του ἡ βασίλισσα Ἀλεξάνδρα
καθ' ὅλα ἴσοι πρὸς τοὺς Σελευκίδας.
Ἰουδαῖοι καλοί, Ἰουδαῖοι ἁγνοί, Ἰουδαῖοι πιστοὶ—πρὸ πάντων.
Ἀλλά, καθὼς ποῦ τὸ ἀπαιτοῦν ἡ περιστάσεις,
καὶ τῆς ἑλληνικῆς λαλιᾶς εἰδήμονες·
καὶ μ' Ἕλληνας καὶ μ' ἑλληνίζοντας
μονάρχας σχετισμένοι—πλὴν σὰν ἴσοι, καὶ ν' ἀκούεται.
Τωόντι ἐτελεσφόρησε λαμπρῶς,
ἐτελεσφόρησε περιφανῶς
τὸ ἔργον ποῦ ἄρχισαν ὁ μέγας Ἰούδας Μακκαβαῖος
κ' οἱ τέσσαρες περιώνυμοι ἀδελφοί του.

ΩΡΑΙΑ ΛΟΥΛΟΥΔΙΑ ΚΙ ΑΣΠΡΑ ΩΣ ΤΑΙΡΙΑΖΑΝ ΠΟΛΥ

Μπῆκε στὸ καφενεῖο ὅπου ἐπήγαιναν μαζύ.—
Ὁ φίλος του ἐδῶ πρὸ τριῶ μηνῶν τοῦ εἶπε,
«Δὲν ἔχουμε πεντάρα. Δυὸ πάμπτωχα παιδιὰ
ἤμεθα—ξεπεσμένοι στὰ κέντρα τὰ φθηνά.
Στὸ λέγω φανερά, μὲ σένα δὲν μπορῶ
νὰ περπατῶ. Ἕνας ἄλλος, μάθε το, μὲ ζητεῖ».
Ὁ ἄλλος τοῦ εἶχε τάξει δυὸ φορεσιές, καὶ κάτι
μεταξωτὰ μαντήλια.— Γιὰ νὰ τὸν ξαναπάρει
ἐχάλασε τὸν κόσμο, καὶ βρῆκε εἴκοσι λίρες.
Ἦλθε ξανὰ μαζύ του γιὰ τὲς εἴκοσι λίρες·
μὰ καί, κοντὰ σ' αὐτές, γιὰ τὴν παληὰ φιλία,
γιὰ τὴν παληὰν ἀγάπη, γιὰ τὸ βαθὺ αἴσθημά των.—
Ὁ «ἄλλος» ἦταν ψεύτης, παληόπαιδο σωστό·

It yielded splendid results, the work
begun by the great Judas Maccabaeus
and his four renowned brothers;
which afterwards continued relentlessly
amid numerous trials and tribulations.
By now, nothing unseemly has remained.
All subjugation to the arrogant
monarchs of Antioch has come to an end.
Behold! King Alexander Jannaeus
and his wife, Queen Alexandra,
equal in every way to the Seleucids.
Righteous Jews, pious Jews, devout Jews—above all.
But, as circumstances require,
also masters of the Hellenic tongue;
and in contact with Greek or Hellenizing
monarchs—yet, be it known, as equals.
Indeed, it yielded splendid,
it yielded glorious results,
the work begun by the great Judas Maccabaeus
and his four renowned brothers.

LOVELY FLOWERS AND WHITE SUCH AS BEFITTED WELL

He walked in the café where they used to go together.—
It was here that his friend had told him three months before:
'We've got no money at all. We are two penniless lads,
reduced to frequenting the cheapest places.
Quite frankly I tell you, I can't go around with you.
If you want to know someone else is after me.'
This 'someone' had promised his friend two suits of clothes
and some silk handkerchiefs.— To win him back again
he moved heaven and earth, and came up with twenty pounds.
His friend returned to him for these twenty pounds;
but at the same time, for their former attachment,
for their former affection, for their profound love.—
This 'someone' was a liar, in fact a total scoundrel;

μιὰ φορεσιὰ μονάχα τοῦ εἶχε κάμει, καὶ
μὲ τὸ στανιὸ καὶ τούτην, μὲ χίλια παρακάλια.

Μὰ τώρα πιὰ δὲν θέλει μήτε τὲς φορεσιές,
καὶ μήτε διόλου τὰ μεταξωτὰ μαντήλια,
καὶ μήτε εἴκοσι λίρες, καὶ μήτε εἴκοσι γρόσια.

Τὴν Κυριακὴ τὸν θάψαν, στὲς δέκα τὸ πρωΐ.
Τὴν Κυριακὴ τὸν θάψαν: πάει ἑβδομὰς σχεδόν.

Στὴν πτωχική του κάσα τοῦ ἔβαλε λουλούδια,
ὡραῖα λουλούδια κι ἄσπρα ὡς ταίριαζαν πολὺ
στὴν ἐμορφιά του καὶ στὰ εἴκοσι δυό του χρόνια.

Ὅταν τὸ βράδυ ἐπῆγεν— ἔτυχε μιὰ δουλειά,
μιὰ ἀνάγκη τοῦ ψωμιοῦ του— στὸ καφενεῖον ὅπου
ἐπήγαιναν μαζύ: μαχαῖρι στὴν καρδιά του
τὸ μαῦρο καφενεῖο ὅπου ἐπήγαιναν μαζύ.

ΑΓΕ Ω ΒΑΣΙΛΕΥ ΛΑΚΕΔΑΙΜΟΝΙΩΝ

Δὲν καταδέχονταν ἡ Κρατησίκλεια
ὁ κόσμος νὰ τὴν δεῖ νὰ κλαίει καὶ νὰ θρηνεῖ·
καὶ μεγαλοπρεπὴς ἐβάδιζε καὶ σιωπηλή.
Τίποτε δὲν ἀπόδειχνε ἡ ἀτάραχη μορφή της
ἀπ' τὸν καϋμὸ καὶ τὰ τυράννια της.
Μὰ ὅσο καὶ νἆναι μιὰ στιγμὴ δὲν βάσταξε·
καὶ πρὶν στὸ ἄθλιο πλοῖο μπεῖ νὰ πάει στὴν Ἀλεξάνδρεια,
πῆρε τὸν υἱό της στὸν ναὸ τοῦ Ποσειδῶνος,
καὶ μόνοι σὰν βρεθῆκαν τὸν ἀγκάλιασε
καὶ τὸν ἀσπάζονταν, «διαλγοῦντα», λέγει
ὁ Πλούταρχος, «καὶ συντεταραγμένον».
Ὅμως ὁ δυνατός της χαρακτὴρ ἐπάσχισε·
καὶ συνελθοῦσα ἡ θαυμασία γυναῖκα
εἶπε στὸν Κλεομένη «Ἄγε ὦ βασιλεῦ
Λακεδαιμονίων, ὅπως, ἐπὰν ἔξω
γενώμεθα, μηδεὶς ἴδῃ δακρύοντας

all he had ever given him   was just one suit of clothes,
and that very reluctantly,   after a thousand pleas.

But now he has no need   either for suits of clothes,
and not, most certainly,   for silken handkerchiefs,
or for twenty pounds   or for twenty piasters.

They buried him on Sunday   morning at ten o'clock.
They buried him on Sunday;   now it's almost a week.

Upon his modest coffin   his friend placed flowers for him,
lovely flowers and white,   such as befitted well
his loveliness and his   two and twenty years.

That night—a job   had come his way, a chance
to earn his bread—   as he went in that café
where they used to go together,   a stab it was, deep in his heart,
the dismal café where   they used to go together.

COME, O KING OF THE LACEDAEMONIANS

Cratisicleia* felt it beneath her to be seen
by the people crying and lamenting;
and she kept on walking in majestic dignity and silence.
Her imperturbable countenance displayed none
of her consuming pains and sufferings.
But even so, for one moment, she could bear it no more;
before embarking on that wretched ship for Alexandria,
she took her son to the temple of Poseidon,
and once they were alone, she embraced him
and kept kissing him, while he was 'in great
pain,' says Plutarch, 'and violent agitation'.
But her stalwart character prevailed;
and regaining her composure, that wonderful woman
said to Cleomenes: 'Come, O King of the
Lacedaemonians, when we are outside
nobody should see that we've been crying,

ἡμᾶς μηδὲ ἀνάξιόν τι τῆς Σπάρτης
ποιοῦντας. Τοῦτο γὰρ ἐφ' ἡμῖν μόνον·
αἱ τύχαι δέ, ὅπως ἂν ὁ δαίμων διδῷ, πάρεισι».

Καὶ μὲς στὸ πλοῖο μπῆκε, πιαίνοντας πρὸς τὸ «διδῷ».

ΣΤΟΝ ΙΔΙΟ ΧΩΡΟ

Οἰκίας περιβάλλον, κέντρων, συνοικίας
ποὺ βλέπω κι ὅπου περπατῶ· χρόνια καὶ χρόνια.

Σὲ δημιούργησα μὲς σὲ χαρὰ καὶ μὲς σὲ λύπες:
μὲ τόσα περιστατικά, μὲ τόσα πράγματα.

Κ' αἰσθηματοποιήθηκες ὁλόκληρο, γιὰ μένα.

Ο ΚΑΘΡΕΠΤΗΣ ΣΤΗΝ ΕΙΣΟΔΟ

Τὸ πλούσιο σπίτι εἶχε στὴν εἴσοδο
ἕναν καθρέπτη μέγιστο, πολὺ παλαιό·
τουλάχιστον πρὸ ὀγδόντα ἐτῶν ἀγορασμένο.

Ἕνα ἐμορφότατο παιδί, ὑπάλληλος σὲ ράπτη
(τὲς Κυριακές, ἐρασιτέχνης ἀθλητής),
στέκονταν μ' ἕνα δέμα. Τὸ παρέδοσε
σὲ κάποιον τοῦ σπιτιοῦ, κι αὐτὸς τὸ πῆγε μέσα
νὰ φέρει τὴν ἀπόδειξι. Ὁ ὑπάλληλος τοῦ ράπτη
ἔμεινε μόνος, καὶ περίμενε.
Πλησίασε στὸν καθρέπτη καὶ κυττάζονταν
κ' ἔσιαζε τὴν κραβάτα του. Μετὰ πέντε λεπτὰ
τοῦ φέραν τὴν ἀπόδειξι. Τὴν πῆρε κ' ἔφυγε.

Μὰ ὁ παλαιὸς καθρέπτης ποὺ εἶχε δεῖ καὶ δεῖ,
κατὰ τὴν ὕπαρξίν του τὴν πολυετῆ,
χιλιάδες πράγματα καὶ πρόσωπα·

or doing anything unworthy of Sparta.
That is the only thing still in our power;
as for our fortunes, they will be with us as god might grant.'

And she entered the ship, on the way towards that 'might grant'.

IN THE SAME SPACE

Surroundings of home, of social clubs, of the neighbourhood,
that I behold, and where I walk; year in year out.

I brought you into being amid joy and amid sorrows:
along with so many events, so many happenings.

And you have come to be entirely a feeling for me.

THE MIRROR IN THE ENTRANCE

The wealthy house had in the entrance hall
a mirror, very large, very old;
bought at least eighty years ago.

An extremely handsome youth, assistant to a tailor
(on Sundays an amateur athlete),
stood there with a package. He handed it
to a member of the household, who carried it inside
to fetch the receipt. The tailor's assistant
remained alone and waited.
He approached the mirror and looked at himself,
straightening his tie. Five minutes later
they brought him the receipt. He took it and departed.

But the old mirror that had seen and seen,
during the long years of its existence,
thousands of objects and faces;

μὰ ὁ παλαιὸς καθρέπτης τώρα χαίρονταν,
κ' ἐπαίρονταν ποῦ εἶχε δεχθεῖ ἐπάνω του
τὴν ἄρτιαν ἐμορφιὰ γιὰ μερικὰ λεπτά.

ΡΩΤΟΥΣΕ ΓΙΑ ΤΗΝ ΠΟΙΟΤΗΤΑ—

Ἀπ' τὸ γραφεῖον ὅπου εἶχε προσληφθεῖ
σὲ θέση ἀσήμαντη καὶ φθηνοπληρωμένη
(ὡς ὀκτὼ λίρες τὸ μηνιάτικό του: μὲ τὰ τυχερὰ)
βγῆκε σὰν τέλεψεν ἡ ἔρημη δουλειὰ
ποῦ ὅλο τὸ ἀπόγευμα ἦταν σκυμένος:
βγῆκεν ἡ ὥρα ἑπτά, καὶ περπατοῦσε ἀργὰ
καὶ χάζευε στὸν δρόμο.—Ἔμορφος·
κ' ἐνδιαφέρων: ἔτσι ποῦ ἔδειχνε φθασμένος
στὴν πλήρη του αἰσθησιακὴν ἀπόδοσι.
Τὰ εἴκοσι ἐννιά, τὸν περασμένο μῆνα τὰ εἶχε κλείσει.

Ἐχάζευε στὸν δρόμο, καὶ στὲς πτωχικὲς
παρόδους ποῦ ὁδηγοῦσαν πρὸς τὴν κατοικία του.

Περνώντας ἐμπρὸς σ' ἕνα μαγαζὶ μικρὸ
ὅπου πουλιούνταν κάτι πράγματα
ψεύτικα καὶ φθηνὰ γιὰ ἐργατικούς,
εἶδ' ἐκεῖ μέσα ἕνα πρόσωπο, εἶδε μιὰ μορφὴ
ὅπου τὸν ἔσπρωξαν καὶ εἰσῆλθε, καὶ ζητοῦσε
τάχα νὰ δεῖ χρωματιστὰ μαντήλια.

Ρωτοῦσε γιὰ τὴν ποιότητα τῶν μαντηλιῶν
καὶ τί κοστίζουν· μὲ φωνὴ πνιγμένη,
σχεδὸν σβυσμένη ἀπ' τὴν ἐπιθυμία.
Κι ἀνάλογα ἦλθαν ἡ ἀπαντήσεις,
ἀφηρημένες, μὲ φωνὴ χαμηλωμένη,
μὲ ὑπολανθάνουσα συναίνεσι.

Ὅλο καὶ κάτι ἔλεγαν γιὰ τὴν πραγμάτεια—ἀλλὰ
μόνος σκοπός: τὰ χέρια των ν' ἀγγίζουν
ἐπάνω ἀπ' τὰ μαντήλια· νὰ πλησιάζουν

the old mirror now rejoiced
and prided itself that perfect loveliness
had been bestowed upon it for a few moments.

HE WAS ASKING ABOUT THE QUALITY—

He came out of the office where he'd been hired
in an insignificant, low-paying job
(his monthly salary no more than eight pounds: tips included),
when the dreary job, over which
he stooped all afternoon, was finished.
He came out at seven, and strolled slowly
and idled around in the street.—Handsome;
and interesting: as he seemed to have attained
the full potential of his sensuous beauty.
He'd turned twenty-nine the previous month.

He kept idling around in the streets and the shabby
back alleys leading to his home.

While passing in front of a small shop
where some goods were on sale,
shoddy and cheap, for working folk,
he saw a face inside, a figure,
that urged him on, and he entered pretending
he was looking for coloured handkerchiefs.

He was asking about the quality of the handkerchiefs
and what they cost in a choked voice,
almost faded to a whisper by desire.
And accordingly came the answers,
absentmindedly, in a subdued voice,
intimating latent consent.

All the while they kept talking about the merchandise,
but their one and only objective: to touch hands
over the handkerchiefs; to draw near

τὰ πρόσωπα, τὰ χείλη σὰν τυχαίως·
μιὰ στιγμιαία στὰ μέλη ἐπαφή.

Γρήγορα καὶ κρυφά, γιὰ νὰ μὴ νοιώσει
ὁ καταστηματάρχης ποῦ στὸ βάθος κάθονταν.

ΑΣ ΦΡΟΝΤΙΖΑΝ

Κατήντησα σχεδὸν ἀνέστιος καὶ πένης.
Αὐτὴ ἡ μοιραία πόλις, ἡ Ἀντιόχεια
ὅλα τὰ χρήματά μου τἄφαγε:
αὐτὴ ἡ μοιραία μὲ τὸν δαπανηρό της βίο.

Ἀλλὰ εἶμαι νέος καὶ μὲ ὑγείαν ἀρίστην.
Κάτοχος τῆς ἑλληνικῆς θαυμάσιος
(ξέρω καὶ παραξέρω Ἀριστοτέλη, Πλάτωνα·
τὶ ρήτορας, τὶ ποιητάς, τὶ ὅτι κι ἂν πεῖς).
Ἀπὸ στρατιωτικὰ ἔχω μιὰν ἰδέα,
κ' ἔχω φιλίες μὲ ἀρχηγοὺς τῶν μισθοφόρων.
Εἶμαι μπασμένος κάμποσο καὶ στὰ διοικητικά.
Στὴν Ἀλεξάνδρεια ἔμεινα ἕξι μῆνες, πέρσι·
κάπως γνωρίζω (κ' εἶναι τοῦτο χρήσιμον) τὰ ἐκεῖ:
τοῦ Κακεργέτη βλέψεις, καὶ παληανθρωπιές, καὶ τὰ λοιπά.

Ὅθεν φρονῶ πῶς εἶμαι στὰ γεμάτα
ἐνδεδειγμένος γιὰ νὰ ὑπηρετήσω αὐτὴν τὴν χώρα,
τὴν προσφιλῆ πατρίδα μου Συρία.

Σ' ὅτι δουλειὰ μὲ βάλλουν θὰ πασχίσω
νὰ εἶμαι στὴν χώρα ὀφέλιμος. Αὐτὴ εἰν' ἡ πρόθεσίς μου.
Ἂν πάλι μ' ἐμποδίσουνε μὲ τὰ συστήματά τους—
τοὺς ξέρουμε τοὺς προκομένους: νὰ τὰ λέμε τώρα;
ἂν μ' ἐμποδίσουνε, τὶ φταίω ἐγώ.

Θ' ἀπευθυνθῶ πρὸς τὸν Ζαβίνα πρῶτα,
κι ἂν ὁ μωρὸς αὐτὸς δὲν μ' ἐκτιμήσει,
θὰ πάγω στὸν ἀντίπαλό του, τὸν Γρυπό.

their faces and their lips, as if by chance;
a momentary contact of their limbs.

Hurriedly and furtively, lest the shopkeeper
sitting in the back were to suspect something.

IF ONLY THEY HAD SEEN TO IT

I've been reduced almost to a homeless pauper.
This fateful city, Antioch,
has eaten up all my money,
this fateful city with her extravagant way of life.

Yet, I am young and in perfect health.
With an admirable mastery of Greek.
(I know Aristotle and Plato inside out,
orators and poets and what have you.)
I'm familiar with military matters,
and have befriended several commanders of the mercenaries.
I'm well-informed about administrative affairs, too.
Last year, I spent six months in Alexandria;
up to a point (and that is useful), I know what's happening there:
Kakergetes'* designs and villainies, et cetera.

Wherefore, I consider myself fully
suited to be of service to this country,
my beloved native land, Syria.

Whatever job they put me in, I'll do my best
to be useful to the country. That's my intention.
If, however, they get in my way with their methods—
we know these busybodies now; need we say more?
If they get in my way, how am I to blame?

I'll turn to Zabinas* first,
and if that moron does not appreciate me,
I'm off to his adversary Grypos;

Κι ἂν ὁ ἠλίθιος κι αὐτὸς δὲν μὲ προσλάβει,
πηγαίνω παρευθὺς στὸν Ὑρκανό.

Θὰ μὲ θελήσει πάντως ἕνας ἀπ' τοὺς τρεῖς.

Κ' εἶν' ἡ συνείδησίς μου ἥσυχη
γιὰ τὸ ἀψήφιστο τῆς ἐκλογῆς.
Βλάπτουν κ' οἱ τρεῖς τους τὴν Συρία τὸ ἴδιο.

Ἀλλά, κατεστραμένος ἄνθρωπος, τί φταίω ἐγώ.
Ζητῶ ὁ ταλαίπωρος νὰ μπαλοθῶ.
Ἂς φρόντιζαν οἱ κραταιοὶ θεοὶ
νὰ δημιουργήσουν ἕναν τέταρτο καλό.
Μετὰ χαρᾶς θὰ πήγαινα μ' αὐτόν.

ΚΑΤΑ ΤΕΣ ΣΥΝΤΑΓΕΣ ΑΡΧΑΙΩΝ ΕΛΛΗΝΟΣΥΡΩΝ ΜΑΓΩΝ

«Ποιὸ ἀπόσταγμα νὰ βρίσκεται ἀπὸ βότανα
γητεύματος», εἶπ' ἕνας αἰσθητής,
«ποιὸ ἀπόσταγμα κατὰ τὲς συνταγὲς
ἀρχαίων Ἑλληνοσύρων μάγων καμωμένο
ποῦ γιὰ μιὰ μέρα (ἂν περισσότερο
δὲν φθάν' ἡ δύναμίς του), ἢ καὶ γιὰ λίγην ὥρα
τὰ εἴκοσι τρία μου χρόνια νὰ μὲ φέρει
ξανά· τὸν φίλον μου στὰ εἴκοσι δυό του χρόνια
νὰ μὲ φέρει ξανὰ — τὴν ἐμορφιά του, τὴν ἀγάπη του.

«Ποιὸ ἀπόσταγμα νὰ βρίσκεται κατὰ τὲς συνταγὲς
ἀρχαίων Ἑλληνοσύρων μάγων καμωμένο
ποῦ, σύμφωνα μὲ τὴν ἀναδρομήν,
καὶ τὴν μικρή μας κάμαρη νὰ ἐπαναφέρει.»

and if that idiot, too, won't employ me,
I'll go right away to Hyrkanos.*

Anyway, one of the three should take me on.

And my conscience is at peace
about the random nature of my choice.
All three of them are equally harmful for Syria.

But, a ruined man, how am I to blame?
I'm trying—poor wretch—to make ends meet.
If only the almighty gods had seen to it,
and had created a fourth man, a good one,
happily I would have sided with him.

ACCORDING TO THE RECIPES OF ANCIENT GRECO-SYRIAN MAGICIANS

'What extract can be found, distilled from
magical herbs,' said an aesthete,
'what extract distilled according to the recipes
of ancient Greco-Syrian magicians,
that for a single day (if its effect
cannot last longer) or even for a little while
might bring back again my twenty-three years;
bring back my friend at twenty-two,
bring back to me his beauty, his affection?

'What extract can be found, distilled according to the
recipes of ancient Greco-Syrian magicians,
that in keeping with this evocation of the past,
might bring back again our little room?'

ΣΤΑ 200 Π.Χ.

«Ἀλέξανδρος Φιλίππου καὶ οἱ Ἕλληνες πλὴν Λακεδαιμονίων—»

Μποροῦμε κάλλιστα νὰ φαντασθοῦμε
πῶς θ' ἀδιαφόρησαν παντάπασι στὴν Σπάρτη
γιὰ τὴν ἐπιγραφὴν αὐτή. «Πλὴν Λακεδαιμονίων»,
μὰ φυσικά. Δὲν ἦσαν οἱ Σπαρτιᾶται
γιὰ νὰ τοὺς ὁδηγοῦν καὶ γιὰ νὰ τοὺς προστάζουν
σὰν πολυτίμους ὑπηρέτας. Ἄλλωστε
μιὰ πανελλήνια ἐκστρατεία χωρὶς
Σπαρτιάτη βασιλέα γι' ἀρχηγὸ
δὲν θὰ τοὺς φαίνονταν πολλῆς περιωπῆς.
Ἆ βεβαιότατα «πλὴν Λακεδαιμονίων».

Εἶναι κι αὐτὴ μιὰ στάσις. Νοιώθεται.

Ἔτσι, πλὴν Λακεδαιμονίων στὸν Γρανικό·
καὶ στὴν Ἰσσὸ μετά· καὶ στὴν τελειωτικὴ
τὴν μάχη, ὅπου ἐσαρώθη ὁ φοβερὸς στρατὸς
ποῦ στ' Ἄρβηλα συγκέντρωσαν οἱ Πέρσαι:
ποῦ ἀπ' τ' Ἄρβηλα ξεκίνησε γιὰ νίκην, κ' ἐσαρώθη.

Κι ἀπ' τὴν θαυμάσια πανελλήνιαν ἐκστρατεία,
τὴν νικηφόρα, τὴν περίλαμπρη,
τὴν περιλάλητη, τὴν δοξασμένη
ὡς ἄλλη δὲν δοξάσθηκε καμιά,
τὴν ἀπαράμιλλη: βγήκαμ' ἐμεῖς·
ἑλληνικὸς καινούριος κόσμος, μέγας.

Ἐμεῖς· οἱ Ἀλεξανδρεῖς, οἱ Ἀντιοχεῖς,
οἱ Σελευκεῖς, κ' οἱ πολυάριθμοι
ἐπίλοιποι Ἕλληνες Αἰγύπτου καὶ Συρίας,
κ' οἱ ἐν Μηδίᾳ, κ' οἱ ἐν Περσίδι, κι ὅσοι ἄλλοι.
Μὲ τὲς ἐκτεταμένες ἐπικράτειες,
μὲ τὴν ποικίλη δρᾶσι τῶν στοχαστικῶν προσαρμογῶν.
Καὶ τὴν Κοινὴν Ἑλληνικὴ Λαλιὰ
ὡς μέσα στὴν Βακτριανὴ τὴν πήγαμεν, ὡς τοὺς Ἰνδούς.

Γιὰ Λακεδαιμονίους νὰ μιλοῦμε τώρα!

IN THE YEAR 200 B.C.

'Alexander, son of Philip, and the Greeks except the Lacedaemonians.'—

We can very well imagine
how indifferent everybody was at Sparta
to this inscription: 'except the Lacedaemonians'—
but naturally. The Spartans were not
to be led and to be ordered about
like prized servants. Anyway,
a pan-Hellenic expedition without
a Spartan king in command
wouldn't seem to them of high repute.
Well, of course, 'except the Lacedaemonians'.

This, too, is an attitude of life. It's understandable.

So, 'except the Lacedaemonians' at Granicus
and then at Issus; and in the final
battle where the awesome army was swept away,
which the Persians had amassed at Arbela,
which set out from Arbela for victory, and was swept away.

And out of that wondrous pan-Hellenic expedition,
the victorious, the most brilliant,
the widely renowned, the praised for glory
as no other has ever been praised,
the incomparable, we came to be:
a new Hellenic world, a great one.

We: the Alexandrians, the Antiochians,
the Seleucians, and the numerous
other Hellenes of Egypt and Syria,
and those in Media and those in Persia, and so many others.
With their extended dominions,
and their various attempts at judicious adaptations.
And the Greek *koine** language—
all the way to outer Bactria* we carried it, to the peoples of India.

Do we need to talk about Lacedaemonians now!

ΜΕΡΕΣ ΤΟΥ 1908

Τὸν χρόνο ἐκεῖνον βρέθηκε χωρὶς δουλειά·
καὶ συνεπῶς ζοῦσεν ἀπ' τὰ χαρτιά,
ἀπὸ τὸ τάβλι, καὶ τὰ δανεικά.

Μιὰ θέσις, τριῶ λιρῶν τὸν μῆνα, σὲ μικρὸ
χαρτοπωλεῖον τοῦ εἶχε προσφερθεῖ.
Μὰ τὴν ἀρνήθηκε, χωρὶς κανένα δισταγμό.
Δὲν ἔκανε. Δὲν ἤτανε μισθὸς γι' αὐτόν,
νέον μὲ γράμματ' ἀρκετά, καὶ εἴκοσι πέντ' ἐτῶν.

Δυό, τρία σελίνια τὴν ἡμέρα κέρδιζε, δὲν κέρδιζε.
Ἀπὸ χαρτιὰ καὶ τάβλι τί νὰ βγάλει τὸ παιδί,
στὰ καφενεῖα τῆς σειρᾶς του, τὰ λαϊκά,
ὅσο κι ἂν ἔπαιζ' ἔξυπνα, ὅσο κι ἂν διάλεγε κουτούς.
Τὰ δανεικά, αὐτὰ δὰ ἦσαν κ' ἦσαν.
Σπάνια τὸ τάλληρο εὕρισκε, τὸ πιὸ συχνὰ μισό,
κάποτε ξέπεφτε καὶ στὸ σελίνι.

Καμιὰ ἑβδομάδα, ἐνίοτε πιὸ πολύ,
σὰν γλύτωνεν ἀπ' τὸ φρικτὸ ξενύχτι,
δροσίζονταν στὰ μπάνια, στὸ κολύμβι τὸ πρωΐ.

Τὰ ροῦχα του εἶχαν ἕνα χάλι τρομερό.
Μιὰ φορεσιὰ τὴν ἴδια πάντοτ' ἔβαζε, μιὰ φορεσιὰ
πολὺ ξεθωριασμένη κανελιά.

Ἆ μέρες τοῦ καλοκαιριοῦ τοῦ ἐννιακόσια ὀκτώ,
ἀπ' τὸ εἴδωμά σας, καλαισθητικά,
ἔλειψ' ἡ κανελιὰ ξεθωριασμένη φορεσιά.

Τὸ εἴδωμά σας τὸν ἐφύλαξε
ὅταν ποῦ τἄβγαζε, ποῦ τἄριχνε ἀπὸ πάνω του,
τ' ἀνάξια ροῦχα, καὶ τὰ μπαλωμένα ἐσώρουχα.
Κ' ἔμενε ὁλόγυμνος· ἄψογα ὡραῖος· ἕνα θαῦμα.
Ἀχτένιστα, ἀνασηκωμένα τὰ μαλλιά του·
τὰ μέλη του ἡλιοκαμένα λίγο
ἀπὸ τὴν γύμνια τοῦ πρωϊοῦ στὰ μπάνια, καὶ στὴν παραλία.

DAYS OF 1908

That year he found himself without a job,
and consequently he lived by playing cards,
backgammon, and on borrowed money.

A job, at three pounds a month, in a small
stationery store, had been offered him.
But he turned it down, without any hesitation.
It wouldn't do. That was no salary for him,
a young man, quite lettered, and only twenty-five.

He scraped together two or three shillings a day.
What could the lad earn playing cards and backgammon,
in the lowly cafés of his social class,
however smartly he played, however much he picked stupid players?
As for loans, that's where he fared worst.
He rarely could find five shillings, more often half of that;
sometimes he'd come down to a shilling.

For about a week, occasionally even longer,
when he escaped the awful all-nighters,
he'd refresh himself at the beach, with a morning swim.

His clothes were in an appalling state.
He always wore the same suit,
a much-faded, light brown suit.

Ah, summer days of nineteen hundred and eight,
aesthetically, the faded light brown suit
is missing from your imagery.

Your imagery has preserved him
as he took off, threw off
those unbecoming clothes and the mended underwear.
And he stood stark naked; consummately handsome; a miracle.
His hair, uncombed, ruffled up;
his limbs somewhat sunburnt,
from the morning's nakedness in the sea, and on the beach.

ΕΙΣ ΤΑ ΠΕΡΙΧΩΡΑ ΤΗΣ ΑΝΤΙΟΧΕΙΑΣ

Σαστίσαμε στὴν Ἀντιόχειαν ὅταν μάθαμε
τὰ νέα καμώματα τοῦ Ἰουλιανοῦ.

Ὁ Ἀπόλλων ἐξηγήθηκε μὲ λόγου του, στὴν Δάφνη!
Χρησμὸ δὲν ἤθελε νὰ δόσει (σκοτισθήκαμε!),
σκοπὸ δὲν τὄχε νὰ μιλήσει μαντικῶς, ἂν πρῶτα
δὲν καθαρίζονταν τὸ ἐν Δάφνῃ τέμενός του.
Τὸν ἐνοχλοῦσαν, δήλωσεν, οἱ γειτονεύοντες νεκροί.

Στὴν Δάφνη βρίσκονταν τάφοι πολλοί.—
Ἕνας ἀπ' τοὺς ἐκεῖ ἐνταφιασμένους
ἦταν ὁ θαυμαστός, τῆς ἐκκλησίας μας δόξα,
ὁ ἅγιος, ὁ καλλίνικος μάρτυς Βαβύλας.

Αὐτὸν αἰνίττονταν, αὐτὸν φοβοῦνταν ὁ ψευτοθεός.
Ὅσο τὸν ἔνοιωθε κοντὰ δὲν κόταε
νὰ βγάλει τοὺς χρησμούς του· τσιμουδιά.
(Τοὺς τρέμουνε τοὺς μάρτυράς μας οἱ ψευτοθεοί).

Ἀνασκουμπόθηκεν ὁ ἀνόσιος Ἰουλιανός,
νεύριασε καὶ ξεφώνιζε: Σηκῶστε, μεταφέρτε τον,
βγάλτε τον τοῦτον τὸν Βαβύλα ἀμέσως.
Ἀκοῦς ἐκεῖ; Ὁ Ἀπόλλων ἐνοχλεῖται.
Σηκῶστε τον, ἁρπάξτε τον εὐθύς.
Ξεθάψτε τον, πάρτε τον ὅπου θέτε.
Βγάλτε τον, διῶξτε τον. Παίζουμε τώρα;
Ὁ Ἀπόλλων εἶπε νὰ καθαρισθεῖ τὸ τέμενος.

Τὸ πήραμε, τὸ πήγαμε τὸ ἅγιο λείψανον ἀλλοῦ.
Τὸ πήραμε, τὸ πήγαμε ἐν ἀγάπῃ κ' ἐν τιμῇ.

Κι ὡραῖα τωόντι πρόκοψε τὸ τέμενος.
Δὲν ἄργησε καθόλου, καὶ φωτιὰ
μεγάλη κόρωσε: μιὰ φοβερὴ φωτιά:
καὶ κάηκε καὶ τὸ τέμενος κι ὁ Ἀπόλλων.

*

IN THE OUTSKIRTS OF ANTIOCH

We were aghast here in Antioch, when we heard
of Julian's latest antics.

Apollo made it clear to him at Daphne!
He would not deliver an oracle (much that we cared!),
he did not intend to utter prophecies, until
his shrine at Daphne had been purified.
He was being disturbed, he said, by the nearby dead.

At Daphne, there were many graves.
One of those buried there
was the miraculous, the glory of our church,
the saintly, the triumphant martyr Babylas.

To him he alluded, him he feared, that false god.
As long as he sensed him close by, he didn't dare
utter his prophecies; not a word.
(They are terrified of our martyrs, those false gods.)

The sacrilegious Julian girded himself,
lost his temper and screamed: 'Pick him up, take him elsewhere,
take out this Babylas immediately.
Imagine! Apollo disturbed.
Pick him up, grab him at once.
Dig him out, take him where you will.
Remove him, away with him. This is no game!
Apollo ordered that the shrine be purified.'

We took it, we removed the sacred relic elsewhere.
We took it away, we removed it lovingly and reverently.

And the shrine thrived well indeed!
It wasn't long before
a great fire blazed; a terrible fire;
and both Apollo and the shrine went up in flames.

*

Στάχτη τὸ εἴδωλο· γιὰ σάρωμα, μὲ τὰ σκουπίδια.

Ἔσκασε ὁ Ἰουλιανὸς καὶ διέδοσε—
τί ἄλλο θὰ ἔκαμνε—πῶς ἡ φωτιὰ ἦταν βαλτὴ
ἀπὸ τοὺς Χριστιανοὺς ἐμᾶς. Ἂς πάει νὰ λέει.
Δὲν ἀποδείχθηκε· ἂς πάει νὰ λέει.
Τὸ οὐσιῶδες εἶναι ποὺ ἔσκασε.

The idol in ashes, to be swept away with the trash.

Julian had a fit, and spread the rumour—
what else could he do—that it was arson,
and we the Christians did it. Well, let him talk.
It has not been proven; let him talk.
The important thing is that he had a fit.

EXPLANATORY NOTES

Since there is no universally accepted system of transliteration, Greek proper names have been rendered into English in the following manner: Latinized spellings in common use are retained (i.e. Phoebus, Ithaca); other names have been transliterated following Greek spelling (i.e. Hedyoinos).

Frequently occurring terms are given in the Glossary.

POEMS 1910 [1897–1909]

The first step

7 *Theocritus*: Theocritus of Syracuse (*c*.310–245 BC) was a well-known poet throughout the Hellenistic world, acclaimed for his pastoral idylls. He spent part of his life in Alexandria. Both Eumenes and the scene appear to be poetical inventions.

Interruption

9 *Metaneira*: queen of Eleusis and mother of Demophon, and Peleus, king of Phthia and father of Achilles, were both said to have intervened in fire rituals, in which, respectively, Demeter (goddess of earthly fecundity) and Thetis (a sea-nymph and mother of Achilles) passed the infants Demophon and Achilles through the smoke and fire of the hearth in order to render them invulnerable and thus immortal. By intervening, they prevented their sons from receiving the full benefits of the ritual, and thus the infants remained mortal and at least in part vulnerable to wounds. The story of Demophon is given in the 'Homeric Hymn to Demeter', lines 230–300; that of Peleus and Thetis in Apollodorus, *The Library*, 3. 170–1. Related poem: 'Perfidy'.

Thermopylae

11 *Thermopylae*: the Battle of Thermopylae, one of the most famous in world history, took place at the end of summer, 480 BC. After a series of unsuccessful attempts to break through, Xerxes' Persian forces (the 'Medes' of the poem), led by the Greek traitor Ephialtes, were guided to the rear of the Greek army. In the final phase of the engagement, the contingent of 300 Spartans, refusing to surrender, was annihilated. Yet the initial inability of the Persians to break through the meagre Greek lines made the defeat appear tantamount to a victory. Simonides' epitaph honouring the Spartan dead of the battle is worth repeating: 'O stranger, go tell the Lacedaemonians that we lie here, obedient to their command.'

Che fece . . . il gran rifiuto

From Dante's *Inferno*, Canto III, line 60. The entire tercet reads as follows: 'Poscia ch'io v'ebbi alcun riconosciuto, | vidi e conobbi l'ombra di colui | che fece per viltate il gran rifiuto.' ('After I had recognized some of them, | I saw and knew the shade of him | who, through cowardice, made the great refusal', tr. H. R. Huse). The lines may refer to Celestine, who was elected pope in 1294 and abdicated five months later. The words 'per viltate' in the middle of the line have been omitted in the title. Some Cavafy scholars believe that this poem reflects the ethical standards of any man who says 'No' to the norms and demands of society, and that it has, therefore, a homoerotic subtext.

Perfidy

The poem has the same mythological background as 'The horses of Achilles', 'The funeral of Sarpedon', and 'Interruption'.

The funeral of Sarpedon

Related poems: 'The horses of Achilles', 'Perfidy'.

21 *Sarpedon*: king of Lycia, allied to the Trojans, who was killed by Achilles' friend Patroclus, son of Menoetius. Sarpedon was the son of Zeus and Laodameia. Apollo was his half-brother. See *Iliad* XVI. 462–501, 666–84.

The horses of Achilles

Related poems: 'The funeral of Sarpedon', 'Perfidy', 'Trojans', 'Interruption'.

23 *the horses of Achilles*: Balios and Xanthos, Achilles' horses, mythological offspring of Zephyros (West Wind) and Podarge. For their origin see *Iliad* XVI. 149–254; for their subsequent story see *Iliad* XVII. 426–47.

POEMS (1905–1915)

Satrapy

The Persian Empire was divided into satrapies, that is, individual provinces governed by a satrap. Cavafy has mentioned that the protagonist of the poem does not have to be identified with the Athenian statesman Themistocles or the Spartan king Demaratus, who both ended up in the Persian court at the end of their political careers in Greece, but that he is more of a symbolic figure. Related poem: 'Demaratus'.

29 *Susa*: an early capital of Persia under the Achaemenids.

Wise men

31 For Philostratus see note to 'If dead indeed'.

The ides of March

A seer had warned Julius Caesar to beware of the Ides of March, that is, the fifteenth day of that month. On 15 March 44 BC Caesar's philosopher and friend Artemidorus vainly tried to hand him a message warning him of the conspiracy that resulted in his murder later that day.

33 *Artemidorus*: Greek philosopher mentioned by both Plutarch and Suetonius in their lives of Julius Caesar.

The god forsakes Antony

The poem refers to the story told by Plutarch in his 'Life of Antony', in which just before the fall of Alexandria and his death, the Roman general and politician Mark Antony heard the sound of many instruments and voices singing, and the cries of people shouting and dancing. This procession seemed to cross the city towards the gate where the enemy was located, and to pass out through it. People assumed this to signify that the god Dionysus had now forsaken him. Related poems: 'In Alexandria, 31 B.C.', 'In a township of Asia Minor'.

Theodotus

Theodotus was an orator, probably from Samos, teacher of Ptolemy XII. He persuaded the Egyptians to kill Julius Caesar's rival Pompey in 48 BC, when the latter had landed in Egypt, having lost the Battle of Pharsala against Caesar's forces. There is no historical certainty that it was Theodotus who brought Pompey's head to Caesar.

Ithaca

37 *Ithaca*: homeland of Odysseus in Homer's *Odyssey*.

Laestrygonians . . . Cyclopes: in the *Odyssey*, the Laestrygonians are fierce giants who destroy most of Odysseus' ships and men. The Cyclopes were a savage race of one-eyed giants inhabiting Sicily. Polyphemus, the most famous of them and the son of Poseidon, god of the sea, was blinded by Odysseus.

Trojans

Related poem: 'The horses of Achilles'.

41 *Priam*: king of Troy, husband of Hecuba and father of Hector, Paris, and Cassandra. He was slain by Neoptolemos, son of Achilles. Homer refers to him often as 'Dardanides', because his family was descended from Dardanos.

King Demetrius

Demetrius I Poliorketes (the Besieger) (336/7–283 BC), king of Macedonia. The poem refers to chapters 44 and 41 of Plutarch's 'Life of Demetrius' and to the dialogue *The Cock* by Lucian of Samosata. Related poem: 'On the march to Sinope'.

43 *Pyrrhus*: (319–272 BC), king of Epirus. When he invaded Macedon in 288 the Macedonian troops deserted Demetrius and went over to his side.

The glory of the Ptolemies

The Ptolemies are the sixteen kings and queens of Egypt, descended from Alexander the Great's general Ptolemy I Soter, who formed the Macedonian dynasty (323–30 BC).

The retinue of Dionysus

Damon is an imaginary character, but the other references and details appear to be consistent with the mythology.

45 *Akratos*: one of the retinue of Dionysus, god of wine. His name means 'unwatered' or 'unmixed' (referring to wine). He was particularly venerated in Athens and Piraeus. In the poem, the retinue also consists of: *Hedyoinos* ('Sweet-wine'), *Methe* ('Stupor'), and the personifications of music, *Molpos* and *Hedymeles* ('Sweet Singer'), of theatre, *Comus*, and of initiation, *Teleté*.

The Battle of Magnesia

Philip V of Macedon, left unassisted by the other Greek states, was defeated by the Romans at the famous Battle of Cynocephalae in 197 BC. The scene of the poem is imaginary and is set seven years later, just after the Battle of Magnesia at Magnesia-by-Sipylos in Syria, where in 190 or early 189 BC the Romans, led by the two Scipio brothers, crossed the Hellespont with a small army of 30,000 men. Antiochus III opposed them with a force of 75,000 men. In the end, the Seleucid monarch's forces were shattered, despite a heroic stand by the phalanx. In the aftermath, the Scipios occupied Sardis.

The displeasure of the Seleucid

The Seleucids were a Greek dynasty ruling Syria, and at various times other Near Eastern territories, from 312 to 64 BC. Related poems: 'Orophernes', 'Of Demetrius Soter', 'If only they had seen to it', 'Envoys from Alexandria'.

47 *Demetrius*: Demetrius Soter, son of Seleucus IV Philopater (162–150 BC) of Syria and grandson of Antiochus the Great, was sent to Rome as a hostage during the reign of his father. The other king referred to in the poem is Ptolemy VI Philometor of Egypt (181–145 BC).

Orophernes

Related poems: 'The Battle of Magnesia', 'The displeasure of the Seleucid', 'Of Demetrios Soter'.

49 *Orophernes*: Orophernes II, supposedly the son of Ariarathes IV of Cappadocia. His mother, Antiochis, was the daughter of Antiochus III the Great of Syria. His grandmother, Stratonike, was the daughter of Antiochus II. Demetrius of Syria put him on the throne of Cappadocia in 157 BC, but three years later he was deposed and fled to Antioch, where he attempted to usurp the throne of his protector.

Alexandrian kings

The ceremony described in the poem is a historical fact; it was a spectacle, well stage-managed by Mark Antony. Alexander and Ptolemy Philadelphos were Antony's sons. Caesarion was thought to be the son of Julius Caesar and Cleopatra. He was executed in 30 BC. Antony had invested the three children with titles and honours. See Plutarch, 'Life of Antony', ch. 54; Shakespeare, *Antony and Cleopatra*, Act III. VI. Related poems: 'The god forsakes Antony', 'Caesarion', 'The ides of March', 'Theodotus'.

Philhellene

From the beginning of Hellenistic times, various Hellenizing rulers commonly added the title 'Philhellene' (lover of Greek culture) to their other surnames.

The footsteps

An earlier version was published as 'The footsteps of the Eumenides'. The poem refers to a passage in Suetonius' 'Life of Nero', ch. 46. Nero was the son of Domitius Ahenobarbus and Agrippina, who later became wife of the emperor Claudius. She poisoned her husband in order to give the throne to her son, who, in turn, had her murdered in AD 59.

57 *Lares*: *Lares familiares* were minor deities of Rome and household patrons. Statues of them were kept in small household shrines called *lararia* (sing. *lararium*).

the Furies: in Classical mythology divine avengers of crime, especially within the family. They are about to punish Nero for having murdered his mother and other members of his immediate kin.

Herod Atticus

57 *Herod Atticus*: (AD 101–77). One of the richest Athenians, renowned sophist, patron of the arts, benefactor of Athens, and friend of the Roman emperor Hadrian.

Alexander of Seleucia: a philosopher, scornfully referred to as 'a clay Plato' by Philostratus in *Lives of the Sophists*, 2 B. 1–15.

Sculptor of Tyana

Related poems: 'Wise men', 'If dead indeed', 'Apollonius of Tyana in Rhodes'.

59 *Tyana*: ancient city in Cappadocia and birthplace of the famous philosopher Apollonius.

Rhea: wife of Saturn and mother of the Olympian gods.

Pompey . . . Scipio Africanus: Roman generals.

Patroclus: the friend of Achilles in the *Iliad*.

Caesarion: see note to the poem 'Caesarion' (p. 219).

Tomb of Eurion

All characters mentioned are imaginary. Other poems with references to the Jews and the relations between the Jews and Hellenism: 'Of the Hebrews', 'Aristoboulos', 'Alexander Jannaeus and Alexandra'.

61 *syenite stone*: reddish granitic rock from Syene (Aswan) in Egypt.

Jewish magistrates: i.e. alabarchs, magistrates of the Alexandrian Jewish community.

Arsinoïte nome: prefecture (*nome*) based around the city of Arsinoe, which was built on the ruins of Crocodeilopolis by Ptolemy Philadelphos, in honour of his wife Arsinoe II. Located at the Fayum oasis, it soon became a city of purely Greek character.

That is the Man

The poem refers to a passage from *The Dream* (9) by Lucian of Samosata (AD 120–200), in which the writer explains how he embarked on his literary career. Culture (Gr. *Paideia*) appeared before him in a dream and promised to attach on him marks of identification so that wherever he goes people will whisper to each other: 'That's the man.' The scene, like the anonymous poet of the story, is fictitious.

63 *Antioch . . . Edessa*: the ancient city of Edessa was the capital of Osroene, in northwest Mesopotamia. Antioch was the capital of Syria and Cavafy's second most favoured city after Alexandria. It is mentioned in a great number of his poems.

Perilous things

Myrtias is a fictional character.

63 *Constans*: Roman emperor, AD 337–50. The youngest son of Constantine the Great, he and his brothers Constantine and Constantius became co-emperors in AD 337 upon the death of their father. In 340 they waged war against each other and Constantine was killed. Constans then ruled his brother's dominions. He was murdered in 350.

Manuel Comnenus

65 *King Manuel Comnenus*: Manuel I Comnenus (son of John II) became emperor of Byzantium in AD 1143. A brave and capable military leader, he fought successfully against the Turks of Iconium (now Konya), the Normans of Italy, and the Hungarians. His defeat at Myriocephalos (1174), though, had disastrous consequences for Byzantium.

POEMS (1916–1918)

Before the statue of Endymion

Related poem: 'Of the Hebrews'.

81 *Endymion*: a mythological character known for his beauty. Selene (the Moon) persuaded Zeus to let her keep him in eternal sleep, so that she could forever preserve his beauty and visit him every night.

Envoys from Alexandria

The quarrelling monarchs are Ptolemy VI Philometor and his younger brother Ptolemy VIII Evergetes, co-rulers of Egypt from 170 to 164 BC. The event in question took place in 164 BC. The scene, at the oracle of Apollo in Delphi, is imaginary. Related poems: 'The displeasure of the Seleucid', 'If only they had seen to it'.

Aristoboulos

83 *Aristoboulos*: Aristoboulos III of Judea was the son of Alexandra and the brother of Miriam, wife of Herod I the Great (73–4 BC), who was declared king of Judea in 40 BC. Aristoboulos was drowned by order of Herod in a swimming-pool (35 BC). Related poem: 'Alexander Jannaeus, and Alexandra'.

Hasmonaeans: members of a religious dynasty to which the Maccabees belonged, named after their ancestor Hasmon. They started the successful revolt against the Seleucids of Syria.

85 *Cyprus and Salome*: Cyprus was the mother of Herod I the Great, who incited her son to commit this murder. Salome was the daughter of Herod Philip, son of Herod the Great and Herodias. She is the one who demanded and received the head of John the Baptist. She was first the wife of her uncle Philip and then of her cousin Aristoboulos, king of Syrian Chalkis.

Caesarion

'Caesarion' was the nickname of Ptolemy XV Caesar, ostensibly the son of Julius Caesar and Cleopatra, who was invested with the title 'King of Kings' by Mark Antony. Following Antony's defeat at Actium in 31 BC the victor Octavian (later the emperor Augustus) ordered Caesarion's execution. Related poems: 'Alexandrian kings', 'The god forsakes Antony', 'In Alexandria, 31 B.C.'.

85 *Berenices*: name of three queens of the Ptolemy family.

87 *Too Many Caesars!*: paraphrases *Iliad* II. 204, 'it's not good to have many kings'.

Nero's term

Nero Claudius Caesar (AD 37–68) was emperor of Rome from 54 to 68. In the year 67 he paid a lengthy visit to the region of Achaea and other parts of Greece. A year later the Roman legions in Spain asked their general Galba to take over as emperor, replacing Nero, who committed suicide shortly thereafter. Related poem: 'The footsteps'.

87 *the Delphic Oracle*: the oracle of Apollo at Delphi, the most important oracular site in the ancient world.

One of their gods

There were several cities by the name of Seleucia. The poem refers to the greatest and most renowned of these, founded in 320 BC on the River Tigris by Seleucus I Nicator, who intended to make it the capital of his empire.

Tomb of Lanes

All characters are imaginary. Of the names, Lanes (two syllables) is Greek; Rhametichos is Egyptian; and Marcus is Roman, while the painter was a native of the North African province of Cyrene.

91 *Hyacinthus*: a mythological character, a mortal with whom Apollo fell in love. Hyacinthus was killed by Zephyros in a fit of jealousy. The flower bearing his name sprang from his blood.

Tomb of Iases

Iases is an imaginary character.

91 *Narcissus*: mythological character, known for his beauty and vanity. Son of the river-god Kephisos, he fell in love with his own reflection in the water and eventually was transformed into the flower that bears his name.

A town in Osroene

Both the scene and the characters are imaginary. Osroene was a kingdom in Mesopotamia. Its capital was Edessa.

93 *Plato's Charmides*: Plato immortalized his uncle Charmides in a dialogue bearing his name, in which Socrates is inspired by the physical beauty of Charmides as a young man. The dialogue is an inquiry into wisdom and temperance.

In the month of Athyr

Leucius is an imaginary character.

93 *Athyr*: The third month of the ancient Egyptian calendar, corresponding to today's October or November, bearing the name of Athyr, goddess of tombs and sensual love.

Kappa Zeta: KZ is 27 in Greek numerals.

For Ammones, who died aged 29, in 610

The characters are imaginary. Both are Egyptians, as is clear from their names (Ammones is named after the ancient Egyptian god Ammon).

Aemilianus Monaë, Alexandrian, A.D. 628–655

Aemilianus Monaë is an imaginary character. Egypt, part of the Byzantine Empire since the fourth century AD, was conquered by the Muslim Arabs in 640–2.

POEMS 1919–1933

Of the Hebrews (A.D. 50)

Ianthes is an imaginary character; he is a Jew with a Greek name. The date in the title indicates that he lived during the reign of the Roman emperor Claudius. Related poem: 'Before the statue of Endymion'.

Imenos

Imenos is an imaginary character.

115 *Michael III*: Byzantine emperor, AD 842–67, known as 'the drunkard'.

Of Demetrius Soter (162–150 B.C.)

Demetrius Soter, king of Syria, was the son of Seleucus IV. He unseated the tyrant Heracleides, and for this was named Soter (Saviour). Conqueror of Judaea, he was defeated by the united armies of Ptolemy Philometor, Ariarathes V, and Attalos II. He spent his youth in Rome as a hostage, while the throne of Syria was occupied first by Antiochus IV Epiphanes and later by his cousin Antiochus V. In 162 BC Demetrius escaped from Italy, recovered his throne, and attempted to restore Syria's strength and influence in the region. Successful at first, he later became a morose alcoholic and was defeated and killed by Alexander Balas, a pretender to the throne, in 150 BC. Related poems: 'The displeasure of the Seleucid', 'Orophernes', 'The Battle of Magnesia', 'Craftsman of craters', 'To Antiochus Epiphanes', 'Temethos, Antiochian, A.D. 400', 'The favour of Alexander Balas', 'Envoys from Alexandria'.

If dead indeed

119 *the Sage*: Apollonius, a Neo-Pythagorean philosopher, magician, and conductor of propitiatory rites, from Tyana in Cappadocia. Details of his life and his fame present distinct parallels to early Christian beliefs about Jesus. It was reputed that he performed miracles and that he disappeared or ascended to heaven either at the Temple of Athena at Lindos in Rhodes or at the Temple of the Minoan goddess Diktynna in Crete. Philostratus based his *Life of Apollonius of Tyana* on the account by Damis, a student of Apollonius.

121 *the aged Justin*: the Byzantine emperor Justin I (*c.*AD 450–527).

Young men of Sidon (A.D. 400)

The epigram quoted in the third stanza is supposed to have been written by the tragedian Aeschylus (several of whose plays are mentioned in stanza 4) as his own epitaph.

121 *Meleager and Crinagoras and Rhianos*: Meleager (fl. *c.*100 BC), a Cynic philosopher and epigrammist from Gadara in Syria; lived in Tyre; died at Kos. About 131 erotic epigrams of his are extant. Crinagoras was a composer of epigrams from Mytilene, born between 70 and 65 BC. He was a friend of Julius Caesar and Augustus. Rhianos (*b.* 275 BC), an Alexandrian epic poet from Crete. Few of his verses survive.

123 *Datis*: a general from Media, who along with Artaphernes, the nephew of Darius, commanded the Persian armies at the Battle of Marathon in 490 BC.

Darius

The scene and the name of the poet Phernazes are imaginary. Related poems: 'Young men of Sidon', 'Demaratus', 'Theodotus'.

125 *Darius, son of Hystaspes*: Darius I (521–486 BC), was, after Cyrus the Great (554–529 BC), the most important of the Achaemenid kings of Persia. It was his armies that were defeated by the Greeks at Marathon in 490 BC.

Mithridates . . . Eupator: Mithridates VI Eupator, king of Pontos, 120–63 BC. Cicero considered him the most formidable opponent of Rome. He ascended the throne in 115 BC. He initiated the Third Mithridatic War (74 BC), but was eventually defeated by the Roman generals Lucullus and Pompey (66 BC) and was driven to suicide.

Amisos: now Samsun, Turkey; important city on the coast of the Black Sea that fell to the Romans in 71 BC.

Anna Comnena

127 *Anna Comnena*: daughter of the Byzantine emperor Alexios I Comnenus. In 1118 she made an unsuccessful attempt to usurp the throne from her brother John II, ostensibly on behalf of her husband Nikephoros Bryennios, whose death in 1136 ended her ambitions. She retired to a monastic life and wrote the *Alexiad*, a biography of her father, from which the quotations in the second stanza are taken.

A Byzantine Nobleman, in exile, composing verses

127 *Botaneiates*: Nikephoros III Botaneiates, emperor of Byzantium. He ousted Michael VII in 1078 and was dethroned by Alexius I Comnenus in 1081. Alexius' wife was Irene Doukaina.

The favour of Alexander Balas

Alexander Balas was king of Syria 150–145 BC. The circumstances of the poem are imaginary. Related poem: 'Of Demetrius Soter'.

Melancholy of Jason, son of Kleander, poet in Commagene, A.D. 595

Jason is an imaginary character. Commagene was a small state within the Hellenistic kingdom of Syria. Later it became part of the Byzantine empire until AD 638, when it was conquered by the Arabs. Its capital was Samosata. Related poem: 'Epitaph of Antiochus, king of Commagene'.

Demaratus

Demaratus was king of Sparta, 510–491 BC. King Cleomenes I—joint king with Demaratus—aided by Leotychides, bribed the Delphic Oracle to state that Demaratus was not a legitimate son of King Ariston. Demaratus fled to the court of Darius I, where he was well received. He informed the Persians about

Greek affairs, accompanying Xerxes during his disastrous campaign against Greece. Related poem: 'Darius'.

From the school of the renowned philosopher

135 *Ammonius Saccas*: neoplatonist philosopher who taught during the third century AD in Alexandria. He left no writings, but his circle of students included famous names like Plotinus, Origen, and Longinus. He died in AD 243.

Craftsman of craters

137 *Magnesian defeat*: see notes to poem 'The Battle of Magnesia' (p. 216).

Those who fought for the Achaean League

The Achaean League was the last attempt of mainland Greeks to present a unified front against the danger of Roman occupation, by reviving in 280 BC an older federal organization of the cities of Achaea. The epigram in the first stanza of the poem is ascribed to an imaginary Greek composer of epigrams, writing in 109 BC about the events of 146 BC.

137 *Diaeus and Critolaus*: generals of the armies of the Achaean League, they were defeated in Corinth in 146 BC by the Roman general Mummius.

Ptolemy Lathyros: Ptolemy IX, nicknamed 'Lathyros' (chickpea), reigned over Egypt and Cyprus (117–81 BC).

To Antiochus Epiphanes

The scene and the young companion of Antiochus IV Epiphanes of Syria (175–163 BC) are imaginary, but the event can be approximately dated to 169/8 BC. Antiochus IV Epiphanes was the son of Antiochus III the Great, who was defeated by the Romans at the Battle of Magnesia in 190 BC. The Macedonians tried to regain their status, but were finally defeated at the Battle of Pydna in 168 BC. Related poems: 'Temethos, Antiochian, A.D. 400', 'Of Demetrius Soter', 'The Battle of Magnesia'.

139 *Tyre*: a famous and prosperous harbour city of Phoenicia.

Julian, noticing negligence

Julian the Apostate, Roman emperor AD 361–3. He was attracted to the old religion and the philosophy of the pagan Greek world at a time when Christianity had already become the official religion of the empire. Julian promoted a new, austere brand of paganism, with roots in neoplatonism. The quotation in the poem comes from a letter written by Julian in AD 363, appointing Theodorus as High Priest of Asia. Related poems: 'Julian in Nicomedia', 'A great procession of priests and laymen', 'Julian and the Antiochians', 'You didn't understand', 'In the outskirts of Antioch'.

143 *Nothing in excess*: this maxim, along with 'know thyself', was inscribed above the gateway of the Delphic Oracle.

Julian in Nicomedia

Julian tried to hide his anti-Christian sentiments before he was pronounced emperor. His brother, Gallus, was executed by the emperor Constantius in AD 354. Related poems: 'Julian, noticing negligence', 'A great procession of priests and laymen', 'Julian and the Antiochians', 'You didn't understand', 'In the outskirts of Antioch'.

145 *Maximus*: Maximus of Ephesus, neoplatonic philosopher and teacher of Julian.

Mardonius: Julian's tutor from an early age.

Nicomedia: city in Asia Minor (now Izmit, Turkey), of great renown in antiquity; the capital of Bithynia.

In Alexandria, 31 B.C.

After the Battle of Actium in 31 BC, Cleopatra endeavoured to hide the defeat from her subjects by staging a triumphal entry into Alexandria. Related poems: 'The god forsakes Antony', 'Alexandrian kings', 'In a township of Asia Minor'.

John Cantacuzenus prevails

The protagonist is imaginary. John VI Cantacuzenus (reigned 1347–54), Byzantine emperor. Under Andronicus III (1328–41), he was in charge of the government. When Andronicus died he became regent, since the new emperor, John Palaeologos, was 9 years old. The dowager empress Anne of Savoy opposed him, and John proclaimed himself emperor. After six years of civil war, John Cantacuzenus and John Palaeologus became joint emperors. Eventually, John Cantacuzenus abdicated, became a monk, and wrote his memoirs. Related poem: 'Of coloured glass'.

149 *Lady Irene's*: see note to 'Of coloured glass' below.

Temethos, Antiochian, A.D. 400

Temethos is an imaginary character. Related poems: 'Epitaph of Antiochus, king of Commagene'.

151 *Samosata*: capital of Commagene, a small state within the Hellenistic kingdom of Syria.

hundred-and-thirty-seventh year . . . of the Greeks: 175 BC, dated from the origin of the Seleucid dynasty by Seleucus I Nikator in 312 BC.

Of coloured glass

153 *John Cantacuzenus*: see notes to 'John Cantacuzenus prevails' above.

Irene . . . Asan: she married John Cantacuzenus in the church at Blachernae palace in Constantinople, since the cathedral church of St Sophia was at the time partly in ruins. Irene's sister, Anne of Savoy, during the course of her confrontation with John Cantacuzenus, exhausted the financial resources of the empire to the point that she had to pawn the crown jewels.

On an Italian shore

The protagonist is imaginary. The poem refers to the events of 146 BC, when the Roman general Mummius sacked Corinth, massacring all the men, burning down the houses, selling the women and children into slavery, and transporting the art treasures of the city to Southern Italy (Magna Graecia). Related poem: 'Those who fought for the Achaean League'.

Apollonius of Tyana in Rhodes

See note to poem 'If dead indeed' (p. 221).

In a township of Asia Minor

The decree, as well as the scene, set in 31 BC, is imaginary.

159 *battle at Actium*: the naval battle of 31 BC, in which Mark Antony was defeated by Octavian.

A priest of the Serapeum

The Serapeum, or Temple of Serapis, in Alexandria, was built by Ptolemy I Soter, *c.*300 BC, rebuilt by Ptolemy III Evergetes, and destroyed by the Christian Byzantine emperor Theodosius in AD 391. The worship of the god Serapis as patron of Alexandria was instituted by the Ptolemies. The priests were usually Greeks.

A great procession of priests and laymen

The emperor Julian the Apostate was killed on 26 June 363, and his successor Jovian, a Christian army commander, reigned for seven months. The procession to which the poem refers took place on Holy Cross Day (14 September) of that year. Related poems: 'Julian, noticing negligence', 'Julian in Nicomedia', 'Julian and the Antiochians', 'You didn't understand', 'In the outskirts of Antioch'.

Julian and the Antiochians

The epigram was written by the emperor Julian, in which he derides the people of Antioch for refusing to comply with his efforts to restore paganism. Julian's phobia of the theatre is known from his own testimony. He wrote that he grew a beard 'to punish his face, which nature had made ugly'. Related poems: 'Julian, noticing negligence', 'Julian in Nicomedia', 'A great procession of priests and laymen', 'You didn't understand', 'In the outskirts of Antioch'.

Anna Dalassene

In her *Alexiad* Anna Comnena, the daughter of the Byzantine emperor Alexios I Comnenus, quotes the chrysobull (imperial decree) in which her father, upon his departure to war, entrusted his mother (Anna's grandmother) with the affairs of the state. Related poem: 'Anna Comnena'.

Greek since ancient times

171 *Antioch*: city built by Seleucus Nikator in 300 BC on the River Orontes. Capital of the Hellenistic kingdom of Syria until 64 BC, it also remained a great city in Christian times. It was destroyed by an earthquake in AD 526.

Inachus: son of Uranus and Thetis. Mythological king of Argos and personification of the river that bears his name in the Argolid.

You didn't understand

The poem is based on an interesting wordplay (*anegnon*, *egnon*, *kategnon*) which is taken from the letters of Julian to Basil of Caesaria (Julian, *Works*, Loeb Classics edn. (1913–23), iii. 286). The Christians responded with yet another wordplay.

In Sparta

Related poems: 'Come, O king of the Lacedaemonians'.

175 *King Cleomenes*: Cleomenes III, king of Sparta 235–219 BC, tried in vain to strengthen the military capabilities of the Spartan state, which was unable to cope with the gradual depletion of its power. Thus he solicited the help of the Egyptian king Ptolemy III ('the Lagid' of stanza 3) in order to fight the Macedonians and the Achaean League. In accordance to the terms of the agreement, the mother (Cratisicleia) and children of Cleomenes were to be sent to Alexandria as hostages. The incident is related in Plutarch's 'Life of Agis and Cleomenes'.

On the march to Sinope

The incident regarding the soothsayer is imaginary, but in it reference is made to the fact that in 301 BC the ancestor of Mithridates V, Mithridates Ktistes, was saved by his friend Demetrius of Macedonia, known as Demetrius I Poliorketes (the Besieger). Related poem: 'King Demetrius'.

185 *Mithridates*: Mithridates V Evergetes, king of Pontos, who was murdered by his wife in 120 BC at Sinope.

Myres: Alexandria, A.D. 340

The scene and characters are fictitious. The date (AD 340) was a time of great political and religious upheaval: the civil war between the sons of the emperor Constantine the Great, and the religious confrontation within Christianity between Orthodoxy and Arianism. This is the longest of Cavafy's published poems.

Alexander Jannaeus, and Alexandra

The resistance movement against the Seleucids began in 167 BC, when Judas Maccabaeus, priest of the Hasmonaean clan, arose against the king of Syria, Antiochus IV Epiphanes. After Judas' death in 160 BC his four brothers (John, Simon, Jonathan, and Eleazar) finally drove the Seleucid garrison out of

Jerusalem in 142 BC, beginning a period of Jewish autonomy. Related poem: 'Aristoboulos'.

191 *Alexander Jannaeus*: of the House of the Hasmoneans (members of the dynasty or family to which the Maccabees belonged, named after the ancestor Hasmon), reigned 103–76 BC.

Come, O king of the Lacedaemonians

The king of Egypt, Ptolemy III, offered Cleomenes assistance in his war against the Achaeans, asking in return that Cleomenes' mother and children be kept as hostages in Egypt. Cratisicleia accepted this sacrifice in a spirit of bravery. Following the Battle of Selasia (222 BC), Cleomenes himself took refuge in the court under the protection of Ptolemy. When Ptolemy III died, his successor executed both Cleomenes' mother and his children. The quotation is from Plutarch's 'Life of Agis and Cleomenes'. Related poem: 'In Sparta'.

195 *Cratisicleia*: the wife of King Leonidas III of Sparta, and mother of Cleomenes III.

If only they had seen to it

The protagonist is imaginary. The probable time of the incident—also imaginary—is between 128 and 123 BC. Related poems: 'Envoys from Alexandria', 'Those who fought for the Achaean League', 'Of Demetrius Soter', 'The favour of Alexander Balas', 'Alexander Jannaeus, and Alexandra'.

201 *Kakergetes*: Kakergetes (malefactor) was the nickname of Ptolemy VIII Evergetes (benefactor). He was also derisively named Physkon (bladder). He was the father of Ptolemy IX Soter, known as Lathyros (chickpea).

Zabinas: the nickname of the alleged son of Alexander Balas, who usurped the throne of Syria 128–123 BC and was killed by Antiochus VIII Grypos (hook-nose) in 123 BC.

203 *Hyrkanos*: John Hyrkanos (134–104 BC) was the son of Simon Maccabeus, king of Judaea.

In the year 200 B.C.

The title of the poem places the scene ten years before the defeat of Antiochus III at Magnesia and three years before the Battle of Cynoscephalae, where the Romans defeated the Macedonians. Alexander the Great sent 300 Persian suits of armour to the Parthenon, with a dedicatory inscription from which the opening line is taken. Granicus (334 BC), Issos (333), and Arbela (331) were the three major battles that decided Alexander's Persian campaign. By that time Sparta was a completely insignificant military power. Related poems: 'The Battle of Magnesia', 'In Sparta'.

205 *koine*: a version of Greek commonly spoken by the Greek-speaking population of eastern Mediterranean countries in the Hellenistic and Roman periods.

Bactria: a Persian satrapy (province) in what today approximately corresponds to southern Uzbekistan.

In the outskirts of Antioch

The Christian martyr Babylas was bishop of Antioch AD 237–50. His remains were removed from his original grave and were reburied near the shrine and oracle of Apollo at Daphne, a suburb of Antioch. The priests of Apollo considered that the shrine had been polluted by this burial, especially since the Christians had built a church over the martyr's tomb. When Julian the Apostate visited Antioch in 362 he ordered that the church be demolished and Babylas' remains carried back to their initial grave. In October of 362, the shrine, along with the famous statue of Apollo, was destroyed by fire, which was attributed to the Christians. Related poems: 'Julian, noticing negligence', 'Julian in Nicomedia', 'A great procession of priests and laymen', 'You didn't understand', 'Julian and the Antiochians'.

GLOSSARY

agora the marketplace of ancient Greek cities. A central area within a city, where the commercial, political, judicial, and religious activities of the citizenry took place

boule a legislative council of ancient Greece, consisting first of an aristocratic advisory body and later of a representative senate

crater a large vessel used by the ancient Greeks primarily for mixing wine; more rarely, it was also used for libations in religious ceremonies, or even displayed in private houses for decoration

demos the body of citizens of an ancient Greek city, who were free and eligible to participate in all the functions of the state

eparch the chief official of a Greek eparchy (a geographical and political division of a Greek state)

ephebe a young man in his early youth

iambic metre in ancient Greek poetry, a metre in which each verse consists of an alternation of short and long syllables. In modern poetry, a metre in which each verse consists of an alternation of unstressed and stressed syllables. Cavafy's poetry used the iambic metre, which is the principal agent of his poetic rhythm

idyll in ancient literature, a short poem in narrative or dialogue form dealing with pastoral or rural life. In modern literature, a narrative poem treating an epic, romantic, or tragic theme

Italiote (1) a Greek inhabitant of ancient Italy; (2) of or relating to the Italiotes

Lagid a descendant of Lagus, father of Ptolemy I

philhellene in Hellenistic and Roman times, one professing or displaying a deep interest in Greek culture

satrapy a province in ancient Persia governed by a satrap, who exercised the powers of a local minor king

Seleucid a descendant of Alexander the Great's general Seleucus I Nicator

sophist one of a class of teachers of philosophy and rhetoric in ancient Greece, prominent about the middle of the fifth century BC for their methods of argumentation. They exercised a considerable impact on ancient Greek culture, but in later centuries, by virtue of their unorthodox opinions and their acceptance of pay for instruction, gradually fell into disrepute

stele (pl. stelae) a slab or pillar of stone carved or inscribed and used for commemorative purposes (such as to mark a grave)

talent any of several units of weight in the ancient world, and also a unit of value equal to the respective unit of weight in gold or silver

tetradrachm an ancient Greek silver coin worth 4 drachmas

CHRONOLOGICAL LIST OF POEMS

The poems are grouped by year of first publication and are also in chronological order within each year. From 1905 onwards the order is as determined by Cavafy.

1897
Walls
An old man
The horses of Achilles

1898
Supplication
The funeral of Sarpedon

1899
Candles
The first step

1901
The souls of old men
Che fece . . . il gran rifiuto
Interruption

1903
The windows
Thermopylae

1904
Perfidy
Waiting for the barbarians
Voices
Desires

1905
Trojans

1906
King Demetrius

1907
The retinue of Dionysus

1908
Monotony

1909
The footsteps
That is the Man

1910
The city
Satrapy

1911
The ides of March
Finished
Sculptor of Tyana
The god forsakes Antony
Ionic
The glory of the Ptolemies
Ithaca
Perilous things

1912
Philhellene
Herod Atticus
Alexandrian kings
Come back
In church

1913
Very seldom
As best you can
Of the shop
I went

1914
Tomb of the grammarian Lysias
Tomb of Eurion
Chandelier
Far away

1915
Wise men
Theodotus
At the entrance of the café
He vows
One night
Morning sea
Painted
Orophernes
The Battle of Magnesia
Manuel Comnenus
The displeasure of the Seleucid

1916
When they are roused
In the street
Before the statue of Endymion

1917
A town in Osroene
Passage
For Ammones, who died aged 29, in 610
One of their gods
In the evening
To sensual pleasure
Grey
Tomb of Iases
In the month of Athyr
So long I gazed—
Tomb of Ignatius
Days of 1903
The tobacconist's window

1918
Caesarion
Body, remember...
Tomb of Lanes
Perception
Nero's term
Envoys from Alexandria
Aristoboulos
In the harbour town
Aemilianus Monaë, Alexandrian, A.D. 628–655
Since nine o'clock—
Outside the house
The next table

1919
The afternoon sun
Has come to rest
Of the Hebrews (A.D. 50)
Imenos
On the ship
Of Demetrius Soter (162–150 B.C.)

1920
If dead indeed
Young men of Sidon (A.D. 400)
That they come—
Darius
Anna Comnena

1921
A Byzantine Nobleman, in exile, composing verses
Their origin
The favour of Alexander Balas
Melancholy of Jason, son of Kleander, poet in Commagene, A.D. 595
Demaratus

I brought to Art
From the school of the renowned philosopher
Craftsman of craters

1922
Those who fought for the Achaean League
To Antiochus Epiphanes
In an old book—

1923
In despair
Julian, noticing negligence
Epitaph of Antiochus, king of Commagene
Theatre of Sidon (A.D. 400)

1924
Julian in Nicomedia
Before they are changed by Time
He came to read—
In Alexandria, 31 B.C.
John Cantacuzenus prevails

1925
Temethos, Antiochian, A.D. 400
Of coloured glass
The 25th year of his life
On an Italian shore
In the dreary village
Apollonius of Tyana in Rhodes

1926
Kleitos' illness
In a township of Asia Minor
A priest of the Serapeum
In the wine taverns—
A great procession of priests and laymen
Sophist leaving Syria
Julian and the Antiochians

1927
Anna Dalassene
Days of 1896
Two young men, 23 to 24 years old
Greek since ancient times
Days of 1901

1928
You didn't understand
A young man of Letters—in his 24th year
In Sparta
Portrait of a 23-year-old man, painted by a friend of the same age, an amateur artist
In a large Greek colony, 200 B.C.
The potentate from Western Libya
Kimon, son of Learchos, 22 years old, student of Greek letters (in Cyrene)
On the march to Sinope
Days of 1909, '10 and '11

1929
Myres: Alexandria, A.D. 340
Alexander Jannaeus, and Alexandra
Lovely flowers and white such as befitted well
Come, O king of the Lacedaemonians
In the same space

1930
The mirror in the entrance
He was asking about the quality—
If only they had seen to it

1931
According to the recipes of ancient Greco-Syrian magicians
In the year 200 B.C.

1932
Days of 1908

1933
In the outskirts of Antioch

INDEX OF GREEK TITLES

Ἄγε ὦ βασιλεῦ Λακεδαιμονίων 194
Αἰμιλιανὸς Μονάη, Ἀλεξανδρεύς, 628–655 μ.Χ. 96
Ἀλεξανδρινοὶ βασιλεῖς 52
Ἀλέξανδρος Ἰανναῖος, καὶ Ἀλεξάνδρα 190
Ἄννα Δαλασσηνὴ 166
Ἄννα Κομνηνὴ 126
Ἀπ' τὲς ἐννιὰ— 78
Ἀπιστία 18
Ἀπὸ τὴν σχολὴν τοῦ περιωνύμου φιλοσόφου 134
Ἀπὸ ὑαλὶ χρωματιστὸ 152
Ἀπολείπειν ὁ θεὸς Ἀντώνιον 34
Ἀπολλώνιος ὁ Τυανεὺς ἐν Ρόδῳ 156
Ἀριστόβουλος 82
Ἂς φρόντιζαν 200

Βυζαντινὸς Ἄρχων, ἐξόριστος, στιχουργῶν 126

Che fece . . . il gran rifiuto 10

Γιὰ νἄρθουν— 122
Γιὰ τὸν Ἀμμόνη, ποὺ πέθανε 29 ἐτῶν, στα 610 94
Γκρίζα 102

Δέησις 6
Δημητρίου Σωτῆρος (162–150 π.Χ.) 116
Διακοπὴ 8
Δύο νέοι, 23 ἕως 24 ἐτῶν 168

Εἶγε ἐτελεύτα 118
Εἰκὼν εἰκοσιτριετοῦς νέου καμωμένη ἀπὸ φίλον του ὁμήλικα, ἐρασιτέχνην 176
Εἰς Ἰταλικὴν παραλίαν 154
Εἰς τὰ περίχωρα τῆς Ἀντιοχείας 208
Εἰς τὸ ἐπίνειον 88
Ἐκόμισα εἰς τὴν Τέχνη 132
Ἐν ἀπογνώσει 140
Ἐν δήμῳ τῆς Μικρᾶς Ἀσίας 158
Ἐν ἑσπέρᾳ 102
Ἐν μεγάλῃ Ἑλληνικῇ ἀποικίᾳ, 200 π.Χ. 178
Ἐν πόλει τῆς Ὀσροηνῆς 92
Ἐν πορείᾳ πρὸς τὴν Σινώπην 184
Ἐν Σπάρτῃ 174
Ἐν τῇ ὁδῷ 98
Ἐν τῷ μηνὶ Ἀθὺρ 92
Ἕνας γέρος 4
Ἕνας θεός των 88
Ἕνας νέος, τῆς Τέχνης τοῦ Λόγου—στὸ 24ον ἔτος του 174
Ἐνώπιον τοῦ ἀγάλματος τοῦ Ἐνδυμίωνος 80
Ἐπέστρεφε 72
Ἐπῆγα 74
Ἐπιθυμίες 2
Ἐπιτύμβιον Ἀντιόχου, βασιλέως Κομμαγηνῆς 142
Ἔτσι πολὺ ἀτένισα— 98
Εὔνοια τοῦ Ἀλεξάνδρου Βάλα 128
Εὐρίωνος τάφος 60

Ζωγραφισμένα 68

Ἡ ἀρρώστια τοῦ Κλείτου 156
Ἡ ἀρχή των 128
Ἡ διορία τοῦ Νέρωνος 86
Ἡ δόξα τῶν Πτολεμαίων 42
Ἡ δυσαρέσκεια τοῦ Σελευκίδου 46
Ἡ κηδεία τοῦ Σαρπηδόνος 20
Ἡ μάχη τῆς Μαγνησίας 44
Ἡ πόλις 28
Ἡ προθήκη του καπνοπωλείου 100
Ἡ σατραπεία 28
Ἡ συνοδεία τοῦ Διονύσου 44
Ἡ ψυχὲς τῶν γερόντων 6
Ἡγεμὼν ἐκ Δυτικῆς Λιβύης 180
Ἡδονῇ 98
Ἦλθε γιὰ νὰ διαβάσει— 146
Ἡρώδης Ἀττικὸς 56

Θάλασσα τοῦ πρωϊοῦ 68
Θέατρον τῆς Σιδῶνος (400 μ.Χ.) 144
Θερμοπύλες 10
Θυμήσου, σῶμα . . . 106

Ἰασῆ τάφος 90
Ἰγνατίου τάφος 92
Ἱερεὺς τοῦ Σεραπίου 160
Ἰθάκη 36
Ἴμενος 114
Ἰωνικὸν 70

Καισαρίων 84
Κατὰ τὲς συνταγὲς ἀρχαίων Ἑλληνοσύρων μάγων 202
Κάτω ἀπ' τὸ σπίτι 104
Κεριὰ 2
Κίμων Λεάρχου, 22 ἐτῶν, σπουδαστὴς Ἑλληνικῶν γραμμάτων (ἐν Κυρήνῃ) 182

Λάνη τάφος 90
Λυσίου γραμματικοῦ τάφος 60

Μακρυὰ 72
Μανουὴλ Κομνηνὸς 64
Μάρτιαι εἰδοὶ 32
Μεγάλη συνοδεία ἐξ ἱερέων καὶ λαϊκῶν 162
Μελαγχολία τοῦ Ἰάσωνος Κλεάνδρου· ποιητοῦ ἐν Κομμαγηνῇ· 595 μ.χ. 130
Μέρες τοῦ 1896 166
Μέρες τοῦ 1901 172
Μέρες τοῦ 1903 106
Μέρες τοῦ 1908 206
Μέρες τοῦ 1909, '10 καὶ '11 186
Μέσα στὰ καπηλειὰ— 160
Μιὰ νύχτα 70
Μονοτονία 36
Μύρης· Ἀλεξάνδρεια τοῦ 340 μ.χ. 186

Νὰ μείνει 110
Νέοι τῆς Σιδῶνος (400 μ.χ.) 120
Νόησις 78

Ὁ βασιλεὺς Δημήτριος 42
Ὁ Δαρεῖος 124
Ὁ Δημάρατος 130
Ὁ ἥλιος τοῦ ἀπογεύματος 110
Ὁ Θεόδοτος 34
Ὁ Ἰουλιανὸς ἐν Νικομηδείᾳ 144
Ὁ Ἰουλιανὸς καὶ οἱ Ἀντιοχεῖς 164
Ὁ Ἰουλιανός, ὁρῶν ὀλιγωρίαν 140
Ὁ Ἰωάννης Καντακουζηνὸς ὑπερισχύει 148
Ὁ καθρέπτης στὴν εἴσοδο 196
Ὀμνύει 74
Ὀροφέρνης 48
Ὅσο μπορεῖς 38
Ὅταν διεγείρονται 96
Οὐκ ἔγνως 172
Οὗτος Ἐκεῖνος 62

Παλαιόθεν ἑλληνὶς 170
Πέρασμα 100
Περιμένοντας τοὺς βαρβάρους 14
Πολὺ σπανίως 66
Πολυέλαιος 74
Πρέσβεις ἀπ' τὴν Ἀλεξάνδρεια 80
Πρὶν τοὺς ἀλλάξει ὁ Χρόνος 146
Πρὸς τὸν Ἀντίοχον Ἐπιφανῆ 138

Ρωτοῦσε γιὰ τὴν ποιότητα— 198

Σ' ἕνα βιβλίο παληὸ— 138
Σοφιστὴς ἀπερχόμενος ἐκ Συρίας 164
Σοφοὶ δὲ προσιόντων 30
Στὰ 200 π.χ. 204
Στὴν ἐκκλησία 64
Στὸ πληκτικὸ χωριὸ 154
Στὸν ἴδιο χῶρο 196
Στοῦ καφενείου τὴν εἴσοδο 70

Τὰ ἄλογα τοῦ Ἀχιλλέως 22
Τὰ βήματα 56
Τὰ ἐπικίνδυνα 62
Τὰ παράθυρα 12
Τείχη 12
Τελειωμένα 32
Τέμεθος, Ἀντιοχεύς· 400 μ.χ. 150
Τεχνουργὸς κρατήρων 136
Τὸ διπλανὸ τραπέζι 104
Τὸ 25ον ἔτος τοῦ βίου του 152
Τὸ πρῶτο σκαλὶ 6
Τὸ 31 π.χ. στὴν Ἀλεξάνδρεια 148
Τοῦ μαγαζιοῦ 66
Τοῦ πλοίου 114
Τρῶες 40
Τυανεὺς γλύπτης 58
Τῶν Ἑβραίων (50 μ.χ.) 112

Ὑπὲρ τῆς Ἀχαϊκῆς Συμπολιτείας πολεμήσαντες 136

Φιλέλλην 54
Φωνὲς 2

Ὡραῖα λουλούδια κι ἄσπρα ὡς ταίριαζαν πολὺ 192

INDEX OF ENGLISH TITLES

A Byzantine Nobleman, in exile, composing verses 127
A great procession of priests and laymen 163
A priest of the Serapeum 161
A town in Osroene 93
A young man of Letters—in his 24th year 175
According to the recipes of ancient Greco-Syrian magicians 203
Aemilianus Monaë, Alexandrian, A.D. 628–655 97
Alexander Jannaeus, and Alexandra 191
Alexandrian kings 53
An old man 5
Anna Comnena 127
Anna Dalassene 167
Apollonius of Tyana in Rhodes 157
Aristoboulos 83
As best you can 39
At the entrance of the café 71

Before the statue of Endymion 81
Before they are changed by Time 147
Body, remember . . . 107

Caesarion 85
Candles 3
Chandelier 75
Che fece . . . il gran rifiuto 11
Come back 73
Come, O king of the Lacedaemonians 195
Craftsman of craters 137

Darius 125
Days of 1896 167
Days of 1901 173
Days of 1903 107
Days of 1908 207
Days of 1909, '10 and '11 187
Demaratus 131
Desires 3

Envoys from Alexandria 81
Epitaph of Antiochus, king of Commagene 143

Far away 73
Finished 33
For Ammones, who died aged 29, in 610 95
From the school of the renowned philosopher 135

Greek since ancient times 171
Grey 103

Has come to rest 111
He came to read— 147
He vows 75
He was asking about the quality— 199
Herod Atticus 57

I brought to Art 133
I went 75
If dead indeed 119
If only they had seen to it 201
Imenos 115
In a large Greek colony, 200 B.C. 179
In a township of Asia Minor 159
In Alexandria, 31 B.C. 149
In an old book— 139
In church 65
In despair 141
In Sparta 175
In the dreary village 155
In the evening 103
In the harbour town 89
In the month of Athyr 93
In the outskirts of Antioch 209
In the same space 197
In the street 99
In the wine taverns— 161
In the year 200 B.C. 205
Interruption 9
Ionic 71
Ithaca 37

John Cantacuzenus prevails 149
Julian and the Antiochians 165
Julian in Nicomedia 145
Julian, noticing negligence 141

Kimon, son of Learchos, 22 years old, student of Greek letters (in Cyrene) 183
King Demetrius 43
Kleitos' illness 157

Lovely flowers and white such as befitted well 193

Manuel Comnenus 65
Melancholy of Jason, son of Kleander, poet in Commagene, A.D. 595 131
Monotony 37
Morning sea 69
Myres: Alexandria, A.D. 340 187

Nero's term 87

Of coloured glass 153
Of Demetrius Soter (162–150 B.C.) 117
Of the Hebrews (A.D. 50) 113
Of the shop 67
On an Italian shore 155
On the march to Sinope 185
On the ship 115
One night 71
One of their gods 89
Orophernes 49
Outside the house 105

Painted 69
Passage 101
Perception 79
Perfidy 19
Perilous things 63
Philhellene 55
Portrait of a 23-year-old man, painted by a friend of the same age, an amateur artist 177

Satrapy 29
Sculptor of Tyana 59
Since nine o'clock— 79
So long I gazed— 99
Sophist leaving Syria 165
Supplication 7

Temethos, Antiochian, A.D. 400 151
That is the Man 63
That they come— 123
The afternoon sun 111
The Battle of Magnesia 45
The city 29
The displeasure of the Seleucid 47
The favour of Alexander Balas 129
The first step 7
The footsteps 57
The funeral of Sarpedon 21
The glory of the Ptolemies 43
The god forsakes Antony 35
The horses of Achilles 23
The ides of March 33
The mirror in the entrance 197
The next table 105
The potentate from Western Libya 181
The retinue of Dionysus 45
The souls of old men 7
The tobacconist's window 101
The 25th year of his life 153
The windows 13
Theatre of Sidon (A.D. 400) 145
Their origin 129
Theodotus 35
Thermopylae 11
Those who fought for the Achaean League 137
To Antiochus Epiphanes 139
To sensual pleasure 99
Tomb of Eurion 61
Tomb of Iases 91
Tomb of Ignatius 93
Tomb of Lanes 91
Tomb of the grammarian Lysias 61
Trojans 41
Two young men, 23 to 24 years old 169

Very seldom 67
Voices 3

Waiting for the barbarians 15
Walls 13
When they are roused 97
Wise men 31

You didn't understand 173
Young men of Sidon (A.D. 400) 121

A SELECTION OF **OXFORD WORLD'S CLASSICS**

A SELECTION OF OXFORD WORLD'S CLASSICS

	Classical Literary Criticism
	The First Philosophers: The Presocratics and the Sophists
	Greek Lyric Poetry
	Myths from Mesopotamia
APOLLODORUS	The Library of Greek Mythology
APOLLONIUS OF RHODES	Jason and the Golden Fleece
APULEIUS	The Golden Ass
ARISTOPHANES	Birds and Other Plays
ARISTOTLE	The Nicomachean Ethics Physics Politics
BOETHIUS	The Consolation of Philosophy
CAESAR	The Civil War The Gallic War
CATULLUS	The Poems of Catullus
CICERO	Defence Speeches The Nature of the Gods On Obligations Political Speeches The Republic and The Laws
EURIPIDES	Bacchae and Other Plays Heracles and Other Plays Medea and Other Plays Orestes and Other Plays The Trojan Women and Other Plays
HERODOTUS	The Histories
HOMER	The Iliad The Odyssey